HEALTH & HAPPINESS *Without Bullshit*

HEALTH & HAPPINESS *Without Bullshit*

Jimmy Mathew

Vitasta

Let Knowledge Spread

Published by
Renu Kaul Verma
Vitasta Publishing Pvt Ltd
2/15, Ansari Road, Daryaganj
New Delhi - 110 002
info@vitastapublishing.com

ISBN 978-93-82711-67-4

Typeset and Cover Design by Vits Press
Illustrations by Aswin Appukuttan
Printed by Vikas Computer and Printers

This book is dedicated
to those early scientists,
who toiled against odds to get at the facts.
They made truth possible, to an extent.

Acknowledgment

Thanks are due to my family. The time spent on this book did not make their life easy.

Thank you readers for your encouragement.

Thanks to Publisher Renu Kaul Verma and editor Veena Batra for their faith and competence.

Thanks Aswin Appukuttan for the illustrations.

Thanks to the many authors and scientists from whom I have collected the basic facts necessary. Without them this book would not have been possible. I have made all efforts to acknowledge them in the body of the text.

Why this book?

When there are so many books already in the market, that supposedly reveal the secret or secrets to health, wealth and happiness, why should you read another book? Why the hell should you waste your time reading this, when it is better to spend that time pursuing success and happiness?

Hey, hold on! What is success? Does success bring happiness? How do you pursue them?

Will you get them if you pursue determinedly?

In fact, what is happiness?

What is the basis of longevity? If you are healthy will you live long? Can you improve your own health, and if so, by how much?

If you live long, will you be happy? Is long life worth it?

Can you answer such fundamental questions like these?

How far does existing scientific knowledge take us on these issues?

More basically, does knowledge help us? Can we overcome our innate nature to modify our thoughts and behaviours to help ourselves?

In fact, is there an innate human nature?

Throwing a firefly's worth of light on problems like these is the lofty aim of this book. I make no claims. It is for you to decide whether I have succeeded.

Then you may well ask—why should I read it?

Because my share from the sale of this book is going to charity. It will be used to support the writing whims of a mad doctor in Kochi, who has the best interests of humanity at heart.

This book has two thrust areas—health and happiness. It is not meant to be a comprehensive exposition of the entire science. That will require a million pages. (And I don't know that much). The attempt is to cover a few important areas of interest that can be applied in our day to day life. I have tried to narrate them in a colourful way, with illustrative examples taken from experience. Whenever possible, I have really strived hard to stick to the 'No Bullshit' rule.

The idea is not so much about what you should do, but about what you should probably know. Who am I to tell you what you should do? But there are some suggestions on what you can—maybe—try. The '*how*' is largely left to you, dear reader. I don't know what your journey is all about. Only you can decide what to do with your life. But you should know what you need to do.

The book is organised in short chapters. Each chapter has a message. It is a quantum of the whole, if you will. You can read any chapter you want and go in any order you choose. But if you read from the beginning to end, you will find that it has a logical sequence to it. But some of you may find it more diverting to browse and read whatever strikes your fancy.

As the topics are only loosely connected, I have given summaries of what I have tried to say in the last few chapters. Try not to skip them.

Some of my personal opinions and my own philosophy of life have crawled into this book. That is intentional. Otherwise it would have been like the concentrated food used by astronauts, without juice and flavour. Some of it, some of you may consider to be 'Bullshit'. Please bear with me.

Without 'Bullshit'?

After my second book, *Blood, Sweat and...Cheers*! was released, many readers,(mainly my wife and my mother) advised me to avoid profanity (most others loved it). Bad words were not in fashion, they said. They will not be very happy with the 'Bullshit' part. Then why did I use this word? What do I mean anyway?

My response is—for one thing, mildly offensive bad words never go out of fashion. They cannot. They resurface again and again, like stars peeping out of a cloudy night sky, to relieve the sheer tedium of ordinary human intercourse.

Secondly, Bullshit is not a bad word. It is just a noun. There is no other word to replace that word. Bullshit is Bullshit. It is what you write when your high school teacher asks you to write a paragraph on 'the human dilemma' or 'factors influencing the Indian Monsoon'. It is what you say when the wife asks you what you were doing in the office staying till late at night. It is what you say when the reporter asks you what you would do if you were elected, when you are contesting the polls.

One of my medical school friends, who considered studying to be a bad habit strictly to be avoided, was asked to write about the 'origin, insertion, relations, nerve supply and action of the Teres Major muscle'. He wrote:

"The Teres Major muscle is a big muscle. It is a major muscle, as its name so eloquently describes. The muscle originated in the remote past during human evolution, for some purpose that it is uniquely adapted for. In fact, I won't be surprised if a similar muscle is found also among apes. That much is its significance. The muscle is connected to bones. It is related to nearby structures, and is covered by skin. Muscles are responsible for movement in humans."

Well, let me tell you that every word of this answer is completely true. But you may note that even non-medical people will find this answer deeply unsatisfying. So did my teachers at medical school, and he failed a record number of times before passing finally. Now he runs a wellness and weight loss clinic in one of the metro cities. He is planning to write a book on 'The secret formula to health, happiness and a trim body'. No, he is not me. I have already written this book.

Recently, I read a self-improvement book that stated:

"The power of thought is enormous. Thoughts are electrochemical discharges of neurons and are thus, a form of energy. According to Einstein's famous equation $E=MC^2$, energy is equal to mass. So thoughts are physical things. They are substances on the fabric of the space-time continuum, capable of influencing the universe. So think positive thoughts. Visualise success. Whatever you visualise; you will be able to achieve. The universal consciousness will help you do it. All the billions of people on this earth are suffering because of this simple fact—they don't realise that thoughts are things."

You will not find these kinds of expressions in this book.

I am not implying that all self-improvement books are like this. Only some are. What is more, I freely admit that it is almost impossible to write a book like this without some stuff that some people would consider Bullshit. So ideally the book's name should be:

'About health and happiness—with as little Bullshit as possible'. But it didn't sound good.

And what is the 'KISS-ASSP' Principle?

KISS—Keep It Simple, Stupid.

ASSP—And Shit Scarce, Please.

It is a very good principle, don't you think?

What am I?

This is a very important question. Why should you listen to me? How do you know that I know what I am talking about?

Let me tell you outright, that I am no official expert on happiness psychology, preventive health or wellness science. But I am a qualified doctor. I got my MBBS from a government medical college in Trichur, and did my Masters in Surgery (MS) from the famed central govt institution of JIPMER. Then I did post-doctoral MCh in Plastic and Reconstructive surgery from Calicut. Right now, I am Professor and Reconstructive Micro Surgeon at Amrita Institute of Medical Sciences at Kochi.

All this doesn't entitle me to go blabbering about happiness and wellness to a wider audience. What does qualify me for that is the fact that I did my MBBS very seriously. No—I didn't top the university or anything. But I knew what made human bodies tick (as far as the science of medicine went). I knew how the brain functioned. Being an avid reader, I could correlate my medical knowledge to the wider world of the social sciences and general biology. I had a knack for the truth.

Right now I am involved in the treatment of overweight and obese patients. Management of chronic diseases like diabetes is important in the life of any specialist who deals with wounds and large non-healing ulcers, related to diabetes or otherwise. I have tried to develop an interest in the preventive aspects of these diseases also.

This is not blowing my trumpet. I am very sorry if it seems that way. I am sure most of my fellow medical men share my abilities. But some may not be that passionate about communicating the Truth to their fellow beings.

I am not being patronising here. Any average literate person can access any fact from the internet now. Many are presented in a simple, easy to understand manner. You can draw your own conclusions. There is nothing wrong with that.

What you may lack is a general holistic view. Medicine and Psychology are inherently vague and inexact sciences.

It takes some training to pour through the thousands of research papers that are coming out every year, read between the lines, look critically at their methodology and zero in on the truth. I have made it a sort of my life's mission to dive for the truth and hold it close.

I also write a bit. Having two of my books out there in the market has given me the confidence to attempt this feat. I also imagine that I have an ability to make things simple. And also interesting. If I am mistaken, don't hesitate to direct your abuse, violent outpourings and dire threats to jimmysurgeon@gmail.com. This would possibly prevent me from unleashing any further attempts on an unsuspecting public in future. But I doubt it. So pitch it strong.

Don't get me wrong. I am no ideal person who follows exactly what I have written. I am not an obsessed pursuer of fitness, or an avid dieter. I am not a long distance runner, or a detached Buddhist seeker of nirvana aspiring to tranquil hours of meditative bliss. I am just an ordinary person like you or me, going about my business, and tending to myself and my family in my own imperfect ways. But I have tried to *find out* what can help me improve my life. I have tried to incorporate these principles as far as is possible into my life. Believe me—it has worked to a small extent. I am sure you will also benefit.

Believe me, I am a thing

Is happiness, a thing?

ONE DAY the teacher asked a class of ten-year-olds what they wanted to become when they grew up.

One boy jumped up. "I want to be a doctor."

"Oh, very good," said the teacher.

Many others followed. 'Teacher', 'Truck driver', 'Singer'. The children came up with many professions. One girl said that she just wanted to be at home and look after the house like her mother.

"That is not bad," said the teacher. She was open to unconventional lines of thought.

"What about you, Prakash?" She asked the quiet boy sitting at the back.

"I just want to be happy," said Prakash. "I want to be happy when I grow up."

The teacher was stumped. "But that is not something that... that..." She fumbled.

✻ 2 ✻

A few months ago I was talking to an old lady, a patient of mine. Her only daughter brought her to me every day for a diabetic foot ulcer that she had. She had a son who ran away from home at the age of sixteen. She had no idea where he was; or even if he was still alive. It had been twenty years now, she said.

"Wherever he is, I just want him to be happy. I hope he is happy," she said.

So, is happiness a thing? Is it a good goal to pursue? Can it be taken as a means to an end?

I should tell you here that by happiness I mean the general level of satisfaction we have with life on a daily basis, and not the momentary elation we feel, for example, immediately after winning the lottery. Subjective wellbeing may be a better term, but we will stick with happiness.

Till a few decades ago, such questions were considered meaningless. It was against objective science, many said. Economists felt that well-being was a measure of wealth. Everybody wanted to study things that could be measured; material things. What was felt by human beings was thought to be less than real.

But as you know, what matters most to us is our subjective state of mind. Unless we exist, we have consciousness, the world doesn't exist for us. Every sensation, every objective truth that we have learnt about the world, is present ultimately in our minds only. So what we feel *matters*. There is no doubt about that.

✻ 3 ✻

That is not all. Modern developments in the field of Brain science, Neural imaging, Behavioural psychology, Economics, Statistics etc. has made things like happiness measurable. And study-worthy. Now we can answer questions like:

Is the sensation of happiness and misery present in particular areas of our brain, and does the activity of each area go up and down with whatever we feel according to the good or bad things that happen to us?

Can these be measured, and is the measurement reliable?

Is happiness something that we have, like Blood Pressure, at a constant level or with fluctuations, but unlike BP, present only when we are awake?

Can people's happiness levels be compared?

Can the happiness levels of different societies, at different times, be compared and studied reliably, according to epidemiological principles?

"Yes" is the answer to all the above questions, according to Richard Layard, an economist and happiness researcher, who wrote *Happiness-lessons from a new science.*

fMRI or functional MRI is a method of scanning the brain which shows the areas that become active and the amount of activity while a person is doing some task. For example, when a person moves his right hand a part of the left motor cortex lights up. When a person is happy a particular area of the brain becomes active, *and the amount of activity correlates with his self reported level of happiness.*

* 4 *

Happiness can be measured by self assessment, on a graded scale, just like doctors measure pain. People can be asked to grade their level of well-being on a scale of zero to ten, from zero for very depressed, to ten corresponding to the highest amount of happiness imaginable. These scales show:

- Good correlation across a particular area.
- Similar proportions among males and females.
- Good similarity to the level of activity of the 'happiness' areas in fMRI.
- Some expected variations across regions, for example, low levels of happiness seen in poverty stricken areas or where there is war, famine or disease.
- Low levels of happiness correlate with incidence of depression, suicides, crime and even road traffic accidents.
- Personal levels of self-reported happiness agree very well with *other* people's assessment of their happiness. As in—'He has always been a very happy guy, I will give him a seven out of ten'.

From these, we can infer that happiness, indeed, is a thing. What kind of thing is it? Is it a good thing? These questions remain to be answered.

✱ 5 ✱

Is happiness a good thing?

IMAGINE YOU are a young man living in a nice city. You are healthy and attractive. You have skills and are professionally qualified. You are attractive to women. Life is good. The future appears bright. You are happy.

One day you realise that your life has been a lie. You are actually a prisoner of artificially intelligent computer beings who keep you in a vat of liquid for their own purposes. The world in which you live is only a virtual reality that the evil forces have programmed into your brain. It is not the twenty-first century and there are no cosy cities anymore. The earth is a hostile, dark, radioactive wasteland with some free humans hiding underground in pathetic conditions.

Some rebels want to rescue you. Would you want to be rescued? This is, of course, the dilemma faced by the protagonist in the epoch movie *Matrix*.

What would you do? What is the meaning of the happiness experienced by you if you are living in a fantasy world, totally out of touch with reality?

Pramod Krishnan (Not his real name of course) was a friend of mine. We were in school together. In our adult life, we had met only a few times. He was doing a successful business. One day his wife called me and said that his behaviour had changed. His usual caution was gone, and he gambled money on many risky ventures, losing much of it. He had started drinking heavily, and that was unusual for him. He suddenly attracted a circle of shady friends and got into drunken fights with others. He developed an excessive interest in other women, much to his wife's dismay.

When I met him, he was the same guy. His personality was the same. He was a reasonably happy person, and outgoing. Now he was excessively happy. He talked incessantly and told many dirty jokes in the presence of his wife and children. Once or twice he broke into spontaneous outbursts of song. When I hinted at his recent unwise behavioural changes, he had no clue what I was talking about.

"I am so happy, man. Life couldn't be better," he said.

It turned out that he had contracted a mental disease called mania. It is a psychiatric illness characterised by a permanently elevated mood. Incessant and excessive happiness for no reason. The patients have extreme self-confidence and believe that they can do no wrong.

A few consultations with a psychiatrist and one month of medicines cured him totally. He started his old life again and rebuilt his business successfully.

The psychiatrist was an old friend of mine. He had done a thesis on psychopaths and their moods. Psychopaths are persons who look and behave absolutely normal. But they have an abnormality—they have no conscience. Self-centered in the extreme, they never think twice about murdering or raping other people. Many are serial killers. Usually extremely intelligent, they manage to fool the authorities into thinking they are reformed. Once released, they may quickly start their old ways again. Unlike my friend Pramod's problem, it is not an episodic illness.

" It is a feature of their personality, and largely incurable, though there are different lines of thought," my psychiatrist friend said.

"But they are always happy. They get angry and frustrated at the retribution society gives for their actions, but they never get depressed," he told me.

More problematic is the fact that some perverts, like sadists, get joy or derive happiness by actively inflicting pain or discomfort on others.

There are drugs, like alcohol, that make you happy. Is that good?

The last one is an easy argument to address. We are talking about long-term life happiness. Drinking will make one happy, but then one has to drink larger amounts, more frequently, to stay high. It is addictive. It is a downward tightening spiral. The money runs out, the wife and kids leave. Society shuns such a person. He gets cirrhosis of the liver. And he is miserable.

So, when you consider this question, perhaps we should modify our definition a bit.

When we say 'happiness', it means long-term life happiness or life satisfaction.

We don't consider meaningless happiness, like that of a mentally challenged person or a person with injury to the prefrontal cortex, as true happiness.

We should always consider other people's happiness or the society's happiness *in addition* to our own while evaluating factors that can increase our happiness.

So, the sadist's happiness doesn't count. He decreases his victim's happiness. The sadist himself may lose his happiness when the society punishes him. A horrible ruler or dictator tramples on an entire community's happiness.

Pramod, with his psychiatric illness of mania, greatly decreased the happiness of his wife and kids and all others near and dear to him.

Is there any further scientific evidence or statistics to support this? Richard Layard lists out the following in his book *Happiness-lessons from a new science.*

- Carol Ryff of the University of Wisconsin has shown ways to measure things that are self-evidently good, like positive relationships, purpose in life, autonomy, self-acceptance and personal growth, and shown that high scores in these correlate with self reported measures of happiness and life-satisfaction.
- Happiness improves our health. There is ample evidence of the fact that happy people are less likely to get long-term chronic diseases and they live longer. One notable study noted the happiness levels of a group in their twenties and found that happier people lived significantly longer. Another study observed that among Oscar nominated film professionals, those that actually got the award lived

an average of four years longer.

- Communities and countries that have less crime, more trust among people, with more equal distribution of wealth, are happier. But countries with an authoritarian regime like party or person dictatorships are less happy.

So, we can cautiously say that generally speaking, happiness is a good thing.

Feelings are complex

AN AVERAGE adult human has 206 bones in his body. All of them are named and mapped and studied in detail. For example, we know all the muscles that attach to these bones and the sites of their attachment. Do we know how many muscles are there in our body? An exact number is difficult to ascertain as some consider groups of smaller muscles in the same region of the body as a single one. There is some variation between individuals also. So, the number varies between 640 and 850. Whatever the count, rest assured that we know everything that one needs to know about even the tiniest of these muscles. The exact bone and site of origin, insertion, nerve supply and action. We know what will happen if one is injured or taken out. If there are variations between people, we even know the percentage of people having that variation in the major populations of the world. The arterial tree has been mapped to perfection. So also the nerves. The various branches, sub-branches and sub-sub-sub branches are given in textbooks in technicolour tree diagrams of breathtaking complexity.

In short, the anatomy of the human body has been studied in exquisite detail by curious and obsessed medical scientists. It also, obviously, has applications.

What about the human mind?

No, I am not going to get into a mind-body debate here. In keeping with our established policy of steering clear of the digestive waste of the male member of the most common ungulate in our part of the world, I will just leave it.

Let us just say that it is generally agreed that the term 'mind' is applied to the sum total of the workings of the human brain.

Compared to the rest of the body, the brain is an enigma. It is a white blob, shaped like a knobby cloud. The consistency is of thick jelly. It is very expensive, though, consuming a whopping 25 to 30 per cent of our total energy expenditure.

All of our body is composed of cells lined like bricks to make up various tissues and organs.

In the brain, the chief functioning cells are the neurons. Unlike in other parts of the body, each cell, the neuron, has to be considered a functional unit. The brain is the ultimate in miniaturised complexity. How well do we know the brain? For instance, how many neurons are there in an average human brain? Many older textbooks site 100 billion (One billion is 1000 million, and one million is 10 lakh).

Dr Suzanne from Brazil wanted to know how that figure was arrived at. She searched the literature and was surprised. Nobody seemed to know. Someone must have just guessed it. No doubt an educated guess. But on what basis? No idea. She decided to count, and find out for herself.

She took four human brains. They had been donated by people to the cause of science after their death (what did you think?). She made a soup out of each, by dissolving it in appropriate chemicals. (The details are boring, believe me. Besides, it might put off the more sensitive readers). Then she counted the nuclei of each neuron using the microscope and a counter like the one used for counting red blood cells. One day she looked up from the microscope (tired as hell, one might suppose), and announced the average figure.

Eighty-five billion. Yup. That is the magic number. The number of the units that determine who we are, what we do—delineates our sense of self. Manufactures our consciousness, our essence that makes us aware of this wonderful thing called existence.

Each neuron has tens of thousands of branching outgrowths that form electrochemical connections with other neurons, forming an immense electrochemical hub that builds up the most complex organisation in the entire known universe. Recent research has hinted that each branch, or dendrite, has independent firing potential that makes each of them into a functional unit. That means trillions. Trillions of units and connections, humming with molecular messengers called neurotransmitters, each manipulating a piece of information in this immense information processing machine, the human brain.

Roger Penrose has suggested, with some backing of evidence, that the cytoskeleton, a branching network of bio molecules in each individual neuron is an information-processing miniature computer on its own. That would make the brain many orders of magnitude more complex than previously imagined.

How the cell, I mean hell, do we study this thing? I expect you want the short answer.

With great difficulty.

For those tiresome readers who are not satisfied with this answer, I offer a partial list. (Never be under the impression that I am an expert in this sort of thing.)

- The details of the neurochemistry, fluorescent tagging, squid neurons, sodium gated channels, and the entire messy field of experimental physiology, I simply omit. I can't do it. I apologise. Feel free to delve into the net and drink to your fill and saturate your poor neurons.
- One can make experimental lesions in animals like monkeys and find out the effects on various parts of the brain. We can use animals to study motivation, aggression, learning etc by designing mazes, rewards,

deterrents and the like. We can study behaviour and how they solve problems and co-operate with each other with careful experiments.

- Due to stroke, trauma, tumours, or with surgery, human patients may lose the function of parts of their brains. The disabilities produced can be observed. Brain imaging is very important in this.
- Modern brain imaging like MRI, PET and indirect image of the EEG enables us to observe human brains in real time. Variations in blood flow tell us when an area of the brain gets activated. Scientists can tell the areas that light up and the sequence in which they do so when a person feels happy doing something, for instance.
- Purely psychological approaches—observing behaviour of subjects, studying self-reported states of the mind, and psychological experiments involving individuals or groups of people. These types of experiments involving observing behaviour under different conditions are very important in psychology.

What have we found out about Happiness?

✻ 14 ✻

Anatomy of a mental state

SURAJ DROVE his new Ford Fiesta through the oppressive morning traffic. It was a Monday. He reflected that he was very happy with life. That was what he had recorded in his diary the previous evening. His friend James, the psychologist, had asked him to. Record his level of happiness every day. Was he miserable, a little sad, happy, very happy or extremely happy? He was doing it for the past one year. It was to help with a research project of James. Most of the days, his entry read 'very happy'. Around eight months back, it had fallen to just 'happy' for a few weeks when he was diagnosed with mild diabetes. He was on treatment now and it was under control. Four months back, for two consecutive weeks, he had written that he was a little sad, and on occasion, miserable. That was during his son's accident at school where he had broken a leg. It was at the same time that there was a spate of lay-offs in his company and there was a strong rumour that he might lose his job. But the storm had passed.

At the moment, he was not feeling so good. Commuting to the office was the one routine thing he hated the most. And that too on a Monday. As he settled into his chair in the office, he felt relieved. He enjoyed the early part of the day and meeting with his team members. Many of them were his friends. But then the Boss called. "Suraj, there is a crisis. The Crysil agreement is not coming through. You are given two days to sort it out. Otherwise we will have to find someone else to do the job."

That really ruined his day. He forgot his lunch as he poured through the necessary files. He reached home late, just in time for dinner. He was just happy, he decided. Not very. Or maybe a little sad?

"Happy Birthday, Daddy," his son announced. His wife was smiling in front of the cake. It was a surprise! He had forgotten his birthday.

Just before going to bed, he thought for a moment. Then he wrote 'very happy' in the Diary.

Happiness is a complex state of the mind. It has a higher processing centre in the left prefrontal cortex that shows more activation with increasing happiness. A corresponding centre in the right prefrontal cortex responds to sadness. It lights up in MRI and PET scans when subjects are shown sad or disturbing images. Pleasurable stimuli, happy memories etc. increase the activation of the area in the left prefrontal cortex.

Stimulation of this area with powerful external magnets is possible. This increases one's happiness and this technique has been used to treat depression.

The human brain can be considered to have three evolutionarily hierarchical parts. The most primitive are the centres involved in breathing, heart rate, basic aggression, sex, chewing and swallowing and certain primitive reflexes. This has traditionally been called the 'R-complex'. The R stands for 'reptilian'. It is an old system. The second one is the

'Limbic system' consisting of the Thalamus, Amygdala etc. This system is well developed in mammals and is concerned with emotions. Positive emotions are pleasure, elation, love, ecstasy, pride, relief, excitement, delicious anticipation etc. Negative emotions are fear, anxiety, depression, jealousy, hate, frustration and the like.

Mammals and birds, and many other animals have cerebral cortex, but it is most well-developed in humans. It is the highest in the hierarchy. It integrates all the inputs from the lower centres and presents a balanced image to our conscious awareness. Each emotion and sensory experience contributes its bit.

Happiness is a state of the mind that is present as a baseline throughout our waking lives. It is a little bit like the temperature of water kept in an oven-cum-refrigerator that can be switched to 'heat at 100 degree for five minutes', 'cool at 2 degree for half-an-hour' etc.

'Heat' episodes are pleasurable experiences, hopeful events and similar 'hap hits' that provide upward spikes in the baseline. Pain, frustration, bereavement etc. are the cooling sessions that generate down spikes. The baseline is relatively stable. But many 'sad hits' in succession drag the baseline down. And vice versa, of course.

The baseline happiness is also influenced by our past memories and anticipation of future ones. They are an important aspect of our mental life, as you can imagine.

So generally speaking, happiness is a single dimension

running from extreme misery to great happiness. But there is another quality of feeling running perpendicular to this line, and that is 'arousal'. So misery can be depressive or agitated. Extreme happiness can be enthusiastic joy or a tranquil contentment.

Happiness is least in the morning and slowly climbs up through upward and downward spikes depending on the various travails of the day. It peaks before bedtime. This is a general trend.

Can we be happy and sad at the same time? No. Because sad feelings dampen our happiness levels.

Are there different types of happiness, like the more 'superior' happiness brought on by virtuous conduct and generosity towards others and the more 'base' happiness brought on by addictive drugs like cocaine and watching pornography? No. Subjectively, such a concept doesn't have validity. But these lower methods of creating 'hap hits' mitigate our long-term happiness, as we shall see.

Our baseline happiness levels depend presumably upon external happy events, and our internal attitudes and predispositions. If we can control them, we have the coveted formula. But when we try to do that, we run into difficulties.

✻ 18 ✻

The Treadmill

RAJESH WAS my friend in high school. He had two passions—travelling and vehicles. He gazed at cars and sleek bicycles. He trekked to the local parks and boarded buses to attend science exhibitions in schools miles way, and I always declined his invitations. He had two pet grouses, a principal source of dissatisfaction in his life—too many responsibilities and too little money. He was being brought up by a single mother and had a baby sister. He was the complaining sort. When his mother gave him a second-hand bicycle, he was thrilled for a day. Then he told me bitterly that due to his mother's financial constraints he had to put up with an old bicycle, which in his opinion, belonged to the pre-independence era. He could tell by the faded sticker on the back, which faintly resembled the British flag.

"Even Sunil, the carpenter's son, has a brand new BSA SLR."

Rajesh was good at studies. He took his responsibilities very seriously. And he worked very hard. He was my batchmate during MBBS. State funded scholarship made him exempt from tuition fee. His boarding was free in the college hostel. I congratulated him on this fact. Most of his problems seemed to be getting over.

"What about my clothes? Do you know how ridiculously expensive the books are in Medicine? I have to have a bike now. I don't know how I will pull on for five years," he retorted.

When he passed commendably after five years, he was a very bitter man. He had to start work immediately. His pay was very good, but all his contemporaries were trying to join specialist residencies. He was expected to support his sister's education, and see that she was married off decently.

"What an unfair world!" he lamented.

Twenty years after our date of joining Medical School, we had a reunion. Rajesh had a successful practice, and was quite rich. He also had an MD in general medicine to his credit. He had travelled to all the important places in India. He came in a brand new Honda city. And he still had a worried look.

"My son says he wants to join Medicine. It will cost crores! I wanted to go on a European tour last year, but couldn't due to money constraints. I wonder when my money problems will be over."

He told me in all seriousness that the BMW he had already ordered would have to be on a bank loan as he was very short of money. He was thinking of going to UAE to earn some more.

"I really don't want to leave, but what choice do I have?" He looked totally helpless. And unhappy.

Each pleasurable experience, good thing got, and achievement has the ability to create upward spikes in our happiness levels. When many such things accumulate and are not offset by bad things happening, our happiness baseline will rise. It is simple mathematics, right? Now we have the magic formula. Just seek out and saturate our lives with external good things, and we become happier and happier. In fact, that is what most of us try to do.

Remember that crucial sentence from the last chapter? No? We do miss the important points now and then. *Our happiness levels also depend on our memories of things past, and the anticipation of things to come.*

Anticipation of things to come is called 'expectations'. Expectations depend on our memory of past experiences. In fact, the past teaches us what to expect of the present.

The American psychologist Harry Helson was the first to realise its importance. He said that each of us has an adaptation level, a baseline, that represents what we expect. I expect a nice meal at lunch time and I get it. I feel neither happy nor unhappy. Suppose there is a very poor person who can afford to eat only dinner. If, one day, he gets to eat my nice lunch, he is very happy. He gets a 'hap hit' because he did not expect it.

One day, I can't eat my lunch and have to go hungry. My mood goes down a little.

The poor man who got only dinner won a lottery and now gets three sumptuous meals a day. I am told that now he has become sad and frustrated and shouts at the cook if his favourite chicken curry is not there with his lunch.

A series of pleasant experiences will produce happiness but will also raise our expectation level. So it becomes increasingly difficult for us to be happy. It is impossible for our experiences to exceed our expectations consistently till eternity. Now we understand that sentence we studied in high school Economics class—'human wants are unlimited'. We are sort of built like that. That is what is happening to people who slowly improve their lot and status in life. They slowly increase their expectations to match their attainments. And their happiness levels are stuck at the same level. It is like running on a treadmill. You are running like mad but are not getting anywhere. This is called 'the hedonic treadmill'.

It makes sense. In fact, many spiritual leaders and philosophers have realised it. Buddha did. He said that desire is the cause of misery. Many of us may say that we know it at a subconscious level.

But studies have shown that most people believe that a 25 per cent increase in their salary will have a sustained effect on their happiness. The same studies have demonstrated that the happiness wears off after a short period when they have hiked their needs to adapt to their new level of earning. Their belief was wrong. In fact, surveys done on lottery winners who have won really big sums of money have showed similar results.

Why did nature bestow such a curse on us?

I know many paraplegics who come for treatment of pressure sores. They are paralysed from the waist down, usually due to spinal cord injury. We would expect them to be miserable. But most of them who had the injury many years before are smiling and happy. Many do useful work sitting at home. Crafts, paintings, computer work—they do it, earn well and supplement the family income. A study done among paraplegics and quadriplegics who have been disabled for twenty years shows only marginal decrease in their level of happiness. Patients with adequate social and family support were just as happy as other people. They have downgraded their expectations. They anticipate less.

The treadmill prevents us from becoming euphoric, but also protects us from wallowing in misery.

So, are we doomed? Is our search for happiness a waste of time? Maybe not. But it cannot be achieved by ignoring or pretending that the treadmill doesn't exist. We have to study it and our prime candidate—happiness—more closely and in greater detail.

What the hell are we?

IT WAS during my med school days that I saw the movie *Predator*. It was memorable. I was not used to Hollywood movies at the time. I didn't know how invincible American soldiers were. If I did, I would have been surprised at their dismay in finding that the island on which they were stranded was inhabited by a devilish unknown being. It hunted humans for fun. How beastly! (It is quite cool when we do the same thing to other species, of course). To top it all, the damn thing was invisible.

I would have thought that the odds were heavily stacked against the army men. But then I didn't know Arnold Schwarzenegger. His rippling muscles and unchanging morose expression should have told me that it was all over for the poor predator. Lot of fighting and trickles of red and green blood (green of course, being the standard colour of the blood of all alien beings) later, the predator is exposed in all his glory. Despite being an alien, he was just a muscled human with a screwed up face. It was very enjoyable. Only problem was I couldn't follow the American accent. I could make out some screams and rapid gibberish in deep bass. In the end, just before Arnold the man was about to kill the monster—there was an exchange I understood perfectly:

Arnold: "What the hell are *you*?"

Predator: "What the hell are *you*?"

I was disappointed that there was no satisfactory answer to this question. The predator just followed it up with an unmistakable human laugh (though loud and irritating). Then there was a huge explosion and fire everywhere. I later learnt that most American action thrillers ended this way.

You may wonder what I am driving at, other than the obvious fact that a certain English slang with mild profanity is a common language throughout the known Universe?

What are we?—Are we a product of our genes? By 'we'

I mean our minds. Our emotions, behaviour, personality—what we are. Or does the environment shape us from childhood? Are we, as children, pristine clay, the world shaping us through the years and our experiences chiselling our fine lines?

Bobby Fishman, aged 39, woke up early that day. He had to go to the University of Minnessota for an appointment. There, he was supposed to meet one Mr Gordon Brown. He had never met him before. He took some time in choosing his clothes. Finally he decided on a light blue formal shirt and jeans. Semi formal—he liked that.

He drove up to the building inside the university in his grey sedan. He noted another grey sedan of the same make as his parked in front. He walked in and there stood Gordon Brown. He was his long lost identical twin. They were given up for adoption soon after birth and were brought up in different homes.

Bobby blinked twice. He had a peculiar feeling that he was staring into a mirror. The same half bald head and chiselled face. Gordon wore a blue formal shirt and jeans. They started to talk, at first hesitantly, and then became increasingly animated. Both had enough common things to talk about. Both were firemen. Both worked at the fire and safety departments in different states. Bobby said that as a child he hated Maths. Gordon laughed and said he did too. "But I bet you were very good at spelling," said Gordon. Yes—that was one thing Bobby was good at, just like Gordon. Bobby took out a beautiful boat made of wood. He had made it for Gordon. Woodworking was his hobby. Gordon got out a wonderfully carved model of an aeroplane and offered it to Bobby. He had made it himself.

"Why don't you come and meet us sometimes? My son James Alan would get a kick out of seeing someone so similar to his father," said Bobby.

"Sure. My son is named James Allen. Slight change for a change! We can have a vacation together—maybe at Pas Grille beach in Florida. It is my favourite place."

"Mine too. I go there at least twice a year," said Bobby.

The above exchange is my version of a small episode played out at the University of Minnesota in the nineties. The twins were part of a study called the 'Minnesota Study of Twins Reared Apart' (MISTRA). All the listed similarities are true except the names and the dramatisation. They have an active twin research centre, though now they cannot study twins reared apart, because adoption agencies take care to keep them together.

The original MISTRA had 81 monozygotic and 56 dizygotic twins. Monozygotic twins (Identical twins) have 100 per cent similar DNA. They have identical genes. Dizygotic twins (Fraternal twins) have only 50 per cent of similarity in their DNA. That is, they are just like normal siblings, but have the same age. Twin studies have a lot to tell us about the heritability of behaviour. Thomas Bouchard was the chief researcher who pioneered these kinds of studies.

Did I mention that both Bobby and Gordon had put on 10 pounds in weight in the last two years?

Another set of monozygotic twins both liked to sneeze in elevators to irritate other occupants. One pair, both males, were into body building and fitness and both ran popular gyms in different locations. Twins of both types, reared together and apart, adopted but unrelated children brought up by the same parents under identical conditions, and all such similar factors have now been studied in strictly controlled conditions. Many of the results have come from massive studies in Scandinavian countries, where the authorities keep detailed databases on their citizens. Steven Pinker, in his book *The blank slate* states that the these studies have used the most thorough and best validated measuring instruments known to psychology. He also lists out the main conclusions from the study:

Identical twins are far more similar than fraternal twins, whether raised apart or together.

Identical twins raised apart are highly similar, sometimes more than when they are raised together.

Biological siblings, whether raised apart or together are far more similar than adoptive siblings raised in the same family.

What are the factors that the scientists studied? Is the influence of genes and the environment measurable in terms of percentages? What is the point of it all to our well-being? How do genes affect behaviour? Is this type of research necessary or can this knowledge be dangerous?

Should we examine these questions?

Yes...because *Veritas Curat*..."The truth shall set you free."

Because we humans have an irresistible urge to get at the truth.

Because through truth alone can we search for solutions.

We have no choice but to wade through the bullshit and get at the nuggets buried. It is our destiny.

Genes and destiny

ROBERT CHANG was a second generation American. He was born and brought up in the United States of America. His parents had migrated from China when they were young. Robert had an interest in Palaeontology, but his parents wanted him to become an electronics engineer. Since he was good in mathematics he didn't mind. Pleasing his parents was important for him. His two uncles and an aunt lived nearby. They also approved of his decision to join Electronics, and were proud of him. He could have gone to a more prestigious University far away, but chose to join the community college nearby to be with his relatives and family.

It was there that he met Jane, his present girlfriend. She was majoring in creative arts, her primary interest. Jane's parents were not particular about what she studied. They were happy that she decided to go to college. She lived near her parents, but wanted to go to the west coast as soon as she finished her studies. "I want to experience other places," she said. Secretly she wanted to be away from her parents for a while, "as they got on her nerves too often." She was quite annoyed when Robert insisted that she meet his parents before sleeping with her. He wanted to meet her parents also.

"What for?" she exploded. "We haven't decided on anything yet."

Robert wanted to go with her to California. But the thought of leaving his family made him miserable. He became a nervous wreck. Jane found him crying in his room one day.

"I really can't see what the problem with you is," she said. "I will stay here for one more year. Then we will see."

Mathew D Liebermann and Baldwin Way of the Psychology Department at UCLA, were reviewing research on the genes that control the brain's serotonin system. Serotonin is a neurotransmitter. Neurotransmitters are chemicals that enable electrical signals to pass across synaptic junctions between neurons. Variation in the level of serotonin has been linked to depression in humans.

Way discovered that individuals of Eastern and Western descent show differentially distributed variations within the regulatory region of the serotonin transporter gene-5-HTTLPR. There are three variants of the gene—short-short, long-short, and long-long. Two-thirds of East Asians have the short-short variant, but only one-fifth of Americans and Western Europeans have it. This is a very significant difference, shown in multiple studies.

This short-short variant of the gene is related to depression and social sensitivity. Risk of depression is greater in people with this variant, who lack adequate social support. Their well-being depends upon the cohesion with and support of their communities. These people are likely to be more sensitive to the social environment in general.

Mathew D Lieberman has elaborated upon these concepts in the chapter titled 'What makes big ideas sticky?' in the book *What's Next.* He theorises that this may be one reason why Orientals are culturally likely to be taught that the society is important. That we are all connected. Needs of your people come first. Buddhism and Confucianism have this slant. People from North America and Western Europe are taught to believe in their own goals, feelings and achievements. Individualism rules here. *I am master of my own destiny*. Controlled by a single god who holds individuals responsible for their own eternal salvation.

In India? We are somewhere in the middle. Less than half of the population has the short-short variation of the gene in India. Buddhism originated here, and then migrated to China.

And we know that it is the only country where communism still thrives.

Meanwhile, Robert and Jane took an apartment in their hometown and are living together. But their problems are not over. Jane likes novelty. She wants to travel to exotic places. She wants to meet new people every day. She gets a hit out of bungee jumping, rock climbing and paragliding. Once she joined a course that taught how to handle poisonous snakes. She gets bored easily. Robert loved his routine job at a local company. Going to a movie is the maximum he can handle by way of excitement. And he steers clear of thrillers and horror movies. He loves to sit with a book near the fireplace in his spare time.

Robert wanted to get a cat as a pet. He was fond of them. Jane suggested a small pit viper. "They are so cute," she insisted.

Dopamine is a neurotransmitter that is released in response to excitement. In optimum levels in the brain, release of this chemical causes small 'hap hits'. It is basically part of a reward system. It makes the person want the surge again. Cocaine and amphetamines release Dopamine. It is associated with attention, alert states and learning. Excess of an *effect* of Dopamine, is unpleasant. Dean Hamer of the National Cancer Institute in Maryland, USA, studied a gene called D4DR. A variation of the gene, the long variant, he found was almost universally found in certain 'novelty junkies'. They constantly seek new experiences and find happiness in taking risks. They are prone to addictions, and are impulsive. Routine just bores them to death. Their brains are less sensitive to the *effects* of Dopamine. So they seek out experiences that maximise its output. A group of people with the short variant are highly sensitive to this neurotransmitter. They quickly become overwhelmed with newness. They can take in very little excitement.

And I have to tell you, everything is not going well with our young couple. Jane now doesn't want to go to California. She wants to go to Malawi. She heard that it was fun fishing in Lake Malawi. There is always the danger, people told her, of a crocodile coming and grabbing at your feet. She can't wait to go. Robert is not very open to the idea. Jane has had many American lovers during her teens. An African is an exciting possibility. Frankly, she finds Robert...well, boring.

Tests and Percentages—blast them!

PEOPLE SEE you as a person. Even if your appearance alters by age, disease or injury, they recognise your personality.

The personality is your feelings, thoughts and attitudes—yes. But other people can assess it only by your behaviour. A measure of personality should be able to predict someone's behaviour, at least in broad terms.

There are five major components to personality. Each component varying across the spectrum of a trait.

- Openness to experience: Someone sticking to a

predictable routine and at the other end seeking constant new experiences.

- Conscientiousness
- Extroversion-Introversion spectrum
- Agreeableness-antagonism spectrum (A trait also deemed likeability)
- Neuroticism-stability: Anxious and fearful to stable and unflappable.

Personality tests asks people to agree or oppose statements. 'Many of my friends talk badly behind my back.' 'I think it is ok not to help a person cross the street when you are too busy,' etc. are examples.

Some may think its validity doubtful. But they are repeatable. Same person gives almost same responses when tested with different sets of statements. It agrees with what other people have to say about a person. They also make accurate predictions, like achievement, stability of marriage, criminality etc.

Heritability of a character can be calculated in twin and adoption studies by looking at the variance, and a thing called the correlation coefficient. I will not go into the maths. Better come to the crux.

The results of a multitude of well done research was summarised by the psychologist Eric Turkheimer as 'the three laws of behavioural genetics'.

First law: All human behavioural traits are heritable. Heritability refers to the inheritance of variation of a trait within the human species. It turns out that intelligence is 60 to 70 per cent heritable, and all the above mentioned personality factors are 50 to 60 per cent heritable.

The second law: The effect of being raised in the same family is smaller than the effect of the genes.

The third law: A good portion of the variation in complex human traits is not accounted for by the effects of genes or families.

What has all this got to do with happiness? For one thing, contentment levels are very similar in separated identical twins, irrespective of their life-circumstances.

Remember a previous chapter about factors influencing happiness? Positive feelings like delight, enthusiasm, excitement and anticipation provide us with 'hap hits'. They push up our happiness baseline. Negative things like fear, hostility, misery, frustration etc. drag it down.

Psychologists Costa and McCrae postulated that happy people are those who have a lot of positive 'hap hits' and less of negative feelings. Unhappy people are those who have more 'down drags' and less of the 'hap hits'. It is obvious, you say. It doesn't take a hot-shot psychology Professor to see that.

Well, they were looking for personality traits that *predispose* people to have these emotions in the first place.

They concentrated on introversion-extroversion and neuroticism-stability. These are independent, highly characteristic and reliably measurable features of personality. They measured the positive and negative 'hits' of a large number of people. At the same time they looked at their measure of these personality variables.

Extroverts had much more positive or happy experiences than introverts. But they did not differ in terms of negative or sad effects. Neurotics on the other hand, had much more negative experiences than stable people. They had no difference in 'hap hits'.

The extroversion-introversion spectrum shows individual differences in their ability to experience positive affect, while the neuroticism-stability dimension measures the natural tendency to have negative experiences. Extroverts are more sociable, and this has something to do with this trait.

Our happiness baseline is a summation of our happy and sad experiences. So, really happy ones have a lot of 'hap hits' but are not affected by the downsides of life. The 'stable extrovert' fits this description. They have the blessed disposition. The 'neurotic introvert' bears a sort of curse. He has few good experiences because of introversion but all trivial travails of life hit him hard due to his neuroticism.

Costa and McCrae did another study regarding this. They tried to predict the happiness of people 10 years after by measuring their personality attributes at a particular time. They ignored all the events in the intervening period of their life. The stable extroverts were much happier than a neurotic introvert.

Other traits may influence our levels of well-being. Being agreeable promotes happiness. Obvious, as other people respond more positively to those with an abundance of this trait. Always trying to please other people and not taking note of one's own intrinsic motivations may make one unhappy. Ones sense of self-worth is totally dependent on other's assessment.

Perfectionism is a character of many. Perfectionists find it very difficult to be happy. They are satisfied with only perfection, and it is an elusive goal. They have to have the best, be the best, and do everything just perfect. It seems that it is better to strive for 'good enough for me' type of satisfaction. It also means that you are kind to yourself.

In summary, certain things, unfortunately, seem to be true.

Our minds are not clay that culture and well-meaning parents and peers can mould to any shape as per requirement.

We have an innate operating system with major traits having a heritability of 50 per cent or more.

Our ability to live happily seems to have a significant innate component.

But let us not get dejected. Instead, our insight into our own inner nature should enable us to open doors. Doors to more opportunities. To give us the ability to improve upon what we have, and to minimise our shortcomings, in an effort to fulfil ourselves. That is what knowledge is for. That is what we humans do. Or should do.

Are we slaves to our genes?

DR SURENDRAN and his wife Meera were friends of my father. They wanted to immigrate to the USA. Everything was ready for them. But they delayed the journey till their only daughter Prabha was five years old. As medical people, they believed that in the first five years the child's basic attitudes and personality were set. Early upbringing was responsible for it—that was the conventional wisdom at that time. Once they were in the States, they spoke only their local language at home. The house was full of books on India and Indian culture. They wasted no opportunity to preach about traditional Indian values. They wanted the affluence and opportunities that America offered, both for themselves and for their daughter. But they wanted Prabha to be brought up as an Indian. The couple wanted her to remain Indian in spirit, throughout her life. That was the crux of their carefully thought out plan.

I am sure you can imagine what happened. Like countless other carefully thought out plans, this one fell flat. She turned as American as the kid next door. After sometime, she stopped speaking her native tongue, even in the house. She rebelled during her teens, and flapped her wings restlessly, resisting all attempts at cultural brainwashing. As a young woman, when she married her black boyfriend and moved out of the house, the parents wondered what they had done wrong.

Their assumption was wrong. They had grossly

overestimated their ability as parents to influence their offspring.

Let us revisit the third law of behavioural genetics again:

A good portion of the variation in complex human traits is not accounted for by the effects of genes or families.

We saw that slightly more than 50 per cent of our traits are innate or genetic. But let us not forget that it leaves a substantial 40 to 50 per cent. A huge window for improvement.

What puzzled researchers in twin and adoption studies was that the 'shared environment' had only a measly 10 per cent effect on the various facets of personality. Shared environment means the parents and immediate family. Going by the example given above, the peers and the general cultural environment has a big influence. More than parents. Many unfortunate immigrant couples have found this out the hard way.

What was even more frustrating was the fact that among twins and siblings, most of the peer group and environment is similar. That still leaves a good 30 per cent of variation between them unaccounted for. What is this mysterious factor?

No one knows for sure. Psychologists call it 'the unique environment'. It could be the spontaneous differences in brain wiring, later accentuated by the person's unique responses to events and experiences. Call it free will. Call it God's will. Whatever you name it, we are not fully determined manufactured cars that will run just as predicted.

This is the conclusion reached by happiness researcher Sonja Leubomirsky who wrote the book *The How of Happiness*. She says that 50 per cent of our contentment levels are fixed by a genetically determined 'set point'. Only 10 per cent of it is due to external life events. According to her educated opinion, 40 per cent of our happiness variability is modifiable, with effort.

The study of subjective well-being is a comparatively new science. It is simply called 'Happiness', though what we mean is long-term life satisfaction, and not momentary elation. It is a stable mental quality of individuals. Therefore it is real.

There can be a criticism. Looking after one's own happiness can be an inherently selfish endeavour. Or it can be meaningless, like that of a person having a mental disease causing elevated mood, or a person with naturally inflated self-esteem. Drugs and alcohol can bring temporary elation. But we are looking at long-term happiness, and that too, of the society as a whole. Happiness of almost everyone should count.

Our personalities and hence happiness levels depend a lot on our genes. An example is the Depression gene 5HTTLR, a variant of which causes depression. But it occurs only if there is lack of social support or severe childhood stress. Some characteristics of our personality, like extroversion, make us prone to be happy. Personality traits are inborn, to a large extent.

But, the brain is not cast in concrete. It has the capacity to change over time. Many lines of research show that our personality traits slowly modify themselves over a lifetime. This is dependent on our accumulated experiences. It should be possible to train ourselves to have a more positive outlook. Sonja Lyubomirsky states that 40 per cent of our happiness is modifiable with our own effort. The belief that we can change also seems to be a crucial factor.

There is a treadmill effect to happiness. It follows an equation with 'attainment versus expectations'. We adapt to many happiness inducing things like money and status. This makes increasing our well-being levels somewhat difficult. But if we study the factors influencing our lasting well-being, it should be possible.

By the eighties and nineties, neuroscientists reached the conclusion that the brain is a fixed machine that is fully formed by five or six years of age. Neurons cannot replicate. They cannot be renewed. Separate brain regions cater to different functions. They cannot be altered. These conclusions have been proved wrong, by modern imaging and methods of study.

The brain is a computational organ that keeps changing throughout our life. New connections are formed and old synaptic connections are pruned away. The prefrontal cortex that is concerned with long-term planning and social functioning goes on growing and maturing till the twenties and early thirties.

The sea gypsies are a tribe in Southeast Asia that practically live in the seas. They learn to swim before they can walk, and dive for collecting sea cucumbers and shellfish. They can hold their breath underwater for record times, *and see clearly* under water. Our pupils dilate under water as a reflex. The sea gypsies constrict their pupils to more than 20 per cent. Constricting pupils is supposed to be a hardwired unconscious reaction.

We know that arm wrestlers have awesome biceps in their competing arm. This is due to the work that it is put to. But do you know that London taxi drivers have measurably bigger posterior hippocampus in their brains to store complex routes and spatial information? This study was done by Eleanor Maguire and Katherine Woollet. It has been proved that new neurons are constantly produced in the Hippocampus, cerebellum and possibly other areas in the adult human brain.

Optometrists can put prismatic lenses in reading glasses that invert images. If you put these glasses on, whatever you see looks upside down. You can read books the wrong side up and amaze your friends. But if you keep wearing them, the brain rearranges the images so that your view of the world rights itself. Walk around like that for some days. Then remove the glasses. Lo! Everything looks upside down! We can read the newspaper upside down without glasses now. The friends will be even more amazed. Fortunately for you, this is temporary.

Brain plasticity and our 40 per cent magical window allows us to modify our own inner selves and make us more contented. That is what we should strive for.

Some things change—Believe me

I DON'T know about you, but I have the distinct impression that I am getting better with time. I am not getting any younger. Some hair is gone. I imagine myself to be strong and flexible, but there is a definite decline from what I was in my twenties.

I am not talking about all that.

I feel settled and mature. Bad things don't throw me into pangs of anxiety or into the pits of depression, as they did before. I have become more outgoing, and I remember being quite introverted as a kid. I have a strong feeling that I am now a more likeable person. (I hope many of my friends and family don't read this!).

Robert Viechtbaur, in 2006, analysed 92 studies done till then about personality changes over time, in a meta-analysis. He found that most people became more confident, warm, and emotionally stable over time. Most became more likeable to other people. Very extroverted became slightly more reflective, while the introverted became more outgoing. That is, regarding introversion and extroversion, people drift to the middle of the spectrum.

There are, to me, two interesting aspects to this phenomenon. One is that most of the changes happen during 20 to 40 years of age, though they also occur later. This seems to be an important period. This is against the idea that personality traits are totally fixed by young adulthood. Drastic changes are perhaps rare, but change is possible throughout life, even in such a strongly genetically determined trait like personality. Secondly this is not just a spontaneous change, but looks as if it is related to life events. Persons engaged in theft, crime and a life of despair have a deleterious effects on one's personality. This suggests that purposeful changes are possible.

Carol S Dweck from Stanford, in 2008, in an article, examined the power of belief. Beliefs are an important characteristic of a person. He asserts that beliefs lie at the heart of personality and adaptive functioning. Personal goals, strivings and beliefs are powerful instruments that can drive change. He states that people who believe that their traits are changeable are more open to listen, willing to confront challenges, persist in difficult tasks, and bounce back from failures easily. Look at this study:

Lisa Blackwell of Columbia University did a study on 700 school students. She divided them into two groups. One group was coached on study methods for eight sessions. The other group, she gave the same eight sessions on study methods, and two hours of something else. Then the academic performance of the students was followed up for a period of six months. The group who got the extra 'something' performed significantly better than the other group, including in maths, a problem area for many students. What was this extra something that had such a magical and prolonged effect?

Just two hours of lectures, graphic presentations, and role-play study on how intelligence is *not* innate. They were shown pictures of neurons sprouting new axons, and works and exercises that show how one can boost ones 'smarts'. Actually, intelligence does have a significant innate component. That was not mentioned.

In fact, praise for innate qualities like intelligence makes kids prone to avoid challenges and decreases effort. Praise for effort makes them eager to learn and perform better.

Research seems to prove that there is power in belief. We had better believe that we can improve ourselves. Otherwise we are doomed.

Some truths are surprising

ON THE desk of my former boss, there was a small board that said:

"The greatest need—common sense."

But it is really surprising how often common sense is wrong. When I was a young adolescent, like most of my peers, I was very concerned about physical beauty. It was my lack of (perceived) height that bothered me the most. Later on, my receding hairline became a source of major worry. I couldn't help envying some of my friends who were tall and handsome, though I was good at concealing it. Many pretty girls clustered around them and I imagined these beautiful friends of mine to be much happier than the plainer population that included me.

By high school, it had become clear to me that there were differences among people in their natural abilities. Some students could do maths effortlessly. Whenever I was doing a maths problem, I tugged and tore at my hair so severely that I am convinced that my baldness which was to develop later was mainly due to this. Intelligence was for real. It was a much-prized possession. Society (and teachers) made that abundantly clear. Whatever one said about different abilities and how everyone is good in his own way, there was a quality called general intelligence that was partly innate. Highly intelligent ones do have it much easier than many others. They should be happier than others, shouldn't they?

They should, but they are not. Studies have consistently shown that intelligence has nothing whatsoever to do with lasting life happiness.

Being beautiful and attractive doesn't make one any happier. This surprising finding was proved quite satisfactorily by Diener and colleagues in 1995. They did rigorous measures of subjective well-being and the physical beauty as objectively assessed by impartial judges who were not aware of the implications of the study. Another surprising study found that fashion models who were highly valued for their beauty were significantly *less* happy than their peers.

What could be the reason for this finding? Aspirations and expectations are probably to blame. We become happy when our life outcomes match or exceed our expectations. If I am intelligent, I expect certain results. I expect better grades and a good job. It doesn't make me happier, because it is expected. On the other hand, I will be disappointed if I am intelligent and only barely pass my exams.

When I am handsome I do expect the society to treat me like a beautiful person (It does. And science has shown that people are not impartial as regards physical beauty). I expect similarly beautiful ones of the opposite sex to be attracted to me. I would be very unhappy if they weren't!

As a young college student, I noted that it was good to be young. I was healthy and vigorous. I could eat whatever I wanted.

I saw that my parents were burdened with responsibilities. Many of them I considered bothersome (including being in charge of someone like me). I was generally free to do whatever I pleased. Old age and the suffocating adult world seemed ages away.

My grandparents were alone. They had some diseases and infirmities of old age. Their mobility was restricted. I imagined that they felt very alone. We visited them frequently and they were overjoyed to see us.

I was sure that this was the happiest period in my life. Things would become worse, I was sure.

I would not have been that surprised if happiness levels remained stable throughout life. Now I know about hedonic adaptation and the 'expectation versus attainment' equation. I would have even expected a slow decline in happiness as we progress through adulthood to old age.

In fact, the *opposite* is true. Happiness levels increase steadily and reach a peak in young adulthood. Middle age shows a dip, when you are less happy in your forties or so. Subjective well-being and satisfaction rise in your fifties and sixties in spite of declining health, diseases of old age and stints in hospitals. They show a decline, in some cases, only after age seventy-five. That too, when adequate social support is not there. When ample supports are there, like in advanced countries, eighties are the happiest years in a person's life!

It is clear that there are many things we don't know about the factors that govern happiness. It is easy to come to a conclusion that you can do nothing much about your happiness baseline. You either have it or you don't.

But that is not true. Abject poverty and continuous misery makes people unhappy. Happiness levels vary across communities and countries. As people are lifted out of poverty, countries like India and China have shown a rise in the subjective well-being of its citizens.

In the west, as also in upper middle class India, material prosperity and conveniences of daily life have improved remarkably, over the past half century. Has that made people happier?

We have data from only western countries. But they tell us something that we, as a developing nation should take note of. What do we want to develop into?

It seems that despite manifold increases in absolute income and purchasing power, most of the European countries and the US have not become happier. In fact, one survey shows that in America, half a century back, the average happiness score was 7.5. A recent estimate puts the value at 7.2. During this period, the average American has become healthier, richer and lives considerably longer. The actual prospect for pursuing leisure has increased. Technology, gadgets and the internet have provided unprecedented opportunities to entertain themselves and relieve boredom. Still the number of citizens suffering from depression has gone up. More people attempt suicide. Crime rates are on the rise. Our well-being is on a stagnant path.

In some countries, especially Scandinavian countries, happiness levels have risen slightly. It seems that there are factors that are at work in the modern world that both increase and decrease our happiness levels. It is important that we examine some important intrinsic and extrinsic factors that determine our well-being, both on a personal and collective level.

"Why is he like this? I thought he was very happy with the pay hike."
"He found out that his colleague got a better raise"

✵ 49 ✵

A question of money

IT WAS 2002. I was in Trivandrum after I had just passed my MS and become a qualified surgeon. Trivandrum was a place crawling with specialists of all disciplines. I got a job as junior surgeon in one of the private hospitals. They gave me ten thousand rupees a month.

I went to a conference in Jaipur the next month. On the train I met a bunch of newly minted software professionals, all four to five years younger than me. We got talking. One asked me about my salary. It is not an impolite query in India. When he heard my answer, he whistled.

"That is so low, man. All of us earn more than Rs 25,000 a month."

This did nothing to lift up my mood. I became depressed. True, as a bachelor, I could live quite comfortably on that money. It was a temporary job. There was a long way to go. My full earning potential was not yet realised. I knew all that. Still I felt incredibly frustrated. Many of my classmates were getting thirty to forty thousand in many other hospitals elsewhere. And these kids...I felt my blood boiling. As a junior Resident while doing my MS at JIPMER, I was getting Rs 15,000 as stipend. I felt doubly pissed off that my income had actually fallen.

I was still brooding angrily when I alighted at the station. Some ten cycle rickshaw wallahs accosted me with incessant Hindi. I wanted a ride to the hotel. But I was so irritated that I decided to walk the four kilometres to the place. Five of the rickshaw men followed me.

"The Hotel Presidency? I will take you, *saab*." The clamour was deafening. I shouted at them to shut up and walked briskly. After a kilometre, I looked back when I heard the sound of wheels rattling in a gutter. One person was still following me. Betel stained teeth smiled beseechingly. I was sweating now. I decided to get in. There were still two or three kilometres to go.

The man strained at the pedals with full force. Thin thighs pistoned up and down. Sweat poured from his face. The sun beat down mercilessly. The light reflected off his nearly bald head.

I got down at the hotel. He collected my luggage and handed it to me. I rummaged in my purse. I was looking for a fifty rupee note.

"Two rupees, *saab*," he said. I stared incredulously. I pushed a twenty rupee note into his hand and said:

"Keep it *bhaiya*." It was as far as my Hindi went.

The look on his face was pure joy and gratitude. And I got a lesson in perspective.

We certainly believe that a big increase in our earnings will make us happy on a long-term basis. Almost all people interviewed across countries felt firmly that a million dollars or roubles or whatever will solve a lot of their problems and they will become permanently happier. But the truth is that it has only a temporary effect. Research among lottery winners has shown that.

Yet, I am not going to tell you that money won't buy you happiness. I am not feeding you the cliché that money doesn't matter. Money does matter. Rich people are happier. Many studies have also shown that. The issue is complex and we see conflicting results. What is happening here?

Abject poverty and misery definitely makes folks unhappy. Rich countries are generally happier. India and China have become happier recently, on an average. But the correlation is not perfect, with income. Some poor African countries are among the unhappiest. But many of the former Soviet countries come at the bottom in the happiness scale, in spite of higher income.

But over the last fifty years, as we discussed earlier, purchasing power and real incomes have risen across the western world, with no increase in happiness.

The chief reason is that we become adapted to increase in the wages. We escalate our needs to keep up with the income. When the money pours in, we want a new house, the new car. We can afford that private school now. And within a year we are back to square one. We have scaled up our aspirations, our needs, and our expectations. We see the happiness treadmill in full form, when it comes to money. Yet, the richest in any society are happier. There is conflicting research on money and happiness. Why?

It is because it is not our absolute earnings that matter, but our relative income. We are always comparing ourselves to our peers, neighbours, relatives. People in our immediate community determine our standard. I am not comparing myself with Mukesh Ambani. But I am acutely aware of the income of my brother-in-law, who is a software engineer. I keenly watch the lifestyle of the lawyer next door. I know that the businessman, who is my wife's best friend's husband, is sending both his kids to an expensive international school. But the fact that the washerwoman's kids are going to the government school down the street doesn't register in my brain.

As an entire community or country becomes richer, the society doesn't become happier because the relative incomes stay the same.

Yet the richer you are, many people in your reference population cannot afford your lifestyle. So your status is elevated slightly. So you are happier. If one is a rich man and all his neighbours, relatives and friends are middle class, he is satisfied. If he moves to a rich neighbourhood, all is lost. Then he and his family have to live up to them. Oh, what an effort!

Another feature of money is that the difference in happiness that it can create depends on how much money you already have. If a man is earning only 3,000 rupees a month, he is really struggling. If he gets 3,000 more a month, it makes a real difference. He is much happier. Another person earning 30,000 per month wouldn't become that happy if he gets an additional 3,000. The man who gets

300,000 a month will not even notice the difference. So, at lower levels of income, money has more power to boost the well-being.

What one is used to getting is very important. If the amount falls you get very frustrated. More than gain, humans just hate losing. That has been shown in surveys. So, if the flow of money becomes lower than a previous level it is big blow. You have become used to the high level that you were getting.

When the basic necessities of life are not met, we are miserable. As our incomes rise, we do become happier. But further increase in income does not increase our happiness linearly. We quickly reach a plateau, from which it is difficult to rise further. What we do with the money, it seems, is very important.

Materialism—what is it?

MY SCHOOL friend Sura went to the Gulf to escape poverty. He toiled for eighteen years at relatively low level jobs and came back with (what he thought) was a lot of money.

To buy a villa in the most expensive part of the city was his first move. When he purchased his second car, a Hyundai Accent, on top of his Maruti Alto, I rolled my eyes. He explained that all his neighbours had better cars.

Most had two, so he had to keep up. The children had to go to the most expensive schools, of course, as their friends in the neighbourhood went to the same school.

His father was a wholesale vegetable merchant. He knew the business well. He wanted his son to invest in it. He knew the turf and had the contacts. What was needed was the money. But Sura started a store for designer jewellery. His wife wanted that. Selling vegetables was not the fashionable thing to do among their circle of high profile businessmen and professionals. What will the Tiger's Club say?

When the store didn't do well, he promptly plunged into debt. The EMIs loomed menacingly. His father had prospered in his own business by then. But he didn't want to help him as he felt that Sura and his family had ignored him after coming back from UAE. He felt that his son was ashamed of him.

Materialism is increasing in the modern world. This is not a mere platitude. There is objective evidence for this. When college students are asked what is most important in life, significantly more reply that it is money and material comforts that matter. Twenty years earlier most used to say meaningful goals and purpose in life is more important. One may argue that they have become more realistic. What is wrong with that? It turns out that there is much that is wrong.

Materialism is not the same as money. Money is money. Materialism is an attitude. It has been studied by many psychologists and has certain features.

Material people believe that possessions will make them happy. They strive to acquire them and it is one of their main life goals. Possessions may include cars, a new house or even a prestigious job. They also are very possessive about them. They envy others who have better things as they see them. They may also be ungenerous—sharing wealth or things is not a priority with them. They want to 'wow' other people with their many acquisitions. Some can be very materialistic even though their income is low.

Research on spending habits and life satisfaction has been done from the 1970s. The commercial interests of big business ensured that it was an important thing to study. The initial assumption was that increased purchase and accumulation of worldly possessions would increase the life satisfaction of material people.

By the 1990s, it had become clear that materialism and spending money on things increased *unhappiness.* It was correlated with anxiety, depression, decreased self esteem and lesser life satisfaction.

Isn't there something uncannily familiar about these findings? Many so called sages had said the same thing. Buddhism considers possessions as active impediments to happiness.

The hedonic treadmill ensures that we become quickly adapted to new things. Ever wondered how long the happiness from a major acquisition like a new car or a new apartment lasts? Eight to twelve weeks is the answer. Then we tend to buy the next big thing, to replicate the high. Compulsive shopping and buying takes on an addictive quality. It becomes a disease.

Material things are very visual and are obvious markers of money and status. It makes others envious. Since it is the perceived relative income and status that all are competing for, they make everyone buy more, hoard more. More things. Better ones. Bigger and expensive. Everyone runs harder on the treadmill. People desperately try to make more money. The virus of materialism spreads. The manufacturers and the advertisers egg us on. The economy is booming, all are happy, they assert.

The increased stress on resources poison the planet, the only one we have. Our limited fresh water reserves are destroyed. Global warming threatens to fry us all out of existence in a few generations.

We need to evolve out of 'more for me' to 'adequate for all of us, today and for tomorrow'. But will human nature allow it?

How to spend money ?

WHEN MY friend Narendran Menon went to Abu Dhabi immediately after MBBS, I was very surprised. When he told me that his only intention of going was to make money, I pursed my lips. He was a good student. Was money his only agenda?

It turned out that he came from a poor family. His younger brother had just got into an engineering school. So he had to make money to help out the family.

He came back after five years and joined the health service. Though he never became a specialist, I have never heard him complain. He had some training in Palliative medicine and he became a sort of activist, doing voluntary work in his spare time.

When he took a big loan and started a business venture with his brother as the active partner, I was again surprised. It was an unexpected move from him. He told me that he wanted to have a large corpus of money or passive income so that he could retire early. He wanted to devote all his energy to an NGO that he wanted to start to strengthen Palliative Care services in the community.

I grew up in those times when the parents said that money was not important. 'Eat well, do your homework. Score well in exams. The money will come.'

Now I know that this is wrong. Money is very important. If I earn about the average in my reference group, I can be reasonably happy. After that point, it becomes increasingly difficult for money alone to increase our happiness. But money doesn't 'come' if you just sit and do what you like. One has to pursue money to an extent. This is a paradox of our times. Balance is critical.

It is extremely crucial for what purpose you are using the money. Money for money's sake could be an evil. When the focus is solely on material possessions, we are in a race to nowhere.

There are at least four ways one can aim to earn and use money that might increase personal happiness and the well-being of the community as a whole.

- To achieve some security and stability: Insecurity is a detriment to happiness. You cannot be satisfied with life when you are wondering where the next meal is coming from. Will you have to move to another city to survive? Are you in danger of losing your job? Will you be able to support your family next month? What will you do if there is a sudden grave illness? Who will support you in your old age?
- Total security is a mirage: We have to take life as it comes. But some security is needed. The problem in countries like India is that personal wealth is seen as the sole answer to all these questions. So people desperately strive to amass wealth. This leads to a materialistic mindset. This is especially true when the forces of modernity tears apart the security offered by family and community. The state has a role in ensuring that some basic security is available to its citizens when the times are hard. Otherwise, no one can be satisfied with an optimum level of earning. Increase in the security and stability is a

potent reason for some of the difference in happiness between the poor and the well-off.

- To be generous: It seems strange, but acts of kindness benefit the giver as well as the recipient. Generosity increases our satisfaction. At the same time, it benefits society. We have to have money, if we have to give some away. To do voluntary community work, you have to afford free time.
- To pursue good personal values and goals: A lack of money may prevent us from following what we believe in. Good goals involve good intentions towards society as well as towards oneself. Building and nurturing family, relationships, and community life are good goals.
- To purchase good experiences: This particular aspect was brought out by Van Boven and colleagues in 2005. Their research suggested that experiences are also commodities that can be purchased by money. And they provide more durable improvements in well-being than material possessions. A family trip to the museum, a series of music classes or taking time out for a course which you always wanted to do are examples. Van Boven says that they win over possessions due to three key characteristics.

Good experiences are less prone to hedonic adaptation. The memory of the summer trip to the grandparents can become even better in retrospect. We instinctively tweak our memories so that they become more positive with time. A new car becomes just another car in three months time.

They are less amenable to comparison. You really can't compare the magic show you went to with the kids with the neighbour's trip to Sri Lanka. Each experience is uniquely our own. Its value is subjective. People love telling one another about their experiences. It has been shown that people don't envy other's prospects of leisure or experiences as much as they do the material things or assets that others possess.

Good experiences are more social. Usually they involve family, friends or the wider community. They are the most important determinants of our sustained well-being.

In fact, for any external factor to have a sustained effect on our life satisfaction, it has to have these three factors. They should be resistant to the terrible treadmill effect; they should leave lasting good memories; we should not be able to decrease their importance by comparing it with others, and they should have a relevance to people close to you, and even the wider society that you are in.

The abyss of endless choice

SUGUN PRABHAKAR paced restlessly in the hostel room. This was an uncomfortable period in his life. His engagement was due in a couple of weeks. The fact that he was going to be permanently hitched to one girl did not make him brim over with happiness. He had more than a dozen girlfriends in Medical School, one after another. None of them lasted more than a few months. Though a variety of reasons lay behind each separation, Sugun knew that none of them matched his standards. Just as he seemed to be settling down with one, another more desirable girl always turned up. He was finally going to exchange rings with Shobha, but was she beautiful enough? She was not a doctor. That was something that he was still not reconciled with.

Then there was this thing about Speciality. Immediately after MBBS, he had got ENT in a good college in the north. He had joined, but had left in a few months. ENT was not for him. He wanted General Medicine. After MD, he wanted to do Cardiology. This was the path to success. Prestige and money was sure to follow. But General Medicine went to the best students. He was always average. He had to make an extra effort in the coming entrance exams.

Now he was rummaging in his closet for the new T-shirt he had purchased a week back. Where was it? It was lost in the hundreds of such shirts piled on the racks. He was going out with his friend Anand for dinner tonight. He had to have that particular shirt. He had to!

Meanwhile, Anand was walking to the quaint heritage restaurant at the hotel. He was also getting engaged in a few weeks. His looming matrimony was arranged by his parents. He had liked the girl the moment he saw her. Now he was always on the phone, talking to her. The anticipation of meeting her next week for an 'arranged date' filled him with pleasure.

Anand did not score well in the entrance exam. So he had joined a good private hospital in the city as a DNB trainee in Ophthalmology. He had to pass a difficult exam after three years, but a DNB was equal to an MD. Some did not consider it prestigious, but this did not bother him. Ophthalmology was good.

He ordered a mutton biriyani, without thinking much. It was good. He had had it before, in the same restaurant. He looked over at Sugun, his friend, who was pouring over the menu for the past ten minutes.

"This is a very tiresome period in our lives, don't you think? I am very agitated," said Sugun.

Anand looked at him in surprise.

Sheena Iyengar is a Canadian of Indian origin who did many studies on choice. She has written a book also on how people choose things. We are so used to thinking that more choice is good. Now we have a glut of choice. The rise of individuality, a loosening of expectations from society, and the rise of big business that inundates us with more choices every day, is seen as highly desirable. Sheena did a study where she gave volunteers the freedom to taste and choose chocolates to buy. When the choices were eight or less, the subjects took their time, tasted each, and made their choices.

Many bought what they liked. But when the choices were many, like 20, most people lost interest. They were mostly picking things at random and hardly bought anything. They were less satisfied, overall, with their experience. She did many similar experiments and had similar results.

David Myers and Robert Lane have found some evidence to suggest that an overabundance of choice leads to depression.

What do humans do when we have to choose? Economists always had the answer. Their rational choice theory states that people think about the various costs and benefits of each choice, especially monetary and material gain, and choose that which will give them maximum benefit—always. But it turns out that everyone doesn't do that. Only some do.

Herbert A Simon was the first psychologist to introduce the concept of Maximisers and Satisficers. Maximsers are a bit like what the Economists imagine people to be. They want to look at all the choices. They want the maximum benefit. They weigh each option carefully and aim for the best. For them, only the Best is good.

For the Satisficers, acceptable is good. They aim for what is satisfactory for them. They look at an array of choices and quickly zero in on one—"Oh that is good enough for me."

Barry Schwartz, Andrew Ward and Sonja Lyubomirsky were the pioneers, who in 2002, established a definite connection between this and happiness. Maximisers had less life satisfaction, happiness, optimism and self-esteem. They suffered from more regrets and depression. The Maximisers are more concerned with social comparison. Many of their choices are influenced by others. Social prestige is one of the major concerns of a Maximiser than his own individual radar.

In an earlier era, the universe of choice was a constrained one. You could only have whatever was available. You could do only what society wanted you to do.

Now, there is a Big Bang of options. And does the Satisficer win?

It depends on your viewpoint. Some studies have shown that Maximisers generally achieve more money and status. Of course, they are not happy with what they have acquired. Take your pick.

Career goals and happiness

SATHYENDRANATH WAS a colleague of my cousin. He was a software professional employed in the same company for the last twenty years. He was good at the particular domain in which he was working and had become a specialist in that particular branch of work. By his early forties he was drawing a 2.5 lakh salary. He and family were settled in a flat in Bangalore. Even though his pay was good, the EMIs kept him on his toes.

The recession hit the company rather badly. The orders from abroad for work in his particular domain dried up. He had become redundant. He was politely asked to leave. The management expressed their regret.

Sathya couldn't find a job for six months. By then, his financial position had become precarious. He sold his flat and moved to a rented one. The rent was astronomical in that part of the city. Finally he got a job offer from a company in Chennai. He had to travel every weekend, while his family stayed in Bangalore for the children and their schools. Learning a new line of work was tough. He was in a much more junior position and drew less salary. A few months into the new job, as he was travelling by bus in between cities, he had a massive heart attack and died.

"Wasn't there a better way to do it?" I asked my cousin.

"The company can't be blamed, really," my cousin asserted. "He had become redundant, and re-training a middle aged man is very difficult. One can't cut his salary. The company can recruit at least five youngsters with the same pay."

"It is all black and white, nowadays, you know," he continued. "The account books and financial logic governs all companies. That is the way of the world now. How else will the economy grow?"

Work is very important for happiness. One study demonstrated that people who had a meaningful job and well defined goals were much happier and lived longer than a group who led a life of idle leisure. Work gives us not only money, but meaning. It defines who we are, to an extent. The satisfaction that we are contributing something to society through our work is very important for our well-being. At work, we have a certain status in the hierarchy. It satisfies our basic need for pursuing status. Some of our colleagues become our friends. Being with, and working at common goals with our friends gives us enormous pleasure.

A UK Cabinet office survey in 2014 assessed the relationship between various jobs and life satisfaction. They found only a moderate link between levels of income and happiness. There are many other factors affecting life happiness. Numerous studies have made this clear during the last many decades.

Flexibility, adaptation to change, ability to switch careers midway, moving between jobs looking for better prospects seems to be what is needed today. Flexibility of a gymnast and the multitasking capability of a juggler are made out to be key skills in the present time. But solid evidence is there to show that stability and security of our job has a direct link to our well-being levels. One becomes better at the job, and it becomes more rewarding with time, provided certain other factors are there. Living in the same place, the same home and having stable relationships, neighbours and friends definitely boosts happiness. The pull of money may make you move, because the treadmill may frustrate you. This may provide only temporary respite, however. The threat of being fired looming overhead doesn't do wonders for your life satisfaction. Instability threatens all relationships including that with your spouse and children.

A callous employer, like a big company that looks at employees only through the eyes of its accountants, definitely is evil. A company cannot function as a faceless computer that doesn't value loyalty and trust. In the long-term, it is a sense of belonging that will keep people motivated.

A boring job is a sure path to unhappiness. An earlier work had demonstrated a clear link between repetitive small clerical jobs and clogging of the arteries or atherosclerosis. Our work should challenge our skills optimally without overwhelming our abilities. The 'Flow' concept was introduced by the scientist Mihaly Csikszentmihalyi. Flow is an activity in which you are so immersed, using your full concentration and skills, and which you enjoy. When in 'Flow' people do not notice the time passing. Teaching a favourite topic, creative writing, doing surgery, designing a building, composing a tune etc. are all some activities that may produce Flow. If your work has opportunities to produce this state, it will make you happier. Of course, Flow doesn't happen only at work. One can have hobbies that generate flow.

A good job gives one some autonomy and sense of control. When you are made to feel just like a spoke in the wheel or a brick in the wall, you don't feel involved. Adequate responsibility, decision making capacity and some control over our time makes a job conducive to well-being.

Our personal values and goals are important. The work that we do must hold meaning for us. It should have a sense of purpose. Values, goals, meaning and purpose are vague and nebulous terms. A physical scientist or a cynic might laugh at them. But they recur again and again in happiness research. A work with purpose may involve improving the society in some way, like medical research or social work. It may also be saving the rain forest, decreasing global warming, rooting out corruption, breeding a rare fish, building a business that will change the world in some way, learning psychology to treat mental illness or to help formulate national policy on the Middle East. Whatever turns you on and has some intrinsic meaning for you. Passion, dear reader, is what it is all about. It should not be about the money alone. If it is for the money alone, it should be a temporary means to earn enough money to...well, follow your intrinsic goals and values. Not to impress somebody else or to fulfil someone else's goals. *The Bhagavad Gita* puts it well—to do somebody else's Karma is the greatest curse.

Work—and drop dead

"HARD WORK never killed anybody". Yes—I have heard it many times. But there is a problem with that statement. The one who uttered it first may have believed it, but it isn't true. It has killed. The Japanese have a word for it—*Kiroshi.* Many in our present day urban societies have dropped dead from exhaustion due to too much work.

Even if it doesn't kill you, it can damage your health. The average blood pressure is higher in countries where people work more. It can kill off relationships and destroy the family. These two are the most important factors that determine long-term life happiness.

What induces people to do too much, and endanger their health and their relationships?

One line of thought is to think about it as a pure addiction. Hard work is highly valued. It boosts self esteem. You get praise and appreciation. One may get a high from the 'Flow' of Mihaly Csikszentmihalyi. You get promoted and gain status. It may also act as an escape route for people with low self esteem, social maladaption, intimacy problems with spouse, and disinclination to invest time in messy family affairs. It is much more socially accepted than plunging into alcoholism, compulsive gambling or drugs. Seen in this light, at least some persons who overwork drastically may be having a sort of psychological illness.

But I don't think that is true of most people. In fact, in certain countries more than half of the affluent and even not so affluent may be overworking. All of them cannot be mad!

There are at least two reasons I can think of that will make people work mindlessly hard.

Unreasonably high goals is definitely one thing. Our society today teaches us that we are all similarly highly endowed with skills. Anybody can achieve anything, if they work hard and with passion. The self-help books exhort us to go all out 'to get what is due' and to 'claim your rightful place in the universe'. All of us are born to rule. Beat everyone else. And thus gain unlimited self-esteem. 'How to become a billionaire in 90 days?' 'Think and become a CEO', are, I believe, popular reads.

The idea that anybody can do anything, and that our opportunities are limitless are two BIG lies of our times. All of us have skills, tastes and limitations. A five-foot-two, twenty-year-old is simply not fit for professional basketball. We have to have some self awareness and decide what we want to do. Unreasonable goals have been found to be a potent source of unhappiness, and even depression. But then you might ask—what if I want to be a Hollywood star? Didn't you just say that personal values and goals have to be followed? Well, strictly speaking, I said that good personal values and goals will increase well-being. You have to decide what is good.

The second reason is the treadmill. Work is a source of money. Work can bring us prestige and status. As we have seen, prestige, status and money can bring happiness to an extent. But we should remember that it is the relative position that actually determines it. So, as everyone in a particular society aspires and gets more, it pressurises every other individual to work more. Everyone runs faster on the treadmill to the detriment of everyone else.

The implications are not pleasant. Our widespread notion is that if somebody works more and earns more, it is his private matter. He is not harming anyone. But the concept of relative status means that when one amasses wealth by working excessively, it actually decreases the relative income of others. It smacks of communism and the need for forced equality.

The problem is that communist countries have always had, according to studies, the unhappiest people in the world. Historically, it has been a vehicle of misery. People want to be autonomous and free. They want to be left free to pursue their goals that may include competing for money and status. What to do now?

Also you may argue that in a developing country like ours, will not people balancing out their ambitions and working only optimally hurt the economy? How can we help people out of poverty without wealth being generated? Doesn't relentless hard work have a role?

Didn't Albert Einstein and Thomas Alva Edison overwork? Did the world wonder whether their families suffered? Does true greatness come from tempering your ambitions? Did Madame Curie think that Radium may ultimately kill her due to radiation sickness?

Did Amitabh Bachchan think that his goal of becoming a star was unreasonable? Didn't great writers resign their secure jobs to follow their passion?

Don't ask me. My narrative has to follow a scientific path. But human beings are not always logical. There are no logical answers to all questions. And discussing some of them requires more talent to throw Bullshit around than I possess.

I love you—now make me happy

WE HAVE big heads. That is what gives us a pain in the neck. Our brains weigh nearly one-and-a-half Kilos, while our closest relatives, the chimps, have only half of that. It also gives women a seductive sway in their hips. The abnormally wide pelvis of the human female is engineered to push out the large cranium of our babies. The brain continues to grow long after birth in humans. Human juveniles take a long while to mature, and it takes a long apprenticeship to learn to navigate the complex society and world of humans. It was not possible for one woman to bring up a clutch of human babies.

The father had to get involved. That was the beginning of the 'human pair-bond'. A whole gamut of complex emotions got birthed. Love, longing, jealousy, betrayal, sacrifice—a universe of feelings and connections burst into existence. The children now knew who the father was. Grandparents, uncles, aunts, nephews and cousins made their appearance. As humans are highly sexed, it was difficult to maintain fidelity. Society had to get involved. It had to officially sanction the union and discourage outsiders from ruining the relationship. Marriage was born.

Once an inevitability of adulthood like receding hairlines and sagging breasts, marriage now evokes mixed feelings. Many of us live in enlightened societies where you have a choice *not to marry*. Many married persons look back with a feeling of 'I wish...'

At least some of us, I am sure, will be surprised to learn that every study and survey conducted till date has confirmed that the married status is good for our well-being. Married people are generally happier in the long run than unmarried ones. Bachelors tend to die much earlier than married men. And divorce is associated with unhappiness. Our close relationships and immediate family are by far the most important determinants of happiness.

Did happiness come first or the married status came first? Do happy people remain married and not the other way round? Comparisons between different nations suggest that it is the married status that came first. A higher divorce rate predicts lower subjective well-being.

The advantages of marriage are many. It provides companionship and love. Sex and a sense of belonging are important. Caring for children and nurturing a relationship are seen as worthy goals that should be pursued. They may provide direction and meaning to our life. In societies where the government does not provide adequate buffer, the family is the prime source of security in old age.

And marriage is an institution definitely under threat. The 'World values survey' is an NGO that has studied people's attitudes and social indicators in 100 countries for the past thirty years. The value people attach to marriage has declined greatly in recent years. The divorce rate has gone up in almost every country. Children brought up by single parents have been shown in some studies to be more prone to anxiety, depression and crime. They are also more likely to have unhappy marriages when they grow up, thus perpetuating the cycle. Countries, governments and religion have made separating progressively easy for couples. Now, in most liberal democracies, it is relatively easy to part ways by mutual consent.

There are many reasons for this. One is the rise of Individualism. The idea that my own attitudes, pleasures and happiness come first, and that society has no role in determining them has both advantages and disadvantages. Individualism has risen because now people can afford to ignore society's norms. Government machinery has made an individual's security more stable. So, in general, people are not that interested in sacrificing much for the sake of their spouse, or even children.

Gender roles have changed. A woman can go out and earn. She is no longer dependent on her husband. That makes it easy to separate.

Society's pressure on a couple to remain married has eased. And there are more distractions. The new work culture leaves families with no time. Time constraints are a big breaker of families. The options have increased. It is possible for partners to have other relationships more easily. These are now increasingly considered personal things in which society should not interfere.

We cannot reverse any of this. When you look at tribal societies, we see that when the woman contributes equally to the resources in a community (as when most of the food comes from gathered stuff, and not by hunting), she has greater status. Separation is common among couples in those societies. In communities like the Inuit, where women are totally dependent, they are treated poorly, and divorce is very rare. We cannot save marriage by treading on the rights and freedom of women. One can argue that stability of marriage at any cost comes with the unhappiness of shackled women.

But the fact remains that close relationships and their stability contribute to our subjective well-being. Like so many things that concern humans and societies, it is the balance among contradictory forces that is probably appropriate. Can we become, by attitude—more giving, sacrificing and generous? Can the rise of individualism be tempered? Is it advisable to do so? These are all questions that we can think about. No sermonising here.

* 76 *

Tribals—simple yet healthy

THE YEAR is somewhere around 50000 BC. The place is somewhere in the Middle East, where there were forests and grasslands at that time. A group of anatomically modern humans had crossed over the narrow sea strait that separated Africa from Asia some thousands of years ago. Similar people were already living in Africa for more than two hundred thousand years. There were numerous groups of such humans scattered over that area. Similar subspecies and related species of Homo(like the Neanderthals), lived in the colder parts of Asia and Europe.

'Anatomically modern' means that if they were to don business suits and walk down the streets of Delhi or Bombay today we would stare only with idle curiosity. "Some foreigners," we would remark.

But this particular group of humans of 50000 years ago, were not dressed in business suits. They were clad in crude unstitched swathes of animal skin, and when the weather was warm, went mostly naked.

The group was of around three hundred men and women, and occupied a circle of crudely built huts. An old man was the chief. He was called simply 'The chief'. They called themselves 'The people'. They firmly believed that the hundred or so square kilometres of wilderness around them was the centre of the earth. This area they claimed as their own. The person called 'The God' had given them the title deed to that territory.

The man, whom we will call Mr Male, was a prominent member of the tribe. He was the husband of one of the Chief's daughters. So he had a high position in the tribe. He was the best archer in the tribe, and this increased his status. He had three children. Some other women wanted to marry him also. Mr Male did not agree, primarily because he didn't want to offend the Chief.

More than fifty people of the tribe were his relatives, either by blood or by marriage. And he could explain precisely how they were related to him. Many others also could be related, but no one knew how. The tribe functioned by a complex code of social ethics that was closely adhered to. Everyone trusted each other. Breach of trust was taken very seriously. Everyone knew everyone else.

The men hunted, the women gathered fruits and vegetables and tended the children. Mr Male had close bonds with many other males. They hunted together. Some were close friends. Women had common groups and supported one another to care for the young. Sometimes there were fights over women, or issues of honour. Rarely did one man murder another. But mostly, they were 'The peoples'. They were one. Mr Male had a sense of belonging and he was ready to die for the tribe.

Sometimes he had to be ready for that. There was an uneasy relationship with other tribes in the area. Some of the neighbouring tribes had similar languages, and they traded things and sometimes women. But occasionally, there were wars too. There were killings and abduction of women. 'The Others' could not be trusted. They were not like 'The People'. Sometimes, they were just like animals. Morally beneath 'The People'. They did not follow the lofty rules laid down by 'The God'.

It is a long time since 50000 BC. A lot has happened since then. The advent of agriculture, the era of technology, the rise of the mega cities has changed our way of life. But it seems that part of our brains and attitudes still belong to the Stone Age.

Those living in the community of their origin, with close relatives living nearby, are happier than displaced people. If you are in a village where you know almost everybody else, you are happier. New immigrants are more prone to depression, suicide and other mental illnesses.

Crime is more common in communities that have a sizeable number of new migrants that are outside the social net. When people feel that others can be trusted, the well-being of a community as a whole increases.

Can you measure trust? The 'World values survey' asked people in a community to respond to the question—what do you think is the percentage of the population that can be trusted in your community? The answers varied widely, ranging from below ten to over seventy. Then some scientists kept loaded purses, that had the addresses of the owner, strewn about in the streets. The percentage of purses that were returned was found to correlate closely with the assessment of the people. Isn't that amazing? We have a surprising knack of assessing others in our neighbourhood. And our appraisal influences our subjective well-being.

Reasonable equality in terms of money and dignity contributes to a community's happiness. In surveys, grossly unequal societies were unhappy. There was more crime, and levels of trust plummeted. In such societies, even the rich and people at the top of the status race were unhappier than similar privileged ones in more egalitarian societies. That is a paradoxical finding. Even though the relative status was high, the inequality so damaged community standards that everyone was rendered unhappier. It is worth repeating that the communist experiment of enforcing equality is counterproductive. Even now the former communist states are unhappier, while the happiest people are from the Scandinavian countries, where equality and dignity is high, and so is individual freedom.

We are at a crucial turning point in history. The population living in cities is overtaking those in the countryside in numbers. By 2050, it is estimated that seventy per cent of the world population will be living in cities. Cities throw up many challenges to one's well-being.

The blood pressure of city dwellers is, on an average, 4 mm higher than those from the villages. The level of stress is more. The lack of green spaces and the crowding jars on our nerves. The stability is less. It is more socially demanding. And most of the added stress comes from—well, other people.

Other people are a great source of companionship, friendship, entertainment and happiness. But usually not strangers. Strangers are perceived as a subconscious threat. Constantly negotiating a world filled with strangers does our Stone Age attitude no good. That is why the security provided by the faceless, yet useful, welfare state doesn't compensate for a more personal community life.

The most important factor that influences happiness in the external world is the people around you. Your spouse, children, close relatives and friends are crucial to happiness. Married people are, in general, happier than divorced and unmarried ones. Troubles in close interpersonal relationships breed potent misery.

Even in this modern world, we crave stability and closeness in our communities. When we are living near our friends and relatives, we are happier. Levels of trust are higher and crime is lower in happier communities. Equality is an important determinant to well-being but forced equality doesn't bring happiness. People are happy under free, autonomous and liberal governments.

Money and status do bring some happiness, but people compete for it. It is the relative levels of these that determine well-being. Material goods, money and status are also very prone to hedonic adaptation. We become used to the increases in a short time. Poverty definitely decreases happiness.

Work is very important. Having the right intrinsic goals is very important. Work is good if it aligns with your goals and has opportunities for personal growth and 'flow'. A life of idle leisure without any goals is perceived by many as meaningless. Stability is important in work.

But because of the 'treadmill' effect, anyone can have too much of a work incentive. As people run ever faster on the treadmill, one can work too much to get ahead in the race for status and money. This will bring happiness down.

One can use money to gain autonomy, freedom, pursue value goals or to purchase worthy experiences. Security got by having enough money can improve well-being.

The invasion of the 'Screens'

THERE WAS a time when I could not get enough of the news. TV Sets had become widespread during my teens. The constant stream of accidents, rapes, killings and street fights kept me riveted to the newspaper and the TV screen. The genocides, progroms, wars and famines going on in different parts of the world, promptly shown live in the living room made me lose my faith in humanity. Earthquakes, floods and storms rampaging in the far removed parts of the globe terrified me.

But I loved it. I spent hours in front of the box. I felt compelled to keep track of what was happening around the world.

I loved the other shows too. The colourful advertisements enticed me with the clothes, foods and high life on offer. The voluptuous models fascinated me with their abundance of beauty and curves. The rating-engineered serials impressed me with the sex, sleaze and deviousness of urban India.

In spite of all this, I had a sneaking suspicion that there was something amiss. Was all this distracting me from leading a full life? Could it be possible that these could be making me feel somehow inadequate? And anxious and unhappy?

The King of Bhutan thought so too. No—he was not concerned about me. He didn't know me. If he did, it was possible that he would have been. He was bothered about his subjects. He was one of the first rulers to describe 'the happiness of the people' as the most important goal of governance, rather than GDP. And Bhutan was one of the happiest societies in the world. The king allowed in television only very late, in the nineties, as he had concerns.

The nineties saw Bhutanese viewing high power ads, American serials and glitzy movies like everyone else.

Crime increased suddenly. Children became unruly, and school authorities were baffled. Affairs increased as marriages collapsed. Happiness levels plummeted as Bhutan began its march to modernity.

This effect was confirmed by some Canadian studies. Different states in Canada had cable television introduced at different times. Each state noticed the same unhappy effects as the Bhutanese.

Watching more than an hour a day of TV has been linked to almost all lifestyle diseases and obesity. It is evident that it makes some contribution to attention deficit disorder in children.

Now the number of screens that we have to encounter has multiplied. Laptops, desktops, android phones and touch screen devices litter the background like cookies in a bake house kitchen. Staring at screens is the norm. A recent study from Michigan University seems to show that social networking sites like Facebook may be contributing to human misery, if we don't use them in moderation. We are getting neck deep in the virtual world. Our inner worlds may not be handling this very well. What could be the reasons?

One major reason could be that it cuts us off from other people. It is clear from much of the science of well-being that the community and society are very important. Our friends and immediate family are crucial to our life, whether we like it or not. Healthy interaction is prevented by the 'screens'. The effect may be worse on developing brains. Neuroscience developments hint that the parts of the prefrontal cortex that are involved with social life continue to develop well into our thirties. We could rapidly become social retards, thanks to modern technology.

Now we have information injected into our consciousness from all over the world. Murders, wars and famines from across the world concern us deeply. The haunting images invade our psyches. Our poor tribal minds can't handle the pain, the threat perception and the anxiety. Any disturbance in our neighbourhood demands our immediate attention. We have to be concerned and anxious. We have to be on our guard. Our survival depends on it. Unfortunately, now the entire world is our neighbourhood. And we can do nothing to stop the nuclear arms race, bomb wielding terrorists or the globe warming. We feel anxious and powerless.

The movies and serials compete for our attention. They rake up violence and sex. Blood flows like water.

Now it has been proved that these things lead to a subtle effect called de-sensitisation. Our subconscious minds do not separate real life from screen life. Our children can't anyway. We become immune to other people's suffering. We become violent. We tend to believe that there are no values. Nobody follows them in the screen world anyway. If they can do it, I can do it. The effects of this are not so subtle.

The sneakiest effect is the one of comparison. The media worlds show a universe of unmatched opulence. We live in the living rooms of the idle rich. We discuss with them the benefits of a BMW over a Jaguar. We see them dine at expensive French restaurants. We travel with them, in our minds, across the globe to picturesque resorts. And we feel greatly diminished in comparison.

I see beautiful girls of all races. They stare at me seductively from the fashion channels. Their scantily clad curves beckon my testosterone ravaged body. All of them are so much more beautiful than my wife, I think. I never knew that so many women were *available* around. Maybe there are; should I look for them?

I am not sure whether my wife will read through the whole book. But for the record, the above paragraph is purely rhetorical and has no similarity to the actual goings-on in my mind at any point.

All about me?

MY FRIEND, Chitra Kinikkara, was the complaining sort. She lacked for nothing, yet she had a fixed morose expression on her face.

"I think I think too much." She told me once.

"Come again, I didn't get that." I gaped.

"You see, I am always thinking. Unnecessarily, I... think..." She explained. "When I get up I think. I am so tired today. Is it a cold coming on? All I want this week is a bad cold. After that blunder at the office I nearly lost my job. What would my boss have thought? He doesn't stand incompetence. That was what Lakshmi told me. Oh, my god! What if I get a fever? Dengue fever is rampant now. It can even turn fatal." She paused. "This is the way I think."

"Then I go to the mirror. And I think—good god, look at my hair. Half of it is gone. The wrinkles are a little bit more prominent today. I look like an old hag already. Suresh still looks so young. No wonder he ogles openly at all the young bimbos that are on the streets nowadays."

I smiled sheepishly. Men ogling at women had nothing to do with the state of their wives. Poor Suresh. I wanted to tell her that. But she was already in her own world, thinking something.

"She is a little crazy," I thought. "Always thinks nonsense."

But that made me observe myself and the way my mind worked for a few days. And I realised that I was doing the same thing, most of the time.

There is a name for this, I learned. It is called self obsessed rumination. It is also called 'overthinking' by people who don't like big words. Studies have shown that the thoughts in a person's mind wander 50 to 70 per cent of the time. It is a default mode of the brain. When you are not actively paying attention to something, your mind wanders. You may think about your past achievements or failures. You may despair or exult about your present situation. You may worry about the future. You may plan and rethink your goals. You may play out various future scenarios in your head. These may be pessimistic or joyful.

Sonja Lubomyrsky and colleagues studied this phenomenon for about a decade. They have come to the conclusion that some people do it more than others. And most of the time the thinking is pessimistic and negative.

When one is ruminating, it feels essential to 'think this through so that you can get around it'. One may feel that this is absolutely crucial for planning one's life or to find a solution. But these scientists say that the effect is predominantly negative. The advantages are minimal.

There is one more interesting thing about this phenomenon. It is almost always all about 'me'. What will happen to me if it turns out this way? I was so embarrassed that day! What did she think about me? I could have done it the other way so that she would have a better impression about me. If he fell ill, how would I handle it?

Humans have a huge jutting forehead. That is one important way our faces differ from those of apes. An area of the brain called the pre frontal cortex is responsible for it. In the last 5 million years of human evolution, when the whole brain enlarged by about three times, the pre frontal cortex swelled about six times. It has something essential to do with being human. But it still is not clear exactly what it does.

It is clear that it is the seat of self awareness. It monitors our deepest thoughts and fears. It is constantly in direct touch with the lower limbic system that generates emotions. It does this via funnily shaped neurons called 'Von Ekonomo' neurons. The effect of each sensation and decision is weighed and our emotional responses are assessed. It is a self monitoring system. The same system models other people's minds and reads their reactions.

The medial prefrontal cortex is the area that generates the constant mental chatter of overthinking. It must have had an important evolutionary function, but at the present time, for most people it is destructive.

There are obvious ways to overcome it. You can distract yourself. A hobby or book may do it. It is seen that overthinking leads to binge eating and binge drinking in some. They are doubtless dangerous ways of distracting oneself. You can start working on a solution, if it is a problem that is bugging you. You can take that essential first step.

You can train your mind to focus your attention elsewhere. This is the secret of the many mental practises espoused by gurus of the major religions.

How to 'de-me' yourself?

'FREEDOM FROM the self'. Ego is supposed to be the chief obstacle to 'Nirvana', according to some Buddhists. A lot of eastern religions exhort that 'freedom from the self' is the path to cosmic realisation. The concept of 'self' is an illusion that has to be dispelled.

Various types of meditation have been extensively studied in recent times. In a famous experiment, Jon Kabat-Zinn gave a course in meditation to employees in a company. He divided them into two groups. One group was put on a waiting list. No therapy was given to them. The other group was given a course in meditation for eight weeks. They were also asked to practice at home. The happiness of each group was measured before and after the course. In addition to questionnaires, EEG was also used.

The results were astonishing. The intervention increased the meditation group's happiness by 20 percentile points. And the results lasted a surprising four months.

In meditation, one sits in a comfortable position and focuses attention on one's breathing or on chanting a mantra. We can think with compassion about the world or fill our mind with god. There is a recent type called 'mindfulness meditation' where you have to sit and concentrate on your own sensations, external and internal—the present moment. Whenever the mind wanders, you have to gently bring it back to the task at hand. There are many variations, but this is the common theme.

Initially, one can concentrate only for a few seconds. Slowly, by training, the time spent in true meditation can be increased.

Another recent strategy is 'mindfulness'. You don't have to sit down and meditate. It can be practiced anywhere. The idea is to be fully aware of the present moment. Soak in your sensations and experiences in a non-judgemental way. You are not supposed to react to what is observed. You can observe your own thoughts also. Just be aware of them. When the mind wanders, gently bring it back to the present.

Sounds whacky? Teaching mindfulness has been shown to decrease the relapse rate of patients suffering from major depression by 50 per cent.

I can think of some other instances when the self ceases to exist and the mind is still. It happens sometimes when one is painting or writing fiction with full concentration. When I play table tennis with Varghese Paul, my friend from college, with girls watching, I try with all my concentration to beat him. I can recall times when a microsurgery is in progress, and I use all my skill to put that severed finger back in.

Yes—it is when you are in the flow of Czikszentmihalyi. It is when your attention is on the present moment. When the mind's focus is not on you.

When you focus attention the lateral prefrontal cortex is acting. Simultaneously, it inhibits the medial part, where the stupid negative mental chatter is going on. It clamps down overthinking.

In meditation and mindfulness technique, you are actively training yourself to direct your attention elsewhere. It is away from the self and destructive rumination. In short, these are not passive relaxation techniques, but active exercises that train our executive higher brain regions to have more control on our own mind.

And the focus is outwards. Away from the self. This is one crucial finding. Selfishly focussing on one's own happiness becomes counterproductive. This is why the intrinsic goals are better if they are directed towards the outside world and other people. The happiest people have their goals in how to serve society or to better the world with their skills. Sounds naive and preachy, doesn't it? But that is the surprising conclusion that we reach.

Extrinsic goals are what other people expect us to have. We try to live up to them. Most of the time they involve money, status and things that are very prone to hedonic adaptation. They are also comparative. You have to be better than the next man. As Richard Layard puts it—"it is not enough that you succeed; others must fail." It is a zero sum game.

Is 'God' a thing?

Looking at the evidence from a purely scientific point of view, I was unnerved by the role played by the 'right attitudes and values'. What is 'right'? It smacks uncomfortably of—well, religion. Look at some facts:

If you hold a grudge, it harms you mentally and physically. When you forgive somebody wholeheartedly, you feel relieved and happy. The ability to forgive boosts well-being.

Showing and feeling gratitude for the small blessings in your life gladdens you. Expressing it to a person whom you owe it to benefits you as much as him.

Selfish focus on yourself and your needs does nothing for your well-being. Caring and concern for others boosts it.

Giving benefits the giver almost as much as the receiver. Kind people are happier.

Of course, it is not that evolution cannot explain these things. It can. In fact, it seems too neat for me, like a 'put up job', as Fred Hoyle the famous physicist once said. He was talking about the universe, not evolution. Let us not go into that and stick to happiness.

In fact, it appears that there is a great deal that religion and a belief in God can do for one's health. Believers are happier, healthier and recover better after adverse life events than others. In one famous study, patients who were religious and had very serious cardiac surgery were three times more likely to be alive six months later.

The believers are more likely to be satisfied with their lives. They cope better with crises. It is one of the most robust findings in happiness research.

Some of the effect can be explained by the fact that religious ones are more likely to be non-smokers or non-alcoholics.

The dominant idea of our scientific times is that the Universe is a faceless indifferent physical system, and we are an accident of nature. The essential meaninglessness of existence is increasingly being accepted at a subconscious level. Whatever be the truth of that assertion (I don't believe it), you have to accept one thing—this view is depressing. Those who believe in God find it much easier to find meaning in their lives.

Organised religions, it is true, have sometimes done more harm than good. They have given a reason for people to fight one against the other on the basis of difference in their beliefs. It is a feature of our tribal mind set—the others are different, hence bad, so kill them.

What we are considering here is the spiritual concept of a personal God. Looking from that angle, as a force that makes people happier, more resilient, and value driven, God is indeed a thing. He has to be considered a good thing, then. But you can argue that this is just a concept.

But happiness is also a concept, right? Yet, it is also a feeling pre-wired into our brain circuits. And hence, we argue that it is real. But then, could God have the same kind of ethereal, platonic existence?

V S Ramachandran, the neuroscientist who wrote *Phantoms in the brain* and many other books was the first to suggest that humans may have what he called a 'God module' in their brains. He studied patients with temporal lobe epilepsy. The recurrent seizures originating from the temporal lobe strengthen the connections in that area. This leads to an amplification of the effects of that brain area on the personalities of these people. 'Hyper religiosity' is the term used to describe one of their personality traits. They are believers, and God holds deep meaning for them. They have visions and mystical leanings. Dr Ramachandran demonstrated that their visceral emotional responses to any other stimuli are blunted, and they have an exaggerated response to spiritual suggestions. They are *oriented* to God.

Michael Persinger from Ontario tried to magnetically

stimulate the portion of the left temporal cortex implicated by Ramachandran in healthy subjects. Most of them had 'religious' visions or felt a mysterious spiritual presence. God?

Seizures or stimulations of this area sometimes lead to sudden visions, that the subjects claim, made them understand the meaning of life and the secret purpose of the Universe.

"I see everything now. I get what it is all about," they say.

Jordan Grafman, from the US National Institute of Neurology, studied the phenomenon in greater detail. He found out that there was a complex interconnected system of brain centres spanning many regions that were involved in spirituality and God. One of them is in the pre frontal cortex. These regions were activated whenever the experimental subjects were asked to ponder moral dilemmas (like would you allow your grandfather to die if by doing that you could save your nephew?), and questions of purpose, meaning of life and God. The same regions were at work in both believers and atheists! That is surely suggestive that something is deeply biological about it.

Whether you want it or not, a conglomeration of neural networks in your brain may be playing God or having a hotline to him. Believe what you will.

The higher areas of our brains are responsible for self awareness and monitoring. We are in a mind wandering state for much of our waking selves whenever we are not devoting our full attention to something. Many of us are prone to excessive negative rumination. This 'overthinking' is depressing.

Whenever our full attention is turned to a task, this mental chatter disappears. Techniques like mindfulness and meditation have been shown to improve well-being. They may act, at least partly, by training our minds to focus our attention in a more acceptable way.

'Good values' and the 'right' goals are important for well-being. Gratitude, forgiveness and kindness are qualities that will bring life satisfaction.

Religious people and believers in God are happier and sometimes healthier than others. They are less prone to stress and bounce back from adverse events more promptly. Latest research has shown that there are some areas of the brain in humans that are specifically concerned with, and that evoke spirituality. These areas are present in atheists also and are active during moral reasoning and thinking about the big questions of life's meaning and purpose.

I will not elaborate on what you should do to increase well-being. This is not that type of self help book. And I am not a certified psychiatrist or a life coach or anything. I am not going to preach about happiness, mainly because I am not qualified to do so. I think many things are self evident from the discussion. If you think that you have severe mental health issues, you should consult a professional. Especially if you are substantially depressed most of the time. This book is not therapy.

But it is clear that you may have to move against some of your instincts and innate drives, and strive towards a greater purpose. This quality is called self-control or self-regulation. For example, to get out of the rat race, you may have to resist the pressures of society to an extent. You may have to rein in your impulsive materialism.

Happiness and health are interrelated. Happiness increases health. But happiness alone is not enough. As I am a qualified medical doctor, in the next section I have given some explicit preventive health advice. Again—if you think you have problems, you should consult a physician and have a personal physical exam, tests and advice.

Healthy life—the fine balance

HEALTH IS a concept that all of us understand instinctively, so there is no point in nitpicking with definitions. It involves at least two things:

A reasonably healthy body without major illnesses.

Feeling good about our own self.

The question we want to examine in this section is:

How much of it is in our control?

Let us talk about bodily health. There are three things, when looked at in a basic way that affect our health.

Environment: Suppose you are desperately poor and can't

afford adequate food of good quality. This is a situational problem for you. It is not easily modifiable. Another example is when your surroundings are highly stressful—war, crimes, other stresses. Or you may be living in a factory area where the water and air are highly polluted.

Physiology and genetics: Our age, gender, and genes affect our health. If your father had a massive heart attack at thirty-five without any previous risk factors, you are likely to have a high possibility of developing heart disease. About that basic fact, you can do nothing. You can always try to offset this by preventive measures.

Plain luck or chance: Or what some of us may call God's will. I can have a serious traffic accident at twenty-five and become crippled for life. I can get a sudden attack of severe meningitis and die the next day. I may get a largely non-preventable cancer like stomach cancer or leukaemia.

Lifestyle: We can modify some of our habits, or change some things in the way we live, that can improve our health. This is basically what we are interested in.

Or can we? Is such a statement the truth? If true, what are the lifestyle factors that affect our health? How can we know for sure?

The plain and simple answer is we can't be absolutely sure. Not in the way we are sure that one plus one is two. Not even in the way an engineer can calculate the stresses in a to-be constructed bridge, or a software specialist can predict the way a program might work.

The only way we can move towards these truths is by doing good epidemiological studies and evaluating these studies critically. Many studies have already been done and a lot are being done continuously. The results keep coming out, every single day. All you have to do is read them and come to your own conclusions.

The problem is, you need a little training and experience to evaluate them. To separate the wheat from the chaff. The real stuff from the bullshit. This I will try to do. But I do not claim to be the foremost expert in this field. I do not claim infallibility.

The basic question is—can we influence our own health by our behaviour? If so, what are the things that we should do?

The Alameda County Health study is one that started in 1965. It enrolled over 7000 people and assessed them by a questionnaire. Then these people were reliably followed up with regular assessment of their health and the diseases they developed. Numerous articles and papers came out of the study—one significant one in 2005. This is an example of a good study. Many other good studies trying to answer similar questions have reached almost the same conclusions.

It turns out that some habits are important predictors of survival.

They are:

- Adequate exercise—Being reasonably active.
- Getting seven to eight hours of sleep every day.

- Maintaining a healthy body weight.
- Limited intake of alcohol.
- No smoking.

Not surprising at all, isn't it? Very basic and obvious.

Not really. They were not that obvious a hundred years ago. Or even fifty years ago. Fortunately, we live in an age in which we know these things. All we have to do is follow these simple rules to have a significant chance at improving our health and longevity.

The take home lesson is that we can affect our own health by our own efforts, to some extent. And these are the things to do. Only problem is the cliché—it is easier said than done.

The not-so-wise conventional wisdom

I WENT to a government public school in Trichur in Kerala. There the boys start smoking early. My friend and classmate Anees Ibrahim started in the sixth standard. I don't know where he got the money to get cigarettes and beedis from, but he was smoking all the time. Whenever the teacher was not in class. During recess. Sometimes he cut classes and chain smoked. After I finished school, he had apparently continued smoking. When I started college, he was working with his father at his shop. When I was around twenty, someone informed me that

Anees had died. He complained of a sudden chest pain and died on the way to the hospital.

"No one knows how he died. He was so young, it couldn't be a heart attack," he told me.

Five thousand years ago, or maybe it was seven thousand, a group of humans in South America learned to cultivate a plant to harvest its leaves. They burnt the leaves, and inhaled the fumes, and found it pleasant for some reason. They considered it a special gift from the creator, healthful and invigorating. The exhaled fumes carried their prayers straight to the good god above, or so they believed.

The plant was tobacco.

After colonisation, the plant was carried and re-planted lovingly by humans. It reached all the corners of the globe, leaving the local people puffing away at its fumes. It was generally considered benign and even life-enhancing. Throughout the industrial revolution and the budding age of reason, Europeans burned and inhaled tons and tons of the dried leaf.

Doctors considered themselves men of science in Europe from the seventeenth century onwards. Throughout the seventeenth, eighteenth and nineteenth centuries, these men of science praised tobacco and smoking for its health enhancing properties. And they puffed away at pipes, cigars, cigarettes, happily, while seeing patients and even when they performed surgeries.

It was in 1929 that a German doctor named Fritz

Lickint found a statistical association between smoking and lung cancer. But it was ignored by most of the world after Germany's defeat in the Second World War. In 1954, a study of forty thousand British doctors over twenty years found a clear link between smoking and lung cancer. Then the world started paying attention.

Today, we know that smoking is a major risk factor in causing: Heart attacks, strokes, emphysema, and cancers of the lung, larynx, mouth, oesophagus and pancreas. It is the number one cause of bladder cancer. It causes diffuse narrowing of blood vessels throughout the body that cause gangrene, leading to requirement of amputation of foot or leg.

WHO estimates that tobacco causes more than five million deaths a year. The US Centre for Disease Control describes tobacco as the single most important preventable risk to human health in developed countries.

In its five thousand year history of rampant use, not once was the devastating nature of tobacco found out by healers, rulers and philosophers, till the systematic studies of the twentieth century. No one was wise enough.

An uncle of mine was in his late sixties when he had his first heart attack. He was immediately taken to the hospital and an emergency Angiogram was done. The doctors discovered significant narrowing in two of the arteries supplying the heart. Immediate angioplasty—dilating of the block, and stenting was done. He was discharged after three days. Now he is back to normal and has resumed all his normal activities.

He had led a very careful life. He never smoked, and drank in strict moderation. He was quite careful about what he ate and kept his weight within normal limits. He walked briskly for an hour a day. He had regular check-ups and tests. He was fanatic about keeping his blood sugar under control as he had mild diabetes.

"What was the point of being so careful all your life, if after all that you get a bloody heart attack?" One of his friends commented. "Wasted most of his life without enjoying himself."

"Yes, that is right." Another of his friends said. "I have smoked throughout my life and eaten whatever I wanted. Never had to stay in a hospital ever. It is all fate I tell you. Trying to change fate is not going to work. That is what all the wise people say."

I talked to my uncle later when he was back to work. He told me about his father who died at the age of forty-five.

"He had chest pain and was admitted in the hospital when he was about forty, as I remember," said my uncle.

"He was a heavy smoker and was very fat. Never cared about how he lived. After coming back from the hospital, he was a sick man. Always breathless. But after that he listened to the doctor and was very careful."

"What did the doctor tell him? Did he stop smoking?"

"The doctor did not stress on that. I don't think at that

time they were aware of all that. So he continued to smoke. He was advised to take rest and eat good food."

"Such as?"

"Lots of milk, butter and eggs. Also plenty of beef liver. Entire goats were bought just to make *rasayanam* with the meat. He also advised us to add ghee to whatever he ate. The doctor told us that was the only way to build up his health. Inspite of all this, my father deteriorated and started having severe chest pains. Breathlessness worsened and he became bedridden towards the end of his life."

"I see."

"The doctor was a good family friend. He came for the funeral and helped us a lot. He was a nice man. He consoled us saying that sometimes you just can't do anything about fate."

When even the medical wisdom of a past age cannot be relied upon, what can we do? How exactly is the truth arrived at in Medicine?

What is the truth?

WE ASSUME that the truth is out there somewhere. Early philosophers like Aristotle believed that truth can be ascertained by logical arguments. The problem is what is—logical may not be true.

"What is the 'TRUTH'? That is the question."

"Well, we can ask my wife. She is an expert at finding out the truth. I am speaking from experience."

All birds walk on two legs.

All mammals walk on four legs.

Man is a bird.

This is the logic fallacy. Aristotle stated that thinking logically, men will have more teeth than women. The fact was accepted as conventional wisdom for over a thousand years before a few sceptics in the budding age of reason decided to count and see for themselves. I am sure there must have been lot of resistance to the idea. "What! equal number of teeth? It cannot be!"

But a philosopher who certainly got close to the truth was Pythagoras. Geometry is as close to the truth as you can get. Mathematical truth.

Scientific truth follows these paths:

Mathematical formulation of theories.

Experiment and observation—then inference.

Just observation and inference.

In clinical medicine, there is little mathematical theorisation. So we might as well forget it. The only mathematics routinely used in clinical studies is Statistics. And we cannot do without statistics.

Can we do experiments in clinical medicine? We can study the effect of drugs or chemicals in cultured cells or tissue systems in a test tube (in vitro). We can give medicines to, or do surgery on, or alter the diet or living conditions of experimental animals like rats and study the effects. This process can be done on human beings also, with strict guidelines, consent, ethical committee approval etc.

These experimental studies are called trials. A Randomised Controlled Trial (RCT) is the most reliable type of trial in which there is randomised allocation of subjects into groups—some will receive one intervention, others a different one or no intervention. It can also be placebo controlled and double blind. Placebo is a benign substance or intervention that has no effect. It is given to the group that is to receive no intervention. Double blind means that neither the patients nor the medical scientists evaluating the study know which group receives which. Then bias can be minimised. A Meta analysis (Statistical evaluation of many trials) of many RCTs provides the highest level of evidence possible in medicine. It is by no means infallible, however.

In studies of lifestyle factors that influence human health and disease, trials have little role. Here, we have to rely on pure observation only studies. Simplifying a bit, these are:

- Case-control studies. To assess the factors leading to lung cancer, we can take a group of people having the disease and a comparable group of normal persons. Then we can assess how many smoked in each group, how many were exposed to pollution etc. and then compare the differences using statistical methods.
- Cohort study: Here we follow-up an entire subset of population and assess characters and habits that might be relevant, on a continuous basis. Then we observe the diseases that develop in that population.

Then do the same comparison. This is a better study design, but much more difficult to do.

- Descriptive studies: In this we just note the diseases affecting a group—for example of obese people and then compare it with the general population of comparable characteristics.

Expert advice and recommendations of a panel of experts comes after these levels of evidence. These are the least reliable in scientific terms. Yet are sometimes necessary to consolidate and evaluate the different study results. Conventional wisdom comes at the very bottom. Sometimes it is right, and sometimes not.

Granny and the Good old times

I WAS seeing my friend's granny after almost twenty years. Our gang used to hang out in his house during our med school days. She was ninety-six. It was nice to see that her intellect was as sharp as ever. I had some questions for her. Nearly a century of memories were not to be wasted. I congratulated her on her robust health and intellect.

"Everything is god's grace," she replied.

"I belong to the old generation," she clarified as if it was not obvious enough. "So, no diabetes and high blood pressure and things like that. I do have mild diabetes and slightly elevated pressure. But that was detected only after I turned seventy-five."

"Great, granny! That is really good. And you raised seven children. It is a remarkable feat. Now we struggle to bring up one or two."

"Actually, I bore ten children. Three died. All before they turned three."

"That is sad. How?" I probed.

"Oh, some illnesses. That time it was very common for young babies to die. Karthiyani had seven children, but only three lived."

She had become rather sober. I didn't want to pursue it further.

"I had to bring them up by myself. The youngest was quite small when my husband died. He was a famous lawyer. You know that, no? He was about forty when he died. Tuberculosis. That time lot of people died of tuberculosis."

"But you did not have any major illnesses. That was a blessing."

"Yes, I was very healthy. Always ready to do two men's work. Today, the women are so lazy."

I looked at my wife, sitting beside me, and thought that it was better not to comment.

"I almost died once. I must have been around thirty-five or so. The doctor, Sankaran Menon, who was trained in England, treated me. He said it was typhoid. One of my cousins also died of typhoid when she was young." She became thoughtful. "And a sister died while giving birth to her second baby. Many women died that way. By god's grace I escaped all that."

"Granny, your father and mother were big landlords, weren't they?"

Granny laughed. "Farmers. We were a farming family. My father worked on the farm till he suddenly collapsed, complained of chest pain and died suddenly."

"Oh! Okay. Did he have hypertension or diabetes?" I asked.

"How do I know? And I told you those days we didn't have these illnesses." Granny was becoming irritated. She turned to my wife.

"He might have become a big doctor, but is still rather stupid. I knew him as a boy."

My wife nodded and sighed. "I know." She said it with an exaggerated roll of her eyes. I quickly tried to change the topic.

"Quite hot these days, isn't it?" I was sweating now.

"We didn't have these kinds of summers in our younger days," Granny said. "The weather was always very pleasant."

Our collective recollections of earlier times are not very reliable. They are coloured by nostalgia of the great and good times that will never return. We yearn for that golden period in history that never existed. Myths, lore and tall tales obscure our search for the truth.

I think we can safely state some self evident truths,

backed by solid historical statistics.

Throughout most of our known history, our major scourges were infectious diseases caused by micro organisms, famine, war, violence, accidents and the very real risks of child bearing and giving birth.

Our lifespan has been increasing steadily. At the time of independence, it was around forty-five. Right now, in Kerala, it is approximately eighty. This trend hasn't stabilised even in the west. The lifespan continues to increase. This is one major reason for the increase in *incidence* of so-called lifestyle diseases. This applies to most cancers, as they are commoner with increase in age.

As screening for diabetes, hypertension etc. were not there during previous ages, and there were no reliable records of causes of death, it is impossible to know the incidence of these diseases.

When infectious diseases and other ancient scourges became less, chronic diseases like heart diseases and diabetes became important. Lifespan increased dramatically over the last few centuries.

But since the beginning of reasonably reliable record keeping in the west, there has been an absolute increase in the incidence of these diseases, as countries become more industrialised and urban. So, the term lifestyle disease may not be a misnomer.

Teasing apart the various causes and aspects of this phenomenon is not easy. We humans have a tendency to mix facts, possibilities, and plain falsehood into a confusing bullshitogenic mix.

We need solid data on all the diseases and causes of death. This we know, in most parts of the world, only for a half century. This data does show an apparent increase in the incidence of chronic diseases. Part of this is due to increase in the lifespan. But studies on migration have shown that people acquire these diseases on arrival in a more developed country. For example, indigenous Africans quickly get diabetes, hypertension and some cancers once they land and live in the US, while back in their motherland, the illnesses are practically unknown. This shows that, while heredity may predispose us to have these diseases, they are products of our present lifestyle. And may be largely preventable.

Clarity by statistics

DR BALAKRISHNAN was a colleague at a hospital where I previously worked. He was in his forties. His father had a heart attack during his fifties. But Bala started regular checkups only recently, and was disconcerted to learn that he had quite high cholesterol levels. It was always above three hundred. The fact was that Bala was already leading a careful life. Exercise, healthy frugal diet, the works. So, it was clear that he had a tendency to high cholesterol. He had to have medicines to lower it.

Though he was a doctor of Modern Medicine, Bala was a big fan of traditional and alternative Medicine. He went to an Ayurvedic practitioner who gave him a herbal mixture. Two tablespoons had to be taken every day at bedtime.

A neighbour knew a homeopath nearby. He was a very famous man. Patients came from far and wide to see him. He was a specialist in chronic diseases, and after a consultation he advised Bala to take two small sugary pills every morning. Bala complied happily.

Around fifty kilometres away from where he was staying, a traditional healer practised. He treated all diseases by massage. Did he have a treatment for hypercholesterolemia? Of course he did. Bala drove there every week for a one hour session of massaging his abdomen by the healer.

"The abdomen is the conduit for cholesterol," the healer said. He was right, of course, though not exactly.

Bala cut down further on his fat intake and tightened his diet. He scaled up the exercise. He took two capsules of fish oil every day which has lots of omega 3 fatty acids, shown to decrease cholesterol levels. He gobbled down a fistful of omega3 rich flaxseeds that taste like mud when chewed, at noon.

"This is proper and scientific," said Bala, a little defensively.

After all this, he checked his cholesterol. It was 290. He checked it again after a week—293. A consistent drop of ten to twenty units from his previous levels was achieved.

He felt it was great.

The Cardiologist friend he had consulted did not think so. "It has to be below 200," he insisted, and prescribed him Atorvastatin, a cholesterol lowering drug, that blocks the enzyme HMG Coenzyme A reductase, a key pathway in cholesterol synthesis. Bala reluctantly started taking ten milligram a day. He continued all the other measures too.

After a month Bala's cholesterol was down to 180. He was very happy. He told me he was going to continue doing all the other things also, in addition to taking the medicine.

"It is the concerted effect of all these measures that brought it down. This is holistic medicine," he said.

A few years back, I was leafing through a very popular women's magazine when I was struck by a headline:

'Anti-ageing effect of rejuvenation massage—proven beyond doubt.'

It was the account of an experiment to prove the effectiveness of a traditional treatment designed to make one younger. The treatment consisted of a carefully designed series of procedures. It was a residential program. The client had to stay for one month. The details of the treatment were described in the article. The salient points were:

A herbal concoction to be drunk three times a day (One glass each).

Whole body massage twice a day with specially designed medicinal oil.

Enema administered once a day (To clean up the system).

Transcendental Meditation (Taught by a master of the art).

Yoga therapy for an hour every day.

A famous fifty-year-old media personality had volunteered for the treatment. He had mild diabetes (Fasting glucose 140 mg per decilitre) and mild hypertension (140/90). He had slightly abnormal blood lipid levels. These and many other details were given.

After one whole month, the writer of the article gleefully reports that the man looked much younger. His diabetes was gone (Fasting sugar 110 mg/dl). Blood pressure was almost normal (130/80). The lipid parameters and cholesterol values were notably improved. Hooray! The treatment worked. The pre-treatment and post-treatment (smiling) photographs were also given. This could convince the most sceptical person.

But if one went carefully through the entire article, it was mentioned in passing that the food was based on a strict diet, rich in fruits and vegetables. At the bottom of a table given in smaller print (pre and post treatment effects) one could see that the client lost around five kilograms of body weight during this period.

The problem is, a seven to ten per cent decrease in body weight can by itself account for all the improvement in blood pressure, sugars, cholesterol etc. Can we reach any conclusion at all from a single person's experience in this kind of thing? The answer is No.

How do we know what factors actually caused the effects, in the cases mentioned? Is the Atorvastatin responsible for correcting Bala's cholesterol levels or are the other things, like the Ayurvedic drugs and the massage contributing to the effect? What is the effect of each factor? Can we quantify the effect of each thing as a percentage?

It is possible, but only if we have hard data of a large number of people. Then we can use statistical methods like multiple regression analysis to assess the contribution of each factor. It is practically impossible to comment on individual cases. The human body, the way it reacts and the sheer amount and variety of variables involved is so complex that sense can only be made out in large numbers. And by using troublesome statistics.

But our minds derive enormous meaning from emotionally charged single events and people. We strive to derive the truth from our own or other people's experiences. This is true in many cases. But quite often, when we are trying to get at the actual scientific truth, it is not enough. We need well designed studies. Even then, these will predict the effect of any one thing on a single person only approximately. But our beliefs do not need the truth.

"Follow your heart—but take your brain with you."

Last when I met Bala, he had discontinued Atorvastatin. Now he gets an extra massage each week to compensate for that. His cholesterol levels? He doesn't know. He has stopped checking for it regularly.

"It is stupid to obsess too much about one's health. It is generally not good to take tablets for a lifetime, isn't it? The important thing is to live healthily and be happy. That is what I believe," he said.

Between obsession and being careful there is a very thin line. But that line is very important. It may mark the difference between life and death. So I cannot agree with Bala.

Those damn genes—again!

MANIKANTAN (NOT the real name, of course. None of the names in this book are) came to the OPD with a diabetic foot. The heel of his right foot was eaten away by infection. His doctor had advised amputation. He had come for a second opinion. He was forty-five.

It was not a bright scene. The pulses of that leg were absent, indicating blocked arteries due to atherosclerosis. Atherosclerosis is a generalised disease process that affects arteries all over the body, which meant he could have....

"He had two attacks also doctor," his wife informed me in an anguished voice, breaking my line of thought. "The first one was five years back. That time they discovered that he had severe diabetes also."

Attack, of course meant 'heart attacks'. These ubiquitous

killers are known in the wider community by that name.

"I don't smoke, not one puff," lamented Manikantan. "No drinks. Strict vegetarian. Look at my lean body, sir," he emphasised, self pity oozing out of each word.

"Was there anybody with similar illnesses in the family? Any heart disease or diabetes?" I asked.

"Absolutely not. My parents and siblings are all healthy. Why did this happen to me?" Pained innocence was etched on his face. I looked at the wife. She was sympathetic, but her expression betrayed a scepticism that was not lost on me.

"When did he stop smoking?" I asked her.

"Only after the first attack. Till then he was smoking four to five packs a day for as long as I can remember. And he never had any control over anything, including food. Of course, after the illnesses he strictly followed the doctor's suggestions. He lost ten kilos," she conceded.

"He never had any health check up before that. So we don't know when he developed the hypertension and diabetes," she concluded.

One of my colleagues in a hospital in Bangalore where I was working at that time was a fanatic about his health. He exercised for an hour a day. The occasional ten kilometer races and half marathons in the city always had him as a participant. He had his own diet plan and kept his BMI at around 21. That was not a mean feat, since he really loved his food. He avoided any added sugar in any of his drinks. Sweet foods and refined carbohydrates were an anathema to him.

Why did he do all this?

He told me that both his father and mother had severe diabetes. His three brothers were diabetics. He wanted to beat his heredity. He was a general physician and used all his knowledge and self-control to pursue this.

He developed diabetes at the age of sixty-two. Many of our colleagues laughed at him secretly behind his back, as his obsession had failed. I decided to ask him about how he felt, directly.

"Do you feel your efforts were useless? You were not able to...well...stave off destiny, so to speak."

"You see, I have been detected with mild diabetes, and a single tablet of Metformin, along with my exercise and diet is enough to control it. My parents were dead in their fifties. And do you know, both my elder brothers died of kidney failure in their sixties? All of them had already developed severe diabetes requiring insulin injections when they were in their forties. And they were not at all regular with the treatment. If I control my disease well, it may not progress to life threatening complications till my eighties and nineties.

"I don't mind that," he continued. "You have to die of something. It may happen before that also. That is god's wish. I may still have developed the disease at thirty, in spite of my efforts. Or I might have developed a cancer or something and died early. I believe we have to do what we can and leave the rest to god."

There is no doubt that many of the factors that affect

our health are beyond our control—one of which is our innate constitution. In other words, our genes, half of which come from the father and half from the mother. They are shuffled by a process called 'crossing over', and then they are handed over to us, in a game of cosmic poker. Does that mean that we are mere pawns in a game of lottery, with our destinies already made? We saw in the previous section, how important our innate constitution is for our mental selves. For our body, surely it will be even more important?

Some science seems to indicate that genes are indeed important. A parent who has developed cardiovascular disease at a young age is considered a major risk factor for heart disease as per the Framingham study findings. If one identical twin has diabetes, the chance that the other will develop it is 90 per cent. If a non-identical twin or a sibling has the disease, the chance that one will contract diabetes is 25 to 50 per cent. A study by Kristina Sundquist of Sweden on 80000 adopted men and women who developed coronary artery disease from 1973 to 2008 seems to indicate that if a biological parent had the disease, the chance that the offspring would get it is 40 to 60 per cent higher.

But if one reviews the studies in the field critically, the scene is fraught with contradictions. Two large studies from North-western University say that a healthy lifestyle has the largest effect on cardiovascular health. One was done on 2300 people followed up for 20 years. Another was done on three generations—famed Framingham study, involving more than 10000 people. Both conclude that only a small proportion of risk factors are inherited.

Till today, more than fifty genes have been found, that contribute to the development of diabetes. Yet researchers conclude that together they constitute only 10 per cent of the heritable component of the disease.

Confusing? It certainly is. There are two reasons for this. One is that in most cases, except in certain rare conditions, a gene very rarely contributes directly to a disease. In most common diseases, a multitude of genes interact in complex ways to exert its effect. To make matters worse, the genes are very much influenced by environmental factors that tend to switch the genes on and off to exert an effect.

The second reason is the controversial but nevertheless true fact that our behaviours are also influenced by our genes. An adopted boy whose biological father is a careful teetotaller and frugal eater may do the same, even in a household populated by alcoholic gluttons who have no concern for their own health.

Ever heard of the gene TMEM163? Well, it is a gene found out first by scientists of the Indian Diabetes Consortium in 2012, a variant of which contributes to the development of diabetes. It is the gene which has been found to have the maximum effect (1.56 times) in the incidence of the disease. Thus, it is a very important gene, apparently. All the ones found till now were involved in the production of Insulin, the peripheral utilisation of glucose etc. But the TMEM163 is found to be involved in the signalling pathways of the brain. The gene product is found only in the brain.

What the hell is it doing in the brain? That is what the scientists are asking. Is it some unknown biochemical mechanism involving the brain? A known mechanism, I would say—the inability to resist that plate of fries and the cola put before you even after knowing that these may not be good for you. Nobody knows yet.

Health can be influenced by our own actions. But we have to first learn what we are dealing with. What are the main chronic conditions affecting us, as a population?

We need studies involving large numbers of people and we need statistics for that. Using conventional wisdom as a guide for prevention can be very misleading. Most of what we know about preventive health is relatively recent in origin.

Even if we do everything possible for maintaining our health and preventing diseases, we may fail. The benefits of good habits are only statistical. There is an increased chance of becoming healthier by our own actions. That is all. There is a lot of chance involved.

Our genetics is very important for our health. We cannot change that. But that doesn't mean that one should not be careful. What we do will definitely influence our bodies. The interaction between genes and the environment is complex.

Knowing our foes

IT WAS the mid-eighteenth century in Hungary. A young doctor joined the Vienna General Hospital's Obstetrics and Gynaecology wing as Chief Resident. His name was Ignaz Semmelweis. There were two maternity units in the hospital, each admitting on alternate days. Poor pregnant mothers from across the country flocked to this hospital to give birth.

At that time, a lot of mothers suffered after delivery from a mysterious illness called 'puerperal fever'. It was very dangerous and killed off a lot of women afflicted. It was caused by 'bad air', 'mysterious humors' and many similar vague things, according to the physicians of the time.

Semmelweis, reviewed the records kept in the hospital. The maternal mortality was quite high—about 7 per cent. But he noticed a curious fact. Unit one had a mortality rate of 10 per cent, and unit 2 had only about 4. This was repeated every month and year. It was a notable difference. There was a notable difference in the administration of the units also.

Unit 1 was run by doctors and medical students. Unit 2 was managed by midwives. Was the difference due to the ineptitude of the so-called highly trained doctors when compared to the lowly midwives?

There was another even more puzzling fact. Some mothers gave birth on the streets, on the way. Then they were brought in for aftercare. They had the least incidence of puerperal fever. The streets were safer than the most modern hospital at that time!

Semmelweis personally observed and recorded the working of each unit. He could find no difference. The skill, care, instruments—everything was scrutinised by him. He could identify nothing. His colleagues were least interested in these matters.

That time it was the common practice for doctors to do and attend autopsies and anatomical studies on dead bodies, and then go straight to the labour rooms to conduct deliveries. It was only when one of Semmelweis' friends died, that he got a clue. He got an accidental injury from a scalpel while doing an autopsy. The finger became swollen, and he developed symptoms identical to puerperal fever and died.

Semmelweis proposed that some unknown 'cadavorous particles' were being transmitted to the patients in the labour room through the contaminated hands of the doctors. He suggested that all doctors and midwives wash their hands in a solution of soda lime before entering the labour room.

The maternal mortality rate plunged by 90 per cent. It even came down to zero for many months—for the first time since the beginning of the institution. Semmelweis was dead right.

But the significance of the discovery was recognised widely only after the efforts of Lois Pasteur in France who discovered that microorganisms cause many diseases.

Joseph Lister in Glasgow was a surgeon who introduced antiseptic techniques into surgery. He had heard of Pasteur's work. For the first time in history, cavity surgeries like appendectomy became tolerably safe. The battle against our ancient enemies, the pathogenic microorganisms, was beginning to be won.

In the 1940s and 1950s, doctors and public health experts in the USA noted that people were dying of heart attacks and heart failure—coronary artery disease. The incidence was increasing. It was reaching epidemic proportions. The National Heart, Lung and Blood Institute decided to study it. The study was started in 1948 in the town of Framingham, Massachusetts. It became the famous 'Framingham Heart study'. It was the first step in identifying a new enemy—chronic lifestyle disease.

A total of 5209 people were enrolled in this well-designed longitudinal cohort study. All the factors thought to be relevant were recorded. These people consented to yearly physical examinations, blood and other tests. The diseases and deaths were recorded. The second generation of these participants were enrolled in 1971. This is an ongoing study and the third generation was added in 2002.

It was a massive and fruitful effort, and spanned three generations of participants. It has, till now, generated more than 1000 medical papers. The term 'risk factor' was first used in this study. The findings have been confirmed by literally hundreds of other studies.

Before the results of this study came trickling in, there was no concept that any of these diseases could be prevented. The clogging of arteries, called atherosclerosis, that causes heart attacks and ischemic stroke was thought to be a normal accompaniment of ageing. Hypertension and increased blood cholesterol also were considered normal as people aged.

This study, and later literally thousands of other studies and supporting data have given faces to our main enemies now. They were quite hazy a mere half a century ago.

Coronary artery disease of the heart is a major cause of death and disability. It is brought on by atherosclerosis—a narrowing of the arteries due to development of 'atheromatous plaques' in the walls of the arteries.

Ischemic stroke is a related illness with the same cause—narrowing due to atherosclerosis in the arteries supplying the brain.

Diabetes is a lifestyle disease leading to disability and death.

Some cancers, like colon, breast and prostate, have some relationship to dietary habits. Some other common cancers, like cervix, lung, head and neck etc. are directly related to unsafe sex, cigarette smoking, tobacco chewing and alcohol.

There are certain other diseases that are silent or not particularly distressing in the early stages. But later, they cause or accelerate the onset of other diseases like heart disease, stroke etc. These diseases can be considered directly lifestyle related.

Hypertension is an increase in arterial pressure and is a

silent killer. It accelerates atherosclerosis and is a main risk factor for coronary artery disease and strokes.

Disorders of blood lipids (fats) include increased cholesterol, LDL, triglycerides and a decrease in HDL.

Diabetes—is a major disease in itself, and a main risk factor for many other diseases. It accelerates atherosclerosis.

Obesity is a dangerous increase in body weight. It directly correlates with all the other diseases. It also has a direct contributing effect on other risk factors, like hypertension, diabetes and hypercholesterolemia.

Modern diseases

CARDIOVASCULAR DISEASE is the number one killer of human beings as of 2012. It includes coronary artery disease and ischemic stroke. The main cause of these diseases can be summed up in one word—Atherosclerosis.

Coronary arteries are arteries supplying the heart. Atherosclerosis causes small bumps in the course of these arteries, leading to narrowing. When it becomes too narrow, it causes chest pain during exertion. This is called Angina.

Sudden rupture of an atheromatous plaque can cause blood to clot over it. This causes sudden block in the blood flow to a portion of the heart. This is called a heart attack. It can lead to sudden death. The shock effect can cause the conducting mechanism of the heart to go haywire. The resulting 'ventricular fibrillation' can stop the heart. This is how sudden deaths happen.

The same mechanism can occur in the arteries supplying the brain. Blockage of blood flow causes deficits like paralysis of one side of the body, or the inability to speak and think clearly. Massive strokes cause death due to brain swelling.

Blood vessels are tubes made up of layers of cells. Endothelium is the smooth innermost lining. Small breaks or injuries in the endothelium cause fats, like cholesterol, to accumulate just beneath it. Later, oxidation of these fats produces chemical substances that are deemed unpleasant by the body.

The immune system recruits white cells called Monocytes to migrate into the area. The Monocytes transform into Macrophages, a type of attacking cell. The macrophages swallow the fat particles and secrete chemicals that initiate a low level inflammation. This causes other cells to accumulate, like fibroblasts and smooth muscle cells, ultimately forming a bump or swelling beneath the endothelium. An atheromatous plaque is born.

As mentioned, these plaques can grow slowly or rapidly, depending on the physiology of the person. They can rupture, cause blood clots and sudden occlusion of the artery. In most modern societies, precursors of these plaques called fatty streaks are found in the arteries by the time of puberty in most people. Most young men have mild to moderate atherosclerosis in their coronary arteries by their thirties. This was demonstrated by an autopsy study done on soldiers killed during the Korean War. In contrast, most people among indigenous hunting tribes still following their ancient way of life, atherosclerosis is almost absent.

Studies have shown many risk factors affecting the process. Increasing age is one. Males are more prone to atherosclerosis and its consequences. Heredity is another significant factor. Either parent with severe disease at a younger age is a risk for the children. But these are all non-modifiable risk factors.

There are other things that we can change or keep in control.

Hypertension—Increased arterial pressure causes small endothelial injuries or degrades the endothelium, making it more prone to the process.

Cigarette Smoking—Chemicals are thought to damage endothelium. Nicotine constricts blood vessels. It is one of the most damaging things you can do to yourself.

Diabetes—Increase in the blood sugar causes chemical changes to happen in the accumulated fat. The sugar attaches to the various chemicals, called glycation. Glycated particles cause much more inflammation. Diabetes also complicates fat metabolism making it more abnormal and atherogenic.

Dyslipidemia—An abnormality in the fat components of the blood. Increased cholesterol and triglycerides promote disease. LDL is a lipoprotein complex that transports fat from the intestine and liver to the tissues through blood. The increase causes deposition of fat under the endothelium. HDL is a lipoprotein that transports fat from the periphery to the liver for storage and utilisation. Increased HDL protects against Atherosclerosis.

Obesity—Increase in body weight due to increase in fat content of the body is a bad thing. It increases hypertension and is a causative factor for diabetes. Fat metabolism abnormalities are common in obese people.

Decreased exercise—Moderate exercise is shown to have a beneficial effect in decreasing the process. Exercise works in complex ways. It decreases other risk factors like diabetes and obesity. It also has many direct benefits, like increasing HDL.

As mentioned in a previous chapter, coronary artery disease reached epidemic proportions in the west in the 1940s and 50s. This prompted the search for the risk factors, and later, aggressive public health campaigns.

This does seem to have had an effect. In the USA, the proportion of people dying from coronary artery disease decreased by 50 per cent by 2000, as compared to 1950. This is a country for which detailed statistics are available.

This reduction is the result of primary, secondary and tertiary prevention. The prevention of risk factors like diabetes, hypertension and lipid abnormalities by better diet, exercise, and cessation of smoking is primary prevention. The timely detection and treatment of the risk factors is the secondary one. Tertiary is the prompt treatment of coronary artery disease once it develops, thus preventing unnecessary deaths and disability.

So, prevention is possible, to an extent. It also means that there are a lot of things that are correct about the advices that are being given.

In India, we are at the upswing of the epidemic. It is yet to show its true frightening proportions.

But, even in the west, two other closely related scourges are gaining ground. And they show no signs of abating. They are Obesity and Type 2 Diabetes Mellitus.

Obesity—symbol of opulence or killer?

IT WAS 1997. I had just finished my MBBS. For a short period I stayed at home. One day I met Raman Menon and his family. It was many years since we had met. Raman Menon was in his early seventies. He had made his fortune in the Middle East. That was his ticket to affluence.

"Hello, you have become a doctor now, eh?" He greeted me effusively. He laughed happily and his huge abdomen moved up and down rhythmically like a balloon caught in the wind. His wife stood smiling by his side. She was also very fat.

"You are still very thin. Why is that? Don't you eat

anything while in Medical School?" He asked me. I smiled politely. My BMI was 24. That put me in the upper range of the normal weight. I was not too thin at all.

"You have hardly changed. Other than a few hairs lost, I suppose," he continued. "Too much cramming and thinking is the reason, I guess?"

"And too much testosterone," I thought. Too many testosterone sensitive hair follicles, to be exact. I didn't want to explain. It was a painful topic.

"You have put on some weight," I said.

"Some?" He looked insulted. "I must have gained at least ten kilos since I last saw you," he said proudly. "I love to eat. Everyone in our family is like that. Otherwise what is the point in being able to afford good food?

"I have blood pressure. The doctor said that I am developing diabetes also. My parents didn't have any of these," he said with satisfaction. "She has both." He indicated his wife.

"My son has diabetes. He is hardly forty." He said that in the same way one would have said he had become a CEO of a big company at that age.

Through most of our history we were able to eat just enough to survive. After widespread agriculture, complex societies with hierarchies sprang up. Surplus food was available, especially for some people, high in the political and religious hierarchy. Still most of the population did not have the luxury of becoming fat. No wonder that fatness was a thing to be proud of. It still is, in many parts of the world. There are places like Mozambique where there are 'fatness farms'. There girls are force fed to become fat and attractive. This kind of mindset is present in our country also, in patches. It is stronger among rural, poorer communities.

We need certain standards to grade fatness. Otherwise how can we measure and study it? The WHO has given some ready criteria. It is based on a measurement called 'body mass index'. It is the value we get if we divide our weight in kilograms by the square of the height in metres. The normal range is between 18.5 and 24.9. Above 25 is considered overweight. 30 or above is deemed obesity. Obesity is officially classified as a disease. Any BMI above 35 is severe obesity.

Obesity is associated with diabetes, hypertension, high cholesterol and high triglyceride levels. These are all risk factors for atherosclerosis and consequent coronary artery disease and stroke. Mortality risks have been studied. Large scale American and European studies have shown that the mortality risk is lowest at a BMI of 20 to 25. A BMI above 32 doubles the mortality rate as shown in a 16 year study in 1995.

Other than the lifestyle diseases mentioned, obesity increases the risk of certain cancers like breast, non-alcoholic liver disease and osteoarthritis. And the list doesn't stop there. The most important and direct link is to diabetes, technically called type 2 Diabetes Mellitus.

Before the 20th century, obesity was a rare disease. Now, it is an epidemic. It was formally declared as an epidemic by WHO in 1997. About 10 per cent of the world population is estimated to be obese. And it doesn't include the merely overweight individuals. In the USA, 30 per cent are obese. The average BMI of an American is 26. It is in the overweight range. The average BMI in societies that still follow the hunter-gatherer lifestyle is between 19 and 21.

India is also following the world trend. The National Family Health Survey data 2007 shows that 5 per cent of the population is morbidly obese. The proportion of people who are overweight ranges from 15 to 30 per cent in various states. Surveys among school children put the figure at 20 to 40 per cent, showing that this is an increasing trend.

But BMI is not a foolproof method of measuring corpulence. What matters is the fat. Arnold Schwarzenegger, in his prime, would have had quite a high BMI, because he is bulked up on muscle, not fat. For such an individual, this measurement falls flat as a risk predictor.

To complicate things further, it seems the type of fat matters. The fat around the waist is more dangerous. And according to studies, visceral fat is the most lethal. It is the fat that accumulates around our intestines and liver, contributing to a large waist and a pot belly. We see many men (especially men, rather than women), with normal weight, but a football like belly straining at the belt. This feature is quite common in Indian men. So, it is suggested by many authorities to measure the waist-hip ratio also, in addition to the BMI, to get some more perspective. Fat is a metabolically active tissue. The belly fat is supposed to be more active, secreting hormones and other chemicals that set up a chronic inflammatory state in the body. This is one important way in which it contributes to many diseases.

Understanding Cancer

I HAD a granduncle, who was a bachelor. He was an amazingly healthy old man. At the age of seventy-eight, he had an attack of abdominal pain and fever. It was just a urinary infection. But the urologist ordered an ultrasound scan. He said that it was important to investigate any urinary infection in men. The scan picked up a nodule—a small one centimetre swelling in the prostate gland. The doctor had a thing called 'Prostate specific antigen' in his blood checked. It was very high. He had Prostate cancer. He was upset. My father was his chief adviser and friend. Both of them consulted some specialists and he was put on regular medicine. I was just a kid at the time. I heard the entire story from my granduncle, who regaled listeners with it, whenever any unfortunate relative was within hearing distance.

He died ten years later of what can only be considered old age. He was eighty-eight. He had pneumonia. When I visited him on one of his last days, he told me again of the wonderful tablets that had saved his life. He pointed to the bedside shelf.

"They are in there," he said.

I had got into MBBS by then. I got curious. I opened the shelf and got the bottle of tablets out, and read the label.It was an uncommon multivitamin brand. The wonder drug!

Cancers are on the rise! The hype is deafening. At the time of writing this, here, in Kerala, the media is going crazy about the 'sudden' epidemic of cancer. Kerala has a much higher incidence than other states. How is that possible? We have the best health indicators otherwise. Our average lifespan is the best in India. Infant mortality is miniscule. Infectious diseases are lower.

The only answer must be westernisation. Urbanisation and air pollution. Hormones in our chicken, pesticides in our vegetables, and the industrial effluents in the drinking water are killing us through that Emperor of all maladies—Cancer. That is how the TV Channels put it.

Let us look to the west then. Cancer incidence has indeed been increasing in affluent countries. It is competing well with cardiovascular diseases. In the United States, it is second to it in the scourges that bring death. In UK and Canada, it is the number one cause of death. In India and less developed countries, cancer incidence and mortality is comparatively very low. Here, we have an epidemic on our hands. But what are the causes?

This is a classic case of how one can be misled by statistics if one is not critical enough. At the beginning of the century, the global lifespan was around forty. Around 1947, Indians had an average lifespan of about forty-five, which has now increased to sixty-five. While in the west, from a mere sixty in the 1960s, an average person is expected to live to an amazing eighty, or even eighty-five. Kerala is nearing these numbers. It is not only that. For many European countries, the demographic transition is over. They have greater number of older people in the population. India is a young country. The percentage of old men and women is much less.

Cancer rates are measured by incidence and *mortality rates.* Incidence is the number of new cases diagnosed per year, per thousand people. Mortality rate is the number of people dying from cancer as a *proportion of total deaths.*

Do you see what I am getting at? When the proportion of old people rises, the incidence of diseases commoner in old age rises. When deaths due to diseases like childhood illnesses, accidents and infections like tuberculosis fall, the mortality rate due to cancer, heart disease etc. rises. This is somewhat true for most lifestyle diseases. Most of them get commoner with increase in age. But this is most true for cancer.

That is because all the common cancers are essentially like degenerative diseases of old age. There are some childhood cancers, and of young adulthood, like some lymphomas, leukaemias, sarcomas and the like, but they are the exceptions to the general rule.

Cancers of the lung, prostate cancer, breast cancer, and cancers of the stomach, colon and rectum—these are the main causes of cancer related disease load in most countries. Cancers of the mouth, throat, larynx, food pipe and the cervix in women are much more common in countries like India, and they are largely preventable.

It is estimated that one third of cancers are preventable, by avoiding smoking, chewing tobacco, areca nuts and excess alcohol. They are mainly lung, mouth, throat, larynx and food pipe cancers. The incidence of all these cancers is not increasing but is declining in some countries due to aggressive campaign against these bad habits.

So we come to the stunning conclusion that almost all the rise in cancer prevalence is due to people living long. Age is the number one risk factor for most common cancers. As we become older, the chance that we may fall prey to the disease rises exponentially. Robert A Weinberg, an expert, put it like this, "If we live long enough, sooner or later, we all would get cancer."

Prostate cancer is a classic case that illustrates this well. It is a disease of old age. It is, usually, a very slow growing cancer. Some experts are of the opinion that if we do autopsy studies of all men dying of whatever cause in their nineties, most of their prostates will be hiding small toffee sized cancers. If detected in extreme old age, most do not require much treatment. That explains the story at the beginning of this chapter.

A few decades ago, lung cancer in the developed world and throat related ones in the rest were the most prevalent ones among males. Now, all over the developed world, it is prostate cancer that is number one. The reasons are clear. Declining tobacco use (this decreases lung cancer), increasing life spans, and increased medical surveillance like ultrasound scans that cause more cases to be discovered are the chief causes.

The truth can be brought out by something called 'age-adjusted mortality rates'. In this one calculates the mortality rate for a particular age only. This takes off the lifespan effect. When you look at the age-adjusted mortality rates, it is seen that they have been falling for most cancers all over the world.

Some cancers, like thyroid cancers seem to be on the increase. This is thought to be almost solely due to better early detection.

Does lifestyle have any influence on cancers at all? Certainly. Smoking, chewing tobacco, and alcohol is responsible for one third of the cancer load. The main cancers that can be prevented to an extent are those of the lung, throat, mouth, wind pipe and food pipe.

What about the others?

There is some evidence that a regular intake of fruits and vegetables has a protective effect against some cancers, like those of colon and rectum. Increased body weight has been linked to an increase in cancer incidence. Reneham and Tyson published a meta-analysis of 141 articles related to Body Mass Index and cancer incidence. They found that many cancers like breast, colon, rectum, food pipe etc. are significantly associated with increase in Body Mass Index. The fatter you are, there is a slightly increased chance of getting many cancers. The effect is slight. It is far less than, say, the relationship between weight and heart disease or diabetes. It is still not clear why there is a relationship at all. It may be due to a curious nexus between physiological ageing and less food. So ultimately, even this effect may be related to age after all.

There is some evidence to link environmental air pollution and lung cancer. This was suggested in a recent study. As for pesticides and other pollutants, apart from certain specific occupational exposures, the evidence has been slight.

Stone age wisdom

A DIARY ENTRY:

"I got up early today. The sun was already spreading its rays in the sky, but it was not seen yet. I felt hungry. The roots and nuts we had stored yesterday were for the children only. Our huts were on top of the hill, and I surveyed the massive

“Cant you SEE that I am the Chief?’

plain below. Bushes dotted the green expanse that stretched to the horizon. This land was good. We, all hundred and forty of us, are here for the past twelve years. More than ten years in one place is unusual for us. The last place had no water towards the end, so we had to leave. An entire two days of walk was needed for one hunting party of ten men to catch a rat or a weasel. The lake had a lot of fish, and when that dried up, life became hard. That is why we had left.

I said goodbye to Sasha, my wife. She was getting ready to go with Masa and other women to gather Mungongo nuts, tuber roots and fruits. She was carrying my younger son Machu. My elder son is old enough to run, and he is going with her. As soon as his whiskers start growing, he will join us for the hunt. Men are mighty hunters. Women do all the gathering stuff. But let me tell a secret though. Most of the time, my belly is filled by the grilled roots and nuts that Sasha brings. My family also gets to eat whatever she brings home. By the ancient rules of our race, all hunted meat and caught fish has to be shared between all the members of the tribe. This is good, as almost every day everyone gets to eat a fistful of meat or fish.

Today we had to wander till the sun went down to find some prey to bring home. Our ten member party managed to catch six lizards, and two of them were as big as a rat. Four of us ran after two large field rats, throwing sticks and axes for a long time, but they got away. Finally, after a long chase, we caught a rabbit. I got him with my spear. I was always good at throwing them. Everyone slapped me on the back. I was very happy.

I was ravenous when I got back as I did not have much to eat after yesterday evening. The whole day I had only a tuber which I dug up and a Kara fruit. I was very tired and my whole body ached from all the walking and running. But I was happy thinking about the food that Sasha would have gathered, and the feast of meat that was to come."

The hypothetical journal entry is by a thirty-year-old male human, around hundred thousand years ago, in one corner of the African continent.

Anatomically, modern humans appeared on earth, as per available fossil evidence, around two hundred thousand years ago. They were a communal species, surviving opportunistically wherever they wandered. They originally evolved in the bush and grassland plains of Africa. With their large brains, they adapted to a variety of environments, and had an omnivorous diet.

But, for most of those two hundred thousand years, they lived by hunting and gathering. They wandered kilometres every day looking for tough roots, seeds, fruits, insects and small animals. Males hunted in packs, making an occasional large kill.

It was only ten thousand years ago that agriculture started in earnest. Only then did grains enter in a big way into our diet. Humans divided into workers and a sedentary ruling class. Even then food in plenty was a luxury.

It was only in the last few centuries that food truly became an indulgence. Work was done by machines and we hardly moved.

Initially our bodies evolved to suit the life of a hunter-gatherer and served us for millennia. Could it be that there is discordance between our modern lifestyle and our bodies? Could it be true that many lifestyle diseases are due to this difference? Then, isn't it logical to think that we could learn how to live by looking at how our early ancestors lived?

Maybe!

Palaeolithic lifestyles

THERE IS some logic in the argument that our bodies and our lifestyles may not be matching. So, the argument goes that if we look at how our Palaeolithic ancestors lived, we can pick up pointers on how to live healthily.

How can we find out how they lived?

We can look at archaeological remains that scientists have dug up from the sites of early human settlements. We find animal bones and fish remains, with marks of stone knives with which the meat was shaved off. Remains of fireplaces tell us that they cooked their food. Coarse seeds, shells of nuts, fibrous roots and seeds of fruits tell us what else they ate. What else do we find at these dwelling sites?

Fossilised buried bodies, some preserved in ice, enable us to open their stomachs and look at the contents. (They sure are thorough, these archaeological chaps). And you know what fossilised chunks of shit are called? Coproliths. (They stick at nothing; I mean, the archeologists). But they tell me that the smell wears off by a few thousand years.

S Boyd Eaton and Melvin J Konner were the first to come out with a paper examining these ideas in 1985. It was published in the prestigious *New England Journal of Medicine*, and was termed Palaeolithic Nutrition. In it, they have put forward the dietary mismatch hypothesis. They say that modern lifestyle diseases like strokes, coronary artery disease, type 2 diabetes and certain types of cancers are caused by a mismatch between our modern diet and the diet and lifestyle of the Palaeolithic age. In 2010, another good article, *'Palaeolithic nutrition: twenty five years later'* came out. It tried to examine how much of that hypothesis is true. It said that it had 'considerable validity'. That is just the way these people speak.

It is generally true that hunter-gatherer societies today have a diet that has the following characteristics:

1. Much lower levels of refined carbohydrates.
2. Much lower levels of Sodium, that is, salt.
3. Comparable or similar levels of fat and cholesterol as our modern diet.
4. Much higher levels of physical activity than ours.

In 2012, Staffan Lindeberg examined all the available

studies upto then and published a review article regarding this subject. A review article is a study that looks at the data of many studies and tries to reach conclusions. He concluded that there is indeed some support and evidence to the theory that the diet of indigenous societies can prevent age-related diseases listed above.

He said that dairy products, margarine, some oils, refined sugar and starch, cereal grains were to be avoided. These currently constitute seventy per cent of our dietary intake.

Then what are we left with? There seems to be hardly anything else.

Well, our ancestors did eat the following:

Lean meat, fish, vegetables, tubers and fruits.

Does that mean we can gobble up pork fat, beef liver, eggs, and seafood by the plateful and remain healthy and fit?

I think we should get some perspective here and look at how our neighbours, the present day aboriginal people actually live.

W R Leonard wrote a piece on food and anthropology in the *Scientific American 2004*. In it he lists out certain populations about whom data is available.

The Kung and Turkana of Africa, the Evenky of Russia, the Quecha of Peru and the Inuit of North America. They differ in their total energy intake by wide margins. The Turkanas take 1,400 calories per day, while the Evenkys consume around 2,800 per day. They also differ in their diet considerably. The Quechas of Peru get 95 per cent of their energy from plant foods, while the Inuits get 96 per cent of their energy from animals and seafood. Of course, the common features do remain, as discussed, like lack of sugar and refined starch.

Yet, all of them have lower levels of hypertension, diabetes, heart disease, etc. than the modern people. Their cholesterol levels are all within normal.

What the hell are we missing here?

Let us look at their average BMI. The indigenous peoples average BMI is around 20. Compare that to the average BMI of modern day USA, which is 26.

"It is a complex conundrum of the mismatch between energy expenditure vis-a-vis energy intake," assert the experts.

In plain English it means that we are eating far more than we expend by exercise.

Better start moving!

I REMEMBER BEING struck by a *National Geographic* programme that I watched years ago. It started with a huge sumo wrestler, weighing 150 kilograms, boasting on camera about his invincible strength. The idea was to have a tug-of-war between him and a tame orangutan. The animal was only one third of the man's size. A moat filled with muddy water separated the participants. The contest started with much fanfare, more boasts and confident assertions by the wrestler. Two tugs and three seconds later, the man plunged into the mud with a tremendous splash. He was not available for comment later. The ape showed its glee by jumping up and down and clapping its hands. But the winner modestly declined to say much.

Man is a puny animal when compared to others of similar or even much smaller size. But their increased strength doesn't necessarily help them. Note that it is the orangutan that is endangered, while the planet is overrun with human beings. The conventional wisdom is that we survive only by our superior and collective brains, weaving strategies and executing them.

However, there is one purely physical feat that we can do much better than most other mammals. No—I am not talking of manual dexterity or ability to make tools. That is due to our brain power and hands.

Can you outrun an antelope galloping across the African savannah? No? What about a hare? Still negative about your abilities? A chicken? I can attest from personal experience that outrunning a chicken is possible for an average person. Initially, the terrified chicken runs much faster and you are about to give up. Many people do. That is the mistake. You keep chasing at a comfortable pace. After a few minutes, it just stops from exhaustion. You can just pick it up.

Apparently, it may be so with most animals, if you are properly trained. There are tribes in central Africa and the Kalahari that routinely run down large prey like deer through a combination of endurance running, tracking skills, and sheer persistence. The hunt is deliberately done at midday under the blistering hot African sun. Some people theorise that this may have been one important way by which early humans obtained their food. No animal, however well-trained, can run for hours and hours, like a marathon runner.

We may argue that only a trained human can do that. Let me ask you—can a trained human match a gorilla or a chimpanzee in a wrestling match? It is not possible. Endurance is natural to us.

How can we be sure? The scientists say we have a lot of clues in our own bodies. Comparative anatomy, they say, can teach us a lot about evolution.

Look at the testes, for example. What I mean is, consider them for a moment. The great Apes are our closest relatives, evolutionarily. Primates, including monkeys are our extended family. Which primate has the largest testes?

If you thought that it is the massive gorilla, you are wrong. It is the chimpanzee. The chimpanzees are the most sexually promiscuous of all primates. Almost the entire male members of the group will mate with a receptive female in heat. The gigantic testes produce copious amounts of sperm, as they compete with those of other males in the female's genital tract.

And who gets the prize for the biggest penis? If you answered chimpanzee, you are dead wrong. It is the human male. The reasons we will come to later.

Ever wondered why we walk on two legs? Again, the main reason is supposed to be that it freed our hands to make tools, thereby driving our superb brain growth. But the Australopithecus were the first humanoids to walk upright, and their brains were only as large as those of the apes today.

The answer appears to be much more complex. On analysis, it appears that running on two legs is much more efficient than on four legs. One important reason is that the front legs of an animal are connected to the chest cavity that bears part of the load. As you run more, you pant. The running interferes with the panting. In the humans our legs are free to run, while our chests are free to pant, independent of each other. What is needed is a superior sense of balance to manage the inherent instability of the bipedal gait.

Another question is why are were naked? That is, comparatively hairless. That is an important difference from all other mammals, except the whales and dolphins. The aquatic mammals need their smooth bodies to reduce drag. There are some who argue that we had a seaside existence in our history that promoted this, but this idea is not bought by most experts. One very likely reason is better heat management while running long distances in the oven-hot African plains.

This also explains our sweating ability. Most medium

mammals of our comparative size cool down by panting. The saliva evaporates and the heat is dissipated through the breath. This is much more inefficient than sweating. And we are designed to sweat copiously. The only problem is that there has to be a wind for this to be optimal. A runner generates his own wind.

If these conjectures are correct, then our sedentary existences may be shockingly out of sync with our bodies. It is likely that there is more than a grain of truth to this theory.

Are you still wondering why we have the largest penis among the primates? If you have a convincing answer, tell me. Or tell the experts. Better still publish it, for you may become famous. Nobody knows the answer, yet.

Being active—the benefits

LACK OF exercise is a definite risk factor in the development of cardiovascular disease, diabetes, obesity, some cancers, and many other diseases.

With both men and women, there is a 20 to 35 per cent of relative risk reduction in all causes of death, including lifestyle diseases for those who do the maximum physical activity.

Moderate exercise is what is recommended by most

“Hey, this is too much work. I will lay off the cakes and pastries instead.”

experts. Exercise can be regarded as either aerobic or muscle-strengthening. Aerobic exercises use our heart and lungs, and include brisk walking, running, cycling and swimming. Push-ups, sit-ups, weight training etc. are the other type. Generally recommended is 30 minutes of moderate exercise, five days a week, and weight training activity for 15 minutes two days a week. How do you know we are doing moderate activity? We should be able to appreciate our heartbeats, will be sweating lightly, but will be able to carry on a normal conversation. More vigorous exercise will have us panting more, and not able to speak other than one or two words at a time.

People planning regular physical activity at middle age should probably have a medical check-up before starting.

One important way in which exercise works is by reducing the incidence of obesity. Excess weight due to accumulation of fat occurs due to taking in more calories as food than we expend by activity. Obviously, exercising expends calories and helps in weight loss. As we have seen, obesity is a risk factor for many diseases, most importantly, diabetes.

Aerobic exercise increases the efficiency of carbohydrate metabolism. Over time, the muscles become more efficient at utilising glucose to create energy. This reduces blood sugar. The blood glucose becomes more easily controlled by the insulin that is secreted by the body. This greater sensitivity to the action of insulin is an important factor in preventing diabetes. Pre-diabetes, a precursor state of diabetes, is characterised by relatively high blood sugar in spite of high circulating levels of insulin. This slowly tires the islet cells in the pancreas and later insulin deficiency occurs. Regular exercise has a preventive effect on the whole process. It is also a treatment for established diabetes, reducing its severity and decreasing the amount of insulin and medicines used to control the disease.

Muscle building exercise is also important. It has some unknown effect on diabetes control. Studies have shown that combining aerobic and muscle building resistance exercises is better at preventing diabetes than either done alone. Muscles use more energy at rest than fat. So more muscle means more energy expended. The increased muscle mass also acts as an endocrine organ, causing many benefits, while abdominal fat secretes chemicals that cause many unwanted effects.

Exercise has great effect on fat metabolism. It very reliably increases the level of HDL in the blood. HDL, as we know, promotes the movement of atherogenic cholesterol into the liver. It also decreases the level of triglycerides in the blood. There is a moderate effect on the LDL levels also bringing it down to a healthier level.

Above all, exercise burns calories and makes you less fat. This is obvious. Less fat means less intra abdominal and visceral fat. That is one important risk factor less contributing to your ill-health.

Apart from effects on physical health, there are

other benefits also. Scientists have found that regular physical activity is a potent treatment for mild to moderate depression. When you exercise, the brain releases 'endorphins'. Endorphins are naturally secreted opiods, similar to morphine and heroin. They create 'the runner's high'—a pleasant feeling of exhilaration and release. It also has an effect on the hypothalamus in the brain that responds to stress via the pituitary and adrenal axis. The physiologic reactivity to stress is modified in a way that damps it down. It has been shown to decrease anxiety and depression and increase self-esteem.

It was in the 1960s that rats were made to exercise regularly on treadmills. Physically they must have become fitter. We don't know. But that was not what was studied. Researchers found that the exercised rat's cerebral cortex became thicker. New cells were being laid down. The effect was strong in the hippocampus, which is a sort of nursery for the formation of new neurons. What is more, these 'runner rats' were better at learning and memory skills, like running mazes, showing that they have actually become smarter. Recently, Japanese researchers at the University of Tsukuba found a possible mechanism for this puzzling effect. They found that exercise rapidly depletes the stores of glycogen, a stored form of glucose that is present in astrocytes in the brain. Astrocytes are neighbour cells to neurons. They envelope, protect and nourish them. Regular exercise drastically increases the amount of stored glycogen in these cells as a form of super-compensation. Want to boost your smarts? Better reach for those running shoes. Or the swimming trunks—whatever.

To underline everything, Marc Hamilton, a leading figure on inactivity physiology, has coined the startling phrase—'sitting is the new smoking'. My god! These researchers won't even let us sit in peace. Many, like him, claim that sitting is an independent risk factor. Any prolonged sitting, as in an office, does actual harm. And it is not offset by any exercise that you may do later in the day. So stand and write those reports. Increase your desk height and prop your computer on it, so that you can stand in front. Fidget. Take a walk. Do anything, but don't sit. Shit!

Many lifestyle interventions work in ways that we cannot predict. One psychiatrist friend told me about a patient suffering from depression who was somewhat resistant to medicines. He advised him to start walking. The improvement was dramatic. He went rapidly off all drugs as his walks became longer. Then, suddenly one day, he was totally cured and announced that he was divorcing his wife.

The walks allowed him an excuse to be away from his nagging wife. The more he walked, the happier he became. Finally, he got to the root of the problem and was fully cured.

Exercise—not a cure-all

COLLEGE HOSTELS are good places to look for real big eaters. I knew two of them during my days there. Jim and Tim—both were famous for their gargantuan appetites. The similar names made it easy to buzz about them.

"Did you see Jim and Tim at the mess yesterday? Each had fifteen rotis."

"And Jim ate two bananas after that, imagine!"

Both had a friendly competition going. We cheered both on. The ability to hog like pigs was indeed considered a worthy feat.

Even though both were twin souls in the matter of downing bucketfuls of the hostel food, there was an important difference between them.

Jim was thin while Tim was very fat.

Perhaps you couldn't call Jim very thin. But he was trim and muscular. He was a fitness freak. He worked out in the gym for an hour every other day. Every morning he put on his running shoes and ran at a steady clip, twenty rounds of the college ground. That was about ten kilometres. He was a district level athlete in the long distance races.

As you might have guessed, Tim was a sedentary animal. Lifting fried legs of chicken shaped like half-dumbbells into his mouth was the maximum he would do by way of exercise. He became fatter and fatter, while Jim seemed to maintain a steady weight and was a pleasing figure, though he became slightly beefy by the time he left college.

Tim tried hard to lose weight. The reasons were obvious. Girls flocked around Jim, while they treated Tim as a comic figure. One thin girl who used to walk with him to the classes started avoiding him. Someone had suggested that it was the gravitational force that attracted her to Tim.

Exercise was the option that Tim chose. Eating less was not a desirable thing to do when one is young and vigorous. That was what was drilled into him when he was a kid. He joined Jim in the gym and started regular running. Of course, he could not match Jim, but he clocked half an hour a day.

The only problem was that Tim saw the exercise as an excuse to eat more. After each run, he felt ravenously hungry. He downed two milkshakes and three eggs immediately after each session. Needless to say, Tim only increased in girth as time passed.

"Exercise is useless!" he fumed.

Jim moved on in life, got married, and his life became busy. He tried to keep up with his fitness regime, but found it impossible to do so. One day, he came down with severe back and knee pain. He had them for years but was continuing to exercise in spite of that. Now it was no longer possible.

I saw them last during the college reunion last year. Both Tim and Jim, now in their late thirties, looked identical—very fat. Obese, to be precise.

Exercise is the new magic word. Eating less is not healthy we are told. In activity lies our salvation. Move. Move...

vigorously. The more you exert, the better it is. One question is—are there any problems associated with exercise?

The number one problem is amply shown by Tim. We tend to overestimate its effects. Worse, we might take it as an excuse to overeat.

Most of the food that we eat is utilised just to keep us alive and our brains humming. It is estimated that eighty per cent of an average persons calories are used up to maintain the Basal Metabolic Rate. When we run at a moderate pace for half an hour we burn around 200 to 300 calories. Tim thought that was enough to make him slimmer. He even assumed that he could eat more, just because he was spending an extra 300 calories a day. One sugar laden, thick, large-sized milkshake contains easily 300 to 500 calories. So, a sweet, simple milkshake was more than enough to offset any benefit he got from his exercise. No wonder he became fatter.

Yes, definitely, like Jim, one can exercise to ones maximum capacity by running two or three marathons a week, and eat all we want. Even then, any excess calories that you take in can lead to weight gain over decades, for it is a slow process. Besides, is it healthy?

Most studies have shown the benefits of moderate exercise but none have shown advantages of severe, vigorous exercise. It is certainly possible to be an unhealthy athlete.

Many marathon runners can develop a kind of fibrosis in the heart that can lead to conduction abnormalities. Premature osteoarthritis is a well-known sequel of overzealous and vigorous exercise. Over a lifetime, it becomes progressively difficult to follow an extremely difficult course of physical activity. The metabolic rate drops as you age, meaning that we need less food as we become older. But we eat the same amount of food. This is the basis of middle age spread, which is absent in traditional societies.

Another thing with exercise is that it is addictive. The release of endorphins is good for your mental health, but one can become dangerously addicted to the 'high' that we get during exercise. This can cause us to continue, even when we are sick, or in pain. We may also become obsessed about it, and neglect our family and social commitments.

So, the trick is to do sustainable, moderate exercise. No more, no less. One recommendation is half-an-hour to one hour of moderate aerobic exercise, like running, brisk walking, cycling, swimming etc. five days a week. It has to be combined with strength exercises, like weight training, two days a week, half an hour each.

Longevity—is it worth it?

WHEN THE Indian Ocean Tsunami hit our shores, the Andaman and Nicobar islands were severely affected. Government officials, when they visited one of the smaller islands after the incident, expected the worst. It was inhabited by a hunter-gatherer tribe that had no contact with modern civilisation. It was feared that most of the members had perished.

But they were surprised to see all of them huddling securely on the most elevated peak on the island. When the water receded as a prelude to the apocalyptic waves, the oldest member of the tribe told the rest:

"This is a battle between the land and the sea. Temporarily, the land has won. But the sea will strike back with unimaginable force. Start climbing the hill—quick."

"How do you know, old one?" asked someone.

"My great-grandfather told me that when I was a boy," said the old man.

Two hundred thousand years ago. That is the time when, the fossil records tell us, anatomically modern humans appeared on the scene. They used primitive stone tools.

But if we want to look at the history of technology, we have to look further back. Homo erectus, our immediate predecessor species started using them two million years ago. That is more than 15 lakh years earlier to us.

The strange fact is that there is no radical difference in technology between early humans and the Homo erectus tools. Stones, shaped stones, flaked stone axes and sharpened long stone knives—millennia after millennia.

Then something happened around fifty thousand years ago. Intricate carved spearheads and stone figurines appeared. Complex tools came on the scene. Exquisite paintings made with a profusion of natural dyes adorned the walls of primitive caves.

It was not only that. The tools, the art and the technology rapidly advanced with each generation. Bows propelled arrowheads. Mammals and other large animals rapidly became extinct, in the face of the rise of a fearsome predator that killed from a distance, and whose stratagems were complex and devious. Population of humans soared as they spread all across the globe. The Neanderthals, a group of cold-adapted, related humans disappeared within a few decades of the rise of our ancestors. They were gone by 30,000 years ago.

The cause of this so called 'great leap forward' is an enduring mystery of human evolution.

Rachel Casperi, from Central Michigan University, is an anthropologist who studied longevity in archaic humans. She has summarised her findings in an article in the 2011 *Scientific American*. She could estimate the ages from fossil teeth wear very reliably.

None of the Neanderthals survived beyond thirty. This is astonishing. In our times, thirty year olds are supposed to be in the prime of their life. Other populations of archaic humans from that time period and before showed the same findings. Rachel calculated a ratio—the 'O/Y ratio' or old versus young ratio, that showed the proportion of older people, old enough to be grandparents. In a group that existed 30,000 years ago or so, the ratio was a very surprising five times that of previous ages. So it is clear that around the time of our 'Great leap forward', the number of old people had a huge surge, nobody is quite sure why. Dr Casperi speculates that the grandparents were significant contributors to the great leap.

Older people have meaningful accumulation of knowledge and experience. They have contributed a lot to the intergenerational transfer of technology and improvement through the ages. They are repositories of traditional wisdom, ties of kinship, and might have contributed to the successful administration of larger groups of people. Larger tribes are more successful.

In short, it is not a crime to want to live long. What we humans are today could possibly be due to our increased longevity.

Studies among centenarians have been done in an attempt to tease apart the secrets to their long life. Such studies have not shown very fruitful results. The centenarians are a very diverse group. Some were very careful. Some not so much and even smoked occasionally. Scientists believe that living till eighty depends on careful habits and heredity, while going on much longer requires an increasing output from the genes.

Even then, certain trends emerge.

They are, as a rule, relatively resistant to the usual lifestyle diseases that increase with age, like hypertension, diabetes, atherosclerosis etc.

They are almost never obese. Most are thin.

Most have been active. But many were not avid fitness freaks.

They tend to take life as it comes (but this could be an effect, not a cause of their long life). What do you expect when one has lived to be hundred?

They tend to have the following metabolic results in their blood tests:

Low levels of circulating Insulin.

Low blood sugar.

Low triglycerides in blood.

This combination of findings indicates very efficient carbohydrate metabolism, and is the opposite of what happens in pre-diabetes or the metabolic syndrome, which is considered to be a precursor of frank diabetes and many other lifestyle diseases.

Can we do anything to increase our longevity? Of course, now that we know many things, like avoiding certain foods. Exercise, and not smoking definitely helps, but what is the most important one? Is there a specific drug, supplement, or lifestyle determinant that will promote average as well as maximum lifespan in people?

'Less is more'—A cure for ageing?

THERE WAS an experiment called 'Biosphere 2'. It involved keeping a few people in a totally enclosed glasshouse for a year. The food was all grown inside. All wastes were recycled, and no food was allowed in from outside.

But there was some unforeseen shortage of food in the enclosure. The inmates were forced to half-starve. They had to survive on 30 to 50 per cent less calories per day than they were accustomed to. But the available food was of high quality, largely consisting of vegetables. Supplements prevented vitamin and mineral deficiencies. Roy Walford was a doctor who was among the participants. He was also responsible for the medical care of the people inside.

He was surprised to observe that all the measurable parameters of health improved in the participants. Their blood pressures went down to healthier levels. Blood sugars plummeted. Pre-diabetic patients reversed their status. The resting pulse rate and body temperature dropped. They lost weight, of course—but they apparently did not become unhealthy.

Back in 1934, Clive McKay of Cornell University did a study on rats that pioneered a truly landmark discovery. He divided a bunch of laboratory rats into two groups. One group was fed normally while the other was given 50 per cent less food than normally needed for rats. But he made sure that they got all the necessary vitamins, minerals etc.

so that they didn't have any deficiencies.

The results were striking. The underfed rats remained active and disease-free well into the rat equivalent of old age. They retained their brain power also and did not show the cognitive decline that ageing inevitably brings. The normally fed rats had become hopelessly senile by that time. Many died. In fact, the average lifespan of food-restricted rats was almost double that of the other group (56 months as opposed to 34 months). Maximum lifespan also increased, demonstrating that there was an actual slowing of the ageing process, rather than *only* a general increase in health.

Why should we be interested in ageing? One can argue that it is health we are concerned about, not the inevitable death. Who wants to stay unhealthy and senile for long?

The issue is that all the chronic diseases and its causes are inextricably linked to ageing. Diabetes and hypertension become much more common as we age. The underlying metabolic processes become unhealthier. For example, the levels of circulating Insulin increase as we become more resistant to its blood sugar lowering action as we age. This happens even when one does not become diabetic. Atherosclerosis is an inevitable accompaniment of ageing. This makes our arteries less pliable and causes Hypertension. We become more susceptible to strokes and coronary artery disease. These same effects are very slowed down in naturally long lived humans—people who live for 100 years or more.

Scientists have been trying to find ways to retard ageing

for close to a century now. But till now, the only partially proven method seems to be the one that was discovered in rats in 1934. This is called Calorie Restriction with Optimal Nutrition. The trick seems to be to reduce your energy intake through food but you should not suffer from the deficiency of any particular essential component. Scientists talk about 'percentage reduction'. A 50 per cent Calorie Restriction means that the animal is fed half of what a normal animal of the same weight would have if given unrestricted access to food.

This strategy has worked in almost all the species that have been studied so far. Fish, spiders, worms, some micro-organisms—it has worked in all of them.

The much awaited results of two studies on Rhesus monkeys were recently released. One showed a benefit in average lifespan and a reduction in age related diseases like diabetes. The other showed only a doubtful effect on longevity, but showed improvement in health. Both studies demonstrated improved test results, like insulin sensitivity, blood sugars, blood pressures and lipid values like cholesterol levels. The animals were on 30 per cent calorie restriction.

On the face of it, the effect is mysterious. The apparent spread across species is even more puzzling. Why should starved beings live longer?

But evolutionarily, it makes sense. When food is plentiful, you gorge. Live life to the full, and mate and reproduce quickly. Produce as many children as possible, because there is a lot of food around. Your descendents will not starve. Then you die. Many with your genes are alive to continue the process of life.

When food is scarce, you starve. This acts as a warning. Times are not good. Don't reproduce now. Just go on living. Live long. You may still be alive when things change and food is again abundant. Then you can still be youthful for a bout of mating and reproducing.

It makes sense. The entire idea may be a way of putting things on hold till the tide turns in your favour.

What about humans? Formal studies like that done on animals are next to impossible. But persons practicing calorie restriction have been studied. One ongoing study CALERIE is looking at subjects put on short-term restriction of 25 per cent. A lot of anecdotal and epidemiological data has been amassed. One example is the inhabitants of the island of Okinawa in Japan. They naturally eat only 70 per cent of the calories that people in other parts of Japan eat. They are culturally tuned to something like 30 per cent calorie restriction. The quality of their diet is good. The Okinawans live significantly longer than others in the rest of the country. They have 40 times the number of above 100 year olds than the rest of Japan.

Certain things are clear:

It makes people thin. It is a sure cure for obesity.

Fifty per cent calorie restriction is almost impossible for a person to practice. Even 25 per cent is very hard. A 10 per cent restriction is a reasonable target.

Severe calorie restriction could be a dangerous practice. It may lead to muscle loss, loss of strength of bones and other as yet unknown problems. Even mild restriction must be undertaken very carefully. There should not be any malnutrition. Adequate intake of proteins, vitamins and minerals should be ensured.

A 10 per cent restriction is nothing but a balanced, frugal diet. It is usually a diet prescribed by nutritionists for an overweight person. Still, to adhere to it over a lifetime, real willpower is needed.

The conspiracy theory

THE SALES figures of a leading toothpaste manufacturer were falling steadily. The three top executives in the sales division were summoned by the CEO.

"Do something. Each of you has to come up with a plan. It has to have a perceptible effect on the sales. Otherwise, I don't have to tell you what is on the line."

With their asses in the line of fire, one went in for aggressive advertising. It had no effect. Another recruited people and did door to door campaigning. Again no spike in the profit margins.

The third guy came up with an ingenious plan. He made the production team agree to increase the diameter of the opening of the tube by a fraction of a millimetre. Every month they increased it bit by bit. The final toothpaste tube had an opening one-and-a-half times the original.

Sales picked up substantially and our hero kept his job. The other two were, in corporate speak, 'let go'. Part of the dismissed person's salaries were added to the perks of our hero.

The other day I was watching a TV programme on American farmers. One farmer was crying in front of a truckload of onions he had produced. They were big, but not big enough for the major shopping mall chains. It was their policy to buy only onions above a particular size. "They say it makes people buy more," lamented the farmer.

These things went through my mind as I sat in front of my friend Avinash at the local cafe. He had gone to the US for a fellowship of one year. He had put on ten kilograms. He was fat now.

"It is very expensive to eat healthily in the States. Burgers, fried chicken and coke are very cheap. And you should see the size of each burger. It is double the size of these things in India. Like the people there. And double servings of cheese and butter with everything you order. How can you allow food to go waste when it is put before you?"

The cafe owner Karunettan came by with two huge glasses of foaming coffee. I tasted it. It was very sugary and creamy. I stared at the man. Usually it was quarter the size, and different.

"What happened to the Kappi, Karunetta?" I asked.

"It is Kappichina. It is the 'passion' now." He meant Cappuccino. And 'fashion'. But that is not the point here.

Is there a conspiracy to make us consume more? To make us devour unhealthy food by the plateful till our eyes bubble and our coronaries clog? You bet there is! Making us unhealthy is not their primary objective, of course. It is only the market relentlessly aiming at the bottom line—more profits. They end up expanding our bottoms and waist lines in the process.

Why does the food industry cater to our most depraved tastes? Because we demand it, of course. We evolved in the unforgiving plains of Africa, constantly wondering where our next meal was coming from. Famine followed times of plenty. Food was a luxury. We were evolved to gorge whenever food was available. The excess fat was stored in subcutaneous deposits around the internal organs like the liver and intestines. Practically nobody became fat, we can presume. The frequent lean times ensured that our ancestors used up their stores periodically. Then they were really hungry for the next buffet. This evolutionary strategy helped them overcome various ice ages and worse. Never in their wildest dreams would they have imagined that their successors, mere 50,000 or so years later, would wallow in so much food.

Our taste buds can distinguish sweet, salt, sour and bitter tastes. Sour and bitter originally were designed to warn us about potentially poisonous substances. 'Hot' is not a taste. It is brought on by the irritation of free nerve endings by certain chemicals. So 'sweet' is one thing that is really designed to encourage us. Sweet means 'good' at a very visceral level. The only sweet things our ancestors ever ate were fruits, and the rare sweet things like the earlier versions of sugar cane and sweet potato. We artificially bred the sugarcane to produce more sugar. Then we got the juice out. After that we took the essence of the sweetness and made it into a fine powder. So we successfully threw out the fibre, the vitamins, the whole lot. The rarity was made into a commodity. Concentrated calories plus taste.

Sodium is an essential mineral we need in bulk. We evolved to value the saltiness of natural foods. Man discovered that it can be mass produced cheaply by evaporating sea water in the sun. Now we routinely ingest five to ten times the required amount of sodium every single day.

We are missing something here. What about fat? And proteins? The puzzle was solved by Japanese researchers when they discovered a new taste bud in humans that is turned on by fat and amino acids from proteins. This new taste was called *Umami*. Some have dubbed it 'Savoury'. Even if we didn't know this, we were already catering to it in a big way. Animals were bred into fatty, bulky brutes. Nuts and seeds were ground and squeezed to take the oil out. The meat was fried in the oil. Monosodium Glutamate or Ajinomoto was used before this scientific discovery. It fires our Umami taste buds. Glutamic acid is an amino acid found in many animal proteins. Our present day food is like pornography. Designed to turn us on. No wonder we can't resist it.

Researchers have found that eating sweet or fatty foods turns on our endogenous opioid system, giving us a high akin to having taken a shot of a drug like morphine. The reward centres in our brains exhort us to repeat the experience. Modern day consumerist culture eggs us on. We follow like hungry wolves, with drooling tongues hanging out.

A friend of mine, a noted environmentalist and scholar, and his daughter came visiting. I accompanied them to the big supermarket nearby. The daughter looked at all the fancy foodstuffs packed and displayed.

"It is their job to display these things so temptingly. It is their job to try to make us buy and eat them." My friend said to his daughter. She looked at him questioningly.

"And it is our job to choose only what is good for us," he completed.

Obesity and overeating?

I ARRIVED a day before the conference. The idea was to spend the day with Vignesh, a friend from my schooldays. He was now running his own software consultancy in Bangalore. It was immediately after my MBBS, and both of us were bachelors. I remembered him as a pleasantly plump boy who smiled while licking at his ice candy.

When I met him at the airport, the smile was in place. He was munching a huge diary milk silk at 6.00 am. There was nothing pleasantly plump about him now. He was decidedly fat. Horribly fat, if one doesn't want to mince words. He must be a hundred kilos, I thought.

I deliberately chose not to comment on his girth. But he brought up the subject himself.

"I am putting on weight. I don't know what to do," he said. "I eat very little," he clarified.

On the way we stopped at a roadside cafe. He ordered the usual. I ordered a pair of idlis and one vada.

"I usually don't have breakfast," he said, sipping his big cup of Cappuchino. "Heavy dieting, you know. My parents are looking for a girl, and my damn fatness is getting in the way."

We went to his private firm where he was the boss. His room was small, but posh, with a refrigerator humming away in a corner.

"I am thirsty," he said, taking out a coke bottle, and pouring out almost half a litre into two glasses. I told him I would take only one-fourth of that. He poured the excess into his own glass.

One of the employees had brought a chocolate cake. Vignesh ate two large pieces. Then, he scooped out icing from the sides and kept licking it off in between sentences.

During tea break, a peon brought in two samosas and

tea. He distractedly ate both, while working on his computer.

At noon he jumped up. "The afternoon is ours! Let us enjoy. First we will go to *Bawarchis* and have mutton biryani and fried chicken. I am starving. I haven't had a thing since morning."

In 2005, Kopelman and Katerson studied and reported that obese people consistently under-report their own food intake, when compared to people of normal weight.

At least some overweight people feel that overeating is not the main cause of their problem. But here I attempt to argue that excess intake of inappropriate food is the primary cause of obesity—except in a small proportion of people.

Take a look at the epidemiology. Before the 20th century, it was not a widespread problem. Now it is more widespread in the rich nations, like the USA. In the richer nations, initially, it was a disease of the upper classes. Later, it migrated to the lower classes. In developing countries, it is still a disease of the privileged rich. In India, the highest rates of the weight problem (30 to 40 per cent) are in Kerala and Punjab. Poorer states like Jharkhand and many north-east states have rates around 10 per cent. This rise parallels the amount of food purchased by people on a per person basis. Data shows that it steadily increased in most parts of the world from 1970s to 2000. The average calorie consumption per person in a country has been shown to correlate closely with the rates of prevalence of obesity. Again, we have to look at the USA, for which carefully done reports are available. From 1970 to 2000, obesity rates in the States increased from 15 to 30 per cent. The average calorie intake in the same period increased by about 336 calories among women and 170 calories in men. Most of this increase was in the form of carbohydrates rather than fat. This fact is of some importance, as we shall see later.

In any region affected by famine, the people are all thin. You can hardly see any overweight person at all.

There is a popular misconception that some of us have a *slower* metabolic rate, and hence don't burn calories well. These become fat. The naturally thin ones, some will have us believe, have a *higher* metabolic rate that evaporates away all the food. This doesn't stand up to scrutiny. As a rule, the obese or overweight have a higher metabolic rate. As they restrict their calories and become thinner, the metabolic rate drops.

And it is not true that it is extremely difficult to lose weight. Have you seen the advertisements of in-house weight loss programs? They are very effective. They will have you live there, prescribe your daily routine and restricted diet. The masters will teach you yoga and exercises. Within a few weeks, you will lost an astonishing amount of weight.

The only problem is, as you return back to your old life and ways, the kilograms slowly creep back in as you fill up to your usual level. And continue on, the flesh piling up gram by gram. It is not losing weight that is difficult, but *maintaining that low weight.*

There is a treatment that is almost guaranteed to lose

weight, and if we are a little careful, keep that weight off permanently. It is usually administered to morbidly obese (that is BMI greater than 40) patients. Some with BMI more than 35, patients with diabetes, hypertension etc. also are offered this treatment. It is called bariatric surgery. The most common bariatric surgery is nothing but removing a major portion of your stomach so that it is a fraction of the previous size. What it does is that it makes you feel absolutely full with a lesser amount of food. Some lose 30 to 40 per cent of their weight with this treatment.

So, taking into account all this, I contend that being obese and overweight is caused by ingested calories exceeding the spent ones on a chronic basis. This is just a medical way of saying that you eat more than you use by exercising.

There is one thing though. There are a number of actual medical diseases that can cause obesity. These include certain hereditary syndromes, hypothyroidism, certain medicines—especially some medicines used for mental diseases etc. But these constitute only a small proportion of overweight people.

The mechanism of overeating

LABORATORY RATS are fed a standard balanced diet—the usual rat feed. Scientists still think that we can learn a lot from rat behaviour. That is why Paul Kenny of Scripps Research Institute gave some rats the option of pastries, cakes, biscuits, sausages and other junk food. They liked it. After some time, the rats stopped eating their usual food and had only the fatty, sugary foods. They gobbled it up. They put on weight and became obese.

If an alarm sounded and then an electric shock was given to a platform that contained rat food while the rats were feeding, they quickly learnt to get off the platform and ran for their lives whenever the alarm blared. But not the obese rats gorging on junk food. They continued to stuff themselves even after the alarm, oblivious to the painful shocks that were sure to follow. This is the same reaction that scientists get when they repeat this sort of experiment with cocaine addicted rats. They continue to take cocaine even after the alarm.

If obesity is due to overeating, why do only some people get it? How do many people remain slim?

To answer, we have to look at the mechanism of appetite control. There are many chemical messengers in the brain, the main one involves a hormone called Leptin. Fat cells secrete Leptin after we have had an adequate meal. This, and many other hormones like Insulin, act on the Hypothalamus in our brains and suppress appetite. And we stop eating. We feel full. We don't become fat.

More than ten years back, some researchers discovered a strain of rat that was obese and prone to diabetes. They found that their Leptin levels were low. They either had low Leptin levels or some problem with the Leptin receptors that prevented its action. Some families of obese humans were also found to have this problem.

This made everyone think that obesity is a disease caused by hormonal imbalance. If your hormones are all wrong, how can self-control help you?

Recently, Paul Kenny, in the *Scientific American* September 2013 issue, said that this concept may be wrong. When you actually do the measurements, very few obese people show a decrease in Leptin levels. In most overweight and obese humans, Leptin and Insulin levels are very *high*. In fact, they are higher than normal.

That means their normal hunger reducing hormones are working normally. Because they eat more than they require, these hormones rise. The body is telling them desperately to stop, but they don't. Why?

Seeing and smelling good food feels good. When we eat tasty food and we are very hungry, it is pure pleasure. The eating process is stimulating the reward centres of our brains. They secrete endorphins, similar in structure to morphine and heroin, and make us feel happy. Dopamine rises in the motivational area of our brains, urging us to continue to seek out and eat more. When we have had enough, the stop hormones kick in and reduce the pleasure that we feel. Leptin and other chemicals act partly by curbing the reward centres of our brains.

In the obese, this control is short circuited. The highly processed, custom made to-be-tasty, modern super yummy designer foods override our natural controls and over stimulate our reward centres. So we keep eating. In short, these foods act similar to dangerous drugs. To make matters worse, they are widely available. It is food addiction.

This addiction model of overeating is increasingly being accepted by experts. Some feel it is not valid. But the bulk of the evidence points the addiction way.

Addiction is when you know that a habit is bad for you, but you can't stop doing it because the short-term pleasure of doing it...well, makes you do it. Again and again. This is exactly what is happening here.

There is evidence that in obese people, the pleasure that they get from a meal is typically less than that in a normal person. This has been seen in imaging studies. This is similar to the tolerance seen in drug addiction, when more and more of the drug is needed to feel the same high.

The brain circuits that are deranged in drug addictions and overeating seem to be very similar.

Many obese people, when they go on a diet, or when they are forced to eat less as after gastric bypass surgery become anxious or depressed. They mimic the withdrawal symptoms seen with normal addictions.

It is a fact that primitive tribal societies had less lifestyle diseases. By looking at these societies, maybe we can learn what to do.

Moderate exercise is good. It protects against many lifestyle diseases. But severe exercise is not sustainable and may be counterproductive.

Longevity is a desired trait in humans. The only experimentally proven method of increasing longevity is eating less, but without developing any deficiencies.

Eating more is the root cause of obesity. Our present commercially driven high sugar and high fat foods are irresistible. The mechanism of obesity is basically an addiction to high calorie food. Eating fewer calories, eating right and moderate exercise are the keys to a healthy and long life.

A little bit about food

I WAIT in the line of the office Canteen almost every day at around 10 am. My intention is to grab a quick coffee in between work. But most of the other employees are here to have their breakfast. It is instructive to watch people order their food.

Sekhar and Madhavan always come together. They order four appams or dosas each. They eat them with sugar or a little chutney. Both never order the Bengal gram or green peas curry that is offered. They are basically gorging on polished carbohydrates. Both are quite overweight and have tummies. They are back at 11.30 for their next food—potato

I am telling you, the pyramid is all wrong !! I am an expert !!

er... Are you sure? I thought you were a nutritionist

filled samosas or sweet honey cakes.

Students come in and have Pepsis and sugared fruit juices at regular intervals. Many are young girls quite conscious of their weight. That is probably the reason why they are sticking to these drinks rather than solid food. As far as I can make out, they are not succeeding.

There are a few really obese individuals who don't seem to eat much. But they trickle in at regular intervals and eat a variety of high energy food like puffs, samosas, fried bananas, and wash them all down with 'healthy' hypersweetened fruit juice.

It is important to know a little bit about food components. Carbohydrates provide energy. They are mainly starches and sugars. Flour from grains, rice and tubers like tapioca and potato have mainly starch. Anything that tastes sweet has sugar in it.

We do require carbohydrates. The old 'food pyramid' has carbohydrates as the base. It is recommended that 60 per cent of your calories should come from them. But now this concept is probably outdated. This traditional pyramid seems to be slightly wrong. Also, there are good carbohydrates and bad ones. The bad ones are to be avoided.

Enter the glycemic index. Some carbohydrate rich foods have a high glycemic index. That means that they are quickly absorbed and are converted rapidly into glucose. They make your blood sugar soar almost as soon as you eat them. The pancreas secretes large quantities of insulin to counter this outpouring. Your blood sugar plummets. You feel hungry again. Repeated eating makes you fat. Increase in body weight increases resistance to the action of Insulin. So the islet cells in the pancreas secrete more and more of it. They get worn out and in time become useless. You are on the path to becoming a diabetic. Of course-this is a highly simplified view of how some develop this disease. Some will have the disease in spite of very careful diet control. Human bodies and genes are unpredictable. All you can do is to try and tweak nature a bit and hope for the best.

Sugar, sugared drinks, and all food made from polished flour are high in glycemic index. Maida is polished wheat flour. Rice flour generally is made from polished grain. Potato and tapioca are high glycemic foods.

Fats and oils are more energy dense than carbohydrates and proteins. Some oils contain essential fatty acids. Oils are indispensible to the body. They have low glycemic index. But some oils in excess cause our lipid values to go haywire, increasing our risks of heart disease. The oils that we generally ingest can be classified as Saturated, Polyunsaturated and Monounsaturated. Butter, ghee, fats from milk, animal fats, and coconut oil are saturated fats. They generally increase LDL and serum cholesterol. Polyunsaturated fats include sunflower oil. Olive oil is Monounsaturated oil. Monounsaturated oils should probably be used more than other oils.

Proteins are the building blocks of the body. They are

used to replace and repair body tissues. Animal muscles, including our own, contain mostly protein. When carbohydrates and fats are not enough, our bodies can turn proteins also into glucose. As the process is slower, the glycemic index of protein rich food is low.

Proteins can be of high quality or low quality. High quality protein is one which contains all the essential amino acids. A low quality protein is deficient in some. The body utilises all the essential amino acids for its building and repair function, at one go. So, much of the low quality protein is changed and wasted as glucose. Only a small part of it can be utilised for its protein function.

All animal proteins—from milk, meat, egg whites etc. are good quality proteins. There are proteins in plant foods also. Legumes like soybean, green gram, Bengal grams, nuts etc. have protein. Grains like wheat and rice have some protein, though not much. Plant proteins are not as balanced as animal proteins. But that can be easily managed by combining grains and legumes at a single meal, and by adding some animal protein like milk, yoghurt, or egg white in the same meal.

Vegetables, greens, fruits provide us with essential vitamins and minerals. They also provide fibre that is very important to prevent constipation, and some studies show, protect against colon cancer and diverticular disease.

Whew! I have mindlessly condensed a lot of food science into the previous paragraphs. I am sure a critic will find a lot of conflicting and contradictory nuances, but I will not give more detail, because it is our aim to keep it simple, rememberable, and doable.

The traditional food pyramid that has been recommended by nutritionists for long had emphasised carbohydrates. Take grains at every meal, they said. They did recommend lots of vegetables and fruits. Avoid oil at all costs they said. It was a kind of low-fat diet that was followed by people who came to know of this.

It worked to a certain extent. Coronary artery disease, that was at its peak in the nineteen fifties and sixties, has actually shown a decreasing trend in the USA. It came down about fifty per cent, as people followed these dietary recommendations.

But something is clearly wrong. The incidence of obesity and excess weight has continued to grow. Diabetes reached epidemic proportions and shows no signs of abating.

It is not very hard to see what has happened. The public did not consume less calories. As I have mentioned earlier, the amount of calories eaten by an average human has gone up. Most of the increase has been of carbohydrates. Sweetened carbonated drinks, sugared fruit juices, polished white breads, biscuits, cookies, cakes, potato chips, French fries and other starch laden alternatives were offered by the food industry and embraced wholeheartedly by the people.

What to bring to the table?

WHAT HAS replaced the food pyramid? Some suggest a plate with three equal portions etched in it. One for good carbohydrates, another for proteins plus some good fat and the last for a generous helping of fruit and vegetables.

Good carbohydrates are made from whole grains. Whole wheat bread or rotis and really brown rice would qualify. We Indians are big grain eaters. We need to limit the portions drastically, even when they are whole grains.

Avoid sugar. Sugar is 'white poison'. Cut it out ruthlessly. Avoid polished flour. Potatoes and tapioca are not at all healthy. They are high glycemic index starches. Remember, potato is not a vegetable. Even carrot is not.

Egg white is good. The white of two eggs can be made into an omelette and eaten every day. Limit whole eggs to two or three a week. Fish is good protein. Almost all dietary research has shown it to be healthy. Chicken without skin is a good source of protein. It is characterised as white meat, predominantly protein, with very little fat between the muscle fibres.

We need to avoid red meat. It has oodles of saturated fat in between the meat. All organ meats, like liver, heart, gizzard, gut etc. are taboo, even when they are from poultry. Prawns, mussels, squid and shellfish are not really fish. Don't bring them to the table.

Nuts are good, if only a small handful is eaten every day.

You have to use a combination of different nuts. Roughly ten or twelve nuts a day is optimal.

Whole milk is not very good. Have half a glass of skimmed milk or yoghurt a day. Butter, ghee, paneer, I know are good for our vegetarian dishes, but not good for our bodies.

Use olive oil or canola oil. If they are too costly for you, use sunflower oil or rice bran oil as the next best options. Palm oil and coconut oil can be used to provide variety. Use them once a week or so. Don't use dalda. It is poison. Officially known as trans-fat, it is a hydrogenated factory produced fat that is not fit for human consumption. Even if we don't use it, bakers and the food industry uses it extensively. Biscuits, bread, pastries, and commercially available fried foods like chips are all swimming in it. Look at the label. If it says trans-fat or hydrogenated oil, throw it out. Better still, don't buy it. But it can be difficult, as many cheaper food joints routinely use hydrogenated oil for all their cooking. In my opinion, it is a crime that should be discouraged by stringent laws.

Have green leafy vegetables and fruits with every meal. Use them to fill up your tummy. Don't cook them too much. There are some fruits that are not so good. Bananas, dates, chiku and very sweet mangoes are to be taken in only small amounts.

Go easy on the salt. Salt is a significant cause of hypertension. A person needs less than half a teaspoon of salt a day. But we take in much more than that.

The worst offenders are the so-called junk foods. Sweet carbonated drinks are a poisonous brew of many useless ingredients that make you take in enormous amounts of raw sugar. Potato chips, pakoras, fried mixtures and the like are nothing but a clever mix of salt, trans-fats and starch in various combinations. Cakes, pastries and biscuits are concoctions of butter, fat, and flour that trigger off feelings in your taste buds that make you crave for more.

Not easy, is it? Today's world is so rife with temptations of good food, that the above list is bound to be depressing. But there is a good side to it. When I said avoid many of the food items, I meant it loosely. You may remember from a previous chapter that there are some tribes like the Eskimos that eat a lot of red meat and very few vegetables, yet still stay healthy. It is the overall quantity and quality of the food in the long-term that determines our health. It is ok to break the rule once in a while. Take red meat once a week. Want to eat prawns every other day? Go ahead and eat them. Eat boiled ones. Eat only three or four small ones. Don't touch the gravy. Want to have a pastry? Have it once a week. Share it with your family so that you eat only a quarter of a full pastry.

In short, eat healthily. Break the rules now and then. But keep your calorie intake below a certain level, on an average.

The battle of the diets

BASIL WAS one of my obese patients. He weighed a whopping 120 kilos on a five foot nine inches frame. One day he rushed into the OPD, jumping (wobbling, actually) with excitement. He had made a new discovery. A weight loss clinic near his house had planned out a diet for him. A thirty kilos loss in three months—they guaranteed that.

"Imagine, I get the money back if I lose less than fifteen kilos in that much time. I can't lose money with this."

It was their famous 'Green-Red-Brown' diet. It was designed by their experts.

One day you can have green vegetables only. Boiled or raw. The next day is the red fruits day. One can have as many tomatoes and apples as one can. Then, vegetables the next day. Then fruits the day after that. Well, you get the general pattern? It is repeated ad infinitum. The only other food allowed is two small whole wheat rotis each day. That is it. It is very simple and easy to follow.

"It is the simplicity that really convinced me," he said.

The program worked. Basil lost 20 kilograms in those three months. The clinic kept the money. But Basil became a nervous wreck. He felt tired and hungry always. Later, he developed tingling sensations in his fingers and toes. He felt giddy and lost his balance and fell down a few times. It was only when muscle weakness prevented him from going to work that he sought medical help. His muscle mass had gone down drastically. He also had anaemia and early vitamin B12 deficiency.

He went off the diet and embarked on an eating binge. Now he weighs 140 kilograms and is scheduled for bariatric surgery.

Recently, diet plans have proliferated like the make of cars on Indian roads after the economic liberalisation of the nineties. I googled 'diets', and on one site got the details of fifty-two separate kinds of diets. Advocates of each one promised that it was the panacea for all the health problems that anybody had. Many more diets are available, I am sure, than those listed.

It all started with the low-fat diet of the nineteen fifties. This was the diet prescribed by health authorities to combat coronary artery disease which had become an epidemic by that time. The diet advocated cutting down all fats and oils drastically. The base of the food pyramid was to be carbohydrates. Fruit and vegetables were very important. Fat was the main villain.

Then, like a backlash, came the very low carbohydrate, protein and fat only diets, like the Atkins diet. Later, these were found to have many problems and now are not recommended.

The vegetarian only (vegan), fruits only (fruitarian) and various fad diets that could be dangerous made the scene confusing.

Some scientists noticed that the inhabitants of places like southern Italy and Greece lived much longer than the general world population. It was said to be due to their diet, which was studied closely. The Mediterranean diet was born.

Many studies have compared various major diets over the years. A recent very good study has, in my opinion, shown the way forward.

It was done in Barcelona, Spain, and included about 7,500 people at high risk for Cardiovascular disease. One group was put on the 'Low-fat diet' and the other on the Mediterranean diet. The end points that were studied were strokes, heart attacks and deaths.

After five years the study was asked to be stopped by the supervising authorities. The Ethical Committee felt that it was not fair to keep one group on a much more dangerous diet. One diet was shown to be much superior to the other in that short period of time.

The diet that won was the Mediterranean diet. One of the problems with the other diet was that it was too difficult to follow. Many did not, and took a standard diet instead. Most of the people put on the Mediterranean diet stuck to it.

The Mediterranean diet has the following characteristics:

Fresh vegetables and fruits with almost every meal.

Whole grain bread is the main carbohydrate. It is eaten in small amounts and is not the mainstay of the diet.

Fish and chicken are the main source of animal protein. Fish is used regularly.

Legumes are eaten liberally. They include pulses, beans and grams.

Zero to four eggs a week.

A small handful of mixed nuts every day.

All cooking done in olive oil. It is the major source of fat. Oil is not very restricted.

A small glass of wine every day.

The people of the Mediterranean basin generally avoid certain foods:

Sugar, pastries, cakes, cookies and baked goods are generally not eaten.

Red meat, like beef, mutton etc. is sparingly used (only once a week).

Milk, butter and other dairy products are avoided.

Polished carbohydrates like maida, white rice, rice flour etc. are not part of their food.

The portion sizes are low. Fewer calories are consumed than the normal western population.

I think that this diet can be taken as a pointer to what one should follow. We should adapt the diet to local conditions. Olive oil is costly. But so is bad health.

Vegetarians would have a problem with the diet. They cannot follow the diet in the exact manner. Some vegetarians do not eat eggs and even milk products. They are called Vegans. Vegans will develop Vitamin B12 deficiency unless they take capsules.

What vegetarians can do is to substitute the fish and chicken with vegetable products. Soya bean, soya paneer and soya chunks are good. Legumes and various kinds of dal and grams can be used in larger amounts. A cup of low fat yoghurt or curd can be used every day. It is largely a question of common sense. One should know what to eat and what to avoid.

The secret of slimming

I AM a reasonably modest man. I don't claim to have made any scientific discoveries. Yet there is one tremendous secret that I have discovered.

They say that if you discover the cure for the common cold, you will become a millionaire. The cure for obesity should definitely come in the same league? If so, I still have a chance.

The secret is a small exercise. A sort of Zen exercise, if you will.

Sit up straight. If you are already standing, remain so. Bring a semi-determined expression to your face. Slight smile is ok, but make sure that you convey the impression that you are serious. Look straight if you are alone or into the eyes of the person with whom you are engaging at the moment.

Move your head horizontally to the left. Then to the right. Do it again. Repeat this exercise many times in rapid succession. Increase the speed towards the end for emphasis. You would have got it now. It is a simple shake of the head. It is not this activity per se that gets your weight under control. It is the timing that is crucial.

Do it whenever someone offers you any junk food. Do it to yourself if you are alone and the thought of that large bag of potato chips or chocolate pastry in the fridge intrudes into your mind. Use it with passion whenever a friend calls you out in between meals for a quick trip to the bakery for a snack of cutlets and cold coffee.

Vigorous use of this exercise is recommended when the item on offer is a cigarette or a second helping of an alcoholic drink. In fact, employ it whenever a second helping of whatever, even healthy food, makes its appearance.

In short, eating less is the secret to weight loss. Eat healthy foods. Follow the Mediterranean diet. Whatever you do, if you ingest more calories than you expend you will put on weight. If you eat less than you lose by way of routine housekeeping functions and by way of exercise, the body will burn fat and the weight will go down. We have discussed that exercise alone is not a good way to do this. So eating less is the only option. Scientifically done, in a safe manner, it may have other benefits also. This is as simple as basic arithmetic.

Why are you not thrilled? Why is not everyone jumping up and down with excitement? Why am I not being nominated for the Nobel Prize?

The reason is, I suspect, that you knew it all along. The entire world knows it, in fact. It is just a matter of putting things in perspective and calling 'a spade a spade' and not a 'funny looking agricultural implement of uncertain use'. It is just a matter of realising that the Emperor is actually walking around in his ugly, hairy nakedness.

One has to do it in a safe manner. If you are really obese and the BMI is above thirty, you need professional help. A doctor has to do a medical check up and some blood tests may be needed. A nutritionist may be useful in planning the daily calorie intake. Graded exercises may have to be started.

If you are just overweight, reducing portion sizes and sticking to healthy food is all that is necessary. If one does a net search, the calorie requirements for your height, gender and activity levels are given. Some sites even give measures for percentage of calorie restriction. You can set your daily calorie restriction for ten per cent depending on your height, and daily activity. That is a relatively safe limit. Let us say, an average Indian male may put his daily quota at 1,800 calories, while a woman can put it at 1,500. It is a guaranteed weight loss program.

How do you calculate calories? For that, a little bit more effort is needed. Again, it is superfluous to list it out here. The internet provides the measures of calories of common foods that can be calculated. If the measures are in grams, there are tables listing the approximate amount equivalent in tablespoons. Believe me; the information is all out there. After some days of daily counting, measuring and calculating, it becomes automatic to look at a meal and get the total calorie count.

As an example, let us take a typical South Indian breakfast—two Idlis, one Vada, some chutney and a plate of black Bengal grams in coconut gravy.

Two Idlis—50 Cal

One moderately large Vada—100 Cal.

One plate of curry and Chutney—200 to 300 Cal. So, the total is 750 Cal. But it can only be approximate.

Sounds like too much work? Well, we have to work for some things. A trim body and robust health does not come cheap. And still, there is no guarantee that you will be healthy. Or even safe from lifestyle diseases. You can only improve the chances. Not interested? Stop reading then. But from the experience of dealing with thousands of patients over many years, I can assure you that the work may be worth it.

Food components are important. Carbohydrates, protein and fats are required by the body. Sugar and plain starch is to be avoided. Whole wheat grains should provide carbohydrates. Fish and legumes are good protein sources. Egg white is good. Legumes can be accompanied by coarse grains. Vegetables and most fruits are good. Nuts in moderation can be taken.

Red meat and high fat dairy products are best avoided. Pastries, cakes, biscuits, puffs, chips and such unnatural foods are not good.

The Mediterranean diet is a good base for planning

healthy eating.

Whatever be the type of food that we eat, if we want to lose weight, the calories have to come down. Otherwise, it is no use. If one is serious enough, one has to learn some calorie counting.

Is dieting sustainable?

MANOJ CAME to me for body shaping. He was in his early thirties and appeared to be of normal weight. But when he took off his shirt, his problem was clear. He had sagging skin on his chest and abdomen. The fat was gone. It was a sign of massive weight loss. It was usual for people who had undergone bariatric surgery. I looked for the surgical scars, but there were none.

"How did you do it?" I asked him. He told me how he went about it. He was advised bariatric surgery. He had developed diabetes and hypertension. But he had decided to do it by diet and exercise alone. Over a three year period, he lost about 50 kilograms. And he had kept it like that, for three years now. The diabetes and the hypertension had disappeared, as if by magic. Now he did not take the medicines for that.

Obesity is a disease with a simple cure. Eat less safely. Exercise in moderation. Spend more energy than you take in and your weight will fall. But it is surprisingly difficult to cure.

Childhood obesity gets carried on to adult life. The number of fat cells increase, and then, never totally disappear. They permanently raise a person's chances of becoming and remaining fat. The wrong habits of eating acquired in childhood are difficult to re-learn.

However fat you are, a loss of three or four kilos are seen by the body as an emergency. The hunger really takes over. You become ravenous. You just can't resist that chunky chocolate cake or that chewy samosa. Once you start, you can't stop. The craving is especially strong for high calorie foods.

The body responds to weight loss by coming down on the basal metabolic rate. You burn less fuel. Your body becomes more efficient at using food. It can function with less food. The extra is stored. Once you start dieting, it becomes *easier* to put on weight.

Still, it is possible, as patients like Manoj are not a rarity. I have interviewed patients like him to uncover the secret. But I have got only certain points.

There was a strong will to succeed in these patients.

They closely monitored their weight—even daily.

Most of them went very slow, putting monthly and yearly targets.

None of them underwent any fad diets.

All of them put intelligence into the effort. They read up on the subject. They could count calories and understand healthy foods. They took it up as a project. They stuck with their resolution till they became *habits.*

They tackled any stress or situation in their lives that was using up too much mental energy. First they toned down their lives, achieved some stability, and then embarked on the project.

They used some common tricks. These include, using smaller plates and portion sizes and eating some protein with every meal. They kept nuts and fruits with them whenever they badly wanted to snack. Most avoided unhealthy foods altogether or had them sparingly.

In short, they used that thing called self-control.

Is self-control a thing?

WALTER MISCHEL and colleagues did an experiment involving four-year-old children in the 1960s. It later became famous as the Marshmallow Test.

He brought in children to a room and left them with a tasty, tempting marshmallow. Then he left the room. The children were alone, but secretly filmed. They could eat the marshmallows right away if they wanted to. But if they waited till he returned without eating them, they would get another. They would have two marshmallows.

Some gobbled the sweet immediately. Some waited for varying periods, but succumbed to temptation in the end.

I am the greatest !
GENES
SELF
CONTROL
INTELLIGENCE
HARD WORK

A few managed to wait the entire fifteen minutes to claim the reward.

Mischel did not stop there. He followed them up through adolescence and young adulthood. Even he was surprised by the results. The ones who showed greater willpower went on to become more academically successful and better at sports. They were more popular and got along with people better. Later they earned higher salaries. They even had a lower body-mass index showing they had healthier eating and lifestyle habits. They were also less prone to drug and alcohol addiction.

A similar but much larger and thorough study was published in 2010, with even more stunning results.

In England, during the Victorian era, willpower was praised. Twentieth century psychologists rejected it. They said it did not exist. But with the marshmallow test, it came back with a vengeance. Roy F Baumister of Florida State University is one of the foremost experts in this field. He says that, however you define success, in terms of money, life satisfaction, or successful family and community life, two attributes are the most important in a person. They are intelligence and willpower. It is indeed a thing—a huge thing.

Baumister says that unlike intelligence, self-control is more amenable to training, rather than being too innate.

The seat of self-regulation is the prefrontal cortex. We discussed it in an earlier chapter. It is connected to self-awareness and self-monitoring, both of which are highly developed in humans. These attributes are present in only a rudimentary form even in apes and highly intelligent dolphins. We are the only creatures that carry around with us an autobiography in our head that is updated every waking second.

Willpower is like a muscle that gets fatigued. If we use up willpower at work, at home we will shout at the kids. We might also polish off that entire chocolate cake in the fridge. This is one reason that we can't diet when we are too stressed, sleep deprived or after a frustrating commute in city traffic. This could be one important mechanism by which stress hurts us. When we live in cities, dealing with strangers take up a lot of willpower. Modern society throws up a lot of choices. Agonising over and deciding between choices depletes our willpower.

But, like a muscle, regular and sustained training strengthens it. Then you have a larger store of willpower. Getting up at a regular time, doing some chores regularly, exercising, and healthy eating, when sustained, improve our self-control over time.

Studies have shown that people who are exceptionally well-regulated are not using their quota of willpower *consciously* most of the time. People with less self-control report actively trying to use their willpower more often. Why is that?

A person with apparent self-control has, over time,

developed his better decisions into *habits*. Once it is a habit, it doesn't take too much willpower to do it.

Once in a while, one has to let go. Indulge. Get drunk, sing in the street, let the hair down a bit. This is important, if the research is to be believed. A lifetime of stringent self regulation will lead to depression. The occasional, harmless, regulated losses in control replenish your willpower stores. Then you are ready to face an unforgiving world with fortitude-and self-control.

First step in self-control is to set a goal. Then list out time periods. What you want achieved in one month, and then in a year. Then comes monitoring. If it is weight control, weigh yourself daily. If you slack one day, make up for it the next day. Keep at it, till your habits are fixed. Don't try to do too much at once.

Set clear goals with bright limits. They should be easy to follow. One should not set conflicting goals. Don't ruminate about them. Don't think much. Just follow them.

Religious people are better at self-control. A higher power that monitors ones behaviour definitely encourages willpower.

Researchers have found clear links between addiction, underachievement and crime to a focus on short-term goals. Short-term goals are important, but you should have your sights really long-term. Again, we have to train ourselves not to brood and overthink about our long-term goals.

***

Bidding goodbye

THIS IS a quick aerial view. I have tried to point out a few interesting sights on the horizon. There are no absolute guidelines and no preaching. Knowledge is joy, and it is also power. We are in an enlightened time in human history when we know a lot about many things. True, we need to know more. But we can try to apply in our daily lives what we already know. How to do it, we are not exactly sure. But I hope this book gives you some food for thought.

If you are able to translate some of the facts presented here into your life, I am happy. But another important aim of this book is to enlighten you on the way science works. How the facts are arrived at in the fields of happiness psychology and medicine in general. As it is not an exact science, one needs some insights into the inner realm of the science to discern fact from Bullshit. Escaping the bullshit of quacks, popular magazines and health advice from half baked sources is not easy. But the core truths are simple. And they are being refined by good science every day. I hope I have succeeded a little in broadening your outlook.

Fundamentals of I

Fundamentals *of* INVESTMENT

Dr. Seema Mahlawat

PRASHANT PUBLISHING HOUSE
DELHI-110094

Published by :

Prashant Publishing House

C-34, 28 Foota Road, Gali-3,
West Karwal Nagar, Delhi-110094
Phone : 011-22963970, Mob. : 9810396373
e-mail.: prashantpublishinghouse@gmail.com

Fundamentals of Investment

First Published 2019

ISBN ISBN:- 978-93-80565-98-9

PRINTED IN INDIA

Published by Mr. R.K. Jha M/s Prashant Publishing House and Published at H.S. Offset House Press, Delhi.

Contents

Preface

Investment is one of the important segment of capital formation. Investment management encourages investor to participate in the security market. The mechanism of the security market is relatively technical and dealing in the market requires skill.

Investment management is the professional management of various securities (shares, bonds and other securities) and assets (e.g., real estate), to meet specified investment goals for the benefit of the investors. Investors may be institutions (insurance companies, pension funds, corporations etc.) or private investors (both directly via investment contracts and more commonly via collective investment schemes e.g. mutual funds or exchange-traded funds).

The term asset management is often used to refer to the investment management of collective investments, (not necessarily) whilst the more generic fund management may refer to all forms of institutional investment as well as investment management for private investors. Investment managers who specialize in advisory or discretionary management on behalf of (normally wealthy) private investors may often refer to their services as wealth management or portfolio management often within the context of so-called "private banking".

The provision of 'investment management services' includes elements of financial statement analysis, asset selection, stock selection, plan implementation and ongoing monitoring of investments. Investment management is a large and important global industry in its own right responsible for caretaking of trillions of dollars, euro, pounds and yen. Coming under the remit of financial services many of the world's largest companies are at least in part investment managers and employ millions of staff and create billions in revenue.

Investment is time, energy, or matter spent in the hope of future benefits actualized within a specified date or time frame. This article concerns investment in finance. In finance, investment is buying or creating an asset with the expectation of capital appreciation, dividends (profit), interest earnings, rents, or some combination of these returns. This may or may not be backed by research and analysis. Most or all forms of investment involve some form of risk, such as investment in equities, property, and even fixed interest securities which are subject, among other things, to inflation risk. It is indispensable for project investors to identify and manage the risks related to the investment. Investment and investing is distinguished from other uses of money (such as saving, speculation, donation, gifting), in that the deployment of money is done for the purposes of obtaining a positive expected return.

In finance, investment is the purchase of an asset or item with the hope that it will generate income or appreciate in the future and be sold at the higher price. It generally does not include deposits with a bank or similar institution. The term investment is usually used when referring to a long-term outlook. This is the opposite of trading or speculation, which are short-term practices involving a much higher degree of risk. Financial assets take many forms and can range from the ultra safe low return government bonds to much higher risk higher reward international stocks. A good investment strategy will diversify the portfolio according to the specified needs.

This is a reference book. All the matter is just compiled and edited in nature, taken from the various sources which are in public domain.

The book will prove useful for investors, policy makers, researchers and all those directly or indirectly, concerned with the functioning of security market.

—*Editor*

1

Introduction

Investment management is the professional management of various securities (shares, bonds and other securities) and assets (e.g., real estate), to meet specified investment goals for the benefit of the investors. Investors may be institutions (insurance companies, pension funds, corporations etc.) or private investors (both directly via investment contracts and more commonly via collective investment schemes e.g. mutual funds or exchange-traded funds).

The term asset management is often used to refer to the investment management of collective investments, (not necessarily) whilst the more generic fund management may refer to all forms of institutional investment as well as investment management for private investors. Investment managers who specialize in advisory or discretionary management on behalf of (normally wealthy) private investors may often refer to their services as wealth management or portfolio management often within the context of so-called "private banking".

The provision of 'investment management services' includes elements of financial statement analysis, asset selection, stock selection, plan implementation and ongoing monitoring of investments. Investment management is a large and important global industry in its own right responsible for caretaking of trillions of dollars, euro, pounds and yen. Coming under the remit of financial services many of the world's largest companies are at least in part investment managers and employ millions of staff and create billions in revenue. Fund manager (or investment adviser in the United States) refers to both a firm that provides investment management services and an individual who directs fund management decisions.

TYPES OF INVESTMENTS

The various types of investment are:

- *Cash investments*: These include savings bank accounts, certificates of deposit (CDs) and treasury bills. These investments pay a low rate of interest and are risky options in periods of inflation.
- *Debt securities*: This form of investment provides returns in the form of fixed periodic payments and possible capital appreciation at maturity. It is a safer and more'risk-free' investment tool than equities. However, the returns are also generally lower than other securities.
- *Stocks*: Buying stocks (also called equities) makes you a part-owner of the business and entitles you to a share of the profits generated by the company. Stocks are more volatile and riskier than bonds.
- *Mutual funds*: This is a collection of stocks and bonds and involves paying a professional manager to select specific securities for you. The prime advantage of this investment is that you do not have to bother with tracking the investment. There may be bond, stock- or index-based mutual funds.
- *Derivatives*: These are financial contracts the values of which are derived from the value of the underlying assets, such as equities, commodities and bonds, on which they are based. Derivatives can be in the form of futures, options and swaps. Derivatives are used to minimize the risk of loss resulting from fluctuations in the value of the underlying assets (hedging).
- *Commodities*: The items that are traded on the commodities market are agricultural and industrial commodities. These items need to be standardized and

must be in a basic, raw and unprocessed state. The trading of commodities is associated with high risk and high reward. Trading in commodity futures requires specialized knowledge and in-depth analysis.

- *Real estate*: This investment involves a long-term commitment of funds and gains that are generated through rental or lease income as well as capital appreciation. This includes investments into residential or commercial properties.

SHORT INVESTMENT

In finance, short selling is the practice of selling assets, usually securities, that have been borrowed from a third party with the intention of buying identical assets back at a later date to return to the lender. The short seller hopes to profit from a decline in the price of the assets between the sale and the repurchase, as the seller will pay less to buy the assets than the seller received on selling them. Conversely, the short seller will incur a loss if the price of the assets rises. Other costs of shorting may include a fee for borrowing the assets and payment of any dividends paid on the borrowed assets. Shorting and going short also refer to entering into any derivative or other contract under which the investor profits from a fall in the value of an asset.

Going short can be contrasted with the more conventional practice of"going long", whereby an investor profits from any increase in the price of the asset.

Concept

To profit from a decrease in the price of a security, a short seller can borrow the security and sell it, expecting that it will be cheaper to repurchase in the future. When the seller decides that the time is right, the seller buys equivalent securities and returns them to the lender. The process relies on the fact that the securities are fungible; the term"borrowing" is used in the sense of borrowing $10, where the same or different $10 note can be returned to the lender assuming the value of the note is the same that it was at the time of the contract's execution. A short seller typically borrows through a broker, who is usually holding the securities for another investor who owns the securities; the broker itself seldom purchases the securities to lend to the short seller. The lender does not lose the right to sell the securities while they have been lent, as the broker will usually hold a large pool of such securities for a number of investors which, as such securities are fungible, can instead be transferred to any buyer. In most market conditions there is a ready supply of securities to be borrowed, held by pension funds, mutual funds and other investors.

The performance of buying back the securities that were sold short is called"covering the short" or"covering the position". A short position can be covered at any time before the securities are due to be returned. Once the position is covered, the short seller will not be affected by any subsequent rises or falls in the price of the securities, as he already holds the securities required to repay the lender.

The terms shorting and going short are also used as blanket terms for tactics that allow an investor to gain from the decline in price of a security. Such tactics are generally based on a derivative contract, such as an option, a future or a similar synthetic position.

For example, a put option consists of the right to sell an asset at a given strike price; the owner of the option therefore benefits when the market price of the asset falls below that price, as he can buy the asset at the lower price and sell it under the option at the strike price. Similarly, a short position in a futures contract means the holder of the position has an obligation to sell the underlying asset later at a given price; if the price falls below the given price, the person with the short position can buy the asset at the lower price and sell it under the future at the higher price.

Worked Example

If shares in C&Company currently trade at $10 per share, a short seller can borrow 100 shares of C&Company and immediately sell those shares for a total of $1,000. If the price of the shares falls to $8 per share, the short seller can buy 100 shares back for $800, return the shares to lender and keep the $200 profit. The lender accepts the return of the same number of shares as it originally lent, despite the fact that the market value of the shares has decreased. However, if the price of the shares in C&Company instead rises to $25 per share following the short sale, and the short seller is required to return the shares, the short seller would have to buy back 100 shares at $2,500 and would incur a loss of $1,500.

Comparison with Long Positions

Short selling is the opposite of "going long". A short seller takes a negative, or "bearish" stance, believing that the price of a security will fall. Investors who employ short selling often use it to allow them to profit on trading in securities which they believe are overvalued, just as traditional long investors attempt to profit on securities which are undervalued by buying them.

Because a short position is the opposite of a long position, many features of the position are reversed in comparison. In particular, the profit is limited to the value of the security, but the loss is unlimited. In practice, as the price of a security rises the short seller will receive a margin call from the broker, demanding that the short seller either cover his short position or provide additional cash in order to meet the margin requirement for the security, which effectively places a limit on the amount that can be lost.

Mechanism

Short selling stock consists of the following:

- The investor instructs the broker to sell the shares and the proceeds are credited to his broker's account at the firm upon which the firm can earn interest. Generally, the short seller does not earn interest on the short proceeds.
- Upon completion of the sale, the investor has 3 days to borrow the shares. If required by law, the investor first

ensures that cash or equity is on deposit with his brokerage firm as collateral for the initial short margin requirement. Some short sellers, mainly firms and hedge funds, participate in the practice of naked short selling, where the shorted shares are not borrowed or delivered.

- The investor may close the position by buying back the shares. If the price has dropped, he makes a profit. If the stock advanced, he takes a loss.
- Finally, the investor may return the shares to the lender or stay short indefinitely.
- At any time, the lender may call for the return of his shares e.g. because he wants to sell them. The borrower must buy shares on the market and return them to the lender. When the broker completes this transaction automatically, it is called a 'buy-in'.

Shorting Stock in the U.S.

In the U.S., in order to sell stocks short, the seller must arrange for a broker-dealer to confirm that it is able to make delivery of the shorted securities. This is referred to as a "locate." Brokers have a variety of means to borrow stocks in order to facilitate locates and make good delivery of the shorted security.

The vast majority of stocks borrowed by U.S. brokers come from loans made by the leading custody banks and fund management companies. Institutions often lend out their shares in order to earn a little extra money on their investments. These institutional loans are usually arranged by the custodian who holds the securities for the institution. In an institutional stock loan, the borrower puts up cash collateral, typically 102% of the value of the stock. The cash collateral is then invested by the lender, who often rebates part of the interest to the borrower. The interest that is kept by the lender is the compensation to the lender for the stock loan.

Brokerage firms can also borrow stocks from the accounts of their own customers. Typical margin account agreements give brokerage firms the right to borrow customer shares without notifying the customer. In general, brokerage accounts are only allowed to lend shares from accounts for which customers have "debit balances", meaning they have borrowed from the account. SEC Rule 15c3-3 imposes such severe restrictions on the lending of shares from cash accounts or excess margin shares from margin accounts that most brokerage firms do not bother except in rare circumstances.

Most brokers will allow retail customers to borrow shares to short a stock only if one of their own customers has purchased the stock on margin. Brokers will go through the "locate" process outside their own firm to obtain borrowed shares from other brokers only for their large institutional customers.

Stock exchanges such as the NYSE or the NASDAQ typically report the "short interest" of a stock, which gives the number of shares that have been legally sold short as a per cent of the total float.

Alternatively, these can also be expressed as the short interest ratio, which is the number of shares legally sold short as a multiple of the average daily volume. These can be useful tools to spot trends in stock price movements but in order to be reliable, investors must also ascertain the number of shares brought into existence by naked shorters. Investors are cautioned to remember that for every share that has been shorted, a 'shadow owner' exists who also is part of the universe of owners of that stock, i.e. Despite not having any voting rights, he has not relinquished his interest and some rights in that stock.

Securities Lending

When a security is sold, the seller is contractually obligated to deliver it to the buyer. If a seller sells a security short without owning it first, the seller needs to borrow the security from a third party to fulfill its obligation. Otherwise, the seller will "fail to deliver," the transaction will not settle, and the seller may be subject to a claim from its counterparty. Certain large holders of securities, such as a custodian or investment management firm, often lend out these securities to gain extra income, a process known as securities lending. The lender receives a fee for this service. Similarly, retail investors can sometimes make an extra fee when their broker wants to borrow their securities. This is only possible when the investor has full title of the security, so it cannot be used as collateral for margin buying.

Sources of Short Interest Data

Time delayed short interest data is available in a number of countries, including the US, the UK, Hong Kong, and Spain. Some market participants believe that stock lending data provides a good proxy for short interest levels. The amount of stocks being shorted on a global basis has increased in recent years for various structural reasons.

Short Selling Terms

Days to Cover is a numerical term that describes the relationship between the amount of shares in a given equity that have been legally short sold and the number of days of typical trading that it would require to 'cover' all legal short positions outstanding. For example, if there are ten million shares of XYZ Inc. that are currently legally short sold and the average daily volume of XYZ shares traded each day is one million, it would require ten days of trading for all legal short positions to be covered.

Short Interest is a numerical term that relates the number of shares in a given equity that have been legally shorted divided by the total shares outstanding for the company, usually expressed as a per cent. For example, if there are ten million shares of XYZ Inc. that are currently legally short sold and the total, number of shares issued by the company is one hundred million; the Short Interest is 10%. If however, shares are being created through naked short selling, "fails" data must be accessed to assess accurately the true level of short interest.

Major lenders:

- Merrill Lynch
- State Street Corporation

- JP Morgan Chase
- Northern Trust
- Fortis
- Citibank
- Bank of New York Mellon Corporation
- UBS AG

Naked

A naked short sale occurs when a security is sold short without borrowing the security within a set time, 3 days in the US. This means that the buyer of such a short is buying the short-seller's promise to deliver a share, rather than buying the share itself. The short-seller's promise is known as a hypothecated share.

When the holder of the underlying stock receives a dividend, the holder of the hypothecated share would receive an equal dividend from the short seller.

Naked shorting has been made illegal except where allowed under limited circumstances by market makers. It is detected by the Depository Trust and Clearing Corporation as a "failure to deliver" or simply "fail." While many fails are settled in a short time, some have been allowed to linger in the system.

In the US, arranging to borrow a security before a short sale is called a locate. In 2005, to prevent widespread failure to deliver securities, the U.S. Securities and Exchange Commission put in place Regulation SHO, intended to prevent investors from selling some stocks short before doing a locate. Requirements that are more stringent were put in place in September 2008, ostensibly to prevent the practice from exacerbating market declines. The rules were made permanent in 2009. Some have defended the practice of naked short selling against these restrictions.

Fees

When a broker facilitates the delivery of a client's short sale, the client is charged a fee for this service, usually a standard commission similar to that of purchasing a similar security.

If the short position begins to move against the holder of the short position, money will be removed from the holder's cash balance and moved to his or her margin balance. If short shares continue to rise in price, and the holder does not have sufficient funds in the cash account to cover the position, the holder will begin to borrow on margin for this purpose, thereby accruing margin interest charges. These are computed and charged just as for any other margin debit.

When a security's ex-dividend date passes, the dividend is deducted from the shortholder's account and paid to the person from whom the stock was borrowed.

For some brokers, the short seller may not earn interest on the proceeds of the short sale or use it to reduce outstanding margin debt. These brokers may not pass this benefit on to the retail client unless the client is very large. This means an individual short-selling $1000 of stock will lose the interest to be earned on the $1000 cash balance in his or her account.

Dividends and voting rights

Where shares have been shorted and the company which issues the shares distributes a dividend, the question arises as to who receives the dividend. The new buyer of the shares, who is the "holder of record" and holds the shares outright, will receive the dividend from the company. However, the lender, who may hold its shares in a margin account with a prime broker and is unlikely to be aware that these particular shares are being lent out for shorting, also expects to receive a dividend.

The short seller will therefore pay to the lender an amount equal to the dividend in order to compensate, though as this payment does not come from the company it is not technically a dividend as such. The short seller is therefore said to be "short the dividend".

A similar issue comes up with the voting rights attached to the shorted shares. Unlike a dividend, voting rights cannot legally be synthesized and so the buyer of the shorted share, as the holder of record, controls the voting rights. The owner of a margin account from which the shares were lent will have agreed in advance to relinquish voting rights to shares during the period of any short sale. As noted earlier, victims of Naked Shorting attacks sometimes report that the number of votes cast is greater than the number of shares issued by the company.

Markets

Futures and Options Contracts

When trading futures contracts, being 'short' means having the legal obligation to deliver something at the expiration of the contract, although the holder of the short position may alternately buy back the contract prior to expiration instead of making delivery. Short futures transactions are often used by producers of a commodity to fix the future price of goods they have not yet produced. Shorting a futures contract is sometimes also used by those holding the underlying asset as a temporary hedge against price declines. Shorting futures may also be used for speculative trades, in which case the investor is looking to profit from any decline in the price of the futures contract prior to expiration.

An investor can also purchase a put option, giving that investor the right to sell the underlying asset at a fixed price. In the event of a market decline, the option holder may exercise these put options, obliging the counterparty to buy the underlying asset at the agreed upon price, which would then be higher than the current quoted spot price of the asset.

Currency

Selling short on the currency markets is different from selling short on the stock markets. Currencies are traded in pairs, each currency being priced in terms of another. In this way, selling short on the currency markets is identical to going long on stocks. Novice traders or stock traders can be confused by the failure to recognize and understand this point: a contract is always long in terms of one medium and short another.

When the exchange rate has changed, the trader buys the first currency again; this time he gets more of it, and pays back the loan. Since he got more money than he had borrowed initially, he makes money. Of course, the reverse can also occur.

An example of this is as follows: Let us say a trader wants to trade with the US dollar and the Indian rupee currencies. Assume that the current market rate is USD $1 to Rs.50 and the trader borrows Rs.100. With this, he buys USD $2. If the next day, the conversion rate becomes USD $1 to Rs.51, then the trader sells his USD $2 and gets Rs.102. He returns Rs.100 and keeps the Rs.2 profit.

One may also take a short position in a currency using futures or options; the preceding method is used to bet on the spot price, which is more directly analogous to selling a stock short.

Risk

It is important to note that buying shares has a very different risk profile from selling short. In the former case, losses are limited but gains are unlimited. In short selling, this is reversed, meaning the possible gains are limited and the seller can lose more than the original value of the share, with, in theory, no upper limit. For this reason, short selling is usually used as part of a hedge rather than as an investment in its own right.

Many short sellers place a "stop order" with their stockbroker after selling a stock short. This is an order to the brokerage to cover the position if the price of the stock should rise to a certain level, in order to limit the loss and avoid the problem of unlimited liability. In some cases, if the stock's price skyrockets, the stockbroker may decide to cover the short seller's position immediately and without his consent, in order to guarantee that the short seller will be able to make good on his debt of shares.

The risk of large potential losses through short selling inspired financier Daniel Drew to warn:

"He who sells what isn't his'n, Must buy it back or go to pris'n"

Short selling is sometimes referred to as a "negative income investment strategy" because there is no potential for dividend income or interest income. One's return is strictly from capital gains.

Short sellers must be aware of the potential for a short squeeze. When the price of a stock rises significantly, some people who are shorting the stock will cover their positions to limit their losses; others may be forced to close their position to meet a margin call; others may be forced to cover, subject to the terms under which they borrowed the stock, if the person who lent the stock wishes to sell and take a profit. Since covering their positions involves buying shares, the short squeeze causes an ever further rise in the stock's price, which in turn may trigger additional covering. Because of this, most short sellers restrict their activities to heavily traded stocks, and they keep an eye on the "short interest" levels of their short investments. Short interest is defined as the total number of shares that have been legally sold short, but not covered.

A short squeeze can be deliberately induced. This can happen when large investors notice significant short positions, and buy many shares, with the intent of selling the position at a profit to the short sellers who will be panicked by the initial uptick or who are forced to cover their short positions in order to avoid margin calls.

Another disadvantage is that if a stock becomes "hard to borrow", which is defined by the SEC and based on lack of availability, a broker will charge a hard to borrow fee daily, for any day the SEC declares a share is hard to borrow. This occurs without any notification to short sellers. Additionally, a broker may be required to cover a short seller's position at any time. The short seller receives a warning from the broker that they are "failing to deliver" stock, which will then lead to the buy-in.

Short sellers have to deliver the securities to their broker eventually. At that point, they will need money to buy them, so there is a credit risk for the broker. To reduce this, the short seller has to keep a margin with the broker.

Short sellers tend to temper overvaluation by selling into exuberance. Likewise, short sellers are said to provide price support by buying when negative sentiment is exacerbated after a significant price decline. Short selling can have negative implications if it causes a premature or unjustified share price collapse when the fear of cancellation due to bankruptcy becomes contagious.

Strategies

Speculation

A seller intentionally takes on directional risk in the belief that the value of the shorted asset will fall.

Hedging

Hedging often represents a means of minimizing the risk from a more complex set of transactions.

Examples of this are:

- A farmer who has just planted his wheat wants to lock in the price at which he can sell after the harvest. He would take a short position in wheat futures.
- A market maker in corporate bonds is constantly trading bonds when clients want to buy or sell. This can create substantial bond positions. The largest risk is that interest rates overall move. The trader can hedge this risk by selling government bonds short against his long positions in corporate bonds. In this way, the risk that remains is credit risk of the corporate bonds.
- An options trader may short shares in order to remain delta neutral so that he is not exposed to risk from price movements in the stocks that underlie his options

Arbitrage

A short seller may be trying to benefit from market inefficiencies arising from the mispricing of certain products.

Examples of this are:

- An arbitrageur who buys long futures contracts on a US Treasury security, and sells short the underlying US Treasury security.

Against the Box

One variant of selling short involves a long position. "Selling short against the box" consists of holding a long position on which the shares have already risen, whereupon one then enters a short sell order for an equal amount of shares. The term box alludes to the days when a safe deposit box was used to store shares. The purpose of this technique is to lock in profits on the long position without having to sell that position. Once the short position has been entered, it serves to balance the long position taken earlier. Thus, from that point in time, the profit is locked in, regardless of further fluctuations in the underlying share price. For example, one can ensure a profit in this way, while delaying sale until the subsequent tax year.

U.S. investors considering entering into a "short against the box" transaction should be aware of the tax consequences of this transaction. Unless certain conditions are met, the IRS deems a "short against the box" position to be a "constructive sale" of the long position, which is a taxable event. These conditions include a requirement that the short position be closed out within 30 days of the end of the year and that the investor must hold their long position, without entering into any hedging strategies, for a minimum of 60 days after the short position has been closed.

The regulatory response

In the US, Regulation SHO was the SEC's first update to short selling restrictions since 1938. It established "locate" and "close-out" requirements for broker-dealers, in an effort to curb naked short selling. Compliance with the regulation began on January 3, 2005. In the US, initial public offering s cannot be sold short for a month after they start trading. This mechanism is in place to ensure a degree of price stability during a company's initial trading period. However, some brokerages that specialize in penny stocks have used the lack of short selling during this month to pump and dump thinly traded IPOs. Canada and other countries do allow selling IPOs short.

In the UK, the Financial Services Authority had a moratorium on short selling 29 leading financial stocks, effective from 2300 GMT, 19 September 2008 until 16 January 2009. After the ban was lifted, John McFall, chairman of the Treasury Select Committee, House of Commons, made clear in public statements and a letter to the FSA that he believed it ought to be extended.

In the US, a similar response was made by the Securities and Exchange Commission with a ban on short selling on 799 financial stocks from 19 September 2008 until 2 October 2008. Greater penalties for naked shorting, by mandating delivery of stocks at clearing time, were also introduced. Some state governors have been urging state pension bodies to refrain from lending stock for shorting purposes.

Soon thereafter, between 19 and 21 September 2008, Australia temporarily banned short selling,, and later placed an indefinite ban on naked short selling. The ban on short selling was further extended for another 28 days on 21 October 2008.Germany, Ireland, Switzerland and Canada banned short selling leading financial stocks, and France, the Netherlands and Belgium banned naked short selling leading financial stocks.

By contrast, Chinese regulators have responded by allowing short selling, along with a package of other market reforms.

An assessment of the effect of a ban on short-selling that was enacted in many countries in the fall of 2008 showed that it had only "little impact" on the movements of stocks, with stock prices moving in the same way as they would have moved anyhow, but the ban reduced volume and liquidity.

By December, countries in Europe were considering to remove the ban, while the ban in the US was already lifted in October 2008. The SEC proposed new restrictions on short selling in April 2009.

Views of short selling

Advocates of short selling say that the practice is an 'essential' part of the price discovery mechanism. Financial researchers at Duke University said in a study that short interest is an indicator of poor future stock performance and that short sellers exploit market mistakes about firms' fundamentals.

Such noted investors as Seth Klarman and Warren Buffett have said that short sellers help the market. Klarman argued that short sellers are a useful counterweight to the widespread bullishness on Wall Street, while Buffett believes that short sellers are useful in uncovering fraudulent accounting and other problems at companies.

Shortseller James Chanos received widespread publicity when he was an early critic of the accounting practices of Enron Corp. Chanos responds to critics of short-selling by pointing to the critical role they played in identifying problems at Enron, Boston Market and other "financial disasters" over the years. Commentator Jim Cramer has expressed concern about short selling and started a petition calling for the reintroduction of the uptick rule.

Individual short sellers have been subject to criticism and even litigation. Short seller Manuel P. Asensio engaged in a lengthy legal battle with the pharmaceutical manufacturer Hemispherx Biopharma. Short seller Anthony Elgindy was subjected to regulatory sanctions before he was sentenced to prison in 2005 for racketeering conspiracy, securities fraud, wire fraud and extortion. His conviction and sentence was later upheld by an appeals court in New York.

LONG TERM INVESTMENT

Planning for your future and retirement relies on planning the right kinds of long term investments. There are many different types of long term financing investments, and everyone needs to have some sort of investments for their future. Planning your retirement and long term investments go hand in hand.

Importance of Long Term Investments

Let's face it. You will not be able to work forever. No matter how healthy you are, there will come a time when you will not be able to work, due to health problems or simply aging. What will you do for an income when the time comes to retire? This is why planning your long term investments carefully is so important. Maybe you think you will be able to rely on Medicare and social security to take care of you during your retirement. Well, if that is your plan, it is time to look at the news. Social security is in trouble.

Politicians are trying to repair the problem, but chances are in another twenty years, or even less, there will be little to nothing left for you in the social security budget.

Finally, you never know what the future is going to hold. Will you stay healthy? Or, will you have some serious medical expenses that you will need to have finances for. Long term investments give you the security to know that in dire circumstances, money is there.

Long Term Investment Strategies

So, you realise that you need to start looking into long term investments.

But where do you start? How do you know which investments are the best long term investments? Should you use a broker, or do it on your own. Here are some of the most tried and true long term investment strategies.

Start by Setting Goals

As with any other type of investing, proper long term investments start by setting proper goals. How much do you want to have when you retire?

What age do you want to retire? How much should you invest monthly to reach that goal? Are you willing to do your own investing, or do you want someone to show you the ropes. Write these goals down to help guide you as you choose your investments.

Choose the Right Firm

If you decide to seek help looking for your investments, choosing the right firm is important. Make sure you choose a firm that will follow your investment goals. They should work with you to find the best investments, not against you. You should feel like you are in control, even with their help.

CAPITAL ACCUMULATION

Capital is wealth that may be in the form of money or property (including real estate, stocks and bonds) owned by an entity (a person or business). In the world of investing, the term capital can be used for assets that are invested in order to gain from a rise in their value. Capital accumulation is the growth in the total value of the capital.

Capital: Related Terms

Here are some terms associated with the concept of capital:

- *Capital Asset*: Any asset used for wealth creation.
- *Capital Gains*: The profits made on selling an asset.
- *Capital Market*: This is the marketplace for securities, such as shares and bonds, where businesses try to raise long term funds.
- *Financial Instruments*: Contracts of various combinations of capital assets, serving as a store of value, unit of account, medium of exchange or standard of deferred payment.
- *Capital Budgeting*: Also known as investment appraisal, it is the planning process that determines the profitability of long term investments.
- *Cost of Capital*: The cost to a borrower when they are loaned money, or the interest rate on a principal amount that has been loaned.
- *Capital Appreciation*: The rise in the market value of an asset the original investment in it.
- *Capital Risk*: The risk of losing the whole or part of the principal amount spent on an investment.

Connotations of Capital Accumulation

The term capital accumulation can have various connotations in different contexts:

- Spending less than what one earns (accumulation in the form of savings).
- Making investments in physical assets such as plants, equipment, machinery and raw materials.
- Investing in contracts of assets on paper.
- Training human capital and increasing its skill base.

There is always a possibility that the return on an investment will differ from expectations. The amount of risk that investors are willing to take is directly proportional to the potential returns on their investments. This is because investors have to be rewarded for taking additional risk. For example, US Treasury bonds are one of the safest and lowest yielding investments. The capital appreciation on stocks is much higher, since they are much more risky (a corporation is more likely to declare bankruptcy than the US government).

COST OF CAPITAL

Cost of capital is the minimal return that investors intend to earn on their investments. For shareholders, the cost of capital is the dividend and capital gains on the share value, while for bondholders it is the interest rate quoted on a bond.

While investing, it is essential to consider the opportunity cost of the invested capital, as it represents the return that is foregone by investors by choosing an alternative investment opportunity that has similar or comparable risk. So, this factor may be considered while calculating the cost of capital.

Calculating Cost of Capital

There are two ways to calculate the cost of capital:

Weighted Average Cost of Capital (WACC)- This is the minimum return that a company must realise from an existing asset base in order to fulfill the needs of its creditors, owners and investors.

Weighted average cost of capital (WACC) for the invested capital contains equal proportions of equity and debt, which is calculated as:

- WACC = (E/F) Re + (D/F) Rb (1-tc)
- Where Total capital invested (F) = D + E and,
- Re = Expected rate of return on equity or cost of equity (%)
- Rb = Expected rate of return on borrowings or cost of debt (%)
- tC = Corporate tax rate (%)
- D = Current value of the firm's total debt and leases
- E = Total market value of equity and equity equivalents

However, if a part of the capital comprises of a preferred stock or an asset with a different cost of invested equity, then the formula may be modified as follows:

- WACC = Wd (1-T) Rd + We Re
- Wd = Debt portion of value
- T = Tax rate
- Rd = Cost of debt (rate)
- We = Equity portion of the total value of a firm
- Re = Rate (Cost) of internal equity

Capital Asset Pricing Model (CAPM) – This model states that investors must be compensated for the risks associated with an investment and time value of money. So, the CAPM calculates the expected return from a security (Es) as follows:

$$Es = Rf + ßs\ (Rm-Rf)$$

Where:

- Rf = Expected risk-free return from the security
- ßs = Sensitivity of the security to market risk
- Rm = Historical returns from financial markets
- (Rm-Rf) = Risk premium of market assets over risk-free assets

Investors are advised to refrain from investing when the expected return falls short of the required return.

INVESTING RISK

In investing parlance, risk refers to the probability of a monetary loss or actual returns from an investment being lower than the expected returns. There is an inverse relationship between investing risk and return. Investment options that are risky need to offer higher returns than those that are less risky in order to attract investors and make it worthwhile to take on the additional risk.

Types of Risks

A US Treasury bond is considered to be among the safest investments and equities are associated with higher risks. However, every investment involves risk, the difference being in the degree and the type.

- *Capital risk*: This refers to the risk of losing the capital invested.
- *Currency risk*: If one holds assets in a foreign currency, changes in the exchange rate can cause fluctuations in the asset value. A decline in the value of the foreign currency vis-à-vis the investor's domestic currency will result in a reduction in the value of the asset in terms of the home currency. This is known as currency risk or exchange rate risk.
- *Liquidity risk*: The risk associated with a delay in the trade of an asset is known as liquidity risk. An asset sale may be difficult due to the small size of the market or low demand, preventing the owner from converting the asset into cash.
- *Credit risk*: The risk associated with the inability of the borrower to repay the principal is known as credit risk. For instance, the owner of a corporate bond could suffer losses in case the issuing company declares bankruptcy and is unable to redeem the bond.
- *Inflation risk:* Inflation erodes the value of a currency. The possibility of the value of an asset declining due to contraction in the purchasing power of a currency is called inflation risk.

- *Interest rate risk*: The possibility of devaluation of an interest-baring asset (such as bonds, stocks and loans) due to a change in the interest rate is known as interest rate risk.
- Market risk: This refers to the possibility of a decline in the value of an investment due to a change in price. Price fluctuations may be caused by changes in the interest rate, foreign exchange rate, inflation or demand and supply situation.
- *Legal risk*: The risk associated with changes in laws and regulations is called legal risk.
- *Counterparty risk*: This refers to the risk of the other party in an agreement defaulting. For instance, the risk faced by an option owner of the other party not selling the underlying asset as agreed is called their counterparty risk.

There are a number of other risks that an investor may be exposed to. Before making a choice of investment, it is critical to understand the risk involved and ways in which one can minimize risk exposure.

BUSINESS INVESTMENT

Business investment refers to the commitment of funds to a business either in an active capacity or as a passive investor. An active investor would provide seed capital or startup capital, pre-IPO funds or franchising finance. However, most people seek business investment opportunities as passive investors, purchasing stocks and bonds. Business investment decisions require a risk-return tradeoff analysis.

Business Investment: Returns

Business investment opportunities are largely contingent on the prospective rate of return or profit of a proposed business venture. The return on investment (ROI) is the ratio of money gained to the amount of funds invested. In case of passive investing (into shares and bonds), the ROI (or rate of return) includes a stream of income (dividends for shares and interest for bonds) as well as capital gains (appreciation in share or bond prices over time). The rate of return from a business investment is more than a function of the expected cash flows and capital appreciation. Since inflation erodes the value of money, it is important to consider the time value of money. The annual percentage return realised on an investment and adjusted for changes in prices on account of inflation or other external effects is known as the real rate of return.

Creation of Business Investment Opportunities

At the international level, the World Bank Group lends around $15-20 billion every year to finance developmental projects in the third world countries. The International Bank for Rural Development (IBRD), International Finance Corporation (IFC) and Multilateral Investment Guarantee Agency (MIGA) offer specific products, such as bonds, loans and guarantees, to potential investors for financing development in the emerging and underdeveloped economies. The IFC aids small and medium enterprises (SMEs) in the developing world by providing capital, equipment, technical assistance and guidance to fund these projects.

The European Bank for Reconstruction and Development (EBRD) and European Investment Bank (EIB) promote the basic and infrastructural sectors in Southeastern Europe in countries like Bosnia and Serbia. The Clean Development Mechanism (CDM) of the Kyoto Protocol, which has been put into operation by the United Nations Conference on Trade and Development (UNCTAD) in the developing countries, also promotes a greener and cleaner world for sustainable development.

Important Business Investment Destinations

Business investment opportunities have been on good ground in India, China, Vietnam. Singapore and the Gulf region. Also, a few African and Latin American countries have been doing well over the past few years. There exist huge business opportunities in Tanzania in Africa in the field of manufacturing, mining and agriculture. In India, the state of Gujarat offers excellent business investment opportunities. The Indian government can be credited with the surge in investment opportunities in the country. Liberalization of the economy since 1991 has opened up sectors such as food processing, chemicals, automobiles, oil and natural gas and telecommunications. Besides, a slew of incentives are being offered to promote investments in the country, including the relaxation of norms for external borrowing, capital goods imports and customs duty reduction and tax deductions for certain sectors.

Investment opportunities in the infrastructural sector, such as roads, ports and civil aviation, are huge in countries like India, as is in the power, coal and renewable energy sectors. With the government allowing most of the Foreign Direct Investment (FDI) via the automatic route in these sectors, business investment opportunities have emerged enabling foreign investors to garnering good returns. An FDI cap in the telecommunications sector has been raised to 100% in case of Internet service providers according to the latest investment policy followed by the Indian government.

The development of the non-oil sector in the Gulf countries entails attractive inward investments. Countries such as Bahrain have various sectors that are attractive for business investment. These include the finance industry, manufacturing and tourism. The government of Bahrain has been actively involved with the private sector for creating investment avenues for investors from across the world. Most of the GCC countries that attract business investment offer a tax-free environment. Investors are permitted to own 100% of the enterprise and there are no restrictions on the movement of capital.

FINANCIAL INVESTMENT

Financial investment is the commitment of funds into financial instruments, such as securities, bonds, real estate and currencies. The term "investment" is closely related to the disciplines of finance and economics and essentially refers to "savings" or "deferred consumption," which involves purchasing an asset or making a deposit in a bank in the hope of future returns. The term "investment" is used differently in economics and finance. By the term investment, an economist refers to real investment, such as in a machine or a house. On the other hand, a finance professional would refer to a financial asset as an investment. Such financial assets could be money that is deposited in a bank or invested in the money market.

Types of Financial Investment

Financial investments are of several types, including equities, debt instruments, derivatives, currencies and real estate. These financial assets are acquired with the expectation of future cash flows and may increase or decrease in value resulting in capital gains or losses to investors.

How is Financial Investment Made?

People invest spare money to offset the effect of inflation on idle cash as well as to benefit from an additional source of income and capital appreciation. Financial investments are typically made indirectly via intermediaries such as banks, insurance companies, mutual funds, pension funds, collective investment schemes and investment clubs. An intermediary generally makes investments using the money from many individuals.

Financial Investment and Exchanges

Exchanges are financial markets where financial products are traded. There are various kinds of exchanges, such as stock exchanges, futures exchanges and commodity exchanges. These exchanges formulate their own rules and procedures for smooth transactions and ensuring fairness for all investors.

The exchanges are guided by regulating agencies. For instance, the Securities and Exchange Commission (SEC) is the watchdog of the American stock market, while the Securities and Exchange Board of India (SEBI) regulates the Indian stock market.

The various markets for financial investment are:

Bond Market – The following products trade in this market:

- Fixed income
- Corporate bond
- Government bond
- Municipal bond
- Bond valuation
- High-yield debt

Stock (Equities) Market – The following financial instruments trade in this market:

- Stock
- Preferred stock
- Common stock
- Registered share
- Voting share

Forex Market – The following financial instruments trade in this market:

- Currency
- Currency futures
- Non-deliverable forward
- Forex swap
- Currency swap
- Foreign exchange options

Derivatives Market - The following financial products trade in this market:

- Credit derivative
- Hybrid security
- Options
- Futures
- Forwards
- Swaps

The broad range of investment opportunities represents varied levels of risks and rewards. Success in financial investment requires good knowledge of investing. Instead, one could seek the help of financial advisors, who use various technical and fundamental analysis tools to manage portfolios.

INVESTMENT STRATEGY

A well-planned investment strategy is essential before having any investment decisions. A business strategy is generally based upon long run period. Formation of business strategy largely dependent upon the factors such as long-term goals and risk on the investment. As the return on investment is not always clear, so the investors prepare the strategy so as to face the ongoing challenges in investment. A balanced investment strategy is generally required in the process of investment, which possesses long time period and some risk tolerance. In the case, when a strategy is aggressive the chance of attaining a higher goal is higher.

An efficient strategy can be obtained from portfolio theory, which shows good estimates on risk and return. Investment Strategy is usually considered to be more of a branch of finance than economics. It is defined as set of rules, a definite behaviour or procedure guiding an investor to choose his investment portfolio. For example, investing in mutual funds has recently emerged as a very favourable investment strategy. An investment strategy is centered on a risk-return tradeoff for a potential investor. High return investment instruments such as real estate and mutual funds usually have more risks associated with it than low return-low risk investment opportunities. Return on investment can be calculated on past or current investment or on the estimated return on future investment.

Symbolically, it can be expressed as:

- Vf/Vi -1 where Vf denotes final investment value and Vi is the initial investment value. ("f" and "i" should be noted as subscripts)

Return on investment (ROI) is profitable when Vf/Vi-1>0 and the investment is deemed to be unprofitable when the value of final investment is less than that of the initial investment. ROI is calculated to be 1 or 100% when the value of the final investment is twice the value of the initial investment.

Types of investment strategies

A passive investment strategy attempted to minimize transaction costs. An active investment strategy guide used to maximize returns based on moves such as proper market timing. This usually mean, "buying in the lows and selling in the highs" or buying investment instruments when they are cheap and selling them off when their price appreciates. This strategy, however, is not very beneficial for small time investors. Small time investors can adopt the buy and hold investment strategy to invest in equities, which although volatile in nature, give favourable long run returns. Investing in equity markets for small time investors is associated with the investors holding on for very long periods. In the case of real estate, the holding period extends the lifespan of the mortgage. Notably, in case of this strategy, indexing or buying a small proportion of all the shares in market index or a mutual fund is a purely passive variant of the strategy.

The strategy of value investing, a classic investment strategy propagated by Benjamin Graham simply concentrates on the strategy that an investor buys shares of a company as if he was buying off the whole company without paying any attention to the stock market scenario or any exterior conditions such as the political climate. At the end of the day, if he can buy the stock at less than that its actual future worth to the buyer, the person is said to have discovered a "value investment." Investment strategies can also denote the investment strategies a national or federal government should follow to bring about economic growth in a country. This can only be achieved by domestic investment as well as significant FDI (Foreign Direct Investment) flows to particular sectors of countries, especially the less developed ones of Asia and Africa. In case of India, infrastructural problems, excessive government intervention, rigid labour laws and corruption are stifling the flow of FDI in the critical sectors. Less developed countries such as those in the Asia- Pacific region and Africa can bring about much needed development in these economies.

An investment strategy in mutual funds is probably the best bet for a profitable investment. Mutual funds is defined as a pool of money supplied by different investors and in turn used by the mutual fund company to invest in various assets such as stocks and bonds. However, a detailed research has to be conducted for choosing the mutual fund companies and only those should be considered which have a professional investment manger.

This will ensure that the funds get channeled towards the right investments. This also applies for investing in stock markets where a decision to invest should follow a through research about the past and current trends of the stock prices and their Net Asset Values (NAV).

Analyses from market researchers about the predicted future trends should also be considered otherwise gains from capital appreciation; capital gain distribution (in case of mutual funds) and dividends might not be realised. Lastly, investment strategies leading to green investments or investments in renewable sources of energy will be the next big thing in the investment spectrum.

INVESTMENT PLANNING

Investment planning focuses on identifying effective investment strategies according to an investor's risk appetite and financial goals. There is a wide variety of investment options, including shares, bonds, mutual funds, bank deposits, real estate and futures and options. Through investment planning, one can identify the most appropriate portfolio mix.

Investment Planning: How it Works

Investment planning begins after you have taken into account your current and expected income level and have laid down your financial goals. The important aspects of investment planning are:

Investors aiming at long-term goals focus on capital growth. A long-term investment will allow you to tide over rough times without changing your plans. Stocks, mutual funds and real estate represent investment options for capital growth. On the other hand, if you're investing to meet a short-term goal or to give you a regular flow of funds to complement your present salary, you should opt for income investments. These investments generate a regular flow of income in the form of dividends and interest and include fixed-income investments, such as bonds and certificates of deposit (CDs). While making a selection, you should consider the tax implications and associated risks.

Risk: Every investment option represents a unique risk-return trade-off. Typically, more risky investments offer higher returns in order to make it worthwhile for investors to take on the additional risk. Investment planning should take into account an investor's risk appetite, which dependents on your current income level, savings, lifestyle and responsibilities.

Determine your investment profile: This can be done by considering your risk appetite.

There are mainly four types of investment profiles:

- *Conservative (Low Risk Tolerance)*: Such portfolios comprise mainly (about 70%) of income assets, such as fixed interest and cash.
- *Balanced (Average Risk Tolerance)*: This refers to portfolios with an equal emphasis on growth and income assets.
- *Growth (High Risk Tolerance)*: Such portfolios comprise mainly (up to 80%) of growth investments, such as stocks and foreign currencies.
- *High Growth or Aggressive (Very High Risk Tolerance)*: This refers to portfolios with more than 90% of the funds in growth investments

Review your investment plan regularly: This helps in fine-tuning a portfolio to suit your current financial situation and a change in risk preference.

INVESTMENT SECURITIES

Investment securities refer to certificates or documents that indicate that you have an interest in a business or have lent money to a company or a government entity. Investment securities are of two types, namely equity securities (such as common stocks) and debt securities (such as bank notes, Treasury bills and bonds). An entity or corporation that issues securities is known as the issuer.

What are the types of Investment Securities?

Here is a list of the main types of investment securities:

Bond: A bond is a type of loan or debt security for a certain period for which the issuer pays interest at a predetermined rate. Bonds can be issued by credit institutions, government agencies, corporations and public authorities. The principal amount is paid back at a later date – the maturity date or maturity.

The issuer can pay the interest on bonds in intervals or as a lump-sum after maturity. Bonds generate fixed income in the form of interest.

Underwriting is the most common method of issuing bonds. Bonds are categorised as follows:

- Bearer and Registered Bonds
- Treasury Bonds
- Treasury Bills
- Treasury Notes
- General Obligation and Revenue Bonds
- Participating Bonds
- Zero Coupon Bonds
- Convertible Bonds
- High Yield (Junk) Bonds
- Indexed Bonds
- Warrant Bond (Bonds with warrants)
- Mortgaged backed Securities

- Commercial Paper
- Sinking Bond Funds

Equities: Also known as shares, this pertains to the amount of ownership you buy in a company. The general public usually opts for equities.

Consider investing in the following:

- Common Stock
- Preferred Stock
- Par Value
- Book Value
- Classes of Stock
- Dividends
- Ex-Dividend
- Stock Splits
- Treasury Stock
- Depository Receipts
- DRIPS

Commodities: Commodities are those goods which are supplied by a number of suppliers irrespective of differentiation in quality. Tea, coffee, petroleum, milk, copper, rice, wheat, and coal are commodities. So, a contract for buying or selling these commodities can be termed as a security.

Derivatives: These are financial instruments that drive their value from direct securities, such as equities and bonds. Derivatives were called as hedging instruments earlier.

Consider the following options:

- Futures
- Swaps
- Index options
- Covered calls
- Uncovered calls
- Warrants
- Repurchase Agreements

INVESTMENT SERVICES

Financial institutions and professional financial advisers offer a host of investment services that are focused on helping their clients meet predetermined financial goals. These investment services may be customised to a client's income levels, circumstances and objectives and focus on wealth creation and protection. Investment services include making, organizing and managing investments and may also encompass financial planning, accounting, life insurance and tax planning.

Types of Investment Services

Prior to the late 1990s, US commercial banks were forbidden by law to offer investment services. The Gramm-Leach-Bliley Act of 1999 made it legal for a bank to offer both commercial and investment services. Over the years, the distinction between commercial and investment banks has blurred.

The types of investment services offered by banks include:

- *Money management*: The first step for any investor is to ascertain the amount of money he has at his disposal for investing and the various financial options available to maximize returns and tax rebates and minimize risks.
- *Portfolio management services*: These services are aimed at investors achieving the right mix of investments, such as stocks, bonds, commodities, derivatives and CDs, depending upon their financial goals and risk appetite. Portfolio management encompasses making a choice between equity and debt, domestic and international investments as well as growth and safety.
- *Retirement planning services*: Once the retirement goals have been laid down, appropriate investments need to be made into pension plans, 401(k) plans and profit sharing plans. One may also need to invest into the financial and money markets to ensure a steady stream of income post retirement.
- *Collective investment portfolio management*: Banks offer advice on collective investments, such as mutual funds,

ETFs and managed funds. One may also need professional advice for investing in hedge funds. Such funds hedge their risks via methods like short selling.

- *Brokerage services*: Investors need brokers to trade in bonds, stocks, foreign currency and derivatives. The brokerage services offered by banks are considered more reliable and are preferred to those offered by individual brokers.

Apart from financial goals, investors may have other priorities that financial institutions providing investment services can take into account. Such priorities may include socially responsible investing, green investing and sustainable investing.

SPECULATION

Speculation refers to making financial decisions by assuming the risk of loss for the potential for increased returns. There is really a very thin line of difference between speculation and investment and between a speculator and an investor. While all investors must speculate (albeit at different degrees), all speculators must invest in order to make profits.

The Difference Between Investment and Speculation

The difference between an investor and a speculator can be seen vis-à-vis the following parametres:

- *Holding period*: While an investor usually has a longer planning horizon and holds the investment for at least a year, a speculator holds the investment for a few days or months.
- *Risk disposition*: While an investor takes on moderate risks, a speculator assumes significantly higher risk.
- *Expectation of returns*: An investor expects moderate returns, while a speculator makes investments that promise high returns.
- *Decision making*: An investor would carefully evaluate the factors impacting the investment. A speculator would depend more on tips and market sentiments.

How Speculation Yields Returns

The degree of speculation tends to rise when the economy is bullish and the markets are buoyant. This is how bubbles are created. A bubble is a phenomenon during which the value of an investment (such as real estate, stock, foreign exchange and petroleum futures) rises substantially. Most of the investments are overpriced in such a scenario, yielding high returns.

Speculation: Dangers

A speculative buying spree, devoid of analytical calculation, aggravates the element of risk. Any downturn in prices can cause panic and excessive selling, resulting in a dramatic plummeting of prices and eventually a market crash. The stock market crisis of 2008 can be attributed to consecutive periods of speculative buying, followed by panic and speculative selling.

How Speculation Helps the Market

Speculation can be a blessing for the economy. This is because speculators inject capital in the market, thereby increasing liquidity. Speculative investments also minimize the risk for arbitrageurs and hedgers.

Benjamin Graham (author of the classic books Security Analysis and The Intelligent Investor and mentor to Warren Buffett) urged people to ignore the market as a whole and focus on the true "value" represented by an investment.

CAPITAL INVESTMENT

A business needs cash to purchase fixed assets, such as land, building, equipment and machinery, as well as to take care of day-to-day operating expenses. The money invested in a business for the purchase of fixed or large assets is called capital investment.

Capital investment decisions are crucial as their impact on a business is long term. Thus, it is important to evaluate the economic feasibility of the investment.

Points to Consider While Making a Capital Investment

While making a capital investment, one must consider its impact on the profitability of the business in the long term. When estimating profitability, one needs to consider the time value of money. This concept is based on the fact that cash in hand is worth more than cash receivable at a future date. This is because currently-available cash can be invested to generate earnings, while the value of cash to be received in future can decline due to inflation.

A capital investment may result in an increase in revenues. However, revenue growth does not necessarily mean positive returns from the investment, since several factors, such as inflation, interest rates on loans and opportunity cost of money, need to be taken into consideration while calculating the returns.

Determining the Feasibility of a Capital Investment

One can determine the economic feasibility of a capital investment through the following steps:

- Discount the cash returns from the investment to reflect the time value of money. Adjusting the future flow of income to the present value would help in judging whether the returns are at least equal to the cost of the debt and equity funds that need to be committed by your business to purchase the asset.
- Calculate the present value of cash required to buy the asset. This value is equal to the purchase price of the asset in most cases. However, this value can be higher in case you wish to build in additional capital to replace or maintain equipment within the facility.
- Calculate the annual benefits or net cash flows within the asset's useful lifetime. The benefits would be the increased net cash flows from the specific investment on an after-tax basis.
- Compute the present value of the annual net cash flows. This will give you an estimate of the amount of net cash flows you would be able to generate through the capital investment.

- The last computation required is the subtraction of the present value of investment derived in step 2 from the net present value of the investment returns calculated in step.
- A capital investment should be approved only if the value in step 5 is positive. A negative figure reflects that the capital investment will result in losses.

INVESTMENT PROPERTIES

A property that you buy with the purpose of generating financial returns is called an investment property. This property could be land, a single apartment or house, a block of flats, a commercial or industrial building. Investment properties generate profitsthrough rental income, capital growth or both. Investment properties are generally not used for residential purposes. You can also generate rental income from your residential home by renting out spare rooms, but this is finding compatible and reliable tenants can be tough. So, buying a separate investment property and using this to generate rental income is usually a better option.

Benefits of Buying Investment Properties

- Investment in property is usually prone to less volatility than shares. The investment in this sector is relatively a safe form of investment.
- The value of your property rises in the long term.
- You become eligible to receive tax deductions. You can include depreciation in the value of the investment property due to wear, tear and obsolescence as deductions in your tax returns.
- You can obtain tax variations and enhance your cash flows.
- You can earn from the rental income.
- You can make use of negative gearing. A negatively geared investment property is one in which the interest on the property loan is higher than the rental income

derived from the property. By indicating the difference between the interest and the rental income as losses incurred on the investment, you can get deductions in your tax returns. This is the legal remedy to reduce your taxes.

By seeking proper advice from qualified experts such as accountants, financiers and quantity surveyors, it is possible to maximize the benefits you receive from your investment property.

INVESTMENT PORTFOLIO

An investment portfolio refers to a collection of investments held by an institution or an individual. This mix of investments may include stocks, bonds, options, futures, gold certificates, currency, real estate or any other instrument that generates returns.

How to Create an Investment Portfolio?

Investment portfolio, as this will determine your overall returns and risk exposure.

- *Set your financial goals*: Financial goals would have to be set taking into account several factors, including your present income, an estimate of your future income, the number of years left for your retirement, your financial responsibilities (such as child's education or aging parents) and the prospects of the economy.
- *Asset allocation*: Any portfolio must include a mix of investments. This is because each financial instrument entails a different combination of risks and rewards. The various financial instruments can be broadly classified into four financial investment vehicles.

An investment portfolio should be balanced and spread over the broad investment classes with varying risk and reward levels. Diversifying the investment portfolio helps to minimize risk exposure, while maximizing potential return. Hence, one would need to have a basic knowledge of the various instruments available for investing.

Avoid rebalancing your portfolio regularly: It is not a good idea to rebalance the investment portfolio too often. This is because risks are lower in the longer term and asset values may be volatile in the short term. So it is better to set an annual or long term rebalancing schedule.

Things to Consider while Creating an Investment Portfolio

Here are a few things you need to keep in mind while building your investment portfolio:

- Take full advantage of your company's investment plans. This may include 401(k), profit sharing and stock options.
- Ensure that you are adequately covered against unforeseen losses through insurance.
- In case you do not have the time to study the various investment vehicles or to stay in touch with changes in regulations and the developments in the economy, consider seeking the services of a financial advisor.
- A good place to begin for a novice investor is a mutual fund, which pools money from several investors and spreads them over various investment vehicles.

2

Investments and Security

INTRODUCTION

Security analysis is a pre-requisite for making investments. In the present day financial markets, investment has become complicated. One makes investments for a return higher than what he can get by keeping the money in a commercial or cooperative bank or even in an investment bank.

In the finance field, it is a common knowledge that money or finance is scarce and that investors try to maximize their return. But the finance theory states that the return is higher, if the risk is also higher.

Return and risk go together and they have a trade off. Most of the investments are risky to some degree. The art of investment is to see that the return is maximised with the minimum of risk, which is inherent in investments. If the investor keeps his money in a bank in savings account, he takes the least risk, as the money is safe and he will get back when he wants it. But he runs the risk that the return in real terms, adjusted for inflation is negative or small and even if positive, it may not come up to his expectations or needs.

In the discussion, we concentrated on the word'Investment'. But for making investment, we need to make security analysis. It then becomes necessary to define properly investment and security analysis at the outset.

FINANCIAL MARKETS AND INVESTMENT

Financial markets have the basic function of mobilising the investments needed by corporate entities. They also performance as market places for investors who are attracted by the returns offered by the investment opportunities in the market. In this context there is a need to understand the meaning of investment and the motives of investment.

Investment may be defined as an activity that commits funds in any financial/physical form in the present with an expectation of receiving additional return in the future. The expectation brings with it a probability that the quantum of return may vary from a minimum to a maximum. This possibility of variation in the actual return is known as investment risk. Thus every investment involves a return and risk.

Investment is an activity that is undertaken by those who have savings. Savings can be defined as the excess of income over expenditure. However, all savers need not be investors. For example, an individual who sets aside some money in a box for a birthday present is a saver, but cannot be considered an investor. On the other hand, an individual who opens a savings bank account and deposits some money regularly for a birthday present would be called an investor. The motive of savings does not make a saver an investor. However, expectations distinguish the investor from a saver. The saver who puts aside money in a box does not expect excess returns from the savings. However, the saver who opens a savings bank account expects a return from the bank and hence is differentiated as an investor. The expectation of return is hence an essential characteristic of investment.

An investor earns/expects to earn additional monetary value from the mode of investment that could be in the form of physical/financial assets. A bank deposit is a financial asset. The purchase of gold would be a physical asset. Investment activity is recognised when an asset is purchased with an intention to earn an expected fund flow or an appreciation in value.

An individual may have purchased a house with an expectation of price appreciation and may consider it as an investment. However, investment need not necessarily represent purchase of a physical asset. If a bank has advanced some money to a customer, the loan can be considered as an investment for the bank. The loan instrument is expected to give back the money along with interest at a future date. The purchase of an insurance plan for its benefits such as protection against risk, tax benefits, and so on, indicates an expectation in the future and hence may be considered as an investment.

From the examples it can be seen that investment involves employment of funds with the aim of achieving additional income or growth in value. The essential quality of an investment is that it involves the expectation of a reward. Investment, hence, involves the commitment of resources at present that have been saved in the hope that some benefits will accrue from them in the future.

TYPES OF INVESTMENTS

Investments may be classified as financial investments or economic investments. In the financial sense, investment is the commitment of funds to derive future income in the form of interest, dividend, premium, pension benefits, or appreciation in the value of the initial investment. Hence, the purchase of shares, debentures, post office savings certificates, and insurance policies are all financial investments. Such investments generate financial assets. These activities are undertaken by anyone who desires a return and is willing to accept the risk from the financial instrument.

Economic investments are undertaken with an expectation of increasing the current economy's capital stock that consists of goods and services. Capital stock is used in the production of other goods and services desired by the society. Investment in this sense implies the expectation of formation of new and productive capital in the form of new constructions, plant and machinery, inventories, and so on. Such investments generate physical assets and also industrial activity. These activities are undertaken by corporate entities that participate in the capital market. Financial investments and economic investments are, however, related and dependent. The money invested in financial investments is ultimately converted into physical assets. Thus, all investments result in the acquisition of some asset, either financial or physical. In this sense, markets are also closely related to each other. Hence, the perfect financial market should reflect the progress pattern of the real market since, in reality, financial markets exist only as a support to the real market.

Characteristics of Investment

The features of economic and financial investments can be summarised as return, risk, safety, and liquidity.

Return: All investments are characterised by the expectation of a return. In fact, investments are made with the primary objective of deriving a return. The expectation of a return may be from income (yield) as well as through capital appreciation. Capital appreciation is the difference between the sale price and the purchase price of the investment. The dividend or interest from the investment is the yield. Different types of investments promise different rates of return. The expectation of return from an investment depends upon the nature of investment, maturity period, market demand, and so on. The purpose for which the investment is put to use influences, to a large extent, the expectation of return of the investors. Investment in high growth potential sectors would certainly increase such expectations. The longer the maturity period, the longer is the duration for which the investor parts with the value of the investment. Hence, the investor would expect a higher return from such investments.

Risk

Risk is inherent in any investment. Risk may relate to loss of capital, delay in repayment of capital, non-payment of interest, or variability of returns. While some investments such as government securities and bank deposits are almost without risk, others are more risky. The risk of an investment is determined by the investment's maturity period repayment capacity, nature of return commitment, and so on.

The longer the maturity period, greater is the risk. When the expected time in which the investment has to be returned is a long duration, say 10 years, instead of five years, the uncertainty surrounding the return flow from the investment increases. This uncertainty leads to a higher risk level for the investment with longer maturity rather than on an investment with shorter maturity.

Safety

The safety of investment is identified with the certainty of return of capital without loss of money or time. Safety is another feature that an investor desires from investments. Every investor expects to get back the initial capital on maturity without loss and without delay. Investment safety is gauged through the reputation established by the borrower of funds. A highly reputed and successful corporate entity assures the investors of their initial capital. For example, investment is considered safe especially when it is made in securities issued by the government of a developed nation.

Liquidity

investment that is easily saleable or marketable without loss of money and without loss of time is said to possess the characteristic of liquidity. Some investments such as deposits in unknown corporate entities, bank deposits, post office deposits, national savings certificate, and so on are not marketable. There is no well-established trading mechanism that helps the investors of these instruments to subsequently buy/sell them frequently from a market. Investment instruments such as preference shares and debentures are marketable. The extent of trading, however, depends on the demand and supply of such instruments in the market for the investors. Equity shares of companies listed on recognised stock exchanges are easily marketable. A well-developed secondary market for securities increases the liquidity of the instruments traded therein. An investor tends to prefer maximisation of expected return, minimisation of risk, safety of funds, and liquidity of investments.

OBJECTIVES OF INVESTMENT

A prudent and consistent saving habit lets income earners to set aside a certain amount of current income for future consumption. Savings kept as cash do not result in an incremental return. Hence, savings are invested in assets with the desired risk -return characteristics. The main objective of an investment process is to minimise risk while simultaneously maximising the expected returns from the investment and assuring safety and liquidity of the invested assets. Investors look for growth/increase in current wealth through investment opportunities. Given an investment environment, an investor's preference will be for investment opportunities that give the highest return.

Investors desire to earn as large returns as possible but with the minimum of risk. Risk can also be stated as the probability that the actual return realised from an investment may be different from the expected return. Financial assets can be grouped into different classes of risk based on the return. Government securities constitute the low risk category as there is very little deviation from expectations and hence are riskless. Shares of corporate entities would form the high-risk category of financial assets as their returns depend on many uncontrollable factors. An investor would be prepared to assume a higher risk only if the expected return is proportionately higher. Hence, there is a trade-off between risk and return.

The objective of safety and liquidity helps an investor to design a retirement plan. This is done to substantiate an investor's earnings beyond the employment tenure. With this in mind, the investor sets aside a part of the current income in growth/income-yielding assets that would give an assured return after a period of time.

Savings kept as idle cash do not become investments since it loses its value over time due to rise in prices. This rise in prices, or inflation, invariably erodes the value of money. Investments are, hence, made with the objective to provide a hedge or protection against inflation over the investment duration. This time value concept necessitates investors to choose asset types that will enable them to retain at least the cash value held at present over a future period. In effect, the real rate of return would be negative if the investment cannot earn a higher return than the inflation rate. For example, if inflation is at an average annual rate of 4 per cent, then the expected return from an investment should be 4 per cent to help savings funds to flow into investment avenues. The objective of investment hence can be stated as giving an expected return from the asset that is higher than the prevalent inflation rate in the economy.

The third objective of investment is the utilisation of tax incentive plans offered by the government. In order to foster investment habits, many economies offer incentives in the form of tax-saving plans. Tax rates are applicable for a fiscal year; therefore, to cut down on immediate tax expenditures as investor would invest in tax- saving investment plans offered by the government. This objective of the investor to reduce present tax payments and hence invest in tax-saving plans can be considered as a short-term investment objective. Tax-saving plans also offer a marginal return to the investors. Based on the tax policies of the country, investment criteria could solely depend on this factor also.

Types of Investors

Investors can be classified on the basis of their risk bearing capacity. Investors in the financial market have different attitudes towards risk and hence varying levels of risk-bearing capacity. Some investors are risk averse, while some may have an affinity for risk. The risk bearing capacity of an investor is a function of personal, economic, environmental, and situational factors such as income, family size, expenditure pattern, and age. A person with a higher income is assumed to have a higher risk-bearing capacity. Thus investor can be classified as risk seekers, risk avoiders, or risk bearers. A risk seeker is capable of assuming a higher risk while a risk avoider choose instruments that do not show much variation in returns. Risk bearers fall in between these two categories. They assume moderate levels of risk.

Investors can also be classified on the basis of groups as individuals or institutions. Individual investors operate alongside institutional investors in the investment market. However, their characteristics are different. Individual investors in any financial market are large in number, but in terms of value of investment they are comparatively smaller. Institutional investors, on the other hand, are organisations with surplus funds beyond immediate business needs or organisation whose business objective is investment. Mutual funds, investment companies, banking and non-banking companies, insurance corporations, and so on are organisations with large surplus funds to be invested in various profitable avenues. While these institutional investors are fewer in number compared to individual investors, their resources are much larger. Institutional investors engage professional fund managers to carry out extensive analysis. Institutional investors and individual investors combine to make the investment market dynamic.

Investment Vs Speculation

Investment and speculation both involve the purchase of assets such as shares and securities, with an expectation of return. However, investment can be distinguished from speculation by risk bearing capacity, return expectations, and duration of trade.

The capacity to bear risk distinguishes an investor from a speculator. An investor prefers low risk investments, whereas a speculator is prepared to take higher risks for higher returns. Speculation focuses more on returns than safety, thereby encouraging frequent trading without any intention of owning the investment. The speculator's motive is to achieve profits through price change, that is, capital gains are more important than the direct income from an investment. Thus, speculation is associated with buying low and selling high with the hope of making large capital gains. Investors are careful while selecting securities for trading. Investments, in most instances, expect an income in addition to the capital gains that may accrue when the securities are traded in the market.

Investment is long term in nature. An investor commits funds for a longer period in the expectation of holding period gains. However, a speculator trades frequently; hence, the holding period of securities is very short.

The identification of these distinctions helps to define the role of the investor and the speculator in the market. The investor can be said to be interested in a good rate of return on a consistent basis over a relatively longer duration. For this purpose the investor computes the real worth of the security before investing in it. The speculator seeks very large returns from the market quickly. For a speculator, market expectations and price movements are the main factors influencing a buy or sell decision. Speculation, thus, is more risky than investment.

In any stock exchange, there are two main categories of speculators called the bulls and bears. A bull buys shares in the expectation of selling them at a higher price. When there is a bullish tendency in the market, share prices tend to go up since the demand for the shares is high. A bear sells shares in the expectation of a fall in price with the intention of buying the shares at a lower price at a future date. These bearish tendencies result in a fall in the price of shares.

A share market needs both investment and speculative activities. Speculative activity adds to the market liquidity. A wider distribution of shareholders makes it necessary for a market to exist.

Investment Vs Gambling

Investment can also to be distinguished from gambling. Examples of gambling are horse race, card games, lotteries, and so on. Gambling involves high risk not only for high returns but also for the associated excitement. Gambling is unplanned and unscientific, without the knowledge of the nature of the risk involved. It is surrounded by uncertainty and a gambling decision is taken on unfounded market tips and rumours. In gambling, artificial and unnecessary risks are created for increasing the returns.

Investment is an attempt to carefully plan, evaluate, and allocate funds to various investment outlets that offer safety of principal and expected returns over a long period of time. Hence, gambling is quite the opposite of investment even though the stock market has been euphemistically referred to as a"gambling den".

MEANING OF SECURITY ANALYSIS

Investment is commitment of funds in the expectation of some positive rate of return. These funds are to be used by another party, user of fund, for productive activity. It can be giving an advance or loan or contributing to the equity or debt capital of a corporate or non-corporate business unit. In other words, investment means conversion of cash or money into a monetary asset or a claim on future money for a return. This return is for saving, parting with saving or liquidity and lastly for taking a risk involving the uncertainty about the actual return, time of waiting and cost of getting back funds, safety of funds, and risk of the variability of the return.

Investment in capital market is made in various financial instruments, which are all claims on money. These instruments may be of various categories with different characteristics. These are all called securities in the market parlance. In a legal sense also, the Securities Contracts Regulation Act, (1956) has defined the security as inclusive of shares, scrips, stocks, bonds, debentures or any other marketable securities of a like nature or of any debentures of a company or body corporate, the Government and semi-Government body etc. It includes all rights and interests in them including warrants, and loyalty coupons etc., issued by any of the bodies, organisations or the

Government. The derivatives of securities and Security Index are also included as securities in the definition in 1998.

In the strict sense of the word, a security is an instrument of promissory note or a method of borrowing or lending or a source of contributing to the funds needed by a corporate body or non-corporate body. Private security for example is also a security as it is a promissory note of an individual or firm and gives rise to a claim on money. But such private securities or even securities of private companies or promissory notes of individuals, partnerships or firms to the extent that their marketability is poor or nil, are not part of the capital market and do not constitute part of the security analysis. In nutshell, securities are financial instruments that have been created to represent a legal obligation to pay a sum in future in return for the current receipt of value. Securities thus represent the cash equivalent received from another person.

DEFINITION OF SECURITY ANALYSIS

For making proper investment involving both risk and return, the investor has to make a study of the alternative avenues of investment- their risk and return characteristics and make proper projection or expectation of the risk and return of the alternative investments under consideration. He has to tune the expectations to his preferences of the risk and return for making a proper investment choice.

The process of analysing the individual securities and the market as a whole and estimating the risk and return expected from each of the investments with a view to identifying undervalued securities for buying and overvalued securities for selling is both an art and a science and this is what is called security analysis.

Security Analysis in both traditional sense and modern sense involves the projection of future dividend, or earnings flows, forecast of the share price in the future and estimating the intrinsic value of a security based on the forecast of earnings or dividends. Thus, security analysis in traditional sense is essentially an analysis of the fundamental value of a share and its forecast for the future through the calculation of its intrinsic worth of the share.

Security Analysis stands for the proposition that a well-disciplined investor can determine a rough value for a company from all of its financial statements, make purchases when the market inevitably under-prices some of them, earn a satisfactory return, and never be in real danger of permanent loss. They encouraged investors to take an entirely different approach by gauging the rough value of the operating business that lay behind the security.

Modern security analysis relies on the fundamental analysis of the security, leading to its intrinsic worth and also risk-return analysis depending on the variability of the returns, covariance, safety of funds and the projections of the future returns. If the security analysis is based on fundamental factors of the company, then the forecast of the share price has to take into account inevitably the trends and the scenario in the economy, in the industry to which the company belongs and finally the strengths and weaknesses of the company itself- its management, promoters' track record, financial results, projections of expansion, diversification, tax planning etc. all these studies are only a part of the total security analysis that the investor should aim at.

Fundamental analysis is about using real data to evaluate a security's value. Although most analysts use fundamental analysis to value stocks, this method of valuation can be used for just about any type of security.

For example, an investor can perform fundamental analysis on a bond's value by looking at economic factors, such as interest rates and the overall state of the economy, and information about the bond issuer, such as potential changes in credit ratings. For assessing stocks, this method uses revenues, earnings, future growth, return on equity, profit margins and other data to determine a company's underlying value and potential for future growth. In terms of stocks, fundamental analysis focuses on the financial statements of a the company being evaluated.

Meaning of portfolio management: A combination of such securities with different risk -return characteristics will constitute the portfolio of the investor. Thus, a portfolio is a combination of various assets and/or instruments of investments. The combination may have different features of risk and return, separate from those of the components. The portfolio is also built up out of the wealth or income of the investor over a period of time, with a view to suit his risk or return preferences to that of the portfolio that he holds. The portfolio analysis is thus an analysis of the risk-return characteristics of individual securities in the portfolio and changes that may take place in combination with other securities due to interaction among themselves and impact of each one of them on others. As referred earlier, portfolios are combinations of assets held by the investors. These combinations may be of various asset classes like equity and debt and of different issuers like Government bonds and corporate debt or of various instruments like discount bonds, warrants, debentures and Blue chip equity or scrip of emerging blue chip companies.

The traditional Portfolio Theory aims at the selection of such securities that would fit in well with the asset preferences, needs and choices of the investor. Thus, a retired executive invests in fixed income Investment management is the professional management of various securities (shares, bonds etc) assets (e.g. real estate), to meet specified investment goals for the benefit of the investors.

Investors may be institutions (insurance companies, pension funds, corporations etc.) or private investors (both directly via investment contracts and more commonly via collective investment plans e.g. mutual funds). The term asset management is often used to refer to the investment management of collective investments, whilst the more generic fund management may refer to all forms of institutional investment as well as investment management for private investors. Investment managers who specialize in advisory or discretionary management on behalf of (normally wealthy) private investors may often refer to their services as wealth management or portfolio management often within the context of so-called"private banking".

The provision of investment management services includes elements of financial analysis, asset selection, stock selection, plan implementation and ongoing monitoring of investments. Investment management is a large and important global industry in its own right responsible for caretaking of trillions of dollars, euro, pounds and yen. Coming under the remit of financial services many of the world's largest companies are at least in part investment managers and employ millions of staff and create billions in revenue.

Securities for a regular and fixed return. A business executive or a young aggressive investor on the other hand invests in new and growing companies and in risky ventures. Modern Portfolio Theory postulates that maximisation of return and or minimisation of risk will yield optimal returns and the choice and attitudes of investors are only a starting point for investment decision and that rigorous risk return analysis is necessary for optimisation of returns.

In risk return analysis, the attitudes and preferences of investors are taken into account as also their risk-return trade off stemming from the analysis of individual securities. The return on portfolio is a weighted average of returns of the individual stocks; and the weights are proportional to each stock's percentage in the total portfolio. Besides the stocks when put together in a basket may not give a total risk which is the mathematical equivalent of total of risks of all the individual stocks, due to the simple reason that the risks of some stocks may be compensated by the risks of other stocks or vice versa.

The risks of some stocks can also be accentuated by those of others in the portfolio. The modern portfolio theory states that the combined risk of a portfolio may be greater or lesser than the sum of the risks of the components of individual securities.

Asset allocation: The different asset classes and the exercise of allocating funds among these assets (and among individual securities within each asset class) is what investment management firms are paid for. Asset classes exhibit different market dynamics, and different interaction effects; thus, the allocation of monies among asset classes will have a significant effect on the performance of the fund. Some research suggested that allocation among asset classes have more predictive power than the choice of individual holdings in determining portfolio return. Arguably, the skill of a successful investment manager resides in constructing the asset allocation, and separately the individual holdings, so as to outperform certain benchmarks (e.g., the peer group of competing funds, bond and stock indices).

Long-term returns: It is important to look at the evidence on the long-term returns to different assets, and to holding period returns (the returns that accrue on average over different lengths of investment). For example, over very long holding periods (eg. 10+ years) in most countries, equities have generated higher returns than bonds, and bonds have generated higher returns than cash. to financial theory, this is because equities are riskier (more volatile) than bonds which are themselves more risky than cash.

Diversification: Against the background of the asset allocation, fund managers consider the degree of diversification that makes sense for a given client (given its risk preferences) and construct a list of planned holdings accordingly. The list will indicate what percentage of the fund should be invested in each particular stock or bond. The theory of portfolio diversification was originated by Markowitz and effective diversification requires management of the correlation between the asset returns and the liability returns, issues internal to the portfolio (individual holdings volatility), and cross-correlations between the returns.

Portfolio analysis includes selection of securities, portfolio construction, revision of portfolio, evaluation and monitoring of the performance of the portfolio.

SECURITIES MARKET

It is needless to say that the financial markets (banks and the securities markets) finance economic growth. They channelise savings to investments and thereby decouple these two activities. As a result, savers and investors are not constrained by their individual abilities, but by the economy's ability to invest and save respectively, which inevitably enhances savings and investment in the economy. To the extent the growth of an economy depends on the rate of savings and investment, financial markets promote economic growth.

The banks and securities markets are two competing mechanisms to channel savings to investment. The securities markets score over banks in the allocational efficiency, as it allocates savings to those investments which have potential to yield higher returns.

This inevitably leads to higher returns to savers on their savings and higher productivity on investments to enterprises. Hence to the extent economic growth depends on the rate of return on investments, securities market promotes economic growth. With this brief background, we propose to talk first about functions of the securities market, then its role and importance in the growth of an economy, then how a liberalized securities market promotes economic growth, then talk about its significance in the Indian economy and finally, significance of the market in the growth of Indian economy.

Functions of Securities Market

The securities market allows people to do more with their savings than they would otherwise. It also allows people to do more with their ideas and talents than would otherwise be possible. The people's savings are matched with the best ideas and talents in the economy. Stated formally, the securities market provides a linkage between the savings and the preferred investment across the entities, time and space. It mobilizes savings and channelises them through securities into preferred enterprises.

The securities market enables all individuals, irrespective of their means, to share the increased wealth provided by competitive enterprises. The securities market allows individuals who can not carry an activity in its entirety within their resources to invest whatever is individually possible and preferred in that activity carried on by an enterprise. Conversely, individuals who can not begin an enterprise they like can attract enough investment form others to make a start and continue to progress and prosper. In either case, individuals who contribute to the investment share the fruits The securities market also provides a market place for purchase and sale of securities and thereby ensures transferability of securities, which is the basis for the joint stock enterprise system.

The liquidity available to investors does not inconvenience the enterprises that originally issued the securities to raise funds. The existence of the securities market makes it possible to satisfy simultaneously the needs of the enterprises for capital and of investors for liquidity. The liquidity the market confers and the yield promised or anticipated on security encourages people to make additional savings out of current income. In the absence of the securities market, the additional savings would have been consumed otherwise. Thus the provision of securities market results in net savings. The securities market enables a person to allocate his savings among a number of investments.

This helps him to diversify risks among many enterprises, which increases the likelihood of long term overall gains. Securities are financial instruments that have been created to represent a legal obligation to pay a sum in future in return for the current receipt of value. Securities thus represent the cash or cash equivalent received from another person. The creation of a security is situation and need specific, and many innovative instruments have been floated in the market. The existence of such financial instruments is, however, within the legal regulations governing the market in which they are floated. The securities market, hence, is place-sensitive. The immediate classification of the securities market can be in terms of national boundaries due to the legal environment. The securities market can be subdivided into national and international markets. However, with technological innovations, international agreements and standards, the line distinguishing a national from an international market is fast disappearing.

National Market

National markets are markets within the boundary of a nation. National markets cater to the financial requirements of the local players. Players from foreign countries are permitted to bring their financial instruments into the national market, subject to their following the rules and regulations imposed by the nation.

There are vast differences in the rules and regulations of the securities market among nations. Each nation has a regulatory authority under whose scrutiny financial instruments are exchanged in that country. The regulatory authority imposes the overall procedure and guidelines to be followed by the players in the national market. National markets sometimes make a difference between pure domestic players and the participation of international players. Hence, there can be a further subdivision of the national market into a domestic segment and a foreign segment.

International Market

International markets are usually referred to as offshore markets. Certain national markets, due to their policy regulations, do not discriminate between the securities issued in its country vis-à-vis other countries. A precise example of an international market is the Euromarket, where the representation of several countries is viewed together. A firm in any one member nation in the European subcontinent could list its securities simultaneously in other countries of the European Union. For example, firm with its headquarters in France, could simultaneously trade its securities in France, Spain, and Germany. This concept of opening the national market to other group countries came to be known as international market.

Domestic Segment: The domestic market caters exclusively to firms registered in a country. The country's regulatory authority controls the domestic market. In India, the Reserve Bank of India along with the Securities Exchange Board of India (SEBI) regulates the functioning of the money market and the capital market, the two types of markets within the umbrella of the domestic market. Based on the economic performance of the country, the domestic markets are also called advanced markets and emerging markets. Advanced markets are usually markets in nations that are economically sound and have also progressed technologically. The US and UK markets are termed as advanced markets. Emerging markets are those in developing nations whose economic progress is forward looking. The Indian market is termed as an emerging market. The domestic markets can be further subdivided into money market and capital market.

Money market: Short-term debt markets are known as money markets. Debt is a fixed income security and represents the borrowing of a market player. Money markets are mostly wholesale markets for financial instruments. Small values are not exchanged in the money market. The minimum value that is exchanged in the Indian money market, for instance, is Rs. 1 million. The large quantum of trade essentially limits the players in the money market to institutional investors such as banks, other financial institutions, government, and large business firms. Here, the players exchange surplus funds at the prevailing interest rates (call rates) for a short duration. The duration could be a day, a week, a month, six months, or a year. This duration indicates the maturity of the instrument. At the time of the issue of the money market instrument as well as at the time of maturity of the instrument, the account transfer of the initial amount along with the interest charges takes place between the players in the money market.

Money market has accommodated within its fold several types of trades. The money market can be differentiated into the call market, treasury bill market, inter-bank market, certificate of deposit market, repo market, commercial paper market, intercorporate deposit market, and commercial bills market

Capital Market

Capital markets exchange both long-term fixed claim securities and residual/equity claim securities. The main economic role of a capital market is to match players who have excess funds to players who are in need of funds. Capital markets also provide liquidity to financial instruments. In this exchange process, there is a valuation of the instruments done by the market for the specific risk assumed by the investors. Risk is prevalent in the capital market since the market valuation process is subject to change. For example, deviation in return is one type of risk prevalent in the instruments traded in the capital market. Besides, the instruments could also have economic risk, liquidity risk, default risk, trading risk, and so on. There are two forms of returns from instruments.

One is the claim on the instrument; the other form of return is due to trade. The claim on the instrument could be fixed or residual. The return through claim is either nil or positive. While fixed claim instruments hardly show any variation in returns, residual claim instruments display fluctuating returns thus exposing the holders to greater risk.

Capital market is the market for securities, where companies and governments can raise long-term funds. The capital market includes the stock market and the bond market. Financial regulators, such as the U.S. Securities and Exchange Commission, oversee the capital markets in their designated countries to ensure that investors are protected against fraud. The capital markets consist of the primary market, where new issues are distributed to investors, and the secondary market, where existing securities are traded.

The capital gain/loss in buying/selling the security is the trade return from the security. Given the risk-return characteristic of the capital market, the expectations of the market participants play a major role in the market price determination of the securities traded. This riskreturn characteristic of the instruments necessitates a subdivision of the capital market into debt market and equity market.

Debt Market

Financial instruments that have a fixed income claim and have a maturity of more than one year are traded in the debt market. Debentures or bonds are examples of debt instruments in the capital market.

Debt instruments may have several distinguishing features. They can be secured or unsecured debt. A secured debt has assets to fall back on while an unsecured debt is subject to more risk. Since an unsecured debt does not have an asset backing, the repayment risk is more. Mortgaged debt refers to a mortgage lien on a group of assets or on a specific asset category. Such a debt is also a secured debt.

Debt can also be categorised as redeemable debt or irredeemable debt. Based on the redemption (repayment) characteristic, it will be stated at the time of issue itself whether the debt will be repaid at maturity. Unless otherwise stated, all debt is usually redeemable debt. Irredeemable debt is a rollover debt, is renewed after maturity. Debt can also be classified as convertible debt or non-convertible debt. Convertible debt implies that the original debt instrument would be converted into another financial instrument at the time of maturity. A non-convertible debt is repaid at the end of the maturity period.

Based on the type of claim on the instrument, debt can be classified as regular interest debt, flexi debt, and zero coupon debt. A debt will bear a fixed claim, which is usually the interest payment made by the issuer to the debt holder. The nominal fixed percentage of interest is specified at the time of issue and the instruments. A flexi debt has the characteristic of changing its interest rate with the prevailing economic environment. The flexible debt is usually associated with inter-bank offer rates. For example, LIBOR (London Inter-bank Offer Rate) is a popular base rate for flexi debt instruments. A zero coupon debt, on the other hand, does not pay regular interest, but issues a document at an offer price and repays the document with value additions that compensates for the regular income through the duration of debt. The debt market distinguishes fresh issues from the subsequent trading of the securities and hence can be further subdivided into primary and secondary markets.

EQUITY MARKET

Equity instruments bestow ownership on the holder of the security. Equity hence implies ownership rights in the corporate entity that has issued the instruments to the public. The claim of the owners of these instruments is residual in nature, that is the owners will have a claim in the distribution of profits and not a fixed interest as in the case of debt instruments. The distribution of dividend out of the profits after payment to debt holders will be decided in the general body meeting of the corporate entity. The corporate will announce the dividend rates. Dividends can be annual or quarterly or extraordinary. Sometimes equity owners also claim additional returns from the firm in the form of bonus shares. Dividend can be distributed either in the form of cash or as new shares.

A stock market, or (equity market), is a private or public market for the trading of company stock and derivatives of company stock at an agreed price; these are securities listed on a stock exchange as well as those only traded privately.

The expression"stock market" refers to the market that enables the trading of company stocks collective shares, other Security finance | securities, and Derivative finance | derivatives. Bonds are still traditionally traded in an informal, Over-the-counter finance | over-the-counter market known as the bond market. Commodities are traded in commodities markets, and derivatives are traded in a variety of markets but, like bonds, mostly'over-the-counter.

The size of the worldwide"bond market" is estimated at Rs45 trillion. The size of the stock market is estimated at about Rs51 trillion. The world derivatives market has been estimated at about Rs480 trillion face or nominal value, 30 times the size of the U.S. economy...and 12 times the size of the entire world economy. It must be noted though that the value of the derivatives market, because it is stated in terms of Notional amount | notional values, cannot be directly compared to a stock or a fixed income security, which traditionally refers to an Actual cash value | actual value. Many such relatively illiquid securities are valued as mark to model | marked to model, rather than an actual market price.

The stocks are listed and traded on stock exchanges which are entities a corporation or mutual organization specialized in the business of bringing buyers and sellers of stocks and securities together.

The stock market is one of the most important sources for companies to raise money. This allows businesses to be publicly traded, or raise additional capital for expansion by selling shares of ownership of the company in a public market. The liquidity that an exchange provides affords investors the ability to quickly and easily sell securities. This is an attractive feature of investing in stocks, compared to other less liquid investments such as real estate.

History has shown that the price of shares and other assets is an important part of the dynamics of economic activity, and can influence or be an indicator of social mood. Rising share prices, for instance, tend to be associated with increased business investment and vice versa. Share prices also affect the wealth of households and their consumption. Therefore, central banks tend to keep an eye on the control and behaviour of the stock market and, in general, on the smooth operation of financial system functions. Financial stability is the raison d'être of central banks.

Exchanges also performance as the clearinghouse for each transaction, meaning that they collect and deliver the shares, and guarantee payment to the seller of a security. This eliminates the risk to an individual buyer or seller that the counterparty could default on the transaction.

The smooth functioning of all these activities facilitates economic growth in that lower costs and enterprise risks promote the production of goods and services as well as employment. In this way the financial system contributes to increased prosperity

Equity instruments can also be of several types. The most distinguishable types of equity are preference equity and common/ or ordinary equity. Preference equity has a preferential claim over dividend payment and/or payment of face value at the time of liquidation (closure) of a corporate. Sometimes a preferential equity may also have a claim for a minimum percentage of dividends when the corporate declares dividend. Common equity instruments do not have such preferential rights. The equity market is also subdivided into the primary market and secondary market.

Primary Market

The primary market is the doorway for corporate enterprises to enter the capital market. The issues of new securities are offered to the public through the primary market. The issue is thus an open public offer to sell the securities. The sale is made at a value predetermined by the firm issuing the security. Sometimes a road show is conducted to feel the pulse of the public in fixing the value for a security. The securities have a face value, which is the denomination in which it is divided. For instance, an instrument could have a face value of Re 1, Rs. 5, Rs. 10, or Rs. 100 in India. This denomination determines the number of units of the security that are offered to the public. The price at which the security is offered to the public is the offer price of the instrument. This price could be equal to or greater or lesser than the face value. When the offer price is greater than the face value, the offer is said to be at a premium. When the offer price is less than the face value, the offer is at a discount. When the two prices are equal, the offer is at par.

The primary is that part of the capital markets that deals with the issuance of new securities. Companies, governments or public sector institutions can obtain funding through the sale of a new stock or bond issue. This is typically done through a syndicate of securities dealers. The process of selling new issues to investors is called underwriting. In the case of a new stock issue, this sale is an initial public offering (IPO). Dealers earn a commission that is built into the price of the security offering, though it can be found in the prospectus. Features Of Primary Market are:-

- This is the market for new long term capital. The primary market is the market where the securities are sold for the first time. Therefore it is also called New Issue Market (NIM).
- In a primary issue, the securities are issued by the company directly to investors.
- The company receives the money and issue new security certificates to the investors.
- Primary issues are used by companies for the purpose of setting up new business or for expanding or modernizing the existing business.
- The primary market performs the crucial function of facilitating capital formation in the economy.
- The new issue market does not include certain other sources of new long term external finance, such as loans from financial institutions. Borrowers in the new issue market may be raising capital for converting private capital into public capital; this is known as'going public'.

Methods of issuing securities in the Primary Market:

- Initial Public Offer;
- Rights Issue (For existing Companies); and
- Preferential Issue.

Several intermediaries have sprung up to help corporate entities to offer their debt and equity instruments to the public. Merchant bankers and underwriters are the major intermediaries who help to match the fund requirement of corporate entities with the surplus fund position of public. The public is re both individual investors and institutional investors.

Sometimes, when the market is dominated by institutions, the market is said to be institutionalised. Once the offer process of the securities to the public is complete, the securities are listed in the markets. The corporate then has to comply with the specific regulations of each local market in which its securities are listed.

Secondary Market

The secondary market refers to the exchange of securities that have been listed through the primary market. The price at which it is traded in the capital market is the market price of the instrument. It is the secondary market that offers tradability to the financial instruments. The number of financial instruments participating in the secondary market hence, cannot exceed the number of financial instruments recorded through the primary market. The secondary market also comes under the regulatory authorities of the market and the main role of the regulator in the secondary market is to safeguard the interest of players in the market. Both individuals and institutions can take part in the secondary market. Brokers and depositories are the main intermediaries in this market, who transact business on behalf of the investors. The brokers can appoint a network of sub- brokers to mobilise investors participation in the market. Depositories help in scripless trading by holding investor accounts in electronic media.

The secondary market is the financial market for trading of securities that have already been issued in an initial private or public offering.[1] Alternatively, secondary market can refer to the market for any kind of used goods. The market that exists in a new security just after the new issue, is often referred to as the aftermarket. Once a newly issued stock is listed on a stock exchange, investors and speculators can easily trade on the exchange, as market makers provide bids and offers in the new stock.

Over a period of time, the secondary market has grown in size and in terms of efficiency. The secondary market may be further sub-divided into the spot market and derivative market.

IMPORTANCE OF THE GOVERNMENT SECURITIES MARKET

GSM constitutes the major segment of the debt market. It not only provides resources to the government for meeting its short-term and long-term needs but also acts as a benchmark for pricing corporate papers of varying maturities. The government securities issues are helpful in implementing the fiscal policy of the government.

It is critical in bringing about an effective and reliable transmission channel for the use of indirect instruments of monetary control. The working of the two of the major techniques of monetary control- Open Market Operations (OMOs) and Statutory Liquidity Ratio (SLR)- are closely connected with the dynamics of this market.

Government securities provide the highest type of collateral for borrowing against their pledge. They have the highest degree of security of capital and the return on each security depends on the coupon rate and period of maturity. They are traded for both long and short-term periods depending on the investment and liquidity preference of the investors. Switches between the short dated and long dated securities take place on the basis of difference in redemption yields.

Issues, Investors, and Types of Government Securities

Government securities are issued by the central government, state governments and semi-government authorities which also include local government authorities such as City Corporations and Municipalities.

The major investors in this market, besides the Reserve Bank, are the national banks as they have to subscribe to these securities to meet their reserve requirements. The other investors are insurance companies, state governments, provident funds, individuals, corporates, non-banking finance companies, primary dealers, financial institutions and to a limited extent, foreign institutional investors and non-resident Indian (NRIs).

These investors can be classified into three segments.

- Wholesale market segment, namely institutional players such as banks, financial institutions, insurance companies, primary dealers, and mutual funds.
- Middle segment comprising corporates, providend funds, trusts, non-banking finance companies, and small cooperative banks with an average liquidity ranging from Rs. 7 crore to Rs. 25 crore.
- Retail segment consisting of less active investors such as individuals and non-institutional investors.

The government securities market is mostly an institutional investors market as standard lots of trade are around Rs. 1 crore and 99 per cent of all trades are done through the Subsidiary General Ledger (SGL) account, which is a kind of depository account held by the Reserve Bank. Individuals cannot open SGL accounts. They have to open SGL-II accounts with a bank or a primary dealer provided they have a huge balance and agree to trade on an ongoing basis.

Government securities are of two types: treasury bills and government dated securities. The latter carry varying coupon rates and are of different maturities. Sometimes, the Reserve Bank converts maturing treasury bills into bonds thereby rolling over the government's debt.

Government Securities Market in the Pre-1991 Period

The Reserve Bank was established in 1935, after which it issued government securities on behalf of the government and sold them to various institutions and the public at large. In the 1930s, the government issued securities at interest rates as low as 2.5 per cent, as the cheap money policy was adopted. After independence, the Reserve Bank was nationalised; since then, it frames the monetary policy, structure of interest rates, programme of borrowing through government securities, and so on instructions from the government.

The programme of borrowing was gradually stepped up in the 1950s to finance development projects in various sectors of the economy. The rates of interest on government securities were also gradually stepped up to enable resource mobilisation. To facilitate this programme of higher borrowings, the Reserve Bank carried out open market operations which helped in creating a genuine market for government securities. Till the 1950s, government securities were more popular with individuals than with institutions.

Since the 1960s and until the 1990s, the government securities market remained dormant. The government was borrowing at preannounced coupon rates from banks which were the predominant group of investors. During the 1980s, the volume of both long-term and short-term debt expanded considerably, especially the latter due to automatic accommodation through the issue of ad hoc T-bills. The Reserve Bank had also little control over some of the essential facets of debt management such as volume and maturity structure of securities to be marketed and the term structure of interest rates. The maturity structure of market loans remained highly skewed in favour of a longer term of more than 15 years. Considering the significance of a vibrant government securities market and for activating an internal debt management policy, a number of measures were announced in the middle of 1991 to reform the government securities market.

Objectives of Reforms in the Government Securities Market

Reforms were undertaken in the government securities market to:

- Increase the operational autonomy of the Reserve Bank;
- Improve institutional infrastructure;
- Improve the breadth and depth of the markets by introducing a variety of new instruments and bring about improvements in the market micro-structure such as yield-based and pricebased auctions, tap about improvements in the market microstructure such as yield-based and price-based auctions, tap loans, preannouncing notified amounts, reissues of dated secrities, announcing calendar of T-bills, liquidity support to primary dealers, and so on;

- Enable sound legal and regulatory framework by amendment to Securities Contracts (Regulation) Act and propose introduction of Government Securities Act;
- Bring in technology related improvements which include initiation of computerisation of Public Debt Offices (PDOs) of the Reserve Bank and of Real Time Gross Settlement System (RTGS);
- Improve transparency and introduce standardised codes for market practices for encouraging standardised accounting norms.

Some Policy Measures Undertaken in the 1990s: The auction system for the sale of medium and long-term securities was introduced from June 3, 1992. Some innovative instruments such as conversion of auction T-bills into term securities, zero coupon bonds, capital indemed bonds, tap stocks and partly paid stock were introduced.

From April 28, 1992, 364-days T-bills auctions were introduced and 91-day T-bills auctions from January 8, 1993. On June 6, 1997, 14- day T-bills were introduced but they were discontinued from May 2001.

Auctions of repurchase agreements (Repo) of dated government securities were introduced from December 1992.

To develop the market, Securities Trading Corporations of India (STCI) was set up in May 1994. it began its operations in June 1994. The most notable policy development in the government securities market during 1994-95 was the delinking of the budget deficit from automatic monetisation by initially limiting the creation of ad hoc Tbills and subsequently discontinuing them. The National Stock Exchange started trading in government securities from June 30, 1994. As a move towards greater transparency, the transactions of government securities through SGL accounts have been made public by the Reserve Bank on a regular basis from September 1, 1994.

A Delivery versus Payment (DVP) system for transactions in government securities was introduced with effect from July

17, 1995. The DVP system synchronises the transfer of securities with cash payment thereby reducing the settlement risk in securities transactions and also preventing the diversion of funds in case of transactions routed through the SGL accounts. In 1999, the computer networking between Reserve Bank's SGL and NSDL was completed, thus enabling electronic settlement for investors having depository accounts with NSDL. The Reserve Bank set up a strong regulatory system which required that every trade must settle with funds and delivery of securities. IOUs and netting were prohibited. Trade reporting of the negotiated deals was made compulsory at the WDM (Ways and means advances) segment of NSF.

In May 1995, the government, for the first time, issued guidelines for non-government provident funds, superannuation funds, and gratuity funds to earmark 25 per cent of their total corpus for investment in central government securities. A well developed government securities market enables other segments of the debt market to develop. As a step towards this, the government went for diversification of instruments-introduction of floating rate bonds indexed to yield on 364-day T-bills. Moreover, it reissued securities of two-year, three-year, five-year, and ten-year maturities at fixed coupon. Further, it permitted commercial banks to retail government securities with non-bank clients.

A plan of Ways and Means Advances (WMA) was introduced effectively from April 1, 1997, to accommodate temporary mismatches between government receipts and payments.

This plan replaced the practice of automatic monetisation of deficit. Foreign Institutional Investors, with a ceiling of 30 per cent investment in debt instruments, have been permitted to invest in government dated securities. In order to facilitate custodial and depository services to FIIs in government dated securities and T-bills, FII investments are now permitted through the SGL account of depositories, in addition to the SGL account of the designated banks, subject to certain conditions.

To encourage retail participation in the primary market for government securities, an allocation of upto 5 per cent has been provided to retail investors on a non-competitive basis. The uniform price auction format for auctions which was confined to the auction of 91-days treasury bills was extended to the auction of dated securities.

The central government issued two floating rate bonds on the basis of uniform price auction on November 21 and December 5, 2001, on an experimental basis. The trading entities have been allowed to sell government securities allotted to them in primary issues on the same day, thus enabling sale, settlement, and transfer on the same day. Some significant steps for further development of the government securities market which the Reserve Bank has taken in 2001-02 are as follows:

- Enhancing fungibility and liquidity through consolidation by re-issuance of existing loans.
- Promoting retailing of government securities and introduction of floating rate bonds.
- Elongation of the maturity profile of outstanding issuance including issuance of bonds with a maturity of 25 years.
- Development of new benchmark government securities by consolidating new issuance in key maturities.
- Setting up of an electronic Negotiated Dealing System (NDS) and Clearing Corporation of India Limited (CCIL) for facilitating trading and settlement in government securities. The NDS (Phase I) was operationalised from February 15, 2002 and CCIL too commenced its operations for clearing and settling of transactions in government securities including repos.
- The Electronic Funds Transfer (EFT) and Real Time Gross Settlement System are being put in force by the Reserve Bank.
- A road map for developing Separate Trading for Registered Interest and Principal of Securities (STRIPS) was prepared, and put on the Reserve Bank's website for comments and suggestions from the market participants.

The government also announced, on February 28, 2001, that comprehensive legislation will be introduced on securitisation and clarification will be issued by the Central Board of Direct Taxes (CBDT) to promote the issuance of Separate Trading Registered Interest and Principal Securities (STRIPS), zero coupon bonds, deep discount bonds, and the like. Retail trading in government securities at select stock exchanges commenced in January 2003.

STRIPS in the Government Securities Market: STRIPS is a process of stripping a conventional coupon bearing security into a number of zero coupon securities which can be traded separately. To emphasise, a 10-year government security can be stripped into a principal component and a set of 20 individual coupons/assuming half yearly coupon payments. Each of these 21 stripped securities can be treated as zero coupon bonds which can be traded at varying yields.

The conversion of one underlying security into a number of zero coupon securities called STRIPS increases the breadth of the debt market and provides a continuous market which ultimately helps in improving liquidity. The creation of securities of varied maturities from a single security satisfies the needs of different investors who have diverse risk profiles and investment horizons.

STRIPS benefits not only investors, but also issuers. STRIPS allows the issuer to issue securities with long-term maturity for any amount. These long-term securities can be stripped to meet the market needs for short-term securities. Moreover, the supply of securities increases with stripping and this boosts the secondary market activity. Further, banks can issue STRIPS against the securities held by them. Thus, STRIPS facilitates the management of the banks' asset-liability mismatches.

Retailing of Government Securities

The existence of a strong retail segment is a prerequisite for the development of the government securities market. Individual can buy government securities from the Reserve Bank's public debt office during auctions. However, most investors are not familiar with the functioning of the government securities market and most of them perceive government securities as an instrument meant for institutional investors. Owing to this, the retail market of government securities did not develop. The Reserve Bank has made efforts to promote retailing of government securities.

Banks are allowed to freely buy and sell government securities on an outright basis at prevailing market prices. They retail government securities to non-bank clients without any restriction on the period between sale and purchase. Further, the interest income on government securities was exempted from the provision of tax deduction at source with effect from June 1997, to facilitate genuine trading in the secondary market.

With no TDS, government securities become an attractive investment for those interested in avoiding TDS, such as senior citizens. One of the major objectives of setting up the primary dealer system and satellite dealer system was to increase the distribution channels and encourage voluntary holding of government securities among a wider investor base.

The Reserve Bank has extended to them a plan for availing liquidity support and the facility of repos (as lenders) for increasing the retail network. With a view to enabling dematerialisation of securities of retail investors, the National Securities Depository Limited (NSDL), Stock Holding Corporation of India Limited (SHCIL) and National Securities Clearing Corporation Limited (NSCCL) were allowed to open SGL accounts with the Reserve Bank. The Reserve Bank allowed NSDL and CDSL to open a second SGL account for depository participants who, in turn, can hold in custody government securities on behalf of the ultimate investors. Retail investment in government securities has been made easy via demat accounts. The procedural hassels have been considerably reduced.

The Reserve Bank encouraged the setting up of mutual funds dealing exclusively in government securities called gilt funds with a view to creating a wider investor base for them. The Reserve Bank provides special liquidity support to the extent of 20 per cent of the investment in government dated securities. A primary dealer sells gilts with a minimum investment of Rs. 25,000 while gilt funds provide access to an individual investor with a low investment minimum of Rs. 5,000. The awareness about gilt funds is rising as they are offering good returns. PNB Gilts is using the Punjab National Bank branch network to popularise government securities with retail investors.

It has tied up with NSDL to work around the problem of physical transfers and has also launched an advertising campaign to inform the public about the advantages of investing in government securities. Gilt funds were managing more than Rs. 3,200 crore as on June 30, 2001.

INFRASTRUCTURE DEVELOPMENT OF THE GOVERNMENT SECURITIES MARKET

The government securities market constitutes the principal segment of the debt market. The development of any market requires the strengthening of the market infrastructure with large number of market players who have divergent perceptions about the market and who would continuously provide liquidity. One of the initiatives taken to develop the government securities market during the first stage of the reform process was the setting up of Securities Trading Corporation of India (STCI). The STCI together with Discount and Finance House of India (DFHI) had the task of developing an active secondary market in government securities.

The Reserve Bank introduced the primary dealer system and satellite dealer system to further strengthen the market infrastructure.

Primary Dealer System

A system of primary dealers was introduced in 1996, to further strengthen the market infrastructure and to make it more liquid and broad based.

The objectives of the introduction of this system were:

- To strengthen the government securities infrastructure;
- To bring about improvements in the secondary market trading, liquidity and turnover in government securities;
- To encourage a voluntary holding of government securities amongst a wider investor base; and
- To make PDs an effective conduit of open market operations.

The major focus of PDs would be on increasing the turnover of government securities rather than becoming a mere repository of this system. Hence, their role would be to performance as market makers by providing two-way quotes in the secondary market, thereby ensuring liquidity and support to the primary market operation. In the long run, this system would facilitate the transfer of market-making activities from the Reserve Bank to primary dealers.

PDs can be subsidiaries of scheduled commercial banks, subsidiaries of all-India financial institutions, companies under Companies Act, 1956 engaged predominantly in government securities market, and subsidiaries of foreign banks/securities firms. Every PD has to maintain minimum net owned funds of Rs.50 crore deployed daily in the government securities market. PDs institutional entities fall in the category of non-banking finance companies. PDs are registered with and regulated by the Reserve Bank of India, irrespective of whether they accept public deposits or not.

Obligations upon PDs Facilities Extended to them: In order to enable PDs to perform their role effectively, the Reserve Bank has cast certain obligations upon PDs which include an annual minimum bidding for dated securities and treasury bills with a minimum success ratio and commitment to underwrite the shortfall (gap) between the subscribed accepted amount and the notified amount. PDs have to achieve an annual turnover of not less than five times of average month-end stocks during the year in dated securities and ten times in treasury bills, within which outright transactions should be three and six times respectively.

To strengthen this system and to make PDs fulfil their obligations, the Reserve Bank extends to them various facilities like access to SGL and current account facility with the Reserve Bank, liquidity support through reverse repos linked to both bidding commitment and performance of PDs in the primary and secondary markets, freedom to deal in money market instruments, facility of transfer of funds from one centre to another under the Reserve Bank's Remittance Facility Plan, exclusive access to open market operations in treasury bills since February 2000 and a switch facility Plan, exclusive access to open market operations in treasury bills since February 2000 and a'switch facility' to swap their medium to long-term dated government securities with 364-day treasury bills during August 2000. Routing operations in the call money market are allowed through all PDs to increase their profitability. PDs are allowed to issue commercial papers (CPs) to raise resources.

The Reserve Bank provides liquidity support to PDs through repos/ refinance against central government securities under three levels. At the first level, normal refinance at bank rate is provided upto a specified amount. A backstop refinance at a variable rate upto a fixed amount is provided at the second level. Finally, discretionary support is extended through Liquidity Adjustment Facility (LAF). The total assured liquidity support for all PDs together is about Rs.4,500 crore for 2002-03 as against Rs.6,000 crore during 2001-02, of which two- third is under the normal facility and one-third under the backstop facility. If any PD in any auction of treasury bills, fails to submit the required minimum bid or submits a bid lower than its commitment, the Reserve Bank will reduce liquidity support to the extent of shortfall/failure in submission of bids for a period of three months from the date so specified by the Bank. For instance, if a bid is short by an amount of Rs.10 crore, liquidity support will be reduced by an amount of Rs.10crore for 3 months.

Act, 1934, the borrowings by commercial/cooperative banks from them is netted for reckoning their demand and time liabilities for computation of cash reserves.

PDs are expected to substantially underwrite the primary issues of government securities and treasury bills. In view of the increasing trend in government borrowings, the role of PDs in enhancing the market for government securities is becoming crucial. PDs give two- way quotes in the Press/Reuters screen and bid in the auctions of 91-day/364-day treasury bils and in the floatation of new loans. PDs are permitted to participate in the call/notice money market, term money market, and bill rediscounting plan both as lenders and borrowers. The system of payment of commission on purchase of securities was replace in 1997-98 by a system of underwriting fees on the amount underwritten by them through competitive bids. The uniform pricing approach is used in accepting bids for underwriting.

The system of underwriting facilitates larger absorption by PDs, keeping in view the Reserve Bank's ultimate objective of moving away from the primary market. The underwriting commitment of each PD is broadly decided on the basis of its size, in terms of its net owned funds, its holding strength, committed amount of bids, and volume of turnover in government securities. In case of auctions of treasury bills, PDs are no longer required to undertake devolvement. Hence, the payment of commission for treasury bills was withdrawn with effect from June 5, 2001-02, a revised plan for bidding and underwriting was announced. PDs are also given a favoured access to the Reserve Bank's OMOs.

Number of PDs DFHI and STCI were accredited as dealers on March 1, 1996. ON June 1, 1996, four more PDs-SBI gilts, PNB gilts, Gilts Securities Trading Corporation Limited, and ICICI Securities -became operational. As on March 31, 2002, there were 18 approved PDs in

the gilts market. The initial six PDs constitute the subsidiaries of RBI/nationalized banks/financial institutions, while the remaining new PDs represent private sector participants. These 18 PDs have net owned funds of over Rs.4,000 crore and total assets of Rs.15,658 crore out of which government securities constitute Rs.12,236 core (78 per cent of total assets).

Primary Dealers Association of India (PDAI)

PDs formed an autonomous, self-regulatory organisation (SRO), Primary Dealers Association of India (PDAI) in 1996. The role of PDAI is

- To promote a liquid debt market and set common standards for market participants;
- To achieve a harmonious integration of different segments of markets;
- To build a healthy relationship between different segments of market participants; and
- To remove some legal, procedural, and administrative bottlenecks in the efficient functioning of the market.

Banks and PDs together formed another autonomous self-regulatory body. Fixed Income Money Market and Derivatives Association of India (FIMMDAI), in 1997.

These two SROs have been proactive and the closely involved in contemporary issues relating to the development of the money market and government securities market. The credit for upgrading the technological infrastructure in these two markets goes to these two SROs. The representatives of the PDAI and FIMMDAI are members of the Technical Advisory Group on Money and Government Securities Markets of the Reserve Bank. The FIMMDAI has now taken over the responsibility of publishing the yield curve in the debt markets. The FIMMDAI prepared the guidelines for standard procedures and documentation to be followed by the participants in the commercial paper market and certificate of deposit (CD) market. Currently, the FIMMDAI is working towards the development of uniform documentation and accounting principles of repo market.

Satellite Dealers: In order to widen the scope for organised dealing and distribution arrangement in the government securities market and to support the system of primary dealers, the Reserve Bank introduced a supporting infrastructure in the form of satellite dealers. SDs form the second tier of trading and distribution of government securities.

The guidelines for registration of satellite dealers in government securities market were announced on December 31, 1996. The guidelines, subsidiaries of scheduled commercial banks and all-India financial institutions (AIFIs) and companies incorporated under Companies Act, 1956 with minimum net owned funds of Rs.5 crore were eligible to be SDs. In pursurance of these guidelines, the Reserve Bank granted approval to 16 entities for registration as SDs in the government securities market. SDs were permitted to issue commercial papers for raising resources and could avail of liquidity support from the Reserve Bank and the facility of ready forward transactions. Some of the satellite dealers were promoted as primary dealers. The network of satellite dealers was created to promote the retailing of government securities but the performance of the satellite dealers was not found to be satisfactory. The Reserve Bank decided to discontinue the system after obtaining the view of the Primary Dealers Association of India. No new SDs will be licensed and existing SDs were required to make action plans satisfactory to the Reserve Bank for termination of their operations as SDs by May 31, 2002.

Measures to Strengthen the Government Securities Market Infrastructure

For bringing about an improvement in trading and settlement in the money market and government securities market, the Negotiated Dealing System (NDS) and Cleaning Corporation of India Limited (CCIL) have been setup.

Negotiated Dealing System: The Reserve Bank introduced NDSE with a view to reforming the secondary market in government securities and money market operations, introducing transparency, and facilitating electronic bidding in auctions. Test turns on the NDS started in November 2001 and phase I was operationalised from February 15, 2002 with 41 participants.

The NDS provides an on-line electronic bidding facility in the primary auctions of central/state government securities, OMOs/LAF auctions. It enables screen -based electronic dealing and reporting of transactions in money market instruments including repo, secondary market transactions in government securities, and dissemination of information on trades with the least time lags.

The NDS is integrated with the Securities Settlement System (SSS), of the Public Debt Office as also with the CCIL to facilitate paperless settlement of transactions in government securities and treasury bills and bring about improvement in services to investors in government securities. Once a trade is done/reported over NDS, it can be settled either through CCIL or directly through RBI-SGL. Settlement through CCIL is on Delivery versus Payment (DVP-II) mechanism. DVP-II refers to settlement of securities on gross basis (trade by trade basis) while funds will settle on net basis.

Banks, primary dealers, and financial institutions having SGL accounts and current accounts with the Reserve Bank are eligible to participate in NDS. It provides an electronic dealing platform for these participants in government securities. It enables the execution of deals in both the computer matching mode or a chat mode for negotiating deals on the system itself. Members are expected to report all the trades negotiated outside the system for settlement. If facilitates member participation in the primary auctions of government securities and treasury bills by submitting their bids/applications for auctions/ floatation through their own terminals or pooled terminals. The pooled terminal facility is provided at all regional offices for use by SGL account holders not having member terminals. NDS is used by the Reserve Bank for extending the liquidity adjustment facility to eligible members. All entities having SGL accounts with the Reserve Bank were advised to become members eligible members of the NDS by May 31, 2002. Till Agusut 5, 2002, 138 SGL account holders were members of NDS. On an average, 526 deals were reported daily on NDS, of which 473 deals for Rs.11,688 crore were ready for settlement during the quarter ended June 2002. These deals comprised money market deals (109 deals for Rs. 8,762 crore), outright government securities trades (344 deals for Rs.2,080 crore) and repo transactions among member participants. The settlement of the government securities transactions through the CCIL constituted 91.3 per cent of the total government securities trades dealt/reported on the NDS.

The NDS has brought about significant improvements in secondary markets also. It has helped in increasing the level of transparency of the dealings in government securities, T-bills, and other instruments. The system has facilitated screen-based trading, provision of on-line trade information, and reporting through trade execution system for settlement.

Clearing Corporation of India Limited: The Clearing Corporation of India Limited (CCIL) was registered on April 30, 2001 under the Companies Act, 1956. The State Bank of India is the chief promoter of CCIL. Its other promoters are banks, financial institutions, and primary dealers. It has been set up as an ordinary, limited liability, non-government company under the Companies Act, 1956 with an equity capital of Rs.50 crore. It functions like a business entity that is subject to corporate tax on its business profits.

It acts as the central counterparty in the settlement of all trades in government securities, treasury bills, money market instruments, repos, inter-bank foreign exchange deals, and derivatives of any kind where the underlying instrument is a security or money market instrument. CCIL is the clearing and settling agency in respect of all trades by institutional players such as banks, DFIs, primary dealers, mutual funds, corporates, and NBFCs who account for more than 98 per cent of the total trades.

In foreign exchange transactions, CCIL resorts to loss allocation mechanism to manage credit and market risk and restricts the membership to authorised dealers only.

To ensure liquidity for uninterrupted settlements, CCIL has arranged rupee securities through member contributions to the SGF, rupee funds through line of credit with various banks, and US dollar funds by way of a fully collateralised line of credit with the settlement bank.

To deal with operational risk, CCIL is developing a fully automated system for processing trades. A Disaster Recovery Site is being set up at the Institute for Development and Research in Banking Technology (IDRBT), Hyderabad, to ensure business continuity in case of a disaster.

The government raises short-term and long-term funds by issuing securities. These securities do not carry no risk and are as good as the government guarantees the payment of interest and the repayment of principal.

The government generates revenue in the form of taxes and income from ownership of assets. Besides these, it borrows extensively from banks, financial institutions, and the public to finance its expenditure in excess of its revenues. Government securities are of two types: treasury bills and government dated securities.

The latter carry varying coupon rates and are of different maturities. Sometimes, the Reserve Bank converts maturing treasury bills into bonds thereby rolling over the government's debt. The interest rates in the primary market are influenced by the prevailing liquidity conditions.

Reserve Bank's intervention by way of devolvement and private placement, and amount and frequency of issues during the year.

With a view to promoting the retail market segment and providing greater liquidity to retail investors, banks were allowed to freely buy and sell government securities on an outright basis at prevailing market prices, without any restriction on the period between sale and purchase.

Banks were permitted to undertake transactions in securities among themselves or with non-bank clients through the members of OTCEI in addition to NSE. The Reserve Bank manages short-term liquidity through repos and reverse repos and long-term liquidity through open market sales to absorb liquidity in conjunction with private placement/devolvement and open market purchases in tight liquidity conditions. A system of primary dealers was introduced in 1 9 9 6, to further strengthen the market infrastructure and to make it more liquid and broad based.

In order to widen the scope for organised dealing and distribution arrangement in the government securities market and to support the system of primary dealers, the Reserve Bank introduced a supportinginfrastructure in the form of satellite dealers. SDs form the second tier of trading and distribution of government securities. For bringing about an improvement in trading and settlement in the money market and government securities market, the Negotiated Dealing System (NDS) and Cleaning Corporation of India Limited have been setup.

3

Investor and Financial Assets

An investor is a person or entity who invests money in various asset classes for financial gain. Investors can be individuals or companies that purchase equity, debt securities, currency, real estate and commodity derivatives to generate income streams, capital appreciation or both.

INVESTOR TYPES

Investors can be categorized as:

- *Individual investors*: These can be anybody looking to invest in shares, bonds, foreign exchange or other securities. Trusts acting on behalf of individuals also come under this category.
- *Investment banks*: These are financial institutions that assist companies in raising funds by issuing equity. These banks perform other financial services, such as trading in equities, foreign exchange, commodities and derivatives, on behalf of their clients. Apart from providing consultancy services to businesses, these banks facilitate corporate restructuring and mergers and acquisitions. Investment banks earn profits by issuing and selling stocks and bonds.
- *Businesses*: These are organizations that make investments in companies requiring funds to either expand into new markets or for new product development. These businesses fund the capital

requirements of such companies in exchange for a stake in the company or for a share of profits generated through these new ventures. The risk is shared equally by the investors and the company that receives the funds.

- *Funds:* These may be hedge funds or mutual funds, in which investors pool in money to invest in securities, such as shares, bonds or commodities. The ownership of these funds may not be publicly tradable.
- *Venture capital funds*: These funds collect money from high net worth individuals (HNWIs) or institutional investors to invest primarily in early-stage, high-potential companies. The pooled money, called venture capital, is invested in such growth companies in exchange for a stake in these firms. The aim of venture capital funds is to realise huge profits during the invested company's IPO (initial public offering) or sale. However, investments in growth firms are inherently risky.
- *Angel investors*: These are either individuals or a group of affluent investors who provide starting capital for a business in exchange for a part ownership or convertible debt. These investors sometimes also provide specific expertise to these new firms. The sole investment purpose of these investors is to generate high returns. Other types of investors are those who collect valuable objects, such as antiques and works of art.

ASSET

An asset is anything of value owned by a person or company. Assets can be converted into cash depending on demand conditions. In accounting, the term "asset" in a balance sheet includes cash, inventories, property rights and goodwill. Assets can be used to generate cash flows.

Types of Assets: Tangible

The various types of assets are:

- *Tangible assets*: These assets have a physical existence, such as equipment, building and real estate. It has two sub-classes:

- *Current assets*: These are cash as well as assets that can be converted into cash, or consumed within a year or within an operating cycle.

These assets include:

- *Cash and its equivalents*: Including currency, deposit accounts, money orders, checks and bank drafts.
- Inventory: Stock of goods held by an organization.
- *Accounts receivable*: The amount owed to an asset holder in exchange for goods and services provided.
- *Short term investments*: Securities bought to be sold in the near future. These investments are aimed at generating income on short-term price movements.
- *Prepaid expenses*: Operating costs paid for services or products to be used in the future.
- *Long-term investments*: These assets are often bought to be held for long term and can include land, special funds, bonds, long-term notes and stocks.

Fixed assets: These assets, such as tools, machinery, land, buildings and furniture, are purchased with the sole aim of generating profits. Fixed assets, also called PPE (property, plant and equipment), are purchased for long term use.

Types of Assets: Intangible

Intangible Assets

Are not present in the physical form, which makes it very difficult to evaluate the m. Thus, these assets cannot be bought and sold at fair value.

These assets include:

- *Patents*: Exclusive rights granted to a person for an invention or a discovery for a specific timeframe.
- *Copyrights*: Legal rights granted to the owner of an intellectual property, granting him/her exclusive rights. No one can use that intellectual property without obtaining permission from the copyright owner.

- *Goodwill*: This is the difference between the current and fair market price of the net asset value (NAV) of a company.
- *Trademark:* A distinguishing attribute by which a company is readily identified.
- *Trade name*: It is a name under which a business trades. This name could be different from the registered or legal name and can be considered as the company's brand.

ANALYSIS OF INCOME-PRODUCING REAL ASSETS

Some equity investments in real assets, such as real estate, can produce income or cash flows. Examples of income-producing real assets are commercial real estate (which consists of office buildings, warehouses, retail outlets such as shopping centers, and guest quarters such as hotels and motels), industrial real estate (which includes industrial parks), residential real estate (which includes manufactured home and apartment complexes), and agricultural real estate (which consists of farms). Income is derived from these properties by renting or leasing them out to users. As with other income-producing assets, real estate may be analysed using the general cash flow model introduced in the *"General Discounted Cash-Flow Model"*

Valuing Real Estate

Income from equity investments in real estate typically consists of rental or lease income less operating, financing, depreciation, and tax expenses. These revenue and expense streams are similar to those for equity investments in general business assets, and the equity valuation models.

Capitalizing Real Estate Cash Flow: Real estate is often valued using an income capitalization method that is similar to P/e ratio analysis. The process consists of estimating current income from the real estate and then dividing through by an appropriate capitalization rate.

Usually, however, real estate values are appraised by capitalizing income before depreciation, interest, and tax expenses (rather than net income after taxes). This income is often called net operating income or cash flow. Net operating income is often capitalized for real estate investments because depreciation is a noncash expense, often arbitrarily determined by using different accounting policies, and may not match the true replacement and repair costs of the fixed asset. In addition, interest expenses can vary widely depending on how much of a property is financed with debt. As a result of different depreciation and interest expenses, there can also be large differences in tax expenses. For instance, assume that a particular property is expected to generate net operating income of $10,000,000 per year. Assume that properties with similar risk and growth prospects have capitalization rates of 8% (e.g., assume that another property with similar risk and growth prospects had annual net operating income of $8,000,000 and a price of $100,000,000). The value of the property would b

Thus, this process of real estate valuation is similar to multiplying the adjusted earnings of a stock by an appropriate P/e ratio that is obtained from stocks with similar growth prospects and risk (with adjusted earnings for real estate being measured before depreciation, interest, and tax expenses).

Both operating income and cash flow growth prospects for real estate investments can be estimated using similar criteria as for stocks. However, for real estate investments, the primary focus is on rental increases net of cash operating expenses. As a result, real estate cash flow growth is often estimated by inflationary expectations that would permit rental increases. Higher inflationary expectations and growth prospects would result in lower capitalization rates, all else being equal, just as higher expected ROEs and dividend growth rates for stocks result in higher P/e ratios.

However, net cash flow growth prospects can be dampened by more than offsetting expectations of cash expense increases. In addition, cash flow growth expectations can also be affected by the possibility of changes in vacancy rates. In particular, the possibility of higher vacancy rates increases the chances of lower future net cash flows and thus results in a higher current capitalization rate. In fact, due to rising expenses, stagnant or failing rental rates, and higher vacancy rates, growth rate forecasts can be negative, resulting in very high capitalization rates. If the possibility of lower cash flows is related to the national economy (as opposed to being caused by a local or regional economic downturn, or being specific to the particular property or location), an even higher capitalization rate might be required by investors because of the higher systematic risk. The higher transaction costs typically incurred on real estate trades can also increase the capitalization rate.

Although growth prospects and risk determine the relative capitalization rate on different parcels of real estate for any moment in time, general changes in capitalization rates over time are largely caused by changes in risk-free interest rates, changes in market risk premiums, and changes in inflation Oust as changes in stock P/e ratios over time are largely determined by the same factors). In addition, general increases in capitalization rates can also result from past real estate building booms that often lead to widespread overbuilding and that can cause expectations of large rises in vacancy rates in the future (20% vacancy rates are often considered high).

Average and median capitalization rates for different property types are printed periodically in various different sources such as *Investment Property & Real Estate Capital Market Report* published by Institutional Real Estate, Inc. For instance, in the summer of 1998, the capitalization rate was 8.55% for office buildings, 8.70% for warehouses, 9.10% for retail outlets, and 8.50% for apartments. There may have been some fear on the part of investors of increased retail sales via the internet long-term, therefore causing more closures of retail outlets and higher vacancy rates for shopping centers and other retail real estate, and the resulting lower cash flow projected in the future from retail real estate investments made investors capitalize existing cash flow at the relatively higher average rate of 9.10%. However, despite the higher cap rate on retail real estate in general, there was also sentiment that some retail real estate would hold up fairly well in a recession, such as retail outlets that include grocery stores (people always need to buy food which can't easily be sold over the internet) and well-located malls with financially strong tenants and popular stores.

At this time, cap rates had been on the rise for virtually all real estate (especially for lodging and resorts, which had cap rates in excess of 10%, possibly because of investor fears that travel needs might be reduced by increased internet competition), as investors began to perceive that growth in revenue and operating cash flow in general were likely to slow.

Computing the Present Value of Real Estate Cash Flows

Real estate can also be valued by forecasting future cash flows from the real estate and discounting at the required return using equation (4-1). The beta of unlevered real estate investments is generally fairly low because the value of unlevered real estate investments is not extremely volatile, and much of the volatility is related to local factors that are not a function of the aggregate economy. However, use of a large amount of debt in a real estate company can magnify the beta several times, as more debt magnifies systematic risk for the same correlation with the market portfolio.

As a result, discount rates for net real estate cash flows measured net of interest expenses would have to be set as a function of the debt/equity ratio of the company. As in the case for stocks in the same industry, betas for real estate investments could be estimated using the betas of publicly traded real estate stocks like equity Real Estate Investment Trusts (REITS) with similar leverage.

However, cash flows from real estate properties are often evaluated before considering the effect of debt financing. If that approach is utilized, it is necessary to estimate cash flows resulting from paying for the entire purchase price of the real estate in cash, assume therefore no debt service or interest payments, and use a very low discount rate (since the unlevered beta would be used). Often, though, it is difficult to separate the purchase decision from the financing decision (which typically has an important effect on after-tax cash flows), and so investors generally need to compute the present value of the cash flows that incorporate the effects of any debt financing (using software like SIA's PROJECT). Regardless of whether cash flows are measured with or without consideration of the effect of debt financing, it is important not to project the same income from a property into the far future. In particular, there is generally some justification for forecasting substantial changes in cash flows in the future. For instance, there is always the possibility of rising vacancy rates. High vacancy rates are more likely as a property ages, deteriorates, becomes obsolete relative to newer properties, and/or is negatively affected by demographic changes such as people and businesses moving out of an area.

It is also necessary to incorporate into the cash flow forecast the likelihood of increases in operating costs. For instance, maintenance expenses are likely to rise as a property ages. Increased marketing and management expenses (to attract and keep tenants) may also become necessary as a property becomes older, as may legal expenses and liabilities.

The probability of rental increases must also be considered. Although some long-term real estate lease payments are fixed, and many rental rates are controlled by government laws, the rental income on many properties is a function of the inflation rate. Even many long-term leasing contracts on real estate are specified to make rental payments as a function of inflation rate. For example, some lease contracts automatically increase the rental payment by the increase in the inflation rate.

When estimating the present value of real estate, a range of values often can be obtained using different scenarios (such as most likely, most optimistic, and most pessimistic). To maximize the probability of purchasing only underpriced properties, an investor might seek to acquire real estate only if it has a value that exceeds the present value under a most pessimistic scenario (one that has a feasible chance of occurrence).

In addition, real estate values can also be estimated under a best possible use criteria. If the value of the real estate under its current use (such as a shopping mail) is less than what it would be worth if it were converted to another use (such as a warehouse), the possibility of conversion should be taken into consideration (perhaps as one possible scenario, with the value computed net of conversion costs, just as the possibility of managing a company better should be considered when evaluating a stock investment).

As with stocks or any other asset, the final expected sales value of real estate should be a function of its expected final cash flow. To estimate that real estate values will go up in accordance with inflation or with past trends is as much a fallacy for real estate as for stocks. Similarly, to expect real estate values to appreciate forever because of limited supply is a further fallacy. Not all land has yet been used (especially in the United States), and new real estate projects are continually being built, while demand often slows or even falls due to economic and demographic changes. When more new real estate is available than demand, prices can fall. In addition, even with no increase in new real estate, prices of existing real estate can be bid up too high relative to cash flow value in a speculative boom, and a real estate depression with failing prices can result, as occurred nationally in the 1870s and 1930s (and as occurs locally and regionally very frequently).

For instance, as a result of economic factors related to speculation and overbuilding in the 1980s and demographic factors relating to declining population growth, several Harvard analysts predicted that, by the year 2007, residential real estate prices would fall about 50% in real terms (i.e., adjusted for inflation) from their 1990 level. The declining real estate prices of the early 1990s seemed to be consistent with that forecast, although prices recovered in the later 1990s.

The outlook for other types of real estate was also forecast to be poor in the 1990s. In particular, some analysts estimated that the excessive amount of office building construction in the 1980s had resulted in a situation where, even if there were no new office building construction, it would take over 10 years before demand for office space increased to the point where all vacant space could be placed into productive use. However, by the late 1990s, these types of real estate had also recovered from that situation.

Demand for both office and hotel space may be restricted in the future by the revolution in communication, which has made it less necessary for firms to maintain a physical presence in many different places and has reduced the need to travel. As a result, the outlook for real estate revenues and prices is uncertain, especially for lodging and retail real estate (as well as possibly for office space as more people are able to work from their own homes).

Cost Approaches to Valuing Real Estate

In addition to the two methods of valuing real estate using expected cash flows (i.e., the present value and capitalization rate appraisal methods), some analysts also consider the replacement cost of the real estate. Replacement cost is often stated in the form of price per square foot of building floor space. The cost appraisal method is similar to using current cost book value to price stocks. If the real estate actually has a cash flow value in excess of the current cost book value, that value should performance as a floor for the price of the real estate. However, if cash inflows are low (perhaps because vacancy rates are high either locally or nationwide), the price of real estate may be far the replacement cost.

Often, it is possible to estimate the value of real estate by comparing it to the price per square foot of similar real estate in a nearby location. However, such a valuation method should be used with great caution because there are usually significant differences between two fairly similar parcels of real estate. In addition, quoted prices of other pieces of real estate may be only the prices at which other real estate owners are willing to sell, and there may be no buyers willing to pay such a high price. In addition, even where a transaction price is quoted, the price may be inflated by special financing subsidies and/or guarantees.

The Relationship Between Real Estate Values, Inflation, and Taxes

Real estate is often glorified as an investment that has major tax advantages and is positively correlated with inflation. Although real estate investment can, in fact, have tax benefits, its reputation as an inflation hedge, at least short-term, may be undeserved.

The Relationship Between Real Estate Values and Inflation

The values of many real estate assets frequently exhibit negative correlation with inflation. In particular, inflation tends to drive up interest rates. Higher interest rates not only increase the discount rate on real estate cash flows, but also often slow economic growth or even result in a recession that can cause an increase in vacancy rates and reduce cash flows from real estate (although higher interest rates may have a partially offsetting effect longer-term by limiting the number of new real estate projects that are begun and thereby reducing the supply of new real estate in the future).

In any event, to the extent that rents do not rise with inflation (sometimes because they are fixed by contract or by state rental laws, as well as for supply-and-demand or macroeconomic reasons), the effect of higher interest rates is not offset by growth in cash flows from real estate investments, and so the value of real estate investments has been found to be negatively correlated with inflation over short monthly or annual intervals.

Tax Factors in Real Estate Investments: When evaluating the value of real estate, depreciation tax shields should also be considered. These arise from noncash depreciation tax deductions on buildings and other properties. These tax deductions shelter from tax a portion of the cash flows from real estate investments and can therefore result in greater net cash flows after tax even while the real estate may be appreciating in price. However, in addition to real estate, depreciation tax shields exist on most fixed assets, including machinery, equipment, airplanes, and other assets into which productive enterprises invest. Although tax factors can enhance investment value, tax considerations alone cannot make real estate an attractive investment (taxes alone cannot make any asset an attractive investment).

Generally, when computing the value of real estate investments, it is only necessary to compute the present value of after-tax cash flows in order to incorporate the effect of depreciation on real estate values. As a result, it is especially useful to value real estate using the discounted cash flow approach.

Real Estate Investors: Because of the tax advantages associated with depreciation tax shields (which increase cash flow even while the underlying investment may be appreciating in value), real estate investments are very popular among individuals. For instance, Institutional Real Estate, Inc. reported in 1998 that private investors held 46.6% of the $687 billion that had been directly invested into large real estate properties in the U.S. A further 22.1% and 0.3% was held by REITs and public real estate limited partnerships, respectively, both of which are investment companies that are set up to pool investors' money into real estate so that investors only pay taxes on the income after the depreciation tax shields (investment companies are not subject to separate income taxation as long as they pay out all income to investors). U.S. institutional investors held only 26.8% of all real estate assets (with life insurance companies owning 5.0%, other financial institutions holding 1.8%, and pension funds owning 20.0%), while foreign investors held the other 4.2% of U.S. real estate.

Real Estate Financing: Because real estate ownership is publicly recorded, and because it is very difficult or impossible for the owner to carry it off with them, it represents very good collateral for loans. Loans with real estate as collateral are generally called mortgages.

Loans collateralized by assets that are expected to have a high value in case of default on the loan typically have relatively low interest rates. As a result, many investors finance their real estate holdings with large amounts of mortgage debt at a low cost. For instance, the $687 billion in large real estate holdings reported by Institutional Real Estate, Inc. in 1998 represented only the equity portion of the investment, which was measured net of $1.054 trillion that was financed with mortgage debt (i.e., of the total $1741 billion invested into large real estate property assets in the U.S., equity investors put up $687 billion while the other $1054 billion was financed with mortgages). Most of real estate financing is provided by financial institutions (e.g., of the $1054 billion in financing for the large real estate properties, 45.1% was provided by banks and mortgage companies, 8.8% by savings institutions, 17.1% by life insurance companies, 2.3% by pension funds, 9.8% by government agencies, and 16.9% by investment companies).

Real Estate Transaction Costs: While real estate investments are widely perceived to have tax and financing advantages, they are also recognized to entail significant transaction cost disadvantages. In particular, because there are so many individual properties, each of which is distinct and different from the others (unlike shares of stock of the same firm), and because real estate is not easily divisible (it is difficult to buy 1/10 of an office building), most real estate is not traded very frequently. As a result, investors may have to wait weeks or even months before being able to conduct a trade on a particular piece of real estate at a reasonable price, and, even after waiting, transaction costs tend to be higher than for other assets such as widely traded stocks of big corporations. Many investors therefore require higher returns on real estate investments because of a positive transaction cost premium in equation.

However, investment companies that invest into real estate provide some opportunity to invest into real estate with less transaction costs. The most important type of real estate investment companies are REITs. Individual shares in the REITs are widely traded each day for small transaction costs that approximate the expenses of trading the stocks of large corporations (with many REITs being traded on the NYSE like industrial stocks). As a result, there should be no transaction cost premium on such forms of real estate investment. As REITs continue to grow in size and buy up ever larger portions of the fixed amount of real estate in existence, they tend to bid up the prices and reduce the transaction cost premiums required on all real estate.

RETURNS ON FINANCIAL ASSETS

People want to maximize expected returns subject to their tolerance for risk. Return is the principal reward in the investment process, and it provides the basis to investors in comparing alternative investments. Measuring historical returns allows investors to assess how well they have done, and it plays a part in the estimation of future, unknown returns.

We often use two terms regarding return from investments, realised return and expected return. Realised return is after the fact return- return that was earned (or could have been earned).

Realised return is history. For example, a deposit of Rs. 5,00,000 in the Punjab National Bank on January 1 in a certificate of deposit at a stated annual interest rate of 5 per cent will be worth Rs. 525000 one year later. The realised return for the year is Rs. 25000 or 5 per cent.

Expected return is the return from an asset that investors anticipate they will earn over some future period. It is a predicted return, and it may or may not occur.

Components of Return

Return on a financial asset, generally, consists of two components. The principal component of return is the periodic income on the investment, either in the form of interest or dividends. The second component is the change in the price of the asset- commonly called the capital gain or loss. This element of return is the difference between the purchase price and the price at which the asset can be or is sold.

The price change may bring a gain or a loss as it may be in any side. The income from an investment consists of one or more cash payments made at specified intervals of time. Interest payments on most bonds are paid either semi-annually or yearly, whereas dividends on common stocks are usually paid on yearly basis. The distinguishing feature of these payments is that they are paid in cash by the issuer to the holder of the asset.

We often use the term yield to express return. Yield refers to the income component in relation to some price for a security. For our purposes, the price that is relevant is the purchase price of the security. The yield on a Rs. 1,000 par value, 6 per cent coupon bond purchased for Rs. 950 is 6.31 per cent (Rs. 1,000 par value, 6 per cent coupon bond purchased for Rs. 950 is 6.31 per cent (Rs. 60/Rs. 950). However, we need to remember that yield is not, for most purposes, the proper measure of return from a security. The capital gain or loss must also be considered.

Equation is a conceptual statement for total return.

Total return = Income + Price change (+/-)

Note that either component of return can be zero for a given security over any given time period.

A bond purchased for Rs. 800 and held to maturity provides both type of income: interest payments and a price change. The purchase of a non-dividend-paying stock that is sold four months later produces either a capital gain or a capital loss, but no income.

Thus, a measure of return must consider both dividend/ interest income and price change.

Returns over time or from different securities can be measured and compared using the total return concept. The total return for a given holding period relates all the cash flows received by an investor during any designated time period to the amount of money invested in the asset. Total return is defined as,

$$r = \frac{(P_{t-1} - P_{t-1}) + D}{P_{t-1}} \times 100$$

where, r = total return, Pt = price of an asset at time,

(t), P_{t-1} = price of an asset at time (t-1), D = dividend or interest income in simple terms.

Example: Tata Steels share's price on June29, 2004 is Rs. 900 (Pt-1) and the price on June 28, 2005 (Pt), is Rs. 950. Dividend received is Rs. 76 (D). Determine the rate of return.

$$r = \frac{(P_{t-1} - P_{t-1}) + D}{P_{t-1}} \times 100$$

$$= \frac{(950 - 900) + 76}{900} \times 100$$

$$= \frac{50 + 76}{900} \times 100$$

$$= 14\%$$

Calculation of Average Returns

The total return is an acceptable measure of return for a specified period of time. But we also need statistics to describe a series of returns. For example, investing in a particular stock for ten years or a different stock in each of ten years could result in 10 total returns, which must be described mathematically.

There are two generally used methods of calculating the average return, namely, the arithmetic average and geometric average. The statistics familiar to most people is the arithmetic average. The arithmetic average, customarily designated by the symbol X = X n, or the sum of each of the values being considered divided by the total number of values.

Example: The return of stock A for four quarters is as follows:

Quarter-I = 10%; Quarter-II= 8%; Quarter-III= -4%; and Quarter IV= 20%. The average return is,

X = {10 + 8 + (-4)} + 20/ 4 = 8.5%

The arithmetic average return is appropriate as a measure of the central tendency of a number of returns calculated for a particular time, such as a year. However, when percentage changes in value over time are involved, the arithmetic mean of these changes can be misleading. For example, suppose an investor purchased a stock in Year 1 for Rs. 50 and it rose to Rs. 100 by year-end. This is a 100 per cent return [(100-50)/50]. Then the stock went from Rs. 100 at the start of Year 2 to Rs. 50 at the end of that year. The return for year 2 is -50 per cent [(50-100)/100)]. The arithmetic average return is 25 per cent [(+100-50)/2)]. But, realistically, if an investor bought a stock for Rs. 50 and held it two years and it was still at Rs. 50, clearly there is no return at all.

From the it is obvious that an analyst should use a different average to describe accurately the true rate of return over multiple periods. The geometric average return measures compound, cumulative returns over time. It is used in investments to reflect the realised change in wealth over multiple periods.

The geometric average is defined as the nth root of the product resulting from multiplying a series of returns together, as in Equation,

$$G = [(1 + r_1)(1 + r_2) \ldots (1 + r_n)]^{1/n} - 1$$

where, r = total return, n = number of periods.

Return relative: On adding 1.0 to each return (r), we shall get a return relative. If the return for a period is 10 per cent (.10), then the return relative is 1.10. The investor has received Rs. 1.10 relative to each Rs. 1 invested. If the return for a period is -15 per cent (-.15) then the return relative is.85 (1-.15). Return relatives are used in calculating geometric average returns because negative total returns cannot be used in the math.

For our stock that started at Rs. 50, rose to Rs. 100, and then dropped to Rs. 50 over a two-year period, the geometric return would be calculated as follows:

Return relative, Year 1 = 1.00 + 1.00 = 2.00

Year 2= –.50 + 1.00 =.50

Geometric average $(G) = [(2.0)*(.5)]^{1/2} - 1$

$= [1.0]^{1/2} - 1$

$= 0.00$

Here, we also need to note that the geometric average rate of return would be lower than the arithmetic average rate of return because it reflects compounding rather than simple averaging.

Risk in Holding Securities

Risk is generally associated with the possibility that realised returns of securities will be less than the returns that were expected. The source of such risk is the failure of dividends (interest) and/or the security's price to materialize as expected.

There are numerous forces that contribute to variations in return- price or dividend (interest). These forces are termed as elements of risk. Some factors are external to the firm and cannot be controlled.

These factors affect large numbers of securities. In investments, those forces that are uncontrollable, external, and broad in their effect are called sources of systematic risk. Other forces are internal to the firm and are controllable to a large degree.

The controllable, internal factors somewhat peculiar to industries and/or firms are referred to as sources of unsystematic risk. That portion of total variability in return caused by factors affecting the prices of all securities is known as systematic risk. Economic, political, and sociological changes are sources of systematic risk.

Their effect is to cause prices of nearly all individual common stocks and/or all individual bonds to move together in the same manner. For example, if the economy is moving towards inflation and corporate profits shift upward, stock prices may rise across a broad front. Nearly all stocks listed on the National Stock Exchange (NSE) move in the same direction as the S & P Nifty index of NSE. that on the average, 50 per cent of the variation in a stock's price can be explained by variation in the market index. Conversely, the portion of total risk that is unique to a firm or industry is called unsystematic risk. Factors such as management capability, consumer preferences, and labour strikes cause unsystematic variability of returns in a firm. Unsystematic factors are largely independent of factors affecting securities markets in general. Because these factors affect one firm, they must be examined for each firm.

Sources of Systematic Risk

As discussed, the main constituents of systematic risk include-market risk, interest rate risk and purchasing power risk.

Market Risk

The price of a stock may fluctuate widely within a short span of time even though earnings remain unchanged. The causes of this phenomenon are varied, but it is mainly due to a change in investors' attitudes towards equities in general, or towards certain types or groups of securities in particular. Variability in return on most common stocks that is due to basic sweeping changes in investor expectations is referred to as market risk.

Risk which is common to an entire class of assets or liabilities. The value of investments may decline over a given time period simply because of economic changes or other events that impact large portions of the market. Asset allocation and diversification can protect against market risk because different portions of the market tend to underperform at different times. also called systematic risk.

The reaction of investors to tangible as well as intangible events causes market risk. Expectations of lower corporate profits in general may cause the larger body of common stocks to fall in price. Investors are expressing their judgement that too much is being paid for earnings in the light of anticipated events. The basis for the reaction is a set of real, tangible events- political, social, or economic.

Intangible events are related to market psychology. Market risk is usually touched off by a reaction to real events, but the emotional unstability of investors acting collectively leads to a snowballing overreaction. The initial decline in the market can cause the fear of loss to grip investors, and a kind of herd instinct builds as all investors make for the exit. These reactions to reactions frequently culminate in excessive selling, pushing prices down far out of line with fundamental value. With a trigger mechanism such as the threat of war, or an oil shortage, virtually all stocks are adversely affected.

Interest-rate risk: The risk of variations in future market values and the size of income, caused by fluctuations in the general level of interest rates is referred to as interest-rate risk. The basic cause of interest-rate risk lies in the fact that, as the rate of interest paid on Indian government securities rises or falls, the rates of return demanded on alternative investment vehicles, such as stocks and bonds issued in the private sector, rise or fall. In other words, as the cost of money changes for risk-free securities, the cost of money to risk-prone issuers will also change.

People normally regard government securities like treasury bills risk- free. The interest rates demanded on these securities are thought to approximate the"pure" rate of interest, or the cost of hiring money at no risk. Interest rates on gilts shift with changes in the supply and demand for government securities. For example, a large operating deficit experienced by the Indian government will require financing. Issuance of added amounts of Indian government securities will increase the available supply. Potential buyers of this new supply may be induced to buy only if interest rates are somewhat higher than those currently prevailing on outstanding issues. If rates on gilts advance from 8 per cent to 8¼ per cent, investors holding outstanding issues that yield 8 per cent will notice a decline in the price of their securities. Because the 8 per cent rate is fixed by contract on these"old" gilts, a potential buyer would be able to realise the competitive 8¼ per cent rate only if the current holder"marked down" the price. As the rate on guilts advances, they become relatively more attractive and other securities become less attractive. Consequently,bond purchasers will buy governments instead of corporates. This will cause the price of corporates to fall and the rate on corporates to rise. Rising corporate bond rates will eventually cause preferred and inturn common stock prices to adjust downward as the chain reaction is felt throughout the system of security yields. Thus the direct effect of increases in the level of interest rates is to cause security prices to fall across a wide span of investment vehicles.

Also there are indirect effects on common stocks. First, lower or higher interest rates make the purchase of stocks on margin (using borrowed funds) more or less attractive. Higher interest rates, for example, may lead to lower stock prices because of a diminished demand for equities by speculators who use margin. Second, many firms, such as public utilities finance their operations quite heavily with borrowed funds. Others, such as financial institutions, are principally in the business of lending money. Advancing interest rates can bring higher earnings to lending institutions whose principal revenue source is interest received on loans. For these firms, higher earnings could lead to increased dividends and stock prices.

Purchasing-power risk: Purchasing-power risk refers to the uncertainty of the purchasing power of the money to be received. In simple terms, purchasing-power risk is the impact of inflation or deflation on an investment. When we think of investment as the postponement of consumption, we can see that when a person purchases a stock, he has foregone the opportunity to buy some goods or service for as long as he owns the stock.

If, during the holding period, prices on desired goods and services rise, the investor actually loses purchasing power. Rising prices on goods and services are normally associated with what is referred to as inflation. Falling prices on goods and services are termed deflation. Both inflation and deflation are covered in the all-encompassing term purchasing-power risk.

Generally, purchasing-power risk has come to be identified with inflation (rising prices); the incidence of declining prices in most countries has been slight. The anticipated purchasing power changes manifest themselves on both bond and stocks.

Unsystematic Risk

Market, purchasing-power, and interest-rate risks are the principal sources of systematic risk in securities; but we should also consider another important category of security risks-unsystematic risks.

Specific risk is a risk that affects a very small number of assets. This is sometimes referred to as"unsystematic risk". In a balanced portfolio of assets there'd be a spread between general market risk and risks specific to individual components of that portfolio. Determination of the extent of exposure to individual risks is made using models such as Treynor-Black in which the optimal share of a security is inversely proportional to the square of its specific risk.

An example would be news that is specific to either one stock or a group of companies, such as the loss of a patent or a major natural disaster affecting the company's operation. The portion of total risk that is unique or peculiar to a firm or an industry, and beyond that affecting securities markets in general is called unsystematic risk. Factors such as management capability, consumer preferences, and labour strikes can cause unsystematic variability of returns for a company's stock.

Examples of Unsystematic Risks

- *Business risk:* Business risk relates to the variability of the sales, income, profits etc., which in turn depend on the market conditions for the product mix, input supplies, strength of competitors, etc. The business risk is sometimes external to the company due to changes in government policy or strategies of competitors or unforeseen market conditions. They may be internal due to fall in production, labour problems, raw material problems or inadequate supply of electricity etc. The internal business risk leads to fall in revenues and in profit of the company, but can be corrected by certain changes in the company's policies.

- *Financial Risk:* This relates to the method of financing, adopted by the company; high leverage leading to larger debt servicing problems or short-term liquidity problems due to bad debts, delayed receivables and fall in current assets or rise in current liabilities. These problems could no doubt be solved, but they may lead to fluctuations in earnings, profits and dividends to share holders. Sometimes, if the company runs into losses or reduced profits, these may lead to fall in returns to investors or negative returns. Proper financial planning and other financial adjustments can be used to correct this risk and as such it is controllable.
- Default or insolvency risk: The borrower or issuer of securities may become insolvent or may default, or delay the payments due, such as interest instalments or principal repayments. The borrower's credit rating might have fallen suddenly and he became default prone and in its extreme form it may lead to insolvency or bankruptcies. In such cases, the investor may get no return or negative returns. An investment in a healthy company's share might turn out to be a waste paper, if within a short span, by the deliberate mistakes of Management or acts of God, the company became sick and its share price tumbled its face value. Other Risks Besides the described risks, there are many more risks, which can be listed, but in actual practice, they may vary in form, size and effect.

Some of such identifiable risks are the Political Risks, Management Risks and Liquidity Risks etc. Political risk may occur due to the changes in the government, or its policy shown in fiscal or budgetary aspects, changes in tax rates, imposition of controls or administrative regulations etc.

Management risks arise due to errors or inefficiencies of management, causing losses to the company. Marketability liquidity risks involve loss of liquidity or loss of value in conversions from one asset to another say, from stocks to bonds, or vice versa. Such risks may arise due to some features of securities, such as callability; or lack of sinking fund or Debenture Redemption Reserve fund, for repayment of principal or due to conversion terms, attached to the security, which may go adverse to the investor. All the types of risks are of varying degrees, resulting in uncertainty or variability of return, loss of income, and capital losses, or erosion of real value of income and wealth of the investor. Normally the higher the risk taken, the higher is the return.

Risk Measurement

Understanding the nature and types of risk is not adequate unless the investor or analyst is capable of measuring it in some quantitative terms. The quantitative expression of the risk of a stock would make it comparable with other stocks. However, the risk measurements cannot be considered fully accurate as it is caused by multiplicity of factors such as social, political, economic and managerial aspects.

Risk is measured by the variability of returns. The statistical tool often used to measure risk is the standard deviation. We know, standard deviation is a measure of the values of the variables around its mean or it is the square root of the sum of the squared deviations from the mean divided by the number of observations. This can be emphasised with an example.

The concepts of variance, standard deviation, covariance and beta coefficients etc., are also used to explain the measure of risk. In the context of portfolio of assets, or investment in any assets risk is inherent in all such dealings. This risk primarily arises first out of parting of your funds or loss of liquidity. Money lent or parted is always having an element of risk. This element is the same as the concept of total risk.

Capital Asset Pricing Model (CAPM)

CAPM uses the concept of Beta to link risk with return. Using CAPM, investors can assess the risk return trade off involved in any investment decision. Beta is a measure of non-diversifiable risk (Systematic Risk). It shows how the price of a security responds to changes in market prices.

The equation for calculation of Beta is,

$R_i = \alpha_i + \beta_i R_m + e_i$

R_i = Estimated return on ith stock

α = Expected return when market return is zero (intercept)

β_i = Beta, a measure of stock's sensitivity to the market index

R_m = Return on market index

e_i = the error term

Using the Beta concept the Capital Asset Pricing Model will help to define the required return on a security. Normally the higher is the risk we take, the higher should be the return as otherwise we avoid risk. So, the higher the, the higher should be the return.

The equation for CAPM is,

$R_i = Rf + \beta i (R_m - Rf)$

Ri is the required return

Rf is the risk free return

R_m is the average market return

B_i is the measure of systematic risk which is non-diversifiable.

Presently, the risk free return is 6% as the Treasury Bill rate and market return is expected to vary with the chosen. Let us take as and expected market return is 18%, then the return on the stock i is as follows:

R_i = 6% + 1.2 (18 - 6)

= 0.06 + 1.2 (0.12)

= 0.06 +.144

= 20.4%

If the investor is risk taker and chooses a Beta of 1.8, then the expected return will be higher as shown.

R_i = 6 + 18 (18-12)

=.06 + 1.8 (.12)

=.06 +.216 =.276 = 27.6%

Security Market Line (SML)

When the Capital Asset Pricing Model is drawn graphically, we get the S.M.L. If the investor wants to decide on an investment with an expected return he would know the level of risk he has to take or alternatively given the level of risk, he has preferred to take. The investor has to assess whether it is worth taking a level of risk, if he has a target return which involves that risk, as he is assumed to be generally risk averse.

Thus, CAPM and SML help the investor in evaluating risk for a return, in making any investment decision. The principle of the higher the risk, the higher is the return is embodied in this Model.

Concept of portfolio Models: Risks in relation to portfolios are also to be understood in the present discussion. Therefore, the concept of Risk in two Major Models used in valuation is related to systematic, unsystematic and total risk. The two models are those of Markowitz and Sharpe which go by the name of Modern Portfolio Theory.

The return on investments in financial assets takes the form of dividend and/or interest income and appreciation in the price of the asset held.

The risk associated with holding common stocks is really the likelihood that expected returns will not materialize. If dividends or price appreciation fall short of expectations, the investor is disappointed. The principal sources behind dividend and priceappreciation uncertainties are factors that are either controllable or not subject to control by the firm.

The sources of systematic risk, include market, interest-rate, and purchasing-power risks. Market risk reflects changes in investor attitudes towards equities in general that stem from tangible and intangible events. Interest-rate risk and purchasing-power risk are associated with changes in the price of money and other goods and services. Increases in interest rates cause the prices of all types of securities to be marked down. Rising prices of goods and services (inflation or purchasing-power changes) have an adverse effect on security prices because the postponement of consumption through any form of investment means less'real' buying power in the future.

The major sources of unsystematic risk affecting the holding of common stocks are business risk and financial risk. Business risk refers to changes in the operating environment of the firm and how the firm adapts to them. Financial risk is related to the debt-andequity mix of financing in the firm. Operating profits can be magnified up or down, depending upon the extent to which debt financing is employed and under what terms.

The various sources of risk in holding common stocks must be quantified so that the analyst can examine risk in relationship to measures of return. A reasonable surrogate of risk is the variability of return.

This proxy measure in statistics is commonly the variance or standard deviation of the returns on a stock around the expected return. Total risk of an investment consists of two components: diversifiable and non-diversifiable risk. The former risk can be almost entirely by holding a large enough mix of carefully selected securities.

The only risk an investor is compensated for taking is thus non-diversifiable risk. Beta measures this risk and can be used to determine the appropriate required return on a security. Conversely, the market risk is considered as non-diversifiable risk.

APPRECIATION

Appreciation is an increase in the value of an asset, such as stocks, options, currency, bonds and real estate, over a specific period of time. It is the amount by which the selling price of an asset is higher than the initial price. This term also encompasses a rise in the value of an asset held in a company's accounting book.

Appreciation may be driven by a sudden spurt in the demand for an asset, the scarcity of supply of the asset or changes in the inflation rate or the interest rate.

How to Measure Appreciation?

Appreciation in the value of an investment option includes:

- Capital appreciation: This is the difference between the actual sale and the purchase price of a financial asset, such as stocks, options, currency and bonds. For example, if an investor purchases 100 shares of a company for $10 per share and sells the same after 12 months for $10.50 per share, then the capital appreciation is $50 ($0.50 per share).
- Interest amount: Interest is generally paid on capital invested in debt instruments, such as bonds and mutual funds, as well as cash investments, such as savings accounts and certificates of deposit (CD). Interest can be either simple or compound. Simple interest is the interest calculated on the principal amount and does not take into account the time value of money (which refers to inflation/deflation and increases or decreases in the purchasing power of the invested capital). Compound interest is calculated on both the principal and the interest accrued over 12 months.

Interest and capital appreciation together form the total return on investment (ROI). For instance, if a bond is purchased at $20 and pays $2 as interest annually and the bondholder sells the bond for $25 after 12 months, then the ROI is $7 ($5 of capital appreciation and $2 as interest).

Different methods are used to calculate interest in varies types of securities:

- *Stock dividends, US mortgages and GIC*: Simple interest is calculated.
- *Bond yields*: Compounds interest every six months.

- *Bond coupons*: Are accrued daily and measured as simple rate.
- *Stock indexes*: Interest compounds annually on the price alone.
- *Stocks and mutual funds*: Compound every time cash flows to/from investors.
- *US normal mortgage*: Interest is measured as simple rate.

RETURN ON INVESTMENT

Return on investment (ROI) is also called the rate of return (ROR) and is a measure of the performance of any investment. It is the ratio between the financial benefit or loss of an investment and the amount of money invested.

Return on Investment: Calculation

The return on investment can be calculated by the following formula:

ROI = (Net Income/Cost of Investment) × 100,

where,

ROI = Return on Investment

Net Income = Income from investment - Cost of Investment

The return on investment is always expressed as a percentage.

For instance, if the cost of investment is $20,000 and the gain from the investment is $22,000, then the net income will be $22,000-$20,000, or $2,000, and the ROI will be ($2,000/ $20,000) × 100 = 0.1 × 100, or 10%.

In case the ROI is negative, it means the cost of investment is higher than the benefits (income) from that investment. This indicates a loss and this investment should not be considered.

ROI and Time

The calculation of ROI does not indicate the duration of the investment. It does not reveal the gestation period.

ROI and the Rule of Thumb

There are certain rules of thumb that make it easy to introduce the concept of time in ROI. These rules assume that the annual rate of return is constant and that the ROI is compounded once a year.

- *Rule of* 72: This indicates how long it would take to double your investment. To calculate this, divide 72 by the ROI. For instance, if the ROI is 10, then the time it would take to double this investment is 7.2 (72/10) years.
- *Rule of* 114: This indicates how long it would take to triple your money. To calculate this, divide 114 by the rate of return. It would take 11.4 (114/10) years to grow your money threefold.
- *Rule* of 144: This calculates how long it will take to grow your money four times. In the example considered, the time taken to quadruple your money is 14.4 (144/10) years.

While these are fairly good estimates, they are by no means accurate. A proper understanding of ROI is a prerequisite for investing wisely. So, don't forget to calculate and compare the ROI of the various investments you are considering.

INVESTMENT COMPANY

An investment company is one that is in the business of investing in securities. Its core business is to hold securities of other companies only for investment purposes. The profits and losses are shared among those who invest in an investment firm as per their portfolio. The performance of the securities is the major factor determining the performance of investment companies.

Types of Investment Companies

The following are the main types of investment companies:

Management Investment Company: Most investment companies are management investment companies, which are engaged in managing portfolios of securities. Management investment companies can be divided into two categories depending upon the types of securities they offer:

- *Open-End Investment Company*: This type of investment company issues new shares on a continuous basis. The shares may be bought from and sold back to the investment company. Open-end investment companies may also be referred to as mutual funds.
- *Closed-End Investment Company*: This type of investment company sells shares in a onetime public offering. The shares are not offered on a continuous basis. Investors can buy and sell the shares in the open market. The demand and supply of the shares of these closed-end funds determine their market value.
- *Unit Investment Trusts (UITs): These investment companies have the following features*:
- A trustee supervises the management of a UIT investment company.
- A predetermined number of shares are sold to unit holders, who become eligible for a share of net income that the main trust generates.
- The securities of UITs are redeemable.
- The portfolio of securities is not managed on a daily basis.

Exchange-Traded Funds (ETFs): These investment companies can be either UITs or open-end investment companies. The goal of ETFs is to attain a return equal to a particular market index.

- *Hedge Funds*: These are investment pools that are private and unregistered. They are not subject to the numerous regulations that protect investors of mutual funds.
- *Face Amount Certificates*: These investment companies are engaged in issuing debt certificates at a fixed interest rate. Such investment companies are rare today. Face amount certificate holders can covert them into cash on

a predetermined date before maturity. Buyers can pay either a lump-sum or periodic installments.

REAL ESTATE INVESTMENT

Real estate investment involves the commitment of funds to property with an aim to generate income through rental or lease and to achieve capital appreciation. Real estate refers to immovable property, such as land, and everything else that is permanently attached to it, such as buildings. When a person acquires real estate, s/he also acquires a set of rights, including possession, control and transfer rights.

Understanding real estate investment is crucial because it usually involves a substantial investment and a long-term one. Moreover, the real estate market can be unpredictable. This is particularly important when one goes beyond buying a home to actually 'investing' in real estate. There are a number of ways in which an investor can participate in the real estate market.

Real Estate Investment: Rental

One can opt for real estate investment with an aim to rent the property out to a tenant. The owner (landlord) earns a continuous stream of rent from the tenant, but is responsible for paying the mortgage, taxes and any costs associated with maintaining the property. The owner also benefits from capital appreciation (a rise in the value of the property over time). The landlord runs the risk of not finding a tenant and could suffer negative monthly cash flows, with mortgage payments and maintenance expenses still to be borne. As compared to owning stocks and bonds, rental real estate requires a significant amount time and effort to be devoted by the landlord.

Real Estate Investment Groups

Real estate investment groups are similar to small mutual funds. They are set up for rental properties. While an investor may own one or more units, a professionally managed company acquires, builds, maintains and lets out all the units on the properties in exchange for a percentage of the monthly rent.

Real Estate Trading

Real estate traders hold properties for only a short span of time (less than four months), aiming to sell them at a profit. This process is called flipping properties. Investors aim at purchasing significantly undervalued or very hot properties. Such owners may or may not invest money into improving the property before putting it back on sale. A bear market could result in substantial losses for a real estate trader, since the investment is large.

INVESTMENT FUND

An investment fund is a firm that pools funds from a number of retail investors and invests the same for a fee. Thus, an investment fund enables investors to gain exposure to a broad range of options. Moreover, the investment fund is able to achieve economies of scale, bringing down the trading costs.

Investment funds are suitable for investors who wish to invest in securities without studying the characteristics of the various options. Private bankers, trust managers or other advisers often direct some or all of the assets of their clients towards fund investments.

In terms of risk and reward an investment fund can range from being ultra-safe, low-yielding bond funds to being highly-leveraged derivative hedge funds.

Types of Investment Funds

Investment funds can be open-ended or closed-ended. An open-ended fund is an investment fund that allows investors to sell their share in the fund whenever they want, whereas closed-ended investment funds require the investment to be kept locked up for a fixed period.

Investment funds can be either of the two types:

- *Private funds*: This type of fund involves up to 50 investors, with each contributing a significant amount of money (not less than $1 million per investor). The money is then invested into a particular class of assets.

Private funds are usually closed-ended funds and are selected by people who have a long-term investment horizon. In this type of investment fund, money managers use their specialized knowledge of the selected asset class to obtain higher returns than that expected from public funds.

- *Public funds*: Public funds offer high flexibility, liquidity and transparency. These funds are required by law to declare their net asset value (NAV) on a regular basis. Most of these funds have an open-ended structure.

Investment Funds in Emerging Markets

The contribution of investment funds in emerging markets has risen dramatically over the past several years. Only a few investment funds, with a total cash flow of $700 million, were investing in listed securities in the emerging markets in 1984. However, within a decade, the capital targeted at emerging markets had risen to more than $100 billion, with close to a thousand funds participating in the change.

Examples of Investment Funds

Some of the high-yielding investment funds are:

- Melchior Japan Opportunities.
- Jupiter Emerging Markets.
- Invesco Perpetual Latin American.
- New Star UK Strategic Income.
- Old Mutual UK Smaller Companies.
- Old Mutual UK Select Mid-cap.
- JPMF UK Dynamic.
- Allianz RCM UK Mid-cap.

INVESTOR RELATIONS

Investor relations refers to communication between a company and the investing community regarding developments that could have a bearing on the company's stock valuation. Investor relations is considered a management responsibility and several disclosures are required by law. Such disclosures may include quarterly or annual financial reports, change in the top management of a company or strategic alliances.

These days, most public traded financial entities and corporations have departments dedicated to investor relations. This department also addresses and resolves queries from potential investors.

The investor relations department may be headed by a treasurer or the chief financial officer. Effective investor relations contributes towards a company's stock achieving fair valuation.

History of Investor Relations

The evolution of investor relations covers three eras, namely 1945 to 1970 (the communication era), 1970 to 2000 (the financial era) and from 2000 onwards (the synergy era).

In the communication era, investor relations and issues were handled by press agents or other publicists. The lack of financial expertise and strategic management were the weak areas of this era. In 1953, it was Ralph Cordiner, the chairman of General Electric, who created a new position for handling shareholder communications, which is today known as 'investor relations.'

In the financial era, professional investors became important. Finance professionals and accountants handled tasks related to investor relations.

In the synergy (current) era, an effective combination of communication and financial skills are utilized to contribute to investor relations.

This two-way communication enables the company and investors to share information and helps to improve understanding on both sides.

Current Trends in Investor Relations

The current trends in investor relations involve the easy flow of information to support investor meets. The Securities and Exchange Commission (SEC) favours the use of electronic communication tools by companies and investors. Popular tools include blogs, electronic shareholder forums and proxies.

Travel budgets have begun to shrink, thanks to conference calls and new web tools that have made shareholder interactions smoother than before. Companies are also eager to let investors access valuable information and provide instant feedback. Increased awareness of transparency requirements and the introduction of XBRL (Extensible Business Related Language) have remarkably impacted the possibilities for further growth and expansion in investor relations.

4

Fundamental Analysis of Equity Investments

First, information sources that are useful in fundamentally analyzing stocks are described. Next, a top-down forecasting method is evaluated for purposes of estimating the relevant financial variables for stock valuation.

These forecasts are needed to predict the future dividends, whose summed present value equals the stock value. Within this valuation context, the usefulness of scenario forecasting is analysed. Relative P/e ratio analysis within this analytical framework is also discussed. Finally, an actual example of stock valuation is provided.

INTEGRATING ECONOMIC, INDUSTRY, AND COMPANY FORECASTS

An overall economic forecast is generally necessary before evaluating a stock.

The economic forecast should include predictions of real economic growth as well as inflation in order to provide perspective on the environment within which industries and companies will likely operate. Such forecasts may be obtained from various forecasting services. For instance, *Value Line* provides forecasts of real GDP growth and inflation up to 5 years in the future inside the flap of its weekly company analysis booklet.

In addition, some qualitative economic information should be obtained in order that the analyst may make forecasts for individual industries. The important qualitative information includes analysis of consumer spending, capital spending, exchange rates, government legislation, and other factors that may affect specific industries. Many business periodicals (such as *Fortune*, *Business Week*, and *Forbes Global Business and Finance*) provide weekly, monthly, or quarterly updates on the economic environment that includes information on various sectors of the economy. For instance, the "Selection & Opinion" part of *Value Line* provides a quarterly report that analyses the economy and qualitatively explains the reasons for its overall economic forecasts.

Information on the economic environment may be used to forecast specific industry factors such as unit sales growth, inflation, and changes in profitability. Some business periodicals regularly provide such information. *Value Line* provides a quarterly analysis of about 100 different industries. *Value Line*'s industry reports include not only a qualitative analysis of each industry but also forecasts of sales, profit margins, and other factors up to 5 years in the future. Forecasts farther in the future are much more difficult to make, although long-term past data—which indicate that real growth in the U.S. has averaged about 3% per year long-term while inflation has averaged about 3% over the last few decades—can be adjusted for the particular situation of each industry (such as by forecasting long-term real unit sales increases in a high-growth industry like electronics above the 3% past average for the economy).

Within the context of economic and industry predictions, it is possible to make predictions for the company whose stock is being investigated. In order to be able to forecast and value future dividends, company market share of industry sales, operating margins, capital structure, taxes, and asset turnover ratios must be predicted. To assist in the analysis, many investment advisory services provide analyses of individual companies and stocks.

Often when making forecasts, analysts categorize companies into groups. Companies whose sales and assets are growing rapidly are often called growth companies, while firms that have been around for a long period of time and whose sales are not growing rapidly are called mature companies. Businesses whose sales fluctuate greatly up and down with the business cycle are referred to as cyclical companies. Firms whose sales are less adversely affected by recessions within a business cycle are called stable companies. The equities of stable companies are often called defensive stocks in recognition of their ability to defend a portfolio against large losses in a recession.

Once the relevant financial variables have been forecast, a pro forma model may be used to value the stock. A general description of such models is provided..

For purposes of individual stock valuation, the "top-down" approach to forecasting for individual companies explained in this part has inherent advantages over alternative methods of analysis, especially for institutional investors operating with many investment analysts. In particular, although a "bottom-up" forecasting method is often used by economists to aggregate the forecasts of individual industries to predict aggregate inflation and economic growth, starting with an aggregate economic forecast (perhaps obtained from a "bottom-up" economic forecast) permits industry and company analysis to be conducted within a unified context. In particular, by assuming the same overall economic and industry environment for each stock in an industry, valuation biases are avoided that are sometimes caused by the application of inconsistent forecasts for the aggregate economy across different stocks.

For instance, if an institutional analyst values one stock based on a forecast of high aggregate economic growth, while another stock is analysed by another analyst at the same institution based on a forecast of low aggregate economic growth, sales and profit margin forecasts will be biased upward for the former stock compared to the latter stock, as will the stock valuation.

Using Different Forecast Inputs In Valuation Models

Guidelines on forecasting individual variables can be obtained from good documentation on good stock valuation software such as SIA. However, because many of the inputs into a valuation model are forecasted variables whose values must be predicted, the analysis is somewhat subjective and imprecise.

As a result, it is often useful to make several feasible scenario forecasts and obtain a value for each scenario. Scenarios can vary because of different operating

and competitive conditions for the firm as well as due to different assumed financial and operating policies. A simple framework for analysis here might be to value the firm using 3 scenarios: most likely, most optimistic, and most pessimistic (with each scenario having an equal chance of occurrence).

The scenario valuation process creates a range of possible values for the security. If the security's price is less than all prices in the feasible range, it should be purchased. If the security's price exceeds all prices in the feasible range, it is overpriced. If the security's price is within the feasible range, it is probably fairly priced. To estimate a single value for a security, the average of all values within the feasible range could be used (the average could be weighted by the probability of each forecasted scenario occurring if different probabilities of occurrence were estimated for each scenario).

In addition to a cash flow valuation of the firm, it is sometimes useful to evaluate the company's value if its assets were sold off in an orderly fashion. Here, the value of the company's assets would be estimated, assuming there was strong demand for such assets from other firms (such as other firms in the same industry). The maximum value that other firms would be willing to pay for such assets would be the current market value of such individual assets, which can be estimated by their replacement cost (which in turn can be estimated by multiplying the historical book value by some factor to allow for inflation in the price of those assets). After subtracting out the value of the liabilities, the net value to the shareholders would be the replacement cost book value. If this value exceeds the cash flow value of the firm, it might be deduced that the firm is mismanaging its assets, and that it should begin an orderly sale of such assets. Such a scenario should be considered when the present value of expected future cash flows is less than the replacement book value.

P/E Ratio Analysis

Many analysts value stocks relative to other stocks, in lieu of, or in addition to valuing stocks in absolute terms using a dividend discount model. In particular, many analysts compare the P/e ratios of stocks (often in the same industry) and determine which should have higher and lower P/e ratios, given the beta, ROE, and other factors that determine P/e ratios. These analysts attempt to determine whether any particular stock is under- or overpriced by observing whether it has a higher or lower P/e than other stocks that theoretically should have a lower or higher P/e.

For instance, if stock XXX has a forecasted ROE of 15% and a beta of 1, while stock YYY has a forecasted ROE of 14% and a beta of 1.1, then XXX should theoretically have a higher P/e. If YYY has a higher P/e, analysts would recommend buying XXX. Stocks can also valued in an absolute sense using P/e ratio analysis.

Although P/e ratio analysis is usually considered to be a rougher method of than discounting dividends with a pro forma model, it can be useful in providing additional insights on a stock's value. For instance, P/e ratio analysis can be used to second-guess (or double-think) a pro forma valuation analysis.

If P/e ratio analysis provides results that are inconsistent with pro forma valuations, it may be useful to reanalyze the forecasts in the pro forma model (or to double check the assumptions in the P/e ratio analysis model).

Analysts sometimes also examine ratios such as Price/Sales Per Share, which may be evaluated like a P/e ratio within the context of an assumed "normal" profit margin in the future, and Price/Equity Book Value Per Share, which may be evaluated like a P/e ratio within the context of an assumed "normal" ROE in the future.

These ratios are especially important to consider for any firm whose reported profits are not believed to be representative of its true long-term earning power (like for firms with distorted or negative reported net). In all cases, investors prefer to pay lower prices per dollar of sales, book value, or earnings per share (all else being equal). A 1996 study by Haugen and Baker indicated that returns were indeed higher on stocks that had higher e/P, sales/price, and equity book/market ratios. Stocks which have such ratios that are relatively high are often referred to as value stocks to reflect the strong current fundamentals, whereas stocks with such ratios that are relatively low are often called growth stocks to reflect the potential growth in fundamental value for which the market appears to be paying.

Dupont Analysis

Because of the importance of ROEs in determining stock values, this ratio is often decomposed into its component parts for further analysis. For instance, to assist in the evaluation and forecast of ROE, the ROE for a company can be computed as,

ROE = ROA/(1- Liabilities/Assets), where

ROA = Return on Assets = Net Income/Assets.

The ROA itself may be decomposed into its component parts of,

ROA = Asset Turnover × Profit Margin, where

Asset Turnover = Sales/Assets, and

Net Profit Margin = Net Income/Sales.

The decomposition of ROE into its component parts is often called Dupont analysis. This form of analysis may be used to pick up trends in the individual components of ROE that can assist in determining the cause of changes in ROE (and thereby assist in forecasting future ROEs).

For instance, assume that a rise in ROE is found to be the result of an increase in the net profit margin. It might be worth investigating whether the cause of the increased profit margin is the company overpricing its products relative to its competitors (which might eventually result in a decline in profitability), or whether the increased profit margin stems from reducing expenditures on quality control and R&D (which would probably force the company to eventually cut prices and profit margins). On the other hand, if the increase in the profit margin stems from improved efficiency, increased capacity utilization, or the development of new products, the increased margin might be sustainable (or could possibly even be increased further).

Alternatively, increases in ROE sometimes result from a rise in a company's Liability/Assets ratio. The Liabilities/Assets ratio can rise because the company took on more debt (perhaps issuing bonds to buy back stock). the benefits of a rise in ROE caused by an increase in financial leverage may be offset by the negative effects of an increase in required returns and an increase in the probability of bankruptcy. On the other hand, an increase in the Liabilities/Assets ratio may be caused by past write-offs that reduced equity while raising liabilities or decreasing asset values. An artificial rise in ROE caused by write-offs in prior years does not imply that the company can reinvest earnings at a higher rate and therefore cannot be expected to continue.

The Effect Of Foreign Operations On Ratios

Because of changes in currency exchange rates, the value of foreign revenue and costs translated into dollars fluctuates as the dollar rises and falls. For instance, a rise in the value of the dollar decreases the value of foreign sales, while a fall in the value of the dollar makes sales denominated in foreign currencies worth more in terms of dollars. Foreign exchange rate changes therefore clearly affect some of the important ratios that make up the ROE.

The Effect of Real Exchange Rate Changes on Turnover Ratios

Changes in exchange rates affect turnover ratios for firms

with foreign sales, through the effect on the numerator. Although the effect of expected domestic inflation can be incorporated into the nominal sales growth forecasts, the effect of foreign sales growth must be measured separately in the estimate of the change in the asset turnover ratios. In particular, nominal foreign sales measured in the domestic currency will grow at a rate that is different than for domestic sales to the extent that foreign inflation rates are different and to the extent that foreign currency exchange rates change. The exchange rates between two currencies can be expected to change by the difference in risk-free interest rates in the two countries (with the currency paying the higher interest being expected to depreciate). As a result, foreign sales translated into the domestic currency may be expected to grow at a rate above the domestic inflation rate by the amount of,

$$U = Rf - RF + MForeign - MUS, \quad (8\text{-}5)$$

where M is the expected future inflation rate in the subscripted country, and RF is the foreign risk-free interest rate in country F. The U calculation represents the difference in real interest rates in the two countries, which in turn forecasts the change in real exchange rates between the two currencies (i.e., the change in exchange rates not offset by differences in inflation rates in the two countries).

For example, 10-year interest rates in Japan were about 0.87%, while 10-year interest rates in the U.S. were 4.52% (with annual compounding). Given the lack of inflation in Japan currently, inflation in Japan might be expected to average 0% over the next 10 years, while the difference between the yields on fixed-rate U.S. Treasury bonds and inflation-indexed U.S. Treasury bonds indicates expected inflation in the U.S. to be 0.88% (with annual compounding).

In this case,

$$U = 4.52\% - 0.87\% + 0\% - 0.88\% = 2.77\% \quad (8\text{-}6)$$

and so nominal sales from a firm's Japanese operations translated into dollars might be expected to grow 2.77% more rapidly than the firm's U.S. sales (assuming the real growth in both the Japanese and U.S. economies were the same).

Thus, asset turnover ratios would rise to the extent of a company's sales exposure to Japan. For instance, if all of a company's sales were in Japan, the ratios would rise by 2.77% per year. However, if only 6% of a company's sales were in Japan, as was the case for Motorola, the turnover ratios would rise by only 2.77%×.06=0.17% (e.g., a 0.17% rise in an asset turnover ratio of 1.09 would lead to an asset turnover ratio of 1.0017 × 1.09=1.0919).

To some extent, however, the existence of foreign capital (such as debt or preferred stock that makes payments in a foreign currency) can offset the effect of foreign exchange rate changes on sales. In particular, assets financed by foreign capital can negate some of the effect of the foreign exchange rate change on asset turnover ratios (because any turnover changes would be offset by an implicit changed cost for those assets financed by such capital). Therefore, an equation that more completely measures the total effect of foreign exchange rate changes is,

Turnover Ratio Change = U[(foreign sales/total sales)-(foreign capital/capital)].

These changes can be added across countries or areas to estimate the total turnover ratio change.

For example, U=0.21% for Motorola's European operations (based on 10-year bond yield differentials with no difference in forecasted inflation), European sales/total sales=19%, and European debt/capital=0%, so that there is a

Turnover Ratio Change = 0.21%(.19 -.00) = 0.04% related to the company's European operations. Adding Motorola's turnover ratio change for Japan (since Motorola had no Japanese yen capital, there would also be no foreign capital adjustment to the 0.17%. U estimated for its Japanese operations) indicates a total turnover change of 0.17% + 0.04% = 0.21%.

The Effect of Real Exchange Rate Changes on Profit Margins

In addition to the effect on turnover ratios, real exchange rate changes as measured by U.also influence the ability of companies to compete and therefore affect their profit margins. For instance, if the real exchange rate of the U.S. dollar rises, the ability of U.S. exporters to compete against foreign firms

is impaired. In particular, a real rise in the value of the U.S. dollar means that dollar costs are rising more rapidly than the foreign currency costs of foreign companies translated into dollars. As a result, the profit margins of U.S. exporters tend to go down at such times (whereas export profit margins would tend to rise when the dollar fell in real terms). Similarly, U.S. companies that compete against foreign imports would be hurt by a real rise in the U.S. dollar as the foreign imports would become more competitive. The effect of exchange rate changes on profit margins is usually much stronger short-term than the effect on asset turnover ratios. However, for companies like Motorola that largely produce in the regions where they sell their products and that hedge much of their remaining currency risk with derivatives like currency options and forward/futures contracts, the effect of currency changes on profit margins are minimized.

EQUITY INVESTMENTS

Different procedure for valuing stocks are presented. The basic framework for valuing a stock is stated to consist of computing the present value of all future expected dividends from the stock. The most sophisticated model estimates future dividends using projected financial statements. However, using a simple model of constant dividend growth, a more subjective valuation procedure is explained in the form of P/e ratio analysis is described in terms of both comparative and absolute valuation.

The Dividend Discount Model

Payments from equity investments in productive enterprises are made in the form of dividends.

To value stocks based only on the present value of all dividends is analogous to valuing bonds using only the present value of all expected interest and principal payments on a bond. Even if one were planning to hold a long-term bond for just one year, the bond would still have to be valued using the present value of all interest and principal payments expected on the bond (even those expected after one year), since the sales price of the bond in one year would be a function of these payments (just as the sales price of a stock to be sold in one year would be a function of all dividends subsequent to that date). It shows that stock values have investor expectations incorporated into them. As a result, stock values will be high for equities with expectations of high future dividends and low for stocks with low expectations, regardless of current dividend levels. Because dividends are paid from earnings, and because earnings and the future potential dividends from them can be increased by retaining more earnings in the business as opposed to paying them out to shareholders, values.it can be extremely high, even for companies that pay low or no dividends currently, or for companies that aren't even earning a profit, if earnings and dividends at some point in the future are expected to be high.

Because stock values are based on expectations, stock values tend to rise and fall with changes in expectations. In particular, if expectations of future earnings and dividends are lowered, stock values will fall, while stock values will rise when forecasts of earnings and dividends are raised. A number of different events can cause investors to change their expectations on future earnings and dividends, including changes in forecasted economic growth, changes in the industry environment, and changes in the company's own operating situation. Changes in a company's operating environment are often revealed in public company announcements (or press releases, as they are commonly called) that often provide information on a company's new products and cost-cutting measures.

Company earnings reports also affect investors' expectations of future earnings, as they provide an indication of the current profit situation of the company. In particular, when reported earnings are less than expected, investors may determine that the company's situation and future earnings potential are not as good as previously thought, and the stock's value may fall as a result (and vice-versa for reported earnings greater than expectations). A stock price decline is possible even if earnings are reported to increase substantially from the earnings of the prior period if the increase is less than expected. For instance, it is not uncommon for a stock price to decline after a 20% increase in reported profits if investors were expecting a larger 30% increase in earnings Dividend announcements can also affect investor expectations. In particular, companies tend to pay out dividends only if they believe that their earning power is maintainable, so that there is no perceived need to lower the dividend in the future. As a result, an increase in the dividend payment is often taken to be a positive statement about the company's ability to earn profits in the future.

However, as with earnings announcements, the effect that dividend announcements may have on stock values depends on whether the dividend is higher or lower than expected. For instance, if the dividend is increased 10%, and investors were expecting a 40% increase, the stock price may fall significantly. A detailed analysis of the mechanical effect of each dividend

Anatomy of a Dividend Payment

Each time a dividend payment is scheduled on a stock, a holder-of-record date and a dividend payment date must be announced by the company. The holder-of- record date is the day on which the bookkeepers figure out who is entitled to the dividend payment that occurs on the future dividend payment date.

All those shareholders who owned stock at the end of the day that is 3 business days prior to the holder-of-record date are entitled to the dividend. The date 2 business days before the holder-of-record date is called the ex-dividend date because the stock sells without claim to the scheduled dividend on that date.

As a result, stock values tend to fall by the approximate amount of a distribution on the ex-date (and tend to rise gradually as an ex-date approaches). Because stock values represent the present value of all expected future cash flows, the announcement of a dividend that is already anticipated does not affect stock values.

The only announcements that affect stock values are those that are not fully anticipated and that result in a change in estimated future dividends (or that result in a change in discount rates it, perhaps because of a change in required liquidity premiums, beta, risk premiums on stocks in general, or risk-free rates). In particular, an announced increase in dividends, if less than expected, can result in a decline in a stock price, just as an announced increase can result in a rise in the stock price if it is not anticipated.

For instance, on October 19, 1998, Baltimore Gas and Electric Company announced a $.42 quarterly dividend that would be paid on January 4, 1999 to holders of record on December 10, 1998. This dividend was the same as paid in prior quarter, and investors may have been expecting some chance of a dividend increase. Possibly as a result of such disappointment, the stock price fell 5/16 (or $0.3125) on October 19,1998 to $31.125 per share.

The ex-dividend date would be December 8, 1998 (a Tuesday) for this dividend. As a result, the stock price could be expected to fall by $0.42, or about 7/16 of a dollar, on December 8, 1998. In particular, investors who held the stock at the end of December 7, 1998 (which is the last business day before the ex-dividend date) would be entitled to the dividend payment on January 4, 1999 regardless of whether they sold the stock on December 8, 1998 or thereafter.

As a result, investors would be willing to pay $.42 less for the stock at the open of trading on December 8 than they did at the close of the day on December 7. Naturally, other news and changes in economic conditions (such as changes in interest rates, market risk premiums, and expectations) could cause the stock to rise or fall in value for other reasons before, during, and after this time interval, but stock prices do tend to fall on the ex-dividend date by approximately the amount of the dividend.

Stock splits, stock dividends (which are, like stock splits, dividends paid in the form of more of the same stock), and spinoffs (which are dividends paid in the form of subsidiary stock spun off to shareholders) have mechanics similar to that of a cash dividend. On the announcement date, a holder-of-record-date and a payment date are specified. On the ex-date (which is 2 business days prior to the announced holder-of-record date), the stock will generally sell in two forms: "cum" shares with the right to the payment of the additional shares, and "ex" shares without the right. The "ex" shares should trade at a price equal to the price of the "cum" shares less the value of the new shares to be received on the payment date (e.g., in the case of a 200% stock dividend or an equivalent 3-for-1 stock split, the price of the "ex" shares would be 2/3 lower than the "cum" shares). After the payment date of the additional shares to those investors holding "cum" shares, the "cum" shares disappear.

On the announcement date of a stock split or dividend, there is generally no effect (as breaking up the company into more pieces does not normally create value unless the price per share was previously so high as to have a transaction cost premium due to higher trading costs and less liquidity).

For instance, when there is no change in expected cash flows upon announcement of a stock split or dividend (i.e., when there is no announcement of an unanticipated increase in the effective cash dividend), studies have found no evidence of a positive effect on shareholder wealth resulting from the announcement.

On the other hand, when there is other fundamental news announced (such as rising earnings and dividends), the stock price does tend to react oust as it does when there is a spin-off that creates value if the sum of the individual parts of a company are perceived to be worth more than the whole).

The Pro Forma Model

Future dividends can be estimated with pro forma balance sheets and income statements. These projected future financial statements may be estimated by making forecasts on variables such as future sales, profit margins, asset turnover ratios, leverage ratios, and dividend payout ratios.

Because dividends cannot generally be estimated out infinitely in the future, equity valuation models often make simplifying assumptions that, at some future period T, the company will pay out all earnings in dividends, and the dividend stream becomes constant forever thereafter.

The stock can therefore be valued by computing the present value of all dividends until the time period T arrives, and by adding this number to the present value of the value of the stock at period T. Since the constant dividend stream represents a perpetuity, the value of the stock at period T will equal the expected constant dividend at that time divided by the required return.

An example of a pro forma model is the STOCK portion of the SIA software, which values a stock as the present value of all dividends estimated over the next 75 years plus the present value of the expected stock price in 75 years.

Each dividend is estimated using pro forma financial statements that require forecasts on 13 different variables, which include sales, profit margins, dividend payout ratios, asset turnover ratios, and leverage ratios.

The expected value of the 75 future dividends and the stock price in 75 years are all adjusted for the risk of bankruptcy (that is set as a function of the *Value Line* safety rank and leverage) and discounted to a present value). A 100% dividend payout ratio is assumed between 66 and 75 years in the future, with a perpetual dividend thereafter equal to the average dividend paid between 66 and 75 years in the future, so that the stock price in 75 years can be computed as this average dividend far in the future divided by the required return.

A study by Callaghan and Murphy has found evidence that deviations of market prices from pro forma model values (using Value Line or past data to Forecast 75 years into the future) are incorporated into risk-adjusted stock returns over the subsequent 5-10+ years. However, such models were not found to be very powerful in predicting short-term stock prices. Other stock valuation models were discovered to be more effective in predicting short-run stock returns (but were insignificantly related to long-term stock returns).

The Constant Growth Model

If dividends are expected to grow at a constant rate g and the term structure of interest rates.

This model can be used to indicate both direct and indirect relationships between equity prices and various variables. It indicates that equity value is a positive function of dividend growth rates and a negative function of the required return.

However, it indicates an unclear relationship between stock prices an inflation. For instance, during periods of inflation, nominal growth rates in earnings and dividends often increase, as sales tend to grow with inflation as do profits if there isn't a decline in the profit margin.

However, investors also often require higher returns on assets (because of higher risk-free rates) during these times to compensate for losses in purchasing power related to the inflation With an increase in both i and g, the effect on V is unclear. Past history indicates that equity prices often fall when inflation rises, indicating that the increase in i is larger than the increase in g (perhaps because inflation also causes the government to tighten monetary policy to slow down the inflation, thus resulting in interest rates rising faster than inflation, and often resulting in a recession that impedes dividend and earnings growth).

While there are also periods when stock prices rise with increasing inflation (that happen when the effect of inflationary profit growth more than offsets the effect of any increase in interest rates), the overall empirical evidence indicates that stock returns are not positively correlated with inflation over short-term one-month or one-year horizons.

Nevertheless, there is some evidence that stock values do rise with inflation over long periods of time after the short-term effects of interest rate increases are factored out. In particular, once interest rates have risen to a higher level, stock prices can grow with a stable inflation rate.

In addition, if inflation declines to a lower level, interest rates can fall, thereby causing the present value of dividends to rise, so that stock values will reflect the higher value of the earnings that have been increased to an inflated level by past inflation.

While the constant growth model can provide insights on some of the important determinants of stock values, a major problem with direct application of value individual stocks is that the computed stock values are very sensitive to small changes in the estimate of g and sometimes lead to ridiculous valuations. For example, for high values of g relative to i, indicates a negative value for the stock, which is not only counterintuitive but also impossible given the fact that the prices of limited-liability assets like stocks cannot fall below zero. In addition, the formula indicates that a stock which pays no dividend currently is worthless.

Because of these facts and because it is very difficult to estimate g precisely for most companies (except for very stable companies), the constant-growth model is generally not practically applicable (except sometimes as a very rough valuation of very stable companies or the stock market as a whole). However, the constant growth model can be used to derive theoretical relationships between value and important fundamental variables like earnings.

The P/E Ratio Model

Price/earnings (P/e) ratios measure the price paid per dollar of earnings. These ratios can be computed as the market price per share of stock divided by the company's earnings per share, as well as by the ratio of the aggregate market value of all the shares outstanding to aggregate net income. P/e ratios are often used in both theory and practice to analyse equities.

General Theory: Using substitution, can be converted into a model that sets value as a function of the company's earnings e. In particular, the numerator actually equals the dividend expected in the next period, i.e., $d_0(1+g)=d_1$, since g represents the periodic expected growth rate in earnings and dividends. The expected dividend d_1, in turn, equals the earnings expected in the next period multiplied by the dividend payout ratio, where the dividend payout ratio is the percentage of earnings paid out in dividends that can be written as d/e.

Thus, the numerator i can be written as $d_1=e_1(d/e)$. This rewriting of equation indicates the amount an investor would be willing to pay for a dollar of the company's earnings in next period. This model of V/e ratios (which equal P/e ratios if V=P, or if the market's valuation or pricing is being analysed) shows that investors are willing to pay more for a dollar of earnings if the earnings and dividends of the company are expected to grow rapidly, and if the discount rate used to compute the present value of the cash flows from the stock is low. The model for V/e ratios can be developed further as a function of operating ratios with an additional assumption. In particular, if a constant return on equity (defined as ROE=earnings/equity) may be forecast for a company, and if future new equity invested into the company may be estimated by a constant earnings retention ratio (1 - d/e), then it is possible to forecast the growth rate in earnings and dividends

ROE and Dividend Growth Rates

$$e_1 = (\text{Equity}_{0)}r,$$

and

$$e_2 = (\text{Equity}_{1)}r,$$

where,

- $\text{Equity}_1 = \text{Equity}_0 + [e_1(1\text{-}d/e)]$,
- which implies from (E-1),
- $\text{Equity}_1 = \text{Equity}_0 + [(\text{Equity}_{0)}r\ (1\text{-}d/e)]$
- $= \text{Equity}_0[1+ \{r(1 - d/e)\}]$.
- Inserting (E-4) into (E-2), we have
- $e_2 = \text{Equity}_0[1 + - d/e)\}]r$.
- Dividing e_2 in (E-5) by e_1 in (E-1), we get

- $e_{2/}e_1 = 1 + [r(1 - d/e)]$, thus implying that earnings grow at a rate equal to $g = r(1 - d/e)$.

If d/e remains constant, dividends will also grow at a rate of g per year.

An numeric example of the proof can be provide using the October 24,2007.

Motorola stock, whose Equity $_0$ = \$22.22, e_1 = \$2.20, and d_1 = \$0.48 (from the most recent Value Line):

From this data, it can be deduced that,

$$r = \$2.20/\$22.22 = 9.9\%, \text{ and}$$

$$d/e = \$0.48/\$2.20 = 21.8\%.$$

we know that,

$$g = 9.9\% \ (1 - .218) = 7.7\%,$$

so that earnings are expected to grow to

$$e_2 = e_1 (1 + g) = \$2.20 \ (1 + .077) = \$2.37$$

in the next year. This same result occurs when the data are input into equation,

$$e_2 = \$22.22[1 = .099x(1 - .218)] \ x.099 = \$2.37, -$$

and, assuming price equals value, its P/e ratio would be 8

The V/e Ratio as a Capitalization Rate

The foregoing formula for V/e ratios can be used for a variety of purposes. One of the most important uses is to determine the value of a stock's earnings. Determining the value of a stock from its earnings is often called capitalizing its earnings, since the value of a stock essentially represents the present value of the shareholder's claim on the company's earnings (whether the earnings are reinvested or paid out in dividends).

The earnings of a company can be capitalized by multiplying them by an appropriate V/e ratio. The inverse of the appropriate V/e ratio is often called the capitalization rate (e.g., a P/e of 20 represents a capitalization rate of 1/20=5%). Since an equityholder has a claim not only to the current dividend yield but also to reinvested earnings, the capitalization rate measures the current earnings yield on a security.

Equities with similar risk and reinvestment potential should have similar capitalization rates. As a result, assuming P=V (and therefore V/e=P/e), it is possible to use the P/e ratio of stocks with similar risk and reinvestment prospects to capitalize the earnings of equities for which the value is not known. For example, assume a new company with an expected future ROE of 17%, a beta of 1.0, and net income of $30 million is not traded and has no market price. If other stocks with expected future ROEs of 17% and betas of 1.0 have P/e's of 15 on average, it is possible to estimate the value of the new firm by multiplying its earnings by a P/e of 15 to get a value of $30,000,000×15=$450,000,000.

The capitalization rate can also be used for other purposes, such as to determine whether the returns on one class of securities will dominate the returns on another. For instance, if one stock has expected future ROEs of 15%, a beta of 1.1, and a P/e ratio of 9, it is a superior investment to a stock with an expected future ROE of 10%, a beta of 1.5, and a P/e ratio of 11.

Even more broadly, the capitalization rate can be used to make rough comparisons of equity investments with other securities. For instance, it can be shown algebraically that an equity (or group of equities) will earn a return higher than some specified interest rate (such as i or Rf,) only if either the ROE or the capitalization rate exceed that rate. If the ROE and the capitalization rate are both greater than the specified interest rate, the equity (or equities) will definitely be expected to earn a higher return than that specified interest rate. These relationships can be used to evaluate whether equities are likely to earn higher returns than other assets like risk-free Treasury securities.

P/e Ratio Adjustments for Earnings Quality: When applying P/e ratio analysis in practice, it is necessary to consider the fact that the earnings portion of the P/e ratio (as well as of the ROE ratio) includes an accounting entry, reported earnings, that may not reflect the true economic or financial earning power of the company.

For instance, accounting earnings can be manipulated by changing accounting procedures for the same cash flow, such as by changing the depreciation method to straight-line from accelerated or by depreciating fixed assets over a longer life as opposed to a shorter life.

Investors are typically willing to pay a higher P/e for companies with more conservative accounting policies, such as ones whose fixed assets are depreciated over a short useful life with accelerated depreciation methods (which result in higher reported depreciation expenses and lower earnings for the same cash flows), and ones that utilize LIFO inventory accounting when prices are rising (which results in higher reported cost of goods sold and lower earnings during such times—when prices are falling, FIFO is more conservative, whereas Average Cost inventory methods are between FIFO and LIFO in all cases).

In addition, investors also tend to be willing to pay more for companies' earnings that are distorted by one-time negative events such as a nonrecurring loss (like from a one-time write-down of fixed asset book values) and pay less for companies' earnings that are distorted by one-time positive events such as a nonrecurring capital gain (like from a one-time gain from the sale of a subsidiary). Any such events that distort reported earnings in comparison to future projected earnings can result in investors valuing the reported earnings differently.

Similarly, investors tend to be willing to pay less for a company's basic earnings per share if the company has issued options on the company's stock (through convertibles, warrants, and employee stock options) that could result in a significant increase in the number of shares outstanding if exercised and thereby dilute earnings per share growth (employee stock options granted by the largest U.S. companies in 1997 alone represented claims on a number of shares equal to about 1.5% of all those outstanding). Note that the *fully diluted earnings per share* reported on financial statements do not fully incorporate the effects of such dilution, as the reported *fully diluted earnings per share* do not take into consideration the effect of dilution resulting from the exercise of options that are currently out of the money but may become in the money in the future if the stock price rises.

P/e ratios, therefore, tend to be a positive function of the quality of earnings, where earnings quality is considered to be higher when more conservative accounting procedures are used, when there are no irregular items that are increasing reported earnings, and when less future dilution is possible. Often, investors attempt to conduct P/e ratio analysis using a normalized earnings figure that adjusts for differences in accounting procedures and irregular items.

For example, an attempt may be made to estimate earnings if companies used the same accounting methods. In addition, analysts often take any nonrecurring items out of reported earnings.

However, at least a portion of irregular write-offs or gains may be kept in the normalized net income figure if such items tend to recur periodically. One simple method for determining exactly how much of a nonrecurring item to retain would be to compute the average of such figures over the last 5 or 10 years.

For companies with a limited history, a shorter average number of years could be used, and/or a value of zero for nonrecurring items could be assumed for years when they were not in existence.

For purposes of comparing companies in the same industry, it is possible to make additional adjustments for earnings quality (examples of general intra industry adjustments. For comparisons in some industries, special adjustments must be made (an example for the financial institution industry is provided. In addition, adjustments for different levels of leverage and different amounts of reinvested capital are also sometimes made (an analysis of these factors is provided If earnings are adjusted for difference in earnings quality, it is not necessary to adjust the resulting adjusted P/e ratio.

P/e Adjustments for Companies in the Same Industry

- For purposes of comparing companies in the same industry, it is often useful to adjust for depreciation differences by adding depreciation back to earnings. Depreciation plus net income is often labeled cash flow because depreciation is a noncash expense. The ratio price/cash flow can then be used like P/e ratios for purposes of comparison.
- In addition, many analysts add a portion of research and development (R&D) expenses back to earnings or cash flow when analyzing P/e or P/cash flow ratios of companies in the same industry. The reason is that R&D expenses often represent long-term investments that normally do not pay off until far in the future, and so investors may be willing to pay the same amount for a pretax dollar of expensed R&D as for a pretax dollar of earnings. However, because R&D is a tax- deductible item, it is necessary to multiply R&D by (1 - Tax Rate) before adding it back to income in order to compute what earnings would have been if R&D had not been expensed.
- Although such adjustments for R&D and depreciation can be useful, it is important to realise that long-term depreciation and R&D expense requirements differ across industries. As a result, any adjustment that adds back into income a recurring expense like depreciation and R&D should only be made when comparing companies in the same industry.

Special P/e Adjustments for Financial Institutions

- For financial institutions such as banks and savings and loan organizations, a special set of items may be considered to be nonrecurring. The major categories are capital gains from loan and security sales and loan write-offs. To compute normalized earnings, some analysts may leave only the average of capital gains from security and other asset sales over the last 10 years in adjusted net income (i.e., the difference between the year's reported capital gains and the average over the last 10 years would be taken out of reported net income). Also, some average of loan loss and other asset write-offs over the last 10 years should probably be kept in adjusted net income.

- In addition, it is possible to adjust the average write-off figure for inadequate loan loss reserves. In particular, a normal loan loss reserve equal to 0.50% of financial institution loans and a normal ratio of 1% for nonperforming assets to loans can be assumed. Subtracting 0.5% of loans from loan loss reserves and 1% from nonperforming assets therefore computes the extraordinary amount for each.

  Assuming a 50% loss per dollar of extraordinary nonperforming assets (more would be assumed for the case of nonperforming unsecured loans), one can then subtract 50% of extraordinary nonperforming assets from the extraordinary loan loss reserve to determine whether the loan loss reserve is sufficient to cover future losses from the extraordinary nonperforming assets. Any amount by which the losses from the extraordinary nonperforming assets exceed the extraordinary loan loss reserves could then be added to the loan write-offs for the current year (which then would then be included as an input in computing the average loan write-off over the last 10 years).
- Moreover, for financial institutions with mortgage or other callable debt, a portion of interest income represents a premium for call risk. Over time such extra income will be offset by lost interest relating to early repayments. As a result, between 0.25% and 0.5% of the book value of callable debt assets should be considered extraordinary and should therefore be subtracted out of net income to compute adjusted income.
- Finally, income related to financial institutions playing the yield curve should be taken out of net to compute adjusted income. Playing the yield curve refers to having long-term assets financed with short-term liabilities and,

as a result, gambling on winning high profits when the yield curve is upward sloping (i.e., when the interest rate on long-term bonds is higher than that on short-term bonds). Since the various theories of interest rates indicate that one can only expect a small profit (if any) from playing the yield curve over the long term, the short-term profits (or losses) that financial institutions gain from playing the yield curve should be taken out of income to compute adjusted net.

The profits (or losses) from playing the yield curve can be estimated by taking the difference between long-term fixed-rate assets and long-term fixed-rate liabilities for the financial institution (as often computed in an interest-rate sensitivity part of the annual report or financial statements) and multiplying that difference by the average difference between long-term and short-term interest rates over the annual report interval.

- These equations indicate that, for a given ROA, more debt can increase the ROE. In actual fact, the ROA is influenced by the amount of debt taken on (insofar as more debt results in more interest payments and lower net profit/assets), and higher debt levels may not increase the ROE if the interest rate on new debt exceeds the pretax operating rate of return on assets.
- Increasing ROEs by increasing leverage might be advantageous to stockholders were it not for two potentially offsetting factors. the higher financial leverage increases the stock beta, and so there is some offset to higher ROE-induced growth rates in future earnings and dividends in the form of a higher discount rate on the higher future cash flows, In addition to the effect of a higher beta and discountrate, higher financial leverage can increase the chance of bankruptcy and thereby reduce the expected value of the future reinvestment opportunities of the firm.

A 1998 empirical study by Walker has indicated that, despite some transitory stockholder gains, there has been little evidence of long-term benefits from leveraged recapitalizations on average. Even in cases where increasing leverage can increase shareholder value long-term, the earnings of companies that have less leverage remain more valuable because they have greater potential to realise such gains from leverage than companies that have already leveraged themselves (one exception to this rule are companies whose stock is heavily controlled by an investor or investors whose concentrated positions in the company result in insufficient diversification and a severe aversion to unsystematic risk that might prohibit even value-enhancing leverage increases). As a result, earnings are generally considered of a higher quality and valued more highly at less leveraged companies (resulting in such companies generally having higher P/e ratios).

- Although the effect of higher leverage on beta and discount rates can be evaluated within the context of a simple quantitative comparison of P/e, beta, and ROE, the effect of higher leverage on the probability of bankruptcy complicates the analysis. companies with high ROEs have high values based on high future reinvestment rates and futurecash flow growth. To leverage those ROEs with more debt increases the chance of bankruptcy (which would put an end to all operations and reinvestment at any extraordinary ROE) and thereby endangers the vary value created by the high ROES. As a result, many companies with high ROEs and future reinvestment prospects (such as pharmaceutical companies and other high technology firms) tend to have very low levels of debt (in order to maximize the probability of being around to earn those high ROES). Although this bankruptcy effect can be (and is often) incorporated into the expected values of the future cash flow projections for pro forma models, P/e ratio analysis requires the analyst to pay a slightly lower multiple of earnings for a company with more debt, all else (beta and ROE) being equal. Thus, investors are willing to pay more for companies with higher ROES, but they pay more for stocks that generate those high ROEs via greater operating profitability than for stocks that generate high ROEs via greater financial leverage.

- In addition, it should also be the per cent of earnings reinvested at the ROE (as denoted by 1-{d/e}) affects the P/e ratio insofar as reinvesting a large amount of funds at a high ROE is worth more to shareholders than reinvesting a small amount of funds at the same ROE. As a result, companies with high ROEs tend to have higher P/e ratios if they reinvest more funds at that high ROE than if they reinvest less funds at that high ROE.
- It is therefore necessary to consider r, 1-{d/e}, accounting earnings quality, B, and debt when conducting P/e ratio analysis. Higher P/e ratios are justified for companies with higher ROES, higher earnings retention rates (if ROE> i), more conservatively reported earnings, lower betas, and lower financial leverage.

Applied P/e Formulas: For direct applied use, many analysts derive various other formulas for P/e ratios using different assumptions on future dividend growth rates or ROEs. Often, these formulas will be based on dividend growth rates that are assumed to vary over more than one time interval. For instance, a 2-stage dividend growth model assumes that dividends will grow at a constant rate for a number of years, often at a very rapid rate, after which the dividend growth is assumed to stabilize to a more normal constant rate. A 3-stage dividend growth model is also sometimes used that assumes the dividend growth rate moves more gradually from its introductory rapid phase to a normal phase over a time period of up to 50 years.

P/E Ratio Analysis With The Discounted Cash Flow Model

Often, forecasts and analysis of a company will produce variable earnings, ROEs, and dividends for a few years (like

5), after which the company will be in a stable growth mode. Once the stable growth mode is reached, it is possible to estimate the V/e ratio for the stock in this time period, and then discount this price and all dividends received until then to compute the present value of the stock.

*The Rel*ationship Between Stock Valuation and Capital Budgeting

- The various models for stock valuation are mathematically and intuitively linked with the formulas and procedures used tomake capital budgeting decisions (such as discounting cash flows). An explanation of the relationship between stock valuation and capital budgeting model.

Capital Budgeting, Cost of Equity, IRR, and NPV

- The equations can be useful for understanding the interrelationship between stock valuation and capital budgeting decisions made by the company. For instance, the discount rate used in capital budgeting models is typically computed as the cost of capital, which in turn is a function of the cost of equity capital. In addition, the value of a stock can be computed as the present value of all capital budgeting opportunities. Estimating the Required Return on Equity Estimates of g for individual firms are generally too unreliable for the formula to be applicable, just such growth estimates are too unreliable for meaningful direct application. However, it may be possible to use the average earnings growth estimate of investment analysts for a large group of stocks in order to estimate the required return on the stock market. Several sources exist for such data, such as the Institutional Broker's Estimate System (IBES), which is available on the Internet for a fee (alternatively, one could use *Value Line* estimated earnings growth). Inserting such an estimate for E(Rm) into equation (4-2) can result in the company using a discount rate to estimate the present value of capital budgeting projects that is similar to that used by investment analysts who are computing the present value of the dividends from the company's stock.

- For instance, the Value Line Industrial Composite page forecasts earnings of 3.35 for the index in 2001 compared to earnings of 2.08 in 1997, implying an annual growth of
- It is important to point out, however, that maximization of ROE does not necessarily maximize stock price. The reason is that the value of the abnormal growth opportunities is a function not only of the ROE but also the amount of money reinvested at that ROE. For example, some companies in industries with low or negative growth (such as tobacco) earn fairly high ROEs because of limited competition and heavy brand-name recognition, but the P/e ratios for such companies are often not correspondingly high because there are few opportunities to reinvest new funds in industries with low or negative growth.
- Another way to look at this phenomenon is to relate Vabnormal growth to NPV and ROE to IRR. A company can invest a small amount of funds at a high IRR and report a very large ROE, but the NPV of the project may be very low because only a small amount is invested. As a result, the Vabnormal growth is very low. For example, the value of a penny invested at a rate of return of 90% for one period is less than a penny, but millions of dollars invested at a rate of 30% typically has a value measured in the millions.
- It is important to point out, however, that maximization of ROE does not necessarily maximize stock price. The reason is that the value of the abnormal growth opportunities is a function not only of the ROE but also the amount of money reinvested at that ROE. For example, some companies in industries with low or negative growth (such as tobacco) earn fairly high ROEs because of limited competition and heavy brand-name recognition, but the P/e ratios for such companies are

often not correspondingly high because there are few opportunities to reinvest new funds in industries with low or negative growth.

- It should also be that reported ROEs, or even forecasted future ROEs, only performance as proxies for a company's true IRR and earnings reinvestment rate. Sometimes there are existing operations that appear to earn an extremely high return on existing capital, but the projected return on new projects or investments may be very low, in which case the ROE may not be a very meaningful indicator of the reinvestment rate. A good example might be a company that has had some major writeoffs which have reduced stockholders' equity very close to zero and the stockholders' equity of companies that have repurchased a large amount of stock at prices that far exceed the book value per share may have their stockholders' equity greatly reduced to a very low level as a result (since the market value of all repurchased shares are subtracted from the balance sheet stockholders' equity account) and may therefore report meaninglessly high (or even negative) ROE figures. In such cases, it may be more useful to back into an ROE estimate based on past (or future projected) earnings growth g using the equation ROE=g/(1-{d/e}). Or alternatively, in cases of companies that do not seem to have potential to invest at rates that exceed required returns (such as for companies that are not in growth industries), it may be appropriate to assume that ROE=i. In other cases where the computed ROE is clearly a poor indication of the true reinvestment rate of the company, it may b[illegible] necessary to construct some subjective estimate, perhaps obtained using a pro forma forecasting model stockholders' equity account) and may therefore report meaninglessly high (or even negative) ROE figures. In such cases, it may be more useful to back into an ROE estimate based on past (or future projected) earnings growth g using the equation ROE=g/

(1-{d/e}). Or alternatively, in cases of companies that do not seem to have potential to invest at rates that exceed required returns (such as for companies that are not in growth industries), it may be appropriate to assume that ROE=i. In other cases where the computed ROE is clearly a poor indication of the true reinvestment rate of the company, it may be necessary to construct some subjective estimate, perhaps obtained using a pro forma forecasting model.

5

Investment Planning Management

WHY IS INVESTING IMPORTANT

One needs to invest to maximize returns on one's savings and also to be able to generate cash flows for meeting several financial needs of the future. One must, however, invest with knowledge and full care in order to not only protect one's hard-earned capital but also generate good returns.

Investment objectives

There are normally three objectives: safety, return and liquidity. This means that one would like an investment to be absolutely safe, while it generates handsome returns and provides high liquidity.

However, it is difficult to maximize all three objectives simultaneously. Typically, one objective trades-off against another. For example, if one wants high returns, one may have to take some risks, or if one wants high liquidity, one may have to compromise on returns. For people who have a regular income, growth-oriented investments, with some risks, are ideal.

Specification of the Financial Goals

Investments are made with certain financial objectives. These objectives should be defined clearly and be measurable in money terms. For example, it is not enough to say "I want to retire comfortably". Such an objective should be stated, as "I want to retire with the ability to spend ₹ 2,00,000 annually, adjusted for inflation".

An investor saves today, to meet certain financial needs tomorrow. Unless the investor is clear about the purpose of saving, his efforts would not result in the desired benefits. An investor should therefore first identify his financial needs.

For example, an investor may have one or more of the following financial needs:

- To retire at age 55 with an annual income of ₹.3,00,000. I am now 35 years of age
- To completely payoff the housing loan by the time I retire 20 years later.
- To pay for my five year old daughter's college education that would cost me ₹ 1,50,000 per year for 4 years.

The first step for an investor is to clearly write down the financial needs. The financial needs would be expressed in terms of the amount required and the future date on which required.

In the above three examples, we would write:

Example	Amount required	When required Number
1	₹ 3,00,000 p.a.	Each year beginning from the 20th year from now
2	₹ 5000 p.m.	For the next 20 years
3	₹ 1,50,000 p.a.	Beginning from 12th year from now till 16th year.

Every investor should take out time and prepare such a statement of financial goals covering as many requirements as possible. This is the basis on which the financial plan would be prepared. If the financial capability is found to be inadequate to meet all these goals then they have to be prioritized.

The investors' financial needs depend on the age, stage in the career path, size of the family, needs of the other family members etc. Some of the needs can be identified with precision while others can only be tentatively determined.

There may be unanticipated needs as well for which provisions have to be made. Sometimes financial needs change with investor's changing circumstances.

In order to prepare a financial plan, these goals have to be stated in clear and determinable terms of age, amounts and time frame. The financial planning process is merely an exercise of allocation of today's money to meet tomorrow's needs. The financial plan is not static. It has to be reviewed from time to time to account for the changing circumstances.

Assessing the Financial Capacity

An investor sets aside some money today to realize the financial goals stated in the financial plan. How much money can be set aside now depends on the present circumstances. This can be understood by understanding the income, assets and liabilities of the individual investor. The balance sheet lists the investor's assets and liabilities. Hopefully, the assets exceed the liabilities and this excess is the net worth. All assets and liabilities should be valued at the current market value instead of any cost basis. For example, if you own an equity share bought at ₹ 1,000 and it is worth ₹.5,000 now, your balance sheet should reflect ₹.5,000.

Balance Sheet of Mr. A as at 31st March 2010

Assets		**Liabilities**	
Cash	80,000	House loan outstanding	6,00,000
Investments	4,00,000	Car loan outstanding	1,00,000
House	8,00,000	Net worth	11,80,000
Car	2,00,000		
Life insurance surrender value	4,00,000		
Total	18,80,000	Total	18,80,000

An investor should live within his means. Means is the income. Out of this income, routine expenses are met. The remaining amount is available for savings.

An investor should prepare a statement of income and expense. It is called "Cash Flow Statement". The sources of income are salary, dividends, interest, self-employment earnings etc.

Cash Flow Statement of Mr. A for the period 1.4.2009 to 31.3.2010

		Expected	Alternate scenarios		
		Disability	**Death**	**Retirement**	
Income	Business income	4,00,000	0	0	
	net/Salary	1,00,000	1,00,000	1,00,000	1,00,000
	Dividends, interest				
	received Others	0	0	0	0
	Total	5,00,000	1,00,000	1,00,00	1,00,000
Expense	Family living	2,00,000	2,50,000	1,50,000	2,00,000
	expenses	20,000	20,000	20,000	20,000
	Insurance premia	35,000	35,000	35,000	35,000
	Loan installments	30,000	30,000	0	0
	Pension	1,50 000	30,000	30,000	30,000
	contribution Taxes				
	Total	4,35,000	32,65,000	2,35,000	2,85,000
Excess (Deficit)		65,000	(2,65,000)	(1,35,000)	(1,85,000)

After identifying the income, an investor should identify the expenses. Expenses are generally grouped into living expenses, payments already committed and taxes.

The excess of income over expenses in each year is the amount available to save. The investor tries to achieve his financial goals subject to his saving capacity. The Cash Flow Statement is prepared under different scenarios. These are death, disability and retirement.

What is investment planning?

The balance sheet shows what the investor owns and what he owes. The cash flow statement shows the money available for making investments. Together, these two statements tell the investor's financial circumstances and the saving potential. Financial planning is the process of meeting as many of the investor's financial needs as possible with his saving potential.

12 Steps to Investing

Before making any investment, you must ensure that you:

- Obtain written documents explaining the investment
- Read and understand such documents

- Verify the legitimacy of the investment
- Find out the costs and benefits associated with the investment
- Assess risk-return profile of the investment
- Know the liquidity and safety aspects of the investment
- Ascertain if the product is appropriate for your specific goals
- Compare the product with other investments opportunities available
- Examine if it fits with other investments you are considering or you have already made,
- Deal only through registered intermediaries
- Seek all clarifications about the intermediary and the investment,
- Explore the options available to you should something go wrong, and then, if satisfied, make the investment.

PROCESS OF INVESTING

As investors, we would all like to beat the market and we would all like to pick "great" investments on instinct. However, while intuition is undoubtedly a part of the process of investing, it is just part of the process. As investors, it is not surprising that we focus so much of our energy and efforts on investment philosophies and strategies, and so little on the investment process.

It is far more interesting to read about how Peter Lynch picks stocks and what makes Warren Buffett a valuable investor, than it is to talk about the steps involved in creating a portfolio or in executing trades. Though it does not get sufficient attention, understanding the investment process is critical for every investor for several reasons:

1. The investment process outlines the steps in creating a portfolio, and emphasizes the sequence of actions involved from understanding the investors risk preferences to asset allocation and selection to

performance evaluation. By emphasizing the sequence, it provides for an orderly way in which an investor can create his or her own portfolio or a portfolio for someone else.

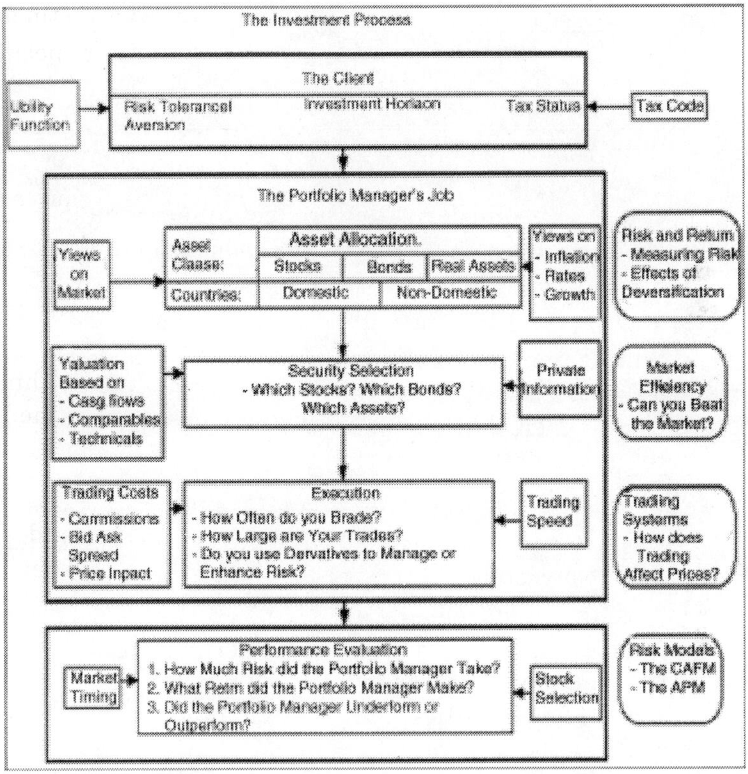

2. The investment process provides a structure that allows investors to see the source of different investment strategies and philosophies. By doing so, it allows investors to take the hundreds of strategies that they see described in the common press and in investment newsletters and to trace them to their common roots.
3. The investment process emphasizes the different components that are needed for an investment strategy to be successful, and by so doing explain why so many strategies that look good on paper never work for those who use them.

Investing well has a secret formula – having the right information, planning and making good choices. The Investment Process is graphically depicted on the next page.

Purchasing Process

From where to purchase the products?

- Brokers: Brokers offer several services like purchase/sale of equity, debt and derivative products, mutual fund units, IPOs etc.
- Banks: Many banks offer facilities for purchase/sale of equity, debt and derivative products, mutual fund units, IPOs etc. physically as well as through their web sites
- Mutual Funds: Almost all Mutual Funds facilitate online and physical buying/selling of mutual funds.
- Stock Exchanges: Close ended mutual funds are traded on stock exchanges and can be brought through brokers. Open ended mutual funds can also be bought/sold on the stock exchange platform.

Steps involved for becoming a capital market investor

- The first requirement is a PAN Card. This is mandatory for all investors.
- The other requirements are a bank account and a demat account. The demat account is normally linked to a bank account in order to facilitate paying in and out of funds and securities.
- The next step is to select a broker and fill a KYC form and enter into a broker-client agreement.
- The broker then allocates a unique client ID, which acts as the identification.
- You are now ready to buy/sell securities.

INCREMENTAL CASH FLOWS

Incremental cash flow is the additional operating cash flow that an organization receives from taking on a new project. A positive incremental cash flow means that the company's cash flow will increase with the acceptance of the project.

There are several components that must be identified when looking at incremental cash flows: the initial outlay, cash flows from taking on the project, terminal cost (or value) and the scale and timing of the project. A positive incremental cash flow is a good indication that an organization should spend some time and money investing in the project.

Incremental Cash Flow and Capital Budgeting

When determining incremental cash flows from a new project, several problems arise: sunk costs, opportunity costs, externalities and cannibalization.

Sunk Costs

These are the initial outlays required to analyze a project that cannot be recovered even if a project is accepted. As such, these costs will not affect the future cash flows of the project and should not be considered when making capital-budgeting decisions. Suppose Newco is considering whether to make an addition to its current plant to increase production. To determine if the new addition is worthwhile, Newco hired a consulting firm for $50,000 to analyze the addition and the effect it will have on production. The $50,000 is considered a sunk cost. If the project is rejected, the $50,000 will still be paid, and if the project is accepted, the $50,000 will not affect the future cash flows of the addition.

Opportunity Cost

This is the cost of not going forward with a project or the cash outflows that will not be earned as a result of utilizing an asset for another alternative. For example, the opportunity cost of Newco's new addition considered above is the cost of the land on which the company is considering putting the new plant addition. As such, it should be included in the analysis of the project.

Externality

In the consideration of incremental cash flows of a new project, there may be effects on the existing operations of the company to consider, known as "externalities." For example, the addition to Newco's plant is for the purpose of producing a new product. It must be considered whether the new product may actually take away or add to sales of the existing product.

Cannibalization

Cannibalization is the type of externality where the new project takes sales away from the existing product.

Changes in Net Working Capital

A change in net working capital is essentially the changes in current assets minus changes in current liabilities. Within the capital-budgeting process, a project typically adds to current assets given additional inventories or potential increases in accounts receivables from new sales. The increases to current assets, however, are offset by current liabilities needed to finance the new project.

Overall, there may be a change to net working capital from the new project.

- If the change in net working capital is positive, the change to current assets outweighs the change in the current liabilities.
- If, however, the change in net working capital is negative, the change to current liabilities outweighs the change in current assets.

Pro Forma Financial Statements

Many companies issue pro-forma financial statements in addition to generally accepted accounting principles (GAAP) - adjusted statements as a way to provide investors with a better understanding of operating results. In legitimate cases, pro forma financial statements take out one-time charges to smooth earnings. However, companies can also manipulate their financial results under the guise of pro-forma financial statements to provide a picture that is rosier than reality. Let's take a closer look at what pro-forma financial statements are, when they are useful and how companies can use them to dupe investors.

What Are Pro-Forma Earnings?

Pro-forma earnings describe a financial statement that has hypothetical amounts, or estimates, built into the data to give a "picture" of a company's profits if certain non-recurring items were excluded. Pro-forma earnings are not computed using standard GAAP and usually leave out one-time expenses that are not part of normal company operations, such as restructuring costs following a merger. Such an expense can be rightfully viewed as a one-time item that does not contribute to the company's representative valuation.

Essentially, a pro-forma financial statement can exclude anything a company believes obscures the accuracy of its financial outlook, and it can be a useful piece of information to help assess a company's future prospects. Every investor should stress GAAP net income, which is the "official" profitability determined by accountants, but a look at pro-forma earnings can also be an informative exercise.

Pro forma earnings figures are inherently different for different companies. There are no universal guidelines that companies must follow when reporting pro forma earnings, which is why the distinction between pro forma and earnings reported using GAAP is very, very important.

GAAP enforces strict guidelines that companies must follow when reporting earnings, but pro forma figures are better thought of as "hypothetical," computed according to the estimated relevance of certain events and conditions experienced by the company. Basically, companies use their own discretion in calculating pro forma earnings, including or excluding items depending on what they feel accurately represents the company's true performance.

For example, net income does not tell the whole story when a company has one-time charges that are irrelevant to future profitability. Some companies therefore strip out certain costs that get in the way. This kind of earnings information can be very useful to investors who want an accurate view of a company's normal earnings outlook, but by omitting items that reduce reported earnings, this process can make a company appear profitable even when it is losing money. We like to call pro forma the "everything-but-the-bad-stuff earnings."

The problem, however, is that there isn't nearly as much regulation of pro-forma earnings as there is of financial statements falling under GAAP rules, so sometimes companies bend or even abuse the rules to make earnings appear better than they really are. Because traders and brokers focus so closely on whether the company beats or meets analyst expectations, the headlines that follow a company's earnings announcements can mean everything. And, if a company missed non-pro-forma expectations but stated that it beat the pro-forma expectations, its stock price will not suffer as badly; it might even go up - at least in the short term.

Problems with Pro Forma

Despite the positive reasoning behind pro-forma statements, there are many ways in which pro-forma earnings can be manipulated. Items often left out of pro forma figures include the following: depreciation, goodwill, amortization, restructuring and merger costs, interest and taxes, stock-based employee pay, losses at affiliates and one-time expenses. The theory behind excluding non-cash items such as amortization is that these are not true expenses and therefore do not represent the company's actual earnings potential. Amortization, for example, is not an item that is paid for as a part of cash flow. But under GAAP, amortization is considered an expense because it represents the loss of value of an asset.

One-time cash expenses are often excluded from pro forma because they are not a regular part of operations and are therefore considered an irrelevant factor in the performance of a company's core activities. Under GAAP, however, a one-time expense is included in earnings calculations because, even though it is not a part of operations, a one-time expense is still a sum of money that exited the company and therefore decreased income. Sometimes companies even take unsold inventory off their balance sheets when reporting pro-forma earnings. Ask yourself this: does producing that inventory cost money? Of course it does, so why should the company simply be able to write it off? It is bad management to produce goods that can't be sold, and a company's poor decisions shouldn't be erased from the financial statements. The Securities and Exchange Commission (SEC) will investigate companies suspected of trying to deceive investors in the pro-forma modification of earnings.

This isn't to say companies are always dishonest with pro-forma earnings; pro forma doesn't mean the numbers are automatically being manipulated. But by being skeptical when reading pro-forma earnings, you may end up saving yourself big money. To evaluate the legitimacy of pro-forma earnings, be sure to look at what the excluded costs are and decide whether these costs should be considering impactful. Intangibles like depreciation and goodwill are okay to write down occasionally, but if the company is doing it every quarter, the reasons for doing so might be less than honorable.

The dotcom era of the late 1990s saw some of the worst abusers of pro-forma earnings manipulations. Many Nasdaq-listed companies utilized pro-forma earnings management to report more robust pro-forma numbers. Taken cumulatively, the difference between GAAP earnings and pro-forma earnings for the dotcom sector during its heyday exceeded billions of dollars.

One of the more notable occurrences of this phenomenon is Network Associates. The company went so far as to exclude its dotcom department's operating earnings. The dotcom department wasn't making or spending pretend money, so why did the company exclude these numbers? No doubt the department was losing money and decided to hide those numbers that reflected poor company strategy from investors.

Benefits of Pro-Forma Analysis

Pro-forma figures are supposed to give investors a clearer view of company operations. For some companies, pro-forma earnings provide a much more accurate view of their financial performance and outlook because of the nature of their businesses. Companies in certain industries tend to use pro-forma reporting more than others, as the impetus to report pro-forma numbers is usually a result of industry characteristics. For example, some cable and telephone companies almost never make a net operating profit because they are constantly writing down big depreciation costs.

In cases where pro-forma earnings do not include non-cash charges, investors can see what the actual cash profit is. For example, recall AOL Time Warner's massive goodwill write-off of about $54 billion in 2002 to reflect the value of AOL's merger with Time Warner in the previous year. With accounting charges nearing $100 billion, Time Warner's GAAP earnings for the year probably would not have been a very good predictor of future prospects - those extraordinary expenses would probably never occur again. Analysis of pro-forma earnings is an important exercise to undertake before considering an investment in a company that reports pro-forma numbers, so be sure to do so.

Also, when a company undergoes substantial restructuring or completes a merger, significant one-time charges can occur. These types of expenses do not compose part of the business's ongoing cost structure and therefore can unfairly weigh on short-term profit numbers. An investor concerned with valuing the long-term potential of the company would do well to analyze pro-forma earnings, which exclude these non-recurring expenses.

Pro-forma financial statements are also prepared and used by corporate managers and investment banks to assess the operating prospects for their own businesses in the future and to assist in the valuation of potential takeover targets. They are useful tools to help identify a company's core value drivers and analyze changing trends within company operations.

Gaap Manipulation

Aside from misusing pro-forma income statements, companies can also mislead investors by creatively classifying their income in several ways, including the following:

- Operating income is not strictly defined under the GAAP because classification lines are often subject to discretion.

Items that are classified into this element can be selectively chosen by management. For example, non-recurring income such as special charges, shareholder class action settlements and unusual events may be included or omitted within the metric to present a value that will please shareholders.

- Sales and gross profits can also be manipulated in many ways within the constraints of the GAAP. For example, companies can classify sales as either the gross amount billed to a customer or expected amounts to be received. Furthermore, sales can also depend on whether or not shipping and handling is treated as a part of revenues. Finally, gross margins can be manipulated by moving certain expenses between SG&A and other costs of sales.
- In the end, these changes create artificially higher or lower income-statement metrics that can mislead shareholders.

The Bottom Line

To sum up, pro-forma earnings are informative when official earnings are blurred by large amounts of asset depreciation and goodwill. But, when you see pro forma, it's up to you to dig deeper to see why the company is treating its earnings as such. Remember that when you read pro-forma figures, they have not undergone the same level of scrutiny as GAAP earnings and are not subject to the same level of regulation.

Although a company reporting pro forma earnings is not doing anything fraudulent or dishonest (because it does report exactly what is and what is not included), it is very important for investors to know and evaluate what went into the company's pro forma calculation, as well as to compare the pro forma figure to the GAAP figure. Often, companies can have a positive pro forma earnings figure while having a negative GAAP earnings figure.

A final cautionary note for when you are analyzing pro forma figures: because companies' definitions of pro forma vary, you must be very careful when comparing pro forma figures between different companies. If you are not aware of how the companies define their pro forma figures, you may be inadvertently comparing apples to oranges. Do your homework and maintain a balanced perspective when reading pro-forma statements. Try to identify the key differences between GAAP earnings and pro-forma earnings and determine whether the differences are reasonable or if they are only there to make a losing company look better. You want to base your decisions on as clear a financial picture as possible.

Operating Cash Flow And Alternative Definitions Of Operating Cash Flow

The cash flow statement summarizes a business's cash inflows and outflows over a period of time. It is important because it is very difficult for a business to manipulate its cash situation. There is plenty that aggressive accountants can do to manipulate earnings, but it's tough to fake cash in the bank. For this reason, some investors use the cash flow statement as a more conservative measure of a company's performance.

Operating cash flow (OCF) is found on the cash flow statement and is calculated through a series of adjustments to net income. OCF is arguably a better measure of a business's profits than earnings because a company can show positive net earnings on the income statement and still not be able to pay its debts. Cash flow is what pays the bills, and OCF can serve as a check on the quality of a company's earnings. If a firm reports record earnings but negative cash, it may be using aggressive accounting techniques.Overview of the Statement of Cash Flows

The statement of cash flows for non-financial companies consists of three main parts:

- Operating flows - The net cash generated from operations (net income and changes in working capital).
- Investing flows - The net result of capital expenditures, investments, acquisitions, etc.
- Financing flows - The net result of raising cash to fund the other flows or repaying debt.

By taking net income and making adjustments to reflect changes in the working capital accounts on the balance sheet (receivables, payables, inventories) and other current accounts, the operating cash flow section shows how cash was generated during the period. It is this translation process from accrual accounting to cash accounting that makes the operating cash flow statement so important.

Accrual Accounting vs. Cash Flows

The key differences between accrual accounting and real cash flow are demonstrated by the concept of the cash cycle.

A company's cash cycle is the process that converts sales (based upon accrual accounting) into cash as follows:

- Cash is used to make inventory.
- Inventory is sold and converted into accounts receivables (because customers are given 30 days to pay).
- Cash is received when the customer pays (which also reduces receivables).

There are many ways that cash from legitimate sales can get trapped on the balance sheet. The two most common are for customers to delay payment (resulting in a buildup of receivables) and for inventory levels to rise because the product is not selling or is being returned.

For example, a company may legitimately record a $1 million sale but because that sale allowed the customer to pay within 30 days, the $1 million in sales does not mean the company made $1 million cash. If the payment date occurs after the close of the end of the quarter, accrued earnings will be greater than operating cash flow because the $1 million is still in accounts receivable.

Harder to Fudge Operating Cash Flows

Not only can accrual accounting give a rather provisional report of a company's profitability, but under GAAP it allows management a range of choices to record transactions. While this flexibility is necessary, it also allows for earnings manipulation. Because managers will generally book business in a way that will help them earn their bonus, it is usually safe to assume that the income statement will overstate profits rather than understate them.

An example of income manipulation is called "stuffing the channel." To increase their sales, a company can provide retailers with incentives such as extended terms or a promise to take back the inventory if it is not sold.

Inventories will then move into the distribution channel and sales will be booked. Accrued earnings will increase, but cash may actually never be received because the inventory may be returned by the customer. While this may increase sales in one quarter, it is a short-term exaggeration and ultimately "steals" sales from the following periods (as inventories are sent back).

The operating cash flow statement will catch these gimmicks. When operating cash flow is less than net income, there is something wrong with the cash cycle. In extreme cases, a company could have consecutive quarters of negative operating cash flow and, in accordance with GAAP, legitimately report positive earnings per share (EPS). In this situation, investors should determine the source of the cash hemorrhage (inventories, receivables, etc.) and whether this situation is a short-term issue or long-term problem.

Cash Exaggerations

While the operating cash flow statement is more difficult to manipulate, there are ways for companies to temporarily boost cash flows. Some of the more common techniques include delaying payment to suppliers (extending payables); selling securities; and reversing charges made in prior quarters (such as restructuring reserves).

Some view the selling of receivables for cash - usually at a discount - as a way for companies to manipulate cash flows. In some cases, this action may be a cash flow manipulation; but it can also be a legitimate financing strategy. The challenge is being able to determine management's intent.

Cash is King

A company can only live by EPS alone for a limited time. Eventually, it will need cash to pay suppliers and, most importantly, the bankers.

There are many examples of once-respected companies who went bankrupt because they could not generate enough cash. Strangely, despite all this evidence, investors are consistently hypnotized by EPS and market momentum and ignore the warning signs.

Investors can avoid a lot of bad investments if they analyze a company's operating cash flow. It's not hard to do, but it is important to do because the talking heads and analysts are all too often focused on EPS.

Alternative Methods of Calculating OCF

The bottom-up approach to operating cash flow takes the company's bottom line–that is, its net income–and adds back non-cash expenses such as depreciation and amortization.

$$OCF = N + D$$

The top-down approach starts with total sales and subtracts only cash expenses (primarily fixed costs, variable costs and taxes), leaving out non-cash expenses such as depreciation and amortization.

$$OCF = S - C - T$$

Because depreciation is tax deductible, it reduces a firm's tax liability. The tax shield method of computing operating cash flow takes this fact into account by multiplying the company's depreciation expense by its tax rate.

$$OCF = (S - C) \times (1 - T) + D \times T$$

Each of these three methods yields the same number for OCF.

Cost Cutting And Asset Replacement

We discussed the use of discounted cash flow as a valuation method for estimating the attractiveness of an investment opportunity. We showed how DCF analysis uses future free cash flow projections and discounts them to arrive at a present value, and how if the present value is higher than the current cost of the investment, the opportunity may be a good one. DCF analysis can be used to determine the value of cost cutting and asset replacement projects under a company's consideration.

Cost Cutting

Cost cutting refers to measures implemented by a company to reduce its expenses and improve profitability. Cost cutting measures may include laying off employees, reducing employee pay, switching to a less expensive employee health insurance programme, downsizing to a smaller office, lowering monthly bills, changing hours of service, restructuring debt or upgrading to more efficient systems.

Let's say a company wants to upgrade its computer system to improve efficiency. While the new computer system will cost money, its purpose is to cut costs. But will it cut costs enough to make the purchase worthwhile? To find out, we can use DCF analysis.

Assume the following:

- Cost of new computer system: $100,000
- Annual savings from improved efficiency: $25,000
- Lifespan of new computer system: 5 years
- Corporate tax rate: 35 per cent
- Depreciation: straight-line basis to zero
- System value in 5 years: $25,000
- Discount rate: 10 per cent

Step 1: Identify capital spending. In this case, it is $100,000.

Step 2: Identify the salvage value of the new computer system using the following calculation:

Salvage Value x (1 -0 35)

Salvage Value = $25,000 x (0.65) = $16,250

Step 3: Calculate the actual annual savings from improved efficiency, taking taxes and depreciation into account. The computer system upgrade will save $25,000 a year. In other words, it will increase operating cash flow by $25,000 a year. On the plus side, the additional depreciation expense of $20,000 a year ($100,000/ 5). Subtracting the depreciation deduction from the increase in operating income gives us $25,000 - $20,000 = $5,000, or earnings before interest and taxes (EBIT). This $5,000 increase in cash flow will be taxed at the company's 35 per cent tax rate, yielding $5,000 x 0.35 = $1,750 in additional tax liability for the company each year. EBIT + Depreciation - Taxes = OCF, so $5,000 + $20,000 - $1,750 = $23,250.

Step 4: Calculate the annual cash flows from undertaking the system upgrade.

Year 0:

-$100,000

Years 1 - 4:

$23,250/yr. = $23,250 x 4 = $93,000

Year 5:

$23,250 + $16,250 salvage value = $39,500

Total: -$100,000 + $93,000 + $39,500 = $32,500

Step 5: Calculate the net present value (NPV) using the discount rate, project life, initial cost and each year's cash flows using an NPV calculator and determine if the upgrade is truly cost-saving. In this case, the discount rate is 10 per cent, the project life is five years, the initial cost is $100,000 and each year's cash flows are provided in step 4. The result is an NPV of -$1,774,24, so the system upgrade would actually not cut costs and thus should not be undertaken.

Asset Replacement

We discussed how to determine a project's cash flows. Here, we'll consider how to analyze those cash flows to determine whether a company should undertake a replacement project. Replacement projects are projects that companies invest in to replace old assets in order to maintain efficiencies. Assume Newco is planning to add new machinery to its current plant.

There are two machines Newco is considering, with cash flows as follows:

Table. Discounted Cash Flows for Machine A and Machine B

Year	0	1	2	3	4	5	6
Cash Flow-Machine A	-5,000	500	1,000	1,000	1,500	2,500	1,000
Discounted Cash Flow	-5,000	461	851	785	1,086	1.670	616
Cumulative Cash Flow	-5,000	-4,539	-3,688	-2,903	-1,817	-147	469
Cash Flow-Machine B	-2,000	500	1,500	1,500	1,500	1,500	1,500
Discounted Cash Flow	-2,000	461	1,277	1,178	1,086	1.002	925
Cumulative Cash Flow	-2,000	-1,539	-262	915	2,002	3,004	3,928

Calculate the NPV for each machine and decide which machine Newco should invest in. As calculated previously, Newco's cost of capital is 8.4 per cent.

Formula:

$$NPV = (\text{Investment}) + \frac{CF_1}{(1+k)^1} + \frac{CF_2}{(1+k)^2} + \frac{\sum CF_t}{(1+k)^t}$$

Answer:

NPV_A = -5,000 + 500 + 1,000 + 1,000 + 1,500 + 2,500 + 1,000 = $469

$(1.084)^1$ $(1.084)^2$ $(1.084)^3$ $(1.084)^4$ $(1.084)^5$ $(1.084)^6$

NPV_B = -2,000 + 500 + 1,500 + 1,500 + 1,500 + 1,500 + 1,500 = $3,929

$(1.084)^1$ $(1.084)^2$ $(1.084)^3$ $(1.084)^4$ $(1.084)^5$ $(1.084)^6$

When considering mutually exclusive projects and NPV alone, remember that the decision rule is to invest in the project with the greatest NPV. As Machine B has the greatest NPV, Newco should invest in Machine B.

METHODS FOR EVALUATING THE CAPITAL EXPENDITURE DECISIONS

One of the drawbacks of non-discounted techniques for evaluating investment criteria is the ignorance of timing of cash inflows and outflows. Another drawback of traditional techniques is that entire cash proceeds are not taken into consideration for analysis. Therefore, improper matching of cash inflows and outflows gives misleading results. Thus discounted payback period, Net present value.

Modified internal rate of return, and Profitability index have been developed to overcome the problems associated with traditional techniques.

Discounted Payback Period

This method has been developed to overcome the limitations of non-discounted payback period. Instead of normal cash inflows, discounted cash inflows are employed to calculate the payback period. It is the time required to recover the initial cost of investment through discounted inflows of a project.

Advantages

The advantages of discounted payback period are:

- It is easy to understand and calculate.
- It takes into account the time value of money.
- This method helps in selection of a profitable project from among mutually exclusive projects very easily.

Disadvantages

The disadvantages of discounted payback period are:

- It does not take into account the cash inflows that occur after the payback period.
- Selection of appropriate rate for discounting the cash flows is another problem.

Net Present Value

This is another method for evaluating the capital expenditure decision using the discounted cash flow method. Under this method a stipulated rate of interest, usually the cost of capital, is used to discount the cash inflows. The Net Present Value (NPV) is calculated by taking a difference between the sum of present value of cash inflows and sum of present value of cash outflows.

Symbolically, NPV of a project can be calculated as follows:

$$NPV = \frac{C_1}{(1+K)^1} + \frac{C_2}{(1+K)^2} + \cdots\cdots + \frac{C_n}{(1+K)^n} - C_o$$

$$= \sum_{t=1}^{n} C_t - C_o$$

Where, C_1, C_2,…………………, C_n = Cash inflows of different years

C_0= Cash outflows of the project.

The following rules should be adopted for accepting or rejecting a project under NPV:

When, NPV > zero – Accept the project.

NPV < zero – Reject the project.

NPV = zero – Be indifferent.

Advantages

The advantages of NPV are:

- It recognizes the time value of money.
- It takes into account the entire series of cash flows for analysis.
- Selection of project under mutually exclusive projects is easy under NPV

Disadvantages

The NPV method also suffers from certain limitations. These are;

- In comparison to traditional method, it is slight difficult to understand and calculate.
- Selection of the discount rate for discounting of cash inflows is another problem of NPV.

Internal Rate of Return

Internal Rate of Return (IRR) method also recognizes the time value of money. Unlike the NPV method a stipulated rate of interest is avoided. This method is also known as Yield on investment. Marginal efficiency of capital and Marginal productivity of capital.

The internal rate of return is that rate of discount which equates the present value of expected cash inflows from a project with present value of cash outflow. In other words, internal rate of return is that rate of discount which makes the net present value of a project equal to zero. Symbolically,

$$C_o = \frac{C_1}{(1+r)^1} + \frac{C_2}{(1+r)^2} + \cdots\cdots\cdots + \frac{C_n}{(1+r)^n}$$

$$C_o - \left\{ \frac{C_1}{(1+r)^1} + \frac{C_2}{(1+r)^2} + \cdots\cdots\cdots + \frac{C_n}{(1+r)^n} \right\} = 0$$

Where, C_0 = Initial outlay of a project

$C_1, C_2, \ldots\ldots C_n$ Expected cash inflows of the project

r = Internal rate of return.

The following rules should be adopted for accepting or rejecting a project under IRR method:

When IRR > Cost of Capital – Accept the project,

IRR < Cost of Capital – Reject the project, and

IRR = Cost of Capital – Be indifferent.

Advantages

The advantages of IRR are summarized below:

- It recognizes the time value of money.
- It considers cash inflows and cash outflows over the entire life of the project.
- In case of mutually exclusive projects, it helps select a project very easily.

Disadvantages

The IRR suffers-from the following disadvantages:

- It involves lengthy and tedious calculations.
- Sometimes a project may have multiple IRR which confuses users.

- Projects selected on the basis of higher IRR may not be profitable in all cases.

Computation of IRR

While computing IRR the following situations may arise:

a. Equal Series Future Cash Inflows:

When the future cash inflows from a project are equal the following steps may be followed for computing the IRR

Step I: Divide the initial cash outflow by annual cash inflow, *i.e.* Payback period.

Step II: Search the nearest discount factor considering the life of the project.

Step III: The rate of interest corresponding to the discount factor gives you the internal rate of return.

Modified Internal Rate of Return

Modified internal rate of return (MIRR) has been developed to resolve some of the problems of IRR. Firstly, IRR assumes that positive cash inflows from a project are reinvested at the same rate of return as that of the project. This is an unrealistic assumption because it will be reinvested at the rate closer to cost of capital. Secondly, more than one IRR can be found if a project has alternative positive and negative cash inflows, which leads to confusion.

However, MIRR gives only one rate. Under MIRR all cash inflows are brought to terminal value using a specific discount rate, generally the cost of capital. MIRR is that rate which equates the terminal value of cash inflows with the compounded value of cash outflows.

The same criteria as used in IRR are used for accepting and rejecting a project in case of MIRR also.

Advantages

Mirr offers the following advantages:

- It recognizes the time value of money.

- It considers cash flows over the entire life of the project.
- It provides a single rate and thus avoids confusion.

Disadvantages

Although this method is better than IRR, it suffers from certain disadvantages, which are:

- It is difficult to understand.
- It involves lengthy and tedious calculations.

Profitability Index:

Profitability index or benefit cost ratio is the ratio of present values of future inflows and outflows of a project. It is a relative measure of an investment decision.

It can be calculated by using the following formula:

PI = Present value of cash inflows/ Present value of cash outflows

The following rules should be followed for accepting or rejecting a project under PI:

When, PI > I, accept the project, and

When, PI < 1, reject the project.

Advantages:

The following are the advantages of PI:

- It is simple to calculate as compared to IRR.
- It recognizes the time value of money.
- It takes into account all cash inflows and outflows of a project.
- It is better than NPV for selection of a project if the projects involve different capital outlays.

Disadvantages

Profitability index suffers from the following disadvantages:

- It is complex to calculate.
- Selection of rate for discounting of cash flows is another problem.

INVESTMENT DECISIONS - CAPITAL BUDGETING

Capital budgeting is vital in marketing decisions. Decisions on investment, which take time to mature, have to be based on the returns which that investment will make. Unless the project is for social reasons only, if the investment is unprofitable in the long run, it is unwise to invest in it now.

Often, it would be good to know what the present value of the future investment is, or how long it will take to mature (give returns). It could be much more profitable putting the planned investment money in the bank and earning interest, or investing in an alternative project.

Capital budgeting versus current expenditures

A capital investment project can be distinguished from current expenditures by two features:

- Such projects are relatively large
- A significant period of time (more than one year) elapses between the investment outlay and the receipt of the benefits..

As a result, most medium-sized and large organisations have developed special procedures and methods for dealing with these decisions. A systematic approach to capital budgeting implies:

- The formulation of long-term goals
- The creative search for and identification of new investment opportunities
- Classification of projects and recognition of economically and/or statistically dependent proposals
- The estimation and forecasting of current and future cash flows
- A suitable administrative framework capable of transferring the required information to the decision level
- The controlling of expenditures and careful monitoring of crucial aspects of project execution

- A set of decision rules which can differentiate acceptable from unacceptable alternatives is required.

The classification of investment projects

- By project size: Small projects may be approved by departmental managers. More careful analysis and Board of Directors' approval is needed for large projects of, say, half a million dollars or more.
- By type of benefit to the firm:
  - An increase in cash flow
  - A decrease in risk
  - An indirect benefit (showers for workers, etc).
- By degree of dependence:
  - Mutually exclusive projects (can execute project A or B, but not both)
  - Complementary projects: taking project A increases the cash flow of project B.
  - Substitute projects: taking project A decreases the cash flow of project B.
- By degree of statistical dependence:
  - Positive dependence
  - Negative dependence
  - Statistical independence.
- By type of cash flow:
  - Conventional cash flow: only one change in the cash flow sign

    e.g. -/++++ or +/—, etc
  - Non-conventional cash flows: more than one change in the cash flow sign,

    e.g. +/-/+++ or -/+/-/++++, etc.

The economic evaluation of investment proposals

The analysis stipulates a decision rule for:

- Accepting or
- Rejecting investment projects

The Time Value of Money

Recall that the interaction of lenders with borrowers sets an equilibrium rate of interest.

Borrowing is only worthwhile if the return on the loan exceeds the cost of the borrowed funds.

Lending is only worthwhile if the return is at least equal to that which can be obtained from alternative opportunities in the same risk class.

The interest rate received by the lender is made up of:

- The time value of money: the receipt of money is preferred sooner rather than later. Money can be used to earn more money. The earlier the money is received, the greater the potential for increasing wealth. Thus, to forego the use of money, you must get some compensation.
- The risk of the capital sum not being repaid. This uncertainty requires a premium as a hedge against the risk, hence the return must be commensurate with the risk being undertaken.
- Inflation: money may lose its purchasing power over time. The lender must be compensated for the declining spending/purchasing power of money. If the lender receives no compensation, he/she will be worse off when the loan is repaid than at the time of lending the money.

Future Values/Compound Interest

Future value (FV) is the value in dollars at some point in the future of one or more investments.

FV consists of:

- The original sum of money invested, and
- The return in the form of interest.

The general formula for computing Future Value is as follows:

$$FV_n = V_o (l + r)^n$$

where

V_0 is the initial sum invested

r is the interest rate

n is the number of periods for which the investment is to receive interest.

Thus we can compute the future value of what V_0 will accumulate to in n years when it is compounded annually at the same rate of r by using the above formula.

6

Investment Companies with Portfolios

Other investment companies such as mutual funds differ from asset-backed securities insofar as their investment holdings can change over time, as the investment company manager is allowed to buy and sell assets for the pool. Mutual funds are the most widely known of this type of investment company. Mutual funds sell shares to the public and use the money to invest primarily into assets for which there is an active resale market (i.e., into assets that can be easily and quickly sold).

Other investment companies with varying portfolios either raise money privately from specified investors (such as unitrusts, private money management companies, and hedge funds) and/ or invest primarily into assets for which there is no active resale market (such as REITs that invest into real estate and venture capital firms that invest into the stock of very small companies).

Some investment companies (such as private money management companies and hedge funds) tend to cater tend to cater to larger investors, while others are offered only to specific tax-exempt investors (e.g., unitrusts are sold to endowment funds and trusts, whose tax-exempt status and desire to spend a stable amount of money each year motivates most unitrusts to be set up to pay out to unitholders a fixed annual percentage of NAV regardless of capital gains and other investment income).

Most such investment companies can be evaluated just as mutual funds are (although there may be less public information available about them). For investment companies with large holdings of illiquid assets, however, it is generally not possible to compute NAV (one exception is a real estate investment company offered by the Teachers Insurance and Annuity Association, or TIAA), and so somewhat different methodologies must be used to analyse these investment companies.

GENERAL CHARACTERISTICS OF MUTUAL FUNDS

mutual funds are organizations that pool investors' money into various investments, of which 85% must be liquid marketable securities for which there is an active resale market. Most mutual funds are members of a family of mutual funds with a single administrative organization (such as Vanguard), which offers many mutual fund choices under the same umbrella, address, and phone number (allowing for ease in transferring money between funds in the same mutual fund family).

Most mutual funds require each new shareholder to initially invest a minimum amount (such as $1000) into the fund (over 25% of all funds in existence in 1997 required minimum initial investments of over $1000). However, many funds have smaller initial minimums for Individual Retirement Accounts (IRAs). Smaller investors can sometimes circumvent any such restrictions by borrowing an amount to meet the initial minimum and then redeeming fund shares to repay the loan. Mutual funds generally allow accounts that have been set up to have less than the initial minimum if the investor enters into an automatic investment plan where some small amount (such as $25 monthly) is periodically invested into the account. Alternatively, it is possible to buy mutual funds through some brokers such as Accutrade (1-800-228-3011) that permit (in return for an initial brokerage fee of about $27) investing as little as $100 into any of over 7600 different mutual funds as long as the investor pledges to invest at least $100 per quarter thereafter (without brokerage fees).

Once the money is raised from investors, the managers of the mutual funds buy and sell assets within a prespecified category of investment as they see fit. Such buying and selling of assets represents portfolio turnover. Turnover is often measured as the total dollar amount of asset sales in a fund divided by the total dollar amount of assets in the fund (so that 200% annual turnover on a fund with $10 million in assets indicates that the fund has sold $20 million in assets over the year, implying that the fund, on average, replaced its assets twice over the year by selling existing security holdings and buying new ones).

Mutual funds can offer expertise in investment selection and diversification within a stated category of permitted investments as well as other services. In return for these services, mutual fund managers levy expense fees on the pool of money in the fund. These expenses are typically levied or accrued daily, although the funds usually quote these expenses on an annualized basis as a per cent of assets. Besides a normal fee levied as a percentage of assets, some funds (such as hedge funds and futures funds) also charge funds a fee equal to a percentage of the profits of the fund.

The expense ratios of mutual funds normally do not include much of the transaction costs of trading. The transaction costs caused by portfolio turnover are typically included in the total prices paid for purchases and in the net prices received for asset sales. As a result, such costs are frequently difficult to measure although they can be approximated by applying 1998 Keim and Madhavan data on institutional trading costs to fund turnover figures.

As mutual funds receive interest and dividends from their investments and earn profits from the sale of investments at prices in excess of the amount paid, they generate income that usually exceeds the expenses they charge their funds. All such net income must generally be paid out to their shareholders in the form of a dividend (and the mutual fund thereby avoids being taxed on the net income). Although such dividends can be paid at any time over the course of the year, mutual fund dividends from regular interest and dividend income are typically paid monthly or quarterly, while gains from the sale of securities are normally paid out only at the end of the year.

Open-end Funds

Some mutual funds called open-end funds also offer an additional service of offering to buy or sell any shares requested at the net asset value per share (NAV) at the end of any business day. NAV is computed as:

NAV = (Market Value of Fund Assets - Fund Liabilities)/ Shares, where the fund's estimate of fair value is used for any non-trading assets held.

Requests to buy or sell shares may be made directly to the fund, often via a toll-free 800 number, or through brokers and financial planners who agree to trade the mutual fund shares for investors (typically for a fee that is charged either to the investor or to the mutual fund).

Payment for fund share redemptions can be made via wire, electronic funds, or mailed check at the request of the shareholder. In addition, many funds (especially those that invest into fixed-income securities) permit shareholders to write checks on their investments (writing a check on a fund results in automatic share sales at net asset value when it clears through to the mutual fund). Regardless of how redemptions are made, open-end mutual funds provide a substantial amount of liquidity to investors by agreeing to redeem shares at net asset value.

Some open-end mutual funds levy an explicit sales fee on purchases and/or sales of shares of the fund. This sales fee is called a load (which can't exceed 8.5% of the investment by U.S. law). Sales fees levied on purchases of open-end mutual fund shares are often called front-end loads. Funds that levy such a front-end fee are normally called load funds. Sales fees that are levied by some mutual funds on share redemptions at the NAV are called back-end loads. Some funds levy only a front-end load or only a back-end load, while other funds levy both. Although the entire load is kept by the mutual fund administrator if the transaction is made directly with the mutual fund, many transactions are made through financial planners and brokers who are paid a portion of the load (typically half).

Some load funds give investors the choice of how they would like to pay their load by offering several different types of shares. For instance, some mutual funds allow investors to purchase A-class shares that levy only a normal front-end load but also permit investors to buy B-class shares that levy no front-end load but instead charge the investor an annual load. In the latter case (the B shares), the load must be paid by the investor directly just for holding the shares (and it is not charged to the mutual fund, so it does not increase the mutual fund's expense ratios). The shares with an annual load would be preferred by more active traders, while the front-end loaded shares might be preferred by long-term investors.

Many back-end loads are reduced or even eliminated for investors who hold the shares for a specified minimum length of time. For instance, many back-end loaded funds levy a 7% fee to sell if the fund is held less than one year, 6% if the fund is held less than 2 years, 5% if the fund is held less then 3 years, etc., until the backend load disappears for investors who have held the shares at least 7 years. Other mutual funds have small back-end loads (like 1%) that disappear if an investor holds the shares just three months.

Many funds do not levy any load and are called no-load funds. However, in practice, any fund without a front-end load is often called a no-load fund if any back-end load is eliminated for investors who hold onto the fund shares long enough.

Some funds pay salespeople (such as brokers and financial planners) for soliciting new shareholders but do not levy any load (neither front-end, back-end, or annual load) directly on investors owning or trading shares. Instead, many of these funds pay the sales fee or commission out of the fund itself in the form of higher daily expenses. Such sales fees (as well as other marketing and distribution costs) charged to the fund as a whole are called 12b-1 expenses and must be disclosed by the mutual fund. These funds are technically no-load funds although they frequently have higher than average annual fees charged to the fund because of the 12b-1 expenses. In 1998, 40% of open-end mutual fund transactions were made directly with the mutual funds. Another 36% were made through full-service brokers, 12% through commercial banks, 7% through financial planners, and 5% through insurance companies and discount brokers (in the future, an increasing share of trades was expected to be made through financial planners and directly with the mutual funds, while a declining share of mutual transactions were forecast through banks and full service brokers).

Closed-End Funds

Open-end mutual funds contrast with closed-end funds which are not required to redeem shares at the net asset value. Although closed-end funds are not obligated to redeem shares, these fund shares may usually be sold to other investors in the market at whatever price the other investors are willing to pay. the price investors are willing to pay for closed-end funds is different from NAV. Some closed-end funds buy up some of their own shares in the market when the price falls far below NAV.

TYPES OF MUTUAL FUNDS

Many mutual funds restrict themselves to only one category of investments such as domestic equities. However, some funds have the freedom to invest in a mixture of asset categories.

For instance, balanced funds can invest in both domestic equities and bonds, while asset allocation funds can invest in most any type of asset (and these latter funds typically diversify into stocks, bonds, real asset investments, and foreign assets).

Other funds are restricted to only a specific subsection of an asset category, such as investment-grade bonds. Some mutual funds even invest in other pools, such as GNMA funds. In 1991, there was $1.347 trillion invested into mutual funds in the U.S. (including $368 billion in equity funds, $439 billion in bond and other fixed-income funds, and $540 billion in money market funds) and $1.375 trillion invested into foreign mutual funds (including $396 billion in French mutual funds, $349 billion in Japanese mutual funds, and $175 billion in German mutual funds, with fixed-income and money market funds making up over 50% of the total). By 1997, there was about $4 trillion invested into U.S. mutual funds, of which over half was invested into stock funds.

There are two general categories of mutual funds: actively managed funds and passively managed funds. Actively managed funds have substantial discretion as to which assets will be purchased by the fund. Passively managed funds are typically restricted to only specified securities with specified weights.

The typical passively managed fund is an index fund, which is constrained to investments in an index of assets (such as the S&P 500) in proportions that approximate the weightings of the index. The purpose of an index fund is to approximately match the performance of the index. Because the assets in the index change from time to time (due to acquisitions and bankruptcies, for instance), the investments of the index fund must be periodically rebalanced.

Such portfolio rebalancing differentiates them from unit investment trusts, which are otherwise very similar insofar as both index funds and unit trusts are passively managed. Another difference between index funds and unit trusts is that some active selection may go into choosing the initial investments for the unit trust, whereas an index fund blindly buys the stocks in an index.

In addition, unit trusts typically have a specified termination date, whereas index funds do not. Although most unit trusts and open-end mutual funds are open-end (agreeing to redeem assets at NAV), there are a few closed-end index funds such as Spiders (an abbreviation for S&P Depository Receipts), which invest into the S&P500, and such as over a dozen different Webs, each of which invests into the equity index of a specified foreign country (like Germany).

Regardless of whether a mutual fund is passively or actively managed, most funds have only one class of stock that shares equally in all the investment income and capital gains of the fund. However, some mutual funds have several classes of stockholders.

For instance, dual funds have one class of shareholders with a claim on the fund's investment income (dividends and interest payments) while another class of shareholders has a claim on the capital gains of the fund.

More recently, a new type of mutual fund has been developed whereby one class of preferred shareholders has a prior claim on the interest income of the fund up to a specified amount that varies with a specified money market interest rate, while the common shareholders of the mutual fund have a claim on all remaining investment income and capital gains. This latter capital structure is especially useful for municipal bond funds, as it gives the preferred shareholders a fairly secure money market interest rate that exceeds high-grade municipal money market rates, while allowing the common shareholders of the fund to obtain a leveraged investment in municipal bonds by essentially "borrowing" at a low tax-advantaged rate (because municipal securities are exempt from federal tax, they tend to have negative terms with yields below the risk-free Treasury rate.

There has been a great deal of discussion about the optimal size of a mutual fund. Although larger mutual funds tend to have lower administrative expenses due to economies of scale, they also often have higher trading costs because of the need to buy so much of a security to obtain a meaningful position. In addition, larger funds find it especially difficult to take significant positions on smaller companies without substantial trading costs. Overall, although it is nearly impossible to start a mutual with less than $1 million in assets, and administrative costs tend to be extremely high for funds with even $10 million in assets, there are many fund managers who believe that it is so counterproductive to be too large that they close their funds to new investors once they reach several billion dollars in assets.

There also exists a type of fund called a fund of funds that pools investors' money for purpose of investing into other mutual funds. Many of these fund of funds are offered by the administrator of a family of mutual funds to invest only into a portfolio of mutual funds in that family. Many funds of funds generally add an extra layer of annual expense (often called a wrap fee) for the service of determining for investors the mutual funds into which they are to invest (as little as 0.08% per year for Fidelity but closer to 2% for others, which is in addition to the annual expenses charged to the funds themselves into which the money is invested). However, some fund administrators (such as Vanguard, Scudder, and T. Rowe Price) do not charge for this service. There was $29 billion invested through such funds of funds in 1998.

Types of Mutual Funds and Similar Investment Companies

- A listing follows for many different types of mutual funds and other investment companies with varying portfolios that exist. Unless otherwise specified, each type may be either closed-end or open-end, depending on the individual investment company.
- Domestic Bond Funds - invest in domestic fixed-income securities (some of the funds may have a specified concentration in bonds with short, medium, or long maturities, while others may have a specified concentration in bonds with either low or high default risk —bond funds specified to invest into debt with higher default risk are often called "high income funds" or "high yield funds").
- *Money market funds**: Invest in money market instruments.
- *Corporate bond funds*: Invest in corporate bonds.
- *Municipal bond funds*: Invest in bonds issued by state and local governments. *government bond funds* - invest in bonds issued by the federal government and/or federal agencies. *mortgage REITs* (real estate investment trusts) - closed-end investment companies that invest into mortgages.

- *Domestic Stock Funds*: Invest in domestic equities
- *Balanced funds*: Invest in stocks and bonds *preferred*
- *Stock funds*: Invest into preferred stocks (usually high-yielding investment grade preferred).
- *Income funds*: Invest in stocks (and/or bonds) with high current yields.
- *Growth funds*: Invest in stocks with low current yields.
- *Small cap funds*: Invest in stocks of companies with smaller market capitaliza-tions (as measured by the market value of all equity, which is computed as the market price times the number of shares outstanding) large cap funds-invest in stocks of larger companies *specialized funds*-invest in stocks of a particular industry (such as health care).
- *Index funds*: Invest into a specified index of stocks (such as the S&P 500).
- *Option funds*: Invest in stocks and options *R&D*
- *Partnerships*: Closed-end investment companies that invest directly in research and development projects (especially related to drug development).
- *Venture capital companies:* Closed-end investment companies that invest in the stock of small companies for which there is no secondary market.
- *Real Asset Funds:* Invest in real assets or companies that produce real investment assets.
- *Real estate funds:* Invest in a portfolio of real estate equities.
- *Precious metals funds:* Invest in companies that mine gold and other precious metals.
- *Equity REITs* (real estate investment trusts) - closed-end investment companies that invest directly into real estate properties.
- *Rreal estate partnerships:* Closed-end investment companies that invest directly into real estate properties.
- *Oil and gas partnerships:* Closed-end investment

companies that invest directly into projects that explore for or pump petroleum.

- *Commodity funds or pools:* Funds that invest in commodity futures contracts.
- *Futures funds or pools:* Funds that invest in commodity and financial futures contracts.
- *Intemational Funds:* Invest in foreign securities
- *International bond funds*: Invest in foreign fixed-income securities.
- *International stock funds*: Invest in foreign equities.
- *Specialized country funds:* Invest in the assets (mostly stocks) of a single foreign country (such as Ireland).
- *Specialized regional funds:* Invest in the stocks of a singly region (such as Europe or Asia).
- *Emerging market funds:* Invest into less developed countries (such as Latin America and Southeast Asia).
- *Total Asset Management Funds:* Invest into several categories of assets (often into all four categories: stocks, bonds, real assets, and foreign assets).
- *Asset allocation funds*: Actively invest into stocks, bonds, and foreign assets, as - well as often into real assets.
- *Hedge funds*: Invest into any assets (including derivatives), taking both long and - short positions (with the positions often being fairly balanced or hedged in order to reduce exposure to systematic risk). The number of investors is usually restricted for regulatory purposes to be under 100, with each investor generally being required to invest at least $250,000 (since 1996, hedge funds have been allowed to have as many as 500 investors if each investor in the fund has a minimum of $5 million in marketable security investments).

  Most hedge funds are closed-end except on specific dates, such as the first business day of the year when redemptions may be made at net asset value. By 1998, there were several thousand hedge funds in existence (including many funds of funds that diversify into different hedge funds) with over $200 billion in assets (some limited empirical evidence indicates that, despite very high management fees, the surviving funds have generated double- digit rates of return on average while having low betas or correlation with the aggregate market portfolio of all assets). -

- *One special note on money market funds: these generally value securities at - cost and thereby maintain a constant NAV of $1 per share. Interest on the funds' investments are accrued to shareholders daily and paid at the end of the month. If there were ever a run by investors to redeem shares of a money market fund after interest rates had risen, the fund might have to sell assets at less than cost, and the NAV could fall below $1. However, despite frequent large gyrations in interest rates, only one money market fund in the U.S. has ever failed to redeem shares at a $1 NAV. As a result, money market funds are often considered to be virtually risk-free investments (as are most diversified portfolios of money market instruments).
- A large number of international mutual funds are also offered in foreign - countries. However, unlike many mutual funds in the U.S., most mutual funds in foreign countries charge an upfront load. For instance, until recently in Germany, there was a typical load of 5% for stock funds, 3% for bond funds, and 1% for - money market funds. Increasing financial integration, deregulation, and competition are changing that situation, however.

EVALUATING INVESTMENT COMPANIES WITH VARYING PORTFOLIOS

An analysis of mutual funds requires an examination of the most important characteristics of each fund. One of the most important functions of mutual funds is to provide diversification, and it is important to ensure that the selection of funds meets the investors' needs. Because most funds concentrate their investments in some particular category of assets (such as stocks), it is generally necessary to choose more than one fund. For instance, to achieve the diversification guidelines, an investor might need to invest into at least 4 different mutual funds: one for domestic equities, one for domestic bonds, one for real assets, and one for foreign assets (with more than these four funds being required if any of the funds has concentration in any individual securities, industries, or foreign regions). Although an investor with limited knowledge could blindly assign equal weights to each category (i.e., 25% into each investment category), or according to the approximate weights of the market portfolio of all securities as estimated i.e., about 20% into U.S. bonds, 20% into U.S. equities, 5% into U.S. real estate, and 55% into foreign bonds and equities), the per cent of wealth allocated to each fund concentrated in an investment category should optimally be set as a function of the type of aggregate fundamental analysis On the other hand, it is also possible to allow professional managers to determine the optimal allocation to each investment category. For instance, if one invested in a balanced fund, there would only be a need for a minimum of 3 different funds, as a balanced fund includes both domestic stock and bond holdings. It is actually possible to select just one fund, if it is an asset allocation fund that diversifies across all investment categories.

When choosing which funds, it is also important to exercise judgment with respect to various other criteria besides diversification. Among the most important information to examine on any fund are the fee or load charged directly to investors for buying or selling shares of the fund, the annual operating expenses charged to the fund for its administration, and the fund's historical performance in maximizing long-term returns net of those expenses. Guidelines for analyzing, researching, and choosing mutual funds and other investment companies with varying portfolios are provided.

Analysis of Mutual Fund Investments

For purposes of selecting a fund for each investment category, it is often useful to investigate 4 fund characteristics:

long-term past performance, annual expenses charged to investors, portfolio turnover, and the existence of a load. Generally, it is thought that, if a fund manager is more skillful than average, the expertise will show up in long-term past performance records in the form of high compounded rates of return. In addition, to the extent that a fund generates excessive expenses for its investors, either through annual expense fees, excessive trading costs, and/or explicit loads to buy or sell the fund's shares, the fund may under perform other funds long-term. Often, higher expenses charged to funds stem from inefficiency and/or the lack of economies of scale and scope (i.e., too few assets over which too many fixed expenses have to be spread), and, at some point, the return from additional trading and management effort does not offset the costs.

These hypotheses have been verified in empirical research that evaluates future returns as a function of the foregoing variables. For instance, empirical research does indicate that funds with good long-term past performance may be more likely to generate future good performance than funds with poor past performance. Performance is often measured by the total compounded rate of return over a long period of time like 4-10 years.

Funds that earned higher compounded rates of return relative to other funds that invest in that category of assets are more likely to do so in the future as well (although they are by no means assured of doing so).

Some studies have also found that funds which charge investors low annual expenses for managing the fund are more likely to provide investors with a higher net return after deducting those expenses. Annual expense ratios are generally compared to theexpense ratios of other funds that invest in that category of assets, and a low ratio would be one that is less than the average. For example, a stock fund with an expense ratio that is lower than the average for all stock funds would be low. Generally, a ratio less than 1% is considered to be fairly low for a stock fund, while a somewhat lower expense ratio would be expected for a bond fund. On the other hand, futures funds and hedge funds typically have extremely high expense ratios equal to 5% or more of assets (largely due to management incentive fees that often are set to take 20% of all profits), and many investors may choose to avoid these types of funds for this reason alone. A 1997 study by Collins and Mack indicates that a mutual fund family typically needs about $20 billion in assets to attain the economies of scale and scope to have the lowest expense ratios, and so investors may want to target only the largest mutual fund families. Some research also indicates that funds with low annual portfolio turnover are more likely to provide investors with higher net returns after deducting the frequently hidden transaction costs of their trading, although not all studies indicate a significant relationship. Like expense ratios, turnover ratios can be compared to the individual and average turnover ratios of other funds that invest into the same category of assets. Turnover ratios under 100% are often considered to be low.

Studies have found that no-load funds are more likely to generate higher net returns than load funds after deducting the sales fee from load fund returns. The load essentially represents compensation to the selling broker, financial planner, or other agent for the time spent helping the investor make investment decisions and choose a fund.

These findings imply that a simple and liquid means of diversifying into an optimal risky portfolio is to pick 4 open-end no-load funds: one that invests into stocks, one that invests into bonds, one that invests into real assets (such as real estate), and one that invests into foreign securities (such as foreign stocks and bonds). The funds would be selected based on the criteria of high compounded returns over a long time interval (like 5-10 years), low expenses, and low turnover, with all comparisons being made relative to other funds that concentrate in that category of assets (like comparing bond funds to other fixed-income funds, international stock funds to other international stock funds, etc.).

Without any knowledge of the relative attractiveness of the four investment categories, it is possible to assign naive equal weights of 25% to each of the 4 funds just to ensure diversification, or use the market weightings (to mimic the overall return on the market portfolio of all assets). However, many investors may prefer to conduct some of the tactical asset allocation analysis to determine the optimal weighting of each investment type in a risky portfolio.

Alternatively, a single no-load asset allocation fund that has good long-term performance, low expenses, and low turnover relative to other asset allocation funds can be chosen. An asset allocation fund typically invests into all 4 investment categories of investments according to the fund manager's own fundamental analysis of the relative attractiveness of each investment type (although many asset allocation funds do not invest a significant amount of money into real estate or other real assets). As a result, selection of an asset allocation fund would be all that investors need to do to construct their risky portfolio p (unless they need some additional real estate assets, which most individuals don't because they already have a large amount of money tied up in the house they are consuming). For instance, TIAA-CREF (1-800-223-1200) offers a no-load asset allocation fund with an initial minimum of only $250 (or $25 for investors agreeing to periodic deductions from their bank accounts) and with extremely low annual expenses of less than 0.50%.

Once investors have chosen optimal risky portfolios of mutual funds, they can then use the guidelines provided for determining the optimal allocation of wealth to that risky portfolio (or use the SIA PORTFOLIO software for a more in-depth analysis within the context of a total financial plan). The remaining amount would be put into risk-free assets. Often, as explained, money market funds are considered to be risk-free assets, so that investors may select a money market fund in order to round out their selection of risky funds to meet their risk-aversion needs.

In all cases, investors can invest into a much larger assortment of mutual funds (as well as other assets), if they are unable to choose a single asset allocation fund or 4 single category funds that are superior to all other risky investment opportunities. For instance, many investors select several stock funds, including some from specific industry sectors, perhaps one that concentrates into growth stocks (with low dividend yields), and one that concentrates into income stocks (with high dividend yields). Choice of specialized funds enables the investor to be more selective in the proportions and timing of investments into various sectors of a given category of asset (like more into growth stocks and biotech stocks when the investor feels that technology stocks are under priced).

In addition to using long-term performance, expenses, and turnover to evaluate mutual fund investments, many investors also analyse the investment strategy of the mutual fund. For instance, some mutual funds use purely quantitative analysis to select stocks, while most funds use a great deal of subjective judgment.

Investors who believe that subjective judgment is the best method of achieving consistently good performance may wish to avoid the funds that employ largely quantitative analysis, regardless of their long-term past performance record. Similarly, many mutual funds have specialized investment strategies that cause them to concentrate in stocks with either high or low P/e stocks.

Investors who believe that stocks with low P/e ratios are more likely to have high value/price ratios would probably prefer to avoid funds with strategies that concentrate in stocks with high P/e ratios. If an investor believes that investments in specific industries or foreign countries are overpriced currently, he or she may choose to avoid funds that have concentrated holdings in those industries or countries. Investors who believe that interest rates are going to fall might weight their portfolios more towards bond mutual funds that hold fixed-income securities with longer maturities.

Investors who believe that yield premiums for default risk are very high might concentrate in funds that invest into bonds with lower credit ratings. In all cases, the subjective judgment can be used to determine whether a mutual fund is investing into assets that have high expected returns relative to their contribution to portfolio risk.

Moreover, some investors consider the size of a fund to be an important decision criteria. For instance, investors who believe that larger funds can have economies of scale and scope should invest into mutual funds with more assets (like over $1 billion). On the other hand, investors who feel that there are only a very limited number of investment opportunities with abnormally high return potential might be inclined to choose funds with a small amount of assets under management (e.g., under $100 million), since smaller funds can more easily concentrate their investments into a limited number of superior investment opportunities without bidding up the price with their purchases.

Some investors may also prefer to invest in funds whose top managers have had good long-term track records with the funds. Such investors might concentrate on funds which have had good long-term past performance and which have had the same managers over that time period. For purposes of conducting this type of analysis, numerous information sources exist.

7

Investment Process Management

An asset or item that is purchased with the hope that it will generate income or appreciate in the future. In an economic sense, an investment is the purchase of goods that are not consumed today but are used in the future to create wealth. In finance, an investment is a monetary asset purchased with the idea that the asset will provide income in the future or appreciate and be sold at a higher price.

The word investment can be defined in many ways according to different theories and principles. It is a term that can be used in a number of contexts. However, the different meanings of "investment" are more alike than dissimilar.

Generally, investment is the application of money for earning more money. Investment also means savings or savings made through delayed consumption. According to economics, investment is the utilization of resources in order to increase income or production output in the future. An amount deposited into a bank or machinery that is purchased in anticipation of earning income in the long run are both examples of investments.

Although there is a general broad definition to the term investment, it carries slightly different meanings to different industrial sectors.

Investment Definition According to economists, investment refers to any physical or tangible asset, for example, a building or machinery and equipment. On the other hand, finance professionals define an investment as money utilized for buying financial assets, for examplestocks, bonds, bullion, real properties, and precious items.

Investment definition according to finance, the practice of investment refers to the buying of a financial product or any valued item with an anticipation that positive returns will be received in the future.

The most important feature of financial investments is that they carry high market liquidity. The method used for evaluating the value of a financial investment is known as valuation.

Definition of investment according to business theories, investment is that activity in which a manufacturer buys a physical asset, for example, stock or production equipment, in expectation that this will help the business to prosper in the long run.

INVESTMENT OBJECTIVE

The options for investing our savings are continually increasing, yet every single investment vehicle can be easily categorized according to three fundamental characteristics - safety, income and growth - which also correspond to types of investor objectives. While it is possible for an investor to have more than one of these objectives, the success of one must come at the expense of others. Let's examine these three types of objectives, the investments that are used to achieve them and the ways in which investors can incorporate them in devising a strategy.

Safety

While no investment option is completely safe, there are products that are preferred by investors who are risk averse. Some individuals invest with an objective of keeping their money safe, irrespective of the rate of return they receive on their capital. Such near-safe products include fixed deposits, savings accounts, government bonds, etc.

Perhaps there is truth to the axiom that there is no such thing as a completely safe and secure investment. Yet we can get close to ultimate safety for our investment funds through the purchase of government-issued securities in stable economic systems, or through the purchase of the highest quality corporate bonds issued by the economy's top companies. Such securities are arguably the best means of preserving principal while receiving a specified rate of return.

The safest investments are usually found in the money market, which includes such securities as Treasury bills (T-bills), certificates of deposit (CD), commercial paper or bankers' acceptance slips, or in the fixed income (bond) market in the form of municipal and other government bonds, and in corporate bonds. The securities listed above are ordered according to the typical spectrum of increasing risk and, in turn, increasing potential yield. To compensate for their higher risk, corporate bonds return a greater yield than T-bills. It is important to realize that there's an enormous range of relative risk within the bond market. At one end are government and high-grade corporate bonds, which are considered some of the safest investments around; at the other end are junk bonds, which have a lower investment grade and may have more risk than some of the more speculative stocks. In other words, it's incorrect to think that corporate bonds are always safe, but most instruments from the money market can be considered very safe.

Income

Some individuals invest with the objective of generating a second source of income.Consequently, they invest in products that offer returns regularly like bank fixeddeposits, corporate and government bonds, etc.

Other Objectives

The safest investments are also the ones that are likely to have the lowest rate of income return or yield. Investors must inevitably sacrifice a degree of safety if they want to increase their yields. This is the inverse relationship between safety and yield: as yield increases, safety generally goes down and vice versa.

In order to increase their rate of investment return and take on risk above that of money market instruments or government bonds, investors may choose to purchase corporate bonds or preferred shares with lower investment ratings. Investment grade bonds rated at A or AA are slightly riskier than AAA bonds, but presumably also offer a higher income return than AAA bonds. Similarly, BBB rated bonds can be thought to carry medium risk but offer less potential income than junk bonds, which offer the highest potential bond yields available but at the highest possible risk. Junk bonds are the most likely to default.

Most investors, even the most conservative-minded ones, want some level of income generation in their portfolios, even if it's just to keep up with the economy's rate of inflation. But maximizing income return can be an overarching principle for a portfolio, especially for individuals who require a fixed sum from their portfolio every month. A retired person who requires a certain amount of money every month is well served by holding reasonably safe assets that provide funds over and above other income-generating assets, such as pension plans, for example.

Growth

While safety is an important objective for many investors, a majority of them invest to receive capital gains, which means that they want the invested amount to grow.There are several options in the market that offer this benefit. These include stocks, mutual funds, gold, property, commodities, etc. It is important to note that capital gains attract taxes, the percentage of which varies according to the number of years of investment.

Growth of Capital

This discussion has thus far been concerned only with safety and yield as investing objectives, and has not considered the potential of other assets to provide a rate of return from an increase in value, often referred to as a capital gain. Capital gains are entirely different from yield in that they are only realized when the security is sold for a price that is higher than the price at which it was originally purchased. Selling at a lower price is referred to as a capital loss. Therefore, investors seeking capital gains are likely not those who need a fixed, ongoing source of investment returns from their portfolio, but rather those who seek the possibility of longer-term growth.

Growth of capital is most closely associated with the purchase of common stock, particularly growth securities, which offer low yields but considerable opportunity for increase in value. For this reason, common stock generally ranks among the most speculative of investments as their return depends on what will happen in an unpredictable future. Blue-chip stocks, by contrast, can potentially offer the best of all worlds by possessing reasonable safety, modest income and potential for growth in capital generated by long-term increases in corporate revenues and earnings as the company matures. Yet rarely is any common stock able to provide the near-absolute safety and income-generation of government bonds.

It is also important to note that capital gains offer potential tax advantages by virtue of their lower tax rate in most jurisdictions. Funds that are garnered through common stock offerings, for example, are often geared toward the growth plans of small companies, a process that is extremely important for the growth of the overall economy. In order to encourage investments in these areas, governments choose to tax capital gains at a lower rate than income. Such systems serve to encourage entrepreneurship and the founding of new businesses that help the economy grow.

KINDS OF INVESTMENTS

There are many kinds of investments, each with its own level of risk and return. The more money you can make from an investment, the higher the risk that you might not get all your money back. So it's good to have a mix of different kinds of investments to spread your risk and get the results you want. And it's important to do your homework and get investment advice so you understand the risks before you hand over your money.

Bank Savings

Savings accounts with New Zealand's major banks are one of the most common and least risky ways to store your money for the short term. Credit unions and building societies also offer savings accounts. When you deposit money in an account you are lending it to the bank, which pays you some interest in return. The interest you can earn is relatively low, so savings accounts are not the best option if you are looking for long-term growth.

Term Deposits

Like savings accounts, term deposits also pay interest. The difference is that you agree to lend your money to the bank for a fixed period of time such as 6 or 12 months in return for a higher rate of interest.

Sometimes you can't withdraw the money during the term of the investment. In other cases you can, but get paid a lower rate of interest. Term deposits are sometimes called 'fixed interest' investments.

Bonds

A bond is like an IOU issued by a government, council, or company. You lend them your money for a number of years, and they promise to pay a certain interest rate – called a coupon. The level of risk involved when investing in bonds depends on the issuer. Unlike term deposits, you can sell your bonds early. However the price you will get can go up and down. Bonds are also sometimes called fixed interest investments.

Shares

When you buy a share, you're buying a small part of a company. If that company makes money, you may be paid a share of the profit, called a dividend. Like house prices, share prices are generally expected to go up over time and give you a 'capital gain' on your money when you sell. However, prices can fall in value as well.

Property

Returns from investing in property come from rental income and from any increase in the value of property over time – called capital gain. Some people view their own home as an investment because it may grow in value. It doesn't have the income that letting property to other individuals or businesses brings. You can invest in commercial property directly, or through managed funds.

Managed Funds and KiwiSaver

A managed fund is a financial product that buys a number of shares and other investments such as property, term deposits, and cash. The buying decisions are made by expert managers.

When you buy units in a managed fund you are spreading your savings across a range of shares or other investments within the fund. That means that your money is 'diversified'. If you are a member of a KiwiSaver scheme you are already investing in a type of managed fund.

Alternatives

Alternatives is a broad term often used to describe investments that fall outside the standard asset classes of cash, bonds, shares and property. Alternatives include commodities, currency and derivatives.

Commodities (including Gold)

These investments don't pay interest or dividends, but do increase and decrease in value which can result in a capital gain. The value of commodities often moves in the opposite direction of other asset classes (e.g. when share prices go down, gold often increases in value, and vice versa), so investors sometimes buy them to try to protect their money.

Currency (Foreign Exchange)

As well as being used to buy goods and services, foreign currency is also used as an investment. Currency investors are looking for higher interest rates overseas, or hoping exchange rates will move in their favour resulting in a capital gain. Investors, including managed funds, may also use currency to protect, or 'hedge', other investments that are invested overseas.

Derivatives (Including options and Futures)

Derivatives are generally only used by more sophisticated investors, such as managed funds. This can be a confusing and complex area of investing. However, derivatives are built on a fairly simple concept - allowing people to protect themselves, or 'hedge', against future price movements. For example a farmer can fix the price today, for the milk they will supply in the future. While at the same time, a supermarket owner can fix the price now for the milk they will receive in the future. Professional investors still use derivatives for this purpose, but can now also use them to invest more efficiently.

Other Alternatives

Other alternatives can include things such as private equity, hedge funds, fine wine, exotic cars and stamps. There are different reasons for buying each one, but, as with all investments, their value can go up or down.

THE INVESTMENT PROCESS

As investors, we would all like to beat the market handily, and we would all like to pick "great" investments on instinct. However, while intuition is undoubtedly a part of the process of investing, it is just part of the process. As investors, it is not surprising that we focus so much of our energy and efforts on investment philosophies and strategies, and so little on the investment process. It is far more interesting to read about how Peter Lynch picks stocks and what makes Warren Buffett a valuable investor, than it is to talk about the steps involved in creating a portfolio or in executing trades. Though it does not get sufficient attention, understanding the investment process is critical for every investor for several reasons:

- The investment process outlines the steps in creating a portfolio, and emphasizes the sequence of actions involved from understanding the investor?s risk preferences to asset allocation and selection to performance evaluation. By emphasizing the sequence, it provides for an orderly way in which an investor can create his or her own portfolio or a portfolio for someone else.
- The investment process provides a structure that allows investors to see the source of different investment strategies and philosophies. By so doing, it allows investors to take the hundreds of strategies that they see described in the common press and in investment newsletters and to trace them to their common roots.
- The investment process emphasizes the different components that are needed for an investment strategy to by successful, and by so doing explain why so many strategies that look good on paper never work for those who use them.

The best way of describing this book is by noting what it does not do. It does not emphasize individual investors or push an investment philosophy. It does not focus heavily on coming up with strategies that beat the market, though there is reference to some of them in the course of the book. Instead, it talks about the process of investing and how this process is the same no matter what investment philosophy one might have. The book is built around the investment process. The process always starts with the investor and understanding his or her needs and preferences.

For a portfolio manager, the investor is a client, and the first and often most significant part of the investment process is understanding the client?s needs, the client?s tax status and most importantly, his or her risk preferences. For an individual investor constructing his or her own portfolio, this may seem simpler, but understanding one?s own needs and preferences is just as important a first step as it is for the portfolio manager. The next part of the process is the actual construction of the portfolio, which we divide into three sub-parts. The first of these is the decision on how to allocate the portfolio across different asset classes defined broadly as equities, fixed income securities and real assets (such as real estate, commodities and other assets). This asset allocation decision can also be framed in terms of investments in domestic assets versus foreign assets, and the factors driving this decision. The second component is the asset selection decision, where individual assets are picked within each asset class to make up the portfolio.

In practical terms, this is the step where the stocks that make up the equity component, the bonds that make up the fixed income component and the real assets that make up the real asset component are picked. The final component is execution, where the portfolio is actually put together, where investors have to trade off transactions cost against transactions speed. While the importance of execution will vary across investment strategies, there are many investors who have failed at this stage in the process.

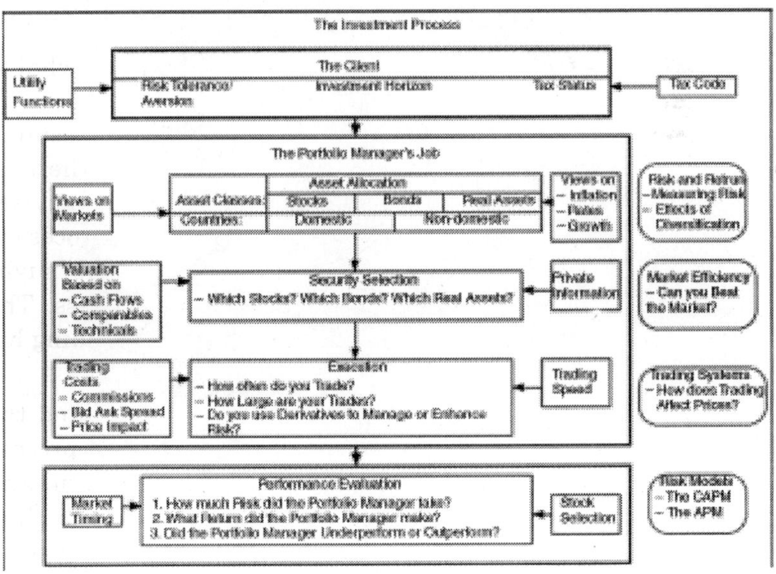

The final part of the process, and often the most painful one for professional money managers, is the performance evaluation. Investing is after all focused on one objective and one objective alone, which is to make the most money you can, given the risk constraints you operate under.

Investors are not forgiving of failure and unwilling to accept even the best of excuses, and loyalty to money managers is not a commonly found trait. By the same token, performance evaluation is just as important to the individual investor who constructs his or her own portfolio, since the feedback from it should largely determine how that investor approaches investing in the future.

Our core investment process is the product of our *Focus on Change* philosophy, and combines asset allocation, security selection, portfolio construction, dealing and risk management.

We believe high-quality research drives outperformance and so we carry out rigorous research in all the major financial markets. We have invested heavily in state-of-the-art technology and have built proprietary systems to add value at every stage. While the investment process for each asset class is different, there are some core elements:

Asset Allocation

The Global Investment Group (GIG) considers where markets are in their own cycles and determines the best allocation of assets, between equities, bonds and other types of investment. This group is made up of senior investment professionals and is responsible for providing overall strategic and tactical focus to our decision-making process. This focus finds expression in theHouse View, which communicates the most favoured and least favoured asset classes in the construction of client investment portfolios.

Security Selection

Our asset managers focus on selecting the best possible individual assets. They analyse the key drivers of prices, assess what's factored in to these prices, and judge what is likely to shift investors' expectations. Combined analyst and portfolio management responsibilities mean our asset managers must have the highest conviction in the assets they recommend. These recommendations can only be included in our portfolios once they've been peer reviewed.

Portfolio Construction

Our asset managers select the most convincing investment ideas to construct portfolios around specific benchmarks, while also taking into account our clients' risk profiles.

Dealing

Our team of experienced dealers finds the best available terms in the market, allowing our asset managers to focus entirely on research and the construction of investment portfolios.

Risk Management

Our investment process doesn't end with the purchase of assets. We continually monitor our portfolios to ensure they are meeting their objectives within the defined risk parameters. We therefore have a dedicated risk management team that measures and monitors risk. In addition, our asset managers play an active role in managing risk within clients' portfolios.

INVESTMENT AND SPECULATION ARE DIFFERENT THINGS

In this series, we'll look at the difference between investment and speculation, and investment and spending.

Even if you're not that much into finance, it's wise to know the basics, not just to make sense of the world and feel smugly superior to pundits (who may represent the lowest known form of life), but more importantly to you personally – to help you make smarter choices with your own money.

Investment vs. Speculation

There is an enormous difference. You'd be surprised how

many people, including many whose jobs it is to know, don't know, at least not in a clear and conscious way.

Aside from plain old ignorance, the reasons are partly cosmetic: "*Investing*" sounds good, while"*speculation*" is a bit of a dirty word. So people prefer to talk about investing even when they're quite obviously speculating.

The confusion is so common that many people don't know what it is they're doing with their money. That's every middle manager who has a few shares of whatever, because that's part of his aspirational identity.

The essential difference is this:

- Investment is based on changes of value.
- Speculation is based on changes of price.

You may now feel there is a grey area between them, where they can mix. You're right if you do. But most of the time, the difference is clear enough to make a binary distinction useful.

For an easy, ideal example, investing is when you buy and plant an apple seedling, wait for it to grow (and/or actively care for it), and then sell the fruit for a steady stream of income, or the grown tree itself for much more. Speculation is buying an apple tree and selling it at a higher price, while it hasn't changed or done anything. Nothing wrong with that, but its important to keep the difference in mind.

Other differences:

- Investment tends to be long term (fundamental value usually grows at ponderous pace), speculation tends to be shorter term. An investor might rebalance his or her portfolio only rarely when conditions change, whereas a speculator might make tens or even hundreds of operations a day and spend much time imagining meaningful information in the random walkof markets.
- Investment is based on fundamentals, speculation on sentiment.
- The strategy of investing is countercyclical, whereas speculation is cyclical. Speculative thinking writ large

> is at work in asset bubbles – when people are buying when prices are already high, hoping they will get even higher, relying on "momentum", and selling in panic when prices drop. By contrast, dips are buying opportunities to an investor, and bubbles the time to cash out. Buying when everybody is selling and selling when everybody is buying helps counteract the excesses and balance prices out through elementary supply and demand. Speculation amplifies market cycles and volatility, investment mellows them out.

While investment is preferable for immediately practical reasons – you're likely to get your ass bitten off by your own mistakes if you speculate heavily – there's nothing inherently wrong with speculation, assuming information symmetry between participants.

For example, when something is worth more to Albert than Bertie, it makes sense for you to buy from Bertie and sell to Albert. It makes even more sense for them to make the trade directly without you, but if one of them needs the money now (and this is more important to him than getting paid more later), and the other doesn't have it yet, and you do, you can help them by buying from Albert and later selling to Bertie at a profit.

The liquidity and time value of money are the two factors missing from popular narratives that explain how everybody won in that scenario. Of course, this is an ideal case and the real world is rather more complicated, and so is the morality of speculation. The point is it *can* be a good thing.

High frequency trading, for instance, is pure speculation, which serves the positive function of providing liquidity to the markets. That's guy-in-tie-speak for *"Whenever you want to sell something, there's somebody buying at a fair price, and vice versa"*. That was not always the case before the robots.

There are criticisms. *"Hurr durr high frequency traders are unfair to mom-and-pop investors who can't compete with supercomputers that make 10,000 trades a second hurr durr!"*

Well, no. The computer infrastructure the HFTs paid for is the reason mom-and-pop investors can make trades for 0.1 cents, rather than 5% of each transaction. Mom-and-pop investors and margin-milking supercomputers are not competitors, they're symbionts, because mom-and-pop are not speculators. Supercomputers and heavily leveraged idiots who think they can beat the market by reading news in a bathrobe are competitors, but the reason the latter end up obliterated is not the supercomputers.

If you have balls of steel, excellent information, the discipline of a zen monk and better yet, a corruptible cousin on the board of a publicly traded company, by all means speculate. If you want to protect and grow your wealth without exposing yourself to too much risk or spending half your free time obsessing over things you can't control, you should invest.

The risk profiles and payoffs bring us to the golden rule of personal finance:

- Invest everything you don't immediately need.
- Speculate only with what you can afford to lose.

Read that until you see it seared into your retinas when you close your eyes, unconsciously assemble the words out of breakfast cereal and mutter it in your sleep.

I'm just gonna say it once more for your benefit:

- Invest everything you don't immediately need.
- Speculate only with what you can afford to lose.

An investor needs a solid, consistent strategy that won't be swayed by "market weather". A speculator needs the opposite – flexibility to adapt to quickly changing conditions.

A successful investor must have a cool head, and make peace with the fact that he will have lower profits than the cowboys during bubbles, or even be ridiculed for insisting on outdated concepts like diversification, due diligence and common sense. But when the cowboys are obliterated by a correction, a rational investor writes off a part of his profits (rarely principal) and carries on.

The strategy for successful investing has been excellently described decades ago and remains constant. If you read one book about this stuff, choose this.

If you read anything else, avoid purported miracle recipes to beating the market, which in a fashion much similar to miracle diets work in one case out of a thousand under the right conditions, for a while, until they don't.

If a book looks anything like "WHAT WALL STREET DOESN"T WANT YOU TO KNOW – HOW I BEAT THE MARKET for two weeks, before I lost everything and had to resort to writing dishonest books", re-read Graham instead.

On Valuations

I'm gonna talk mainly about stocks, because non-speculative, reasonably safe bonds barely return inflation these days.

Buy companies with long term growth prospects, and those you believe are undervalued or overlooked by the market.*

*A relatively new type of buying opportunity is a dip after a blue chip company's inevitable corruption scandal in China. Since nothing big happens in China without corruption, scandals say basically nothing about the ethics of the company. Corruption scandals in China mean that somebody higher up in the Party asked for a huge bribe, didn't get it and retaliated by blowing the whistle on his underlings and western imperialist pigdogs.

"But the Party launched an anti-corruption initiative..."

No, the Party launched a corruption *consolidation* initiative, to ensure money flows in pre-designed channels up the chain of command, without independent structures, side branches, pools and eddies. Different things. But I digress.

There is, on average, a degree of correlation between price and value of a stock, but its far from absolute. The interesting stuff happens precisely in the exceptions – the cheap good, which you need to buy, and the expensive bad, which you recommend to people on Yahoo Finance (an eerily perfect name).

Cheap doesn't have to mean undervalued. Many cheap companies are simply bad.

By the same token, expensive doesn't have to mean overvalued. Many expensive companies are really good and deserve the valuations.

Valuations reflect future expectations more than the present, which is how companies that lose money can still be massively valuable if they're losing money *for the right reasons* (we'll get to that in a minute). This also explains Tesla, which is valued like a company ten times its size, because it has the potential to turn the car industry inside out within a decade, and also because it is currently the only way to buy stock in Elon Musk, which is difficult to overvalue.

In fact, when a growth company spends more money than it makes, that's a good thing – it means it has more ideas than capital, which means good things for the future when the investments it is now making start to pay off. That's an *excellent* thing. It's much better than a mature company sitting cluelessly on a hoard of cash, because it ran out of ideas.

While the latter may seem like a conservative investment, it's actually incredibly unsafe.Stagnant behemoths are riskier investments in any longer term view than well-selected growth companies.

INVESTMENT AND SPECULATION

Investment

Investment is time, energy, or matter spent in the hope of future benefits actualized within a specified date or time frame. This article concerns investment in finance.

In finance, investment is buying or creating an asset with the expectation of capital appreciation, dividends (profit), interest earnings, rents, or some combination of these returns. This may or may not be backed by research and analysis. Most or all forms of investment involve some form of risk, such as investment in equities, property, and even fixed interest securities which are subject, among other things, to inflation risk. It is indispensable for project investors to identify and manage the risks related to the investment. Investment and investing is distinguished from other uses of money (such as saving, speculation, donation, gifting), in that the deployment of money is done for the purposes of obtaining a positive expected return.

Overview

In finance, investment is the purchase of an asset or item with the hope that it will generate income or appreciate in the future and be sold at the higher price. It generally does not include deposits with a bank or similar institution. The term investment is usually used when referring to a long-term outlook. This is the opposite of trading or speculation, which are short-term practices involving a much higher degree of risk. Financial assets take many forms and can range from the ultra safe low return government bonds to much higher risk higher reward international stocks. A good investment strategy will diversify the portfolio according to the specified needs.

The most famous and successful investor of all time is Warren Buffett. In March 2013 *Forbes* magazine had Warren Buffett ranked as number 2 in their Forbes 400 list. Buffett has advised in numerous articles and interviews that a good investment strategy is long term and choosing the right assets to invest in requires due diligence. Edward O. Thorpwas a very successful hedge fund manager in the 1970s and 1980s that spoke of a similar approach. Another thing they both have in common is a similar approach to managing investment money. No matter how successful the fundamental pick is, without a proper money management strategy, full potential of the asset cannot be reached. Both investors have been shown to use principles from the Kelly criterion for money management. Numerous interactive calculators which use the Kelly criterion can be found online. In contrast, dollar (or pound etc.) cost averaging and market timing are phrases often used in marketing of collective investments and can be said to be associated with speculation.

Investments are often made indirectly through intermediaries, such as pension funds, banks, brokers, and insurance companies. These institutions may pool money received from a large number of individuals into funds such as investment trusts, unit trusts, SICAVs etc. to make large scale investments. Each individual investor then has an indirect or direct claim on the assets purchased, subject to charges levied by the intermediary, which may be large and varied. It generally, does not include deposits with a bank or similar institution. Investment usually involves diversification of assets in order to avoid unnecessary and unproductive risk.

History

The Code of Hammurabi (around 1700 BC) provided a legal framework for investment, establishing a means for the pledge of collateral by codifying debtor and creditor rights in regard to pledged land. Punishments for breaking financial obligations were not as severe as those for crimes involving injury or death.

In the early 1900s purchasers of stocks, bonds, and other securities were described in media, academia, and commerce as speculators. By the 1950s, the term investment had come to denote the more conservative end of the securities spectrum, while speculation was applied by financial brokers and their advertising agencies to higher risk securities much in vogue at that time. Since the last half of the 20th century, the terms speculation and speculator have specifically referred to higher risk ventures.

Value Investment

Business revolves around the factor of investing; financially, time, in the future and successful investors will generally focus on certain fundamental metrics for their gains. Avalue investor is aware that when considering the health of a company, the fundamentals associated with it, are a highly influencing factor. They include aspects related to financial and operational data, preferred by some of the most successful investors; for example, Warren Buffett and George Soros. The financial details, such as, earnings per share and sales growth, are essential aids for an investor in determining stocks trading below their worth.

The price to earnings ratio (P/E), or earnings multiple, is a particularly significant and recognized fundamental ratio, with a function of dividing the share price of stock, by itsearnings per share. This will provide the value representing the sum investors are prepared to expend for each dollar of company earnings. This ratio is an important aspect, due to its capacity as measurement for the comparison of valuations of various companies. A stock with a lower P/E ratio will cost less per share, than one with a higher P/E, taking into account the same level of financial performance; therefore, it essentially means a low P/E is the preferred option.

An instance, in which the price to earnings ratio has a lesser significance, is when companies in different industries are compared. An example; although, it is reasonable for a telecommunications stock to show a P/E in the low teens; in the case of hi-tech stock, a P/E in the 40s range, is not unusual. When making comparisons the P/E ratio can give you a refined view of a particular stock valuation.

For investors paying for each dollar of a company's earnings, the P/E ratio is a significant indicator, but the price-to-book ratio (P/B) is also a reliable indication of how much investors are willing to spend on each dollar of company assets. In the process of the P/B ratio, the share price of a stock is divided by its net assets; any intangibles, such as goodwill, are not taken into account. It is a crucial factor of the price-to-book ratio, due to it indicating the actual payment for tangible assets and not the more difficult valuation, of intangibles. Accordingly, the P/B could be considered a comparatively, conservative metric.

Debt Equity and Free Cash Flow

For investment purposes, an essential factor relates to how a company finances its assets, especially if it involves a sizable value stock and is a situation in which debt/equity ratio has a significant influence. Similar to the P/E ratio, the debt/equity ratio, indicates the proportion of financing, a company has obtained from debt; for example, loans, bonds and equity, such as, the issuance of shares and stock, which vary between industries. An indication to investors that all is not financially sound with a company, relates to above-industry debt/equity figures, particularly if an industry is experiencing a challenging, adverse business environment.

A factor that sometimes remains unaware to investors is that the earnings of a company generally do not equal the amount of cash generated. This is due to companies reporting their financials utilising, Generally Accepted Accounting Principles (GAAP). It is a standard framework of guidelines for the financial accounting practices used in any given jurisdiction. International Financial Reporting Standards (IFRS) are commonly used, worldwide.

Free cash flow is a metric that determines for an investor the sum of actual cash remaining in a company after deduction of any capital investments. In general, it is preferable to for a company to boast a positive free cash flow, but similar to the debt-equity ratio, this metric assumes greater significance in a difficult business environment. Finance

Basics of the Profit Line

Arguably, the most commonly utilized valuation metric is Earnings Before Interest, Tax, Depreciation and Amortization, generally referred to as "EBITDA." This metric relates to the basic profits made, prior to the influences and intricacies of accounting deductions becoming issues of the true profit line of a company. This particular metric is recognized as the primary standard of private mergers and acquisitions.

For a company competing in a high growth industry, an investor could expect a significant acquisition premium, which is a buyout offer, several times over the most recent EBITDA. In various instances, it has been known for private equity firms, to pay multiples of up to 6-8 times the EBITDA. However, some buyers could make the decision that even given these relatively high valuations, the offer from a buyer does not take into consideration past expenditures and future potential product growth.

In certain cases, an EBITDA may be sacrificed by a company, in order for the pursuance of future growth; a strategy frequently used by corporate giants, such as, Amazon,Google and Microsoft, among others. This is a business decision that can impact negatively on buyout offers, founded on EBITDA and can be the cause of many negotiations, failing. It may be recognized as a valuation breach, with many investors maintaining that sellers are too demanding, while buyers are regarded as failing to realize the long-term potential of, expenditure or acquisitions.

Capital Gains Taxes

The amount you pay in taxes for long term investments, investments that span over a year long term, and short term investments such as those that are below a year are different. The long term investments range from Zero to twenty percent for capital gains and they are regulated by what tax bracket you are in for income taxes. For the zero to fifteen percent income tax bracket you could qualify for the zero percent long-term capital gains rate. The next bracket is the fifteen to twenty percent income tax bracket where you are set at fifteen percent capital gains tax for long term investments. The next bracket is between twenty and 39.6 percent and that leads to a twenty percent capital gains tax however with these numbers you should add 3.8 percent for the health care surtax. The short term capital gains tax is also related to your total taxable income and is taxed at the same rate as your income and ranges from ten to 39.6 percent.

SPECULATION

Speculation is the practice of engaging in risky financial transactions in an attempt to profit from fluctuations in the market value of a tradable good such as a financial instrument, rather than attempting to profit from the underlying financial attributes embodied in the instrument such as capital gains, interest, or dividends. Many speculators pay little attention to the fundamental value of a security and instead focus purely on price movements. Speculation can in principle involve any tradable good or financial instrument. Speculators are particularly common in the markets for stocks, bonds, commodity futures, currencies, fine art,collectibles, real estate, and derivatives.

Speculators play one of four primary roles in financial markets, along with hedgers who engage in transactions to offset some other pre-existing risk, arbitrageurs who seek to profit from situations where fungible instruments trade at different prices in different market segments, and investors who seek profit through long-term ownership of an instrument's underlying attributes.

History

With the appearance of the stock ticker machine in 1867, which removed the need for traders to be physically present on the floor of a stock exchange, stock speculation underwent a dramatic expansion through the end of the 1920s. The number of shareholders increased, perhaps, from 4.4 million in 1900 to 26 million in 1932.

Speculation and Investment

The view of what distinguishes investment from speculation and speculation from excessive speculation varies widely among pundits, legislators and academics. Some sources note that speculation is simply a higher risk form of investment. Others define speculation more narrowly as positions not characterized as hedging. The U.S. Commodity Futures Trading Commission defines a speculator as "a trader who does not hedge, but who trades with the objective of achieving profits through the successful anticipation of price movements." The agency emphasizes that speculators serve important market functions, but defines excessive speculation as harmful to the proper functioning of futures markets. Financial speculation is unproductive and sterile in economic and human terms and so is guilty of encouraging all those factors that leads the economic system to its ruin. Gambling in general and stock market speculation in particular constitute the basis of unproductive speculation. Unproductive speculation can be criticised in a moral context.

According to Ben Graham in *The Intelligent Investor*, the prototypical defensive investor is "...one interested chiefly in safety plus freedom from bother." He admits, however, that "...some speculation is necessary and unavoidable, for in many common-stock situations, there are substantial possibilities of both profit and loss, and the risks therein must be assumed by someone." Thus, many long-term investors, even those who buy and hold for decades, may be classified as speculators, excepting only the rare few who are primarily motivated by income or safety of principal and not eventually selling at a profit.

Speculation is condemned on ethical-moral grounds as creating money from money and therby promoting the vices of avarice and gambling.

8

Investment Choices in the Capital Market

Among all investment options available, securities are considered the most challenging as well as rewarding. But investment in securities requires considerable skill and expertise and carries the risk of loss if the choice of securities is not right or they are not bought/ sold at right time.

There are a large variety of instruments referred to as securities in common parlance. These include:

- Shares, scrips, stocks, bonds, debentures, debenture stock or other marketable securities of a like nature in or of any incorporated company or other body corporate;
- Derivative;
- Units or any other instrument issued by any collective investment scheme to the investors in such schemes;
- Security receipts;
- Units or any other such instrument issued to the investors under any mutual fund scheme;
- Any certificate or instrument issued to investor by any issuer being a special purpose distinct entity which possesses any debt or receivable including mortgaged debt assigned to such entity and acknowledging beneficial interest of such investor in such debt or receivable including mortgage debt as the case may be;
- Government securities;

- Such other instruments as may be declared by the central government to be securities;
- Rights or interest in securities.

Different securities carry different risk-return profiles. Generally, higher risks carry higher returns and vice-versa. The risk could be in the form of credit risk (counter party may default payment as it may not have integrity), return risk (the return from the investment may depend on several contingent factors) and liquidity risk (it may be difficult to convert security into cash).

Investment decisions are based upon the investors' life cycle stages and other factors such as liquidity, safety, return on investments, tax savings, active involvement required to manage the investment, and minimum amount requirement for selecting the instruments.

It is not always possible to meet all financial goals with available savings. If savings are limited but the needs are substantial, then the savings should be invested in avenues that would offer high returns. But usually, high return also means high risk. All investors are not in a position to take high risks.

There are investment opportunities that are high on risk and there are investment opportunities that are low on risk. Each is called an asset class. An investor allocates his savings to one or more asset classes depending upon his circumstances.

This decision is called the asset allocation decision. Asset allocation decision is perhaps the most important decision in the investment process. The essence of asset allocation lies in the fact that, over time, it can determine up to 90 per cent of the portfolio's return.

How much risk an investor can take depends on his financial circumstances and the mental make-up. Every investor must know his own unique risk profile and then make the investment decisions.

As such, the questions he should ask himself are:

- What kind of investor am I?

- Am I prepared to take high risks?
- Am I averse to taking risks?

There are scientific methods by which an investor can understand his risk profile. For example, answering the following set of questions could give him an idea about his risk profile:

Your age is

- Between 25-35
- Between 35-50
- Between 50-65
- Above 65

Your position is best described by

- You are self-dependent and do not support anybody
- You have dependent(s)
- Nearing retirement
- Retired

How much of the following needs have been taken care of? (Fully, partially, not at all)

- Insurance
- Retirement
- Children's education
- Housing

What proportion of your current expenses is funded from investments?

- Nil
- Up to 15 per cent
- Between 15 per cent and 30 per cent
- Between 30 per cent and 50 per cent
- More than 50 per cent

Your earnings in the future will

- far exceed inflation
- be marginally ahead of inflation
- keep pace with inflation
- not keep pace with inflation

When the price of the share you have purchased drops steeply you would

- Sell your investment
- Sell part of your investment
- Do nothing
- Buy more of the same investment

Each of the above questions would impact the risk profile of an investor. For example, lower the age, greater is the expected willingness to take risks. This is because younger people have a lifetime of earnings ahead of them and thus can afford to take higher risks with their present savings. Similarly, in case a person does not have any dependents, he can take more risk.

At the very basic level, there are three asset classes from which to choose from based upon an investors' risk profile. They are equity, debt and cash. Equity is risky, debt has low risk and cash has even lower risk. Within each of the above asset classes, the investor has to select specific instruments for investment.

Financial circumstances and the investor profile dictate the investment avenues for an investor. Financial instruments vary in terms of the liquidity, safety, and returns they offer. The challenge in making the investment decision is to choose the right combination of instruments keeping in mind the financial situation and investor profile.

Each investment option has some advantages and some limitations. For example, while bank savings account would be highly liquid (you can withdraw whenever you like), investment in Public Provident Fund would be difficult to withdraw.

Risks are generally positively correlated with probability of returns. For example, returns in equity shares can be high, but the associated risks are also relatively higher than other options. Risks can be classified into unsystematic and systematic. Unsystematic risks are those that can be minimized by diversifying one's portfolio. For example, instead of investing in the shares of steel companies alone, one could invest into other sectors like Pharmaceuticals and Software. In this situation, your portfolio may not be terribly affected even if the steel sector were to register a mediocre performance. On the other hand, systematic risks are those that cannot be minimized through portfolio diversification. For example, a Korean investor could not possibly have minimized or eliminated his loss due to the currency crisis in South East Asia, through a strategy of diversification of his portfolio.

The character of the investor is also important. Some investors have the time and the knowledge to study their investment portfolios carefully- these could be called as 'active' investors. Others do not intend to watch their investments regularly, due to lack of time or knowledge or inclination, and are looking for essentially safer avenues for parking their funds.

CAPITAL MARKET

Capital Market is one of the significant aspect of every financial market. Hence it is necessary to study its correct meaning. Broadly speaking the capital market is a market for financial assets which have a long or indefinite maturity. Unlike money market instruments the capital market intruments become mature for the period above one year. It is an institutional arrangement to borrow and lend money for a longer period of time. It consists of financial institutions like IDBI, ICICI, UTI, LIC, etc. These institutions play the role of lenders in the capital market. Business units and corporate are the borrowers in the capital market. Capital market involves various instruments which can be used for financial transactions. Capital market provides long term debt and equity finance for the government and the corporate sector. Capital market can be classified into primary and secondary markets. The primary market is a market for new shares, where as in the secondary market the existing securities are traded. Capital market institutions provide rupee loans, foreign exchange loans, consultancy services and underwriting.

A capital market is a market for securities (equity and debt), where business enterprises (companies) and governments can raise long-term funds. It is defined as a market in which money is provided for periods longer than a year (raising of short-term funds takes place on other markets like the money market). Financial regulators, such as SEBI and RBI regulate and oversee the capital market in their designated jurisdictions to ensure an orderly development of the market and protection of investors. Capital market can be classified into primary market and secondary market. In the primary market, new stocks and bonds are sold by companies to investors. In the secondary market, the existing issued securities are sold and bought among investors or traders through a stock exchange. Capital market development is essential for the economic development of a country. The objective of economic activity in any country is to promote the well-being and standard of living of its people, which depends upon the distribution of income in terms of goods and services in the economy. For the growth process in the economy, production plays a vital role. Production of output depends upon material inputs, human inputs, and financial inputs. Material inputs are in the form of raw materials; plant, and machinery etc., Human inputs are in the form of intellectual, managerial and labour manpower. Financial inputs are in the shape of capital, cash, credit etc. The proper availability and utilization of these inputs promotes the economic growth of a country.

The financial inputs, among other sources, emanate from the capital market system. The capital market thrives with investors' confidence based upon their return on investment as well as from anticipated capital appreciation from their investment.

Investors are a heterogeneous group; they comprise wealthy and middle class, educated and illiterate, young and old, expert and lay man. However, all investors need protection; not protection for assured growth of their investments but protection from malpractices and frauds. An investor typically has three objectives: safety of the invested money, liquidity of the invested money and returns on the investments. There can often be conflicts in the objective of allowing raising of capital for economic development on one hand and protection of investors on the other. However, it is beyond debate that unless the interests of investors are protected, raising of capital would be difficult. An efficient capital market should, therefore, provide a mechanism for efficient raising capital as well as have adequate safeguards to protect the interests of the investors.

In the Indian scenario, efforts were made right since Independence, to create a healthy and efficient capital market through legislative measures. The Capital Issues (Control) Act, 1947 was the first piece of legislation passed in India to control the capital market. Subsequently, The Companies Act was enacted in 1956.

The watershed event in this direction was in 1992 when the Capital Issues Control Act was replaced by the Securities and Exchange Board of India Act, 1992. This Act provides

"For the establishment of a Board to protect the interests of investors in securities and to promote the development of, and to regulate, the securities market and for matters connected therewith or incidental thereto."

SEBI has given priority to both the development, promotion and regulation of the capital market and to investor protection. Its greater focus on investor protection has earned it the name of the Watchdog of the capital market. SEBI strongly believes that investors are the backbone of the capital market as they are the providers of the capital for the economic growth of the country and also are the fulcrum around which the trading in securities takes place.

SEBI has laid down guidelines for almost all constituents of the capital market-from issuers on one hand to stock exchanges on the other hand and all other intermediaries like stock brokers, merchant bankers and underwriters. It also regulates the intermediary fund managers like mutual funds, portfolio managers and collective investment schemes.

Alert to the changing markets-both domestic and international, SEBI continuously revises its various guidelines and regulations.

In the primary market, the focus is on regulation through disclosures. Starting of with the Disclosure and Investor Protection (DIP) Guidelines, SEBI has recently converted these guidelines into the Issue of Capital and Disclosure Requirements) Regulations) (ICDR). These Regulations prescribe detailed norms and directions on disclosures.

However, many investors, especially small investors, do not possess adequate expertise/ knowledge to take informed investment decisions. Many of them are not aware of the risk-return profiles of various investment products. A large number of investors are not fully aware of the precautions they should take while dealing with the market intermediaries. Many are not familiar with the market mechanisms and practices as well as with their rights and obligations.

In the last decade, far-reaching developments have taken place in the capital market. These have impacted the issuers, the intermediaries as well as the investors. The present capital market is significantly different from what it used to be even in the nineties, leave aside the period prior to that. However, new challenges emerge almost on a daily basis. These are substantially fuelled by the huge rewards that the capital market has the potential to offer compared to any other form of investment. At the same time, wrong investment decisions can lead to huge losses too. As such, this market requires considerable skill and expertise, and a higher-than-normal risk profile

Different securities carry different risk-return profiles. Generally, higher risks carry higher returns and vice-versa. The risks may be in the form of credit risk (counter party may default on payment), return risk (the returns from the investment depends upon several contingent factors) and liquidity risk (it may be difficult to convert the securities into cash]. While the counter party risk has been significantly mitigated by the regulator, the other two risks are market-related risks.

Various investment options are available in the capital market and an investor should choose the right products based upon his life cycle stage and upon various parameters like liquidity, safety, returns and taxes, He of course needs to decide whether he has the skills and time for active management of his investments or would he rather pass on this responsibility to a mutual fund or a portfolio manager.

Investors do not have any control over the day to day activities of any company. Investor cannot guide the fate or destiny of the money invested. An investor to that extent is quite fragile. Worse, he is exposed to additional risks if the promoters of the company siphon off or misutilize his money. There are, no doubt, laws some of which are adequate to protect the interests of investors, but inadequacies of certain legislative measures have come to light wherein innocent investors have been deprived of their hard earned money.

"Investor protection" is a very popular phrase which all those concerned with regulation of the capital market use these days, be it SEBI, stock exchanges, investors associations, and even the companies themselves. The term "Investor Protection" is a wide term encompassing various measures designed to protect the investors from malpractices of companies, merchant bankers, depository participants and other intermediaries.

"Investors Beware" should be the watchword of all programmes for mobilization of savings for investment. As all investments have some risk element, this should be borne in mind by the investors. If caution is thrown to the winds, they have only to blame themselves.

DEFINITION OF 'CAPITAL MARKETS'

Markets for buying and selling equity and debt instruments. Capital markets channel savings and investment between suppliers of capital such as retail investors and institutional investors, and users of capital like businesses, government and individuals. Capital markets are vital to the functioning of an economy, since capital is a critical component for generating economic output. Capital markets include primary markets, where new stock and bond issues are sold to investors, and secondary markets, which trade existing securities.

The Capital Markets

Selling securities to investors in the various capital markets provides the means for corporations, governments and government agencies to satisfy their need for capital, thus providing investors the opportunity to profit by trading capital for securities, which are transferable claims on the assets of the entity that originally sold the securities.

More specifically, securities are financial assets that are transferable claims on the real assets of the issuer of the securities. The capital markets, a.k.a. securities markets, consist of the primary capital markets where securities are first sold to institutional investors and the various stock, bond and commodities exchanges where securities are subsequently traded. There are two primary types of securities: debt and equity. Equities include common stock and preferred stock. Debt securities include bonds, convertible bonds, commercial paper, short-term government debt and certificates of deposit. A third type of security, derivatives, derive their value from some underlying asset that may be another security, a tangible asset, the option to buy or sell an asset at a predetermined price or a contract to buy or sell an asset at a predetermined price. However, derivatives are not used as a means for raising capital, rather, they are typically used as a means of hedging, financial engineering or speculating.

Mutual funds are securities comprised of pools of other securities that may be debt, equities or derivatives. With the exception of commodities funds, mutual funds typically restrict their use of derivatives to hedging. Commodities funds use derivatives extensively to either model an index or to model a portfolio of their own design, thus eliminating the unnecessary expense and inconvenience of actually taking possession of the commodities in their portfolios.

Corporations, government agencies and municipal governments raise capital by selling their securities in the primary capital markets to institutional investors. After this initial sale the securities are traded in the secondary capital markets, which is where individual investors buy and sell securities. The U.S. Treasury sells its securities directly to institutional and individual investors. After it's initial sale, Treasury debt also is sold in the secondary market. CDs also are sold directly to institutional and individual investors.

Nearly all U.S. equities are traded on one of the three U.S. stock exchanges: The New York Stock Exchange, the American Stock Exchange and the Nasdaq. These exchanges and the lesser-known exchanges make up the secondary market for equities, which serve both individual and institutional investors.

The New York and American stock exchanges are physical auction-type exchanges where securities are traded at bid and asked prices and liquidity is provided by specialists who make up any imbalances between buy and sell orders. The specialists provide liquidity by keeping inventories of the stocks in which they specialize and by setting the bid price to maintain a balance between supply and demand (*i.e.*, sell orders and buy orders). When a balance can't be maintained, they absorb any excess sell orders and add to their inventories or sell from their inventories to cover excess buy orders. The bid-ask spread is the market specialists' profit, which compensates them for providing liquidity to these capital markets.

The Nasdaq, which stands for National Association of Securities Dealers Automated Quotation System, was formed in 1971 by the National Association of Securities Dealers (Nasd) then subsequently sold in 2000 and 2001, at which time it became The Nasdaq Stock Market. The Nasdaq also operates on a bid-ask basis but it is a fully automated electronic system. Liquidity is provided to this capital market by brokerages who act as dealers that fulfill the same function as the specialists on the physical exchanges. The dealers are said to make a market in the stocks in which they specialize and are thus known as market makers. They, too, are compensated for this service by the bid-ask spread.

Mutual fund shares are sold and redeemed by the fund companies and an exact balance is maintained between sales and redemptions by issuing or dissolving shares, thus there is no need for secondary capital markets for these securities. Individuals can deal directly with the mutual fund companies or through a discount or full-service broker. In the case of no load mutual funds, there will never be a charge for purchases or redemptions, but trades made through a discount brokerage may be subject to a transaction fee and trades made through a full-service brokerage will always be subject to a transaction fee. Individuals can buy and sell Treasury bonds through the U.S. Treasury's Treasury Direct service, which is the Treasury's exclusive capital market. Individuals must trade corporate and municipal bonds through a brokerage in one of the secondary capital markets. Mutual funds and other institutional investors can purchase corporate and municipal bonds in the primary market and have more options than individuals for trading existing issues of all types of bonds.

Whenever the need for capital arises, corporations, governments and government agencies will return to the capital markets to sell more debt and/or equity securities. Occasionally, corporations will use excess cash to buy back a portion of their outstanding common stock or callable bonds, or issue new debt when interest rates drop and use the proceeds to "call back" their older, higher interest callable bonds. When high-interest bonds are called and replaced with bonds that have a lower coupon, the companies' cost of capital is decreased assuming there is no concurrent change in the company's capital structure. There are a number of opinions as to what effect these actions could have on a company's stock under various scenarios. That issue is beyond the scope of this subsection.

The U.S. Federal Reserve Board of Governors' Federal Open Market Committee (FOMC) will from time to time buy Treasury debt in the capital markets as part of its monetary policy. By purchasing Treasury debt on the open market, the Fed increases the money supply.

This is usually done to decrease interest rates and stimulate the economy. It also is done to ward off deflation, which is extremely rare. So rare, indeed, that it hasn't happened since the Great Depression, although we were close, by some accounts, in the early and late 2000s and looking at a distinct possibility in the early 2010s. Increasing the money supply for any reason other than to keep pace with ordinary economic expansion is inflationary, so there needs to be a good reason to do it, like reviving a faltering economy or countering deflation.

ROLE OF CAPITAL MARKET

The primary role of the capital market is to raise long-term funds for governments, banks, and corporations while providing a platform for the trading of securities. This fundraising is regulated by the performance of the stock and bond markets within the capital market.

The member organizations of the capital market may issue stocks and bonds in order to raise funds. Investors can then invest in the capital market by purchasing those stocks and bonds. The capital market, however, is not without risk.

It is important for investors to understand market trends before fully investing in the capital market. To that end, there are various market indices available to investors that reflect the present performance of the market.

Regulation of the Capital Market

Every capital market in the world is monitored by financial regulators and their respective governance organization. The purpose of such regulation is to protect investors from fraud and deception. Financial regulatory bodies are also charged with minimizing financial losses, issuing licenses to financial service providers, and enforcing applicable laws.

The Capital Market's Influence on International Trade

Capital market investment is no longer confined to the boundaries of a single nation. Today's corporations and individuals are able, under some regulation, to invest in the capital market of any country in the world. Investment in foreign capital markets has caused substantial enhancement to the business of international trade.

The Primary and Secondary Markets

The capital market is also dependent on two sub-markets – the primary market and the secondary market. The primary marketdeals with newly issued securities and is responsible for generating new long-term capital. The secondary market handles the trading of previously-issued securities, and must remain highly liquid in nature because most of the securities are sold by investors. A capital market with high liquidity and high transparency is predicated upon a secondary market with the same qualities.

Efficient Capital Market

An efficient capital market is a market where the share prices reflect new information accurately and in real time. Capital market efficiency is judged by its success in incorporating and inducting information, generally about the basic value of securities, into the price of securities.

This basic or fundamental value of securities is the present value of the cash flows expected in the future by the person owning the securities. The fluctuation in the value of stocks encourage traders to trade in a competitive manner with the objective of maximum profit.

This results in price movements towards the current value of the cash flows in the future. The information is very easily available at cheap rates because of the presence of organized markets and various technological innovations. An efficient capital market incorporates information quickly and accurately into the prices of securities.

In the weak-form efficient capital market, information about the history of previous returns and prices are reflected fully in the security prices; the returns from stocks in this type of market are unpredictable.

In the semistrong-form efficient market, the public information is completely reflected in security prices; in this market, those traders who have non-public information access can earn excess profits.

In the strong-form efficient market, under no circumstances can investors earn excess profits because all of the information is incorporated into the security prices.

The funds that are flowing in capital markets, from savers to the firms with the aim of financing projects, must flow into the best and top valued projects and, therefore, informational efficiency is of supreme importance. Stocks must be efficiently priced, because if the securities are priced accurately, then those investors who do not have time for market analysis would feel confident about making investments in the capital market.

Eugene Fama was one of the earliest to theorize capital market efficiency, but empirical tests of capital market efficiency had begun even before that.

Venture Capital Market

Venture Capital is an age old concept but the Venture Capital Market has developed in the recent decades. The term venture capital denotes the act of investment in the areas of high risk, in order to get some high returns. The developments in the venture capital market has taken place in the US markets mainly.

The market of venture capital, in the past, was disconnected and may be identified as individualized to some extent. In the recent times only, the market has been shaped and the market became matured.Venture Capital Markets are a boon for those who want to set up new business.

At the same time, if an existing business wants to develop, the venture capitalists are there to provide financial assistance. These capitalists have their own business interest behind the assistance. These people want to have a share of the huge profits by the business in the future.

Because of this, only those businesses are selected which are supposed to develop rapidly in the future. For this purpose, the venture capitalists have their own team of people to identify the appropriate opportunities.

The modern concept of venture capital should be grateful to General Doriot because he was the person who founded the

American Research and Development Fund. This was done to provide financial assistance to the activities of developing new technologies in the US universities. At the same time, the commercial use and financial benefits from such technologies were also considered seriously.

With the commercial success of the concept of venture capital, big players entered the venture capital market of United States of America. The giant companies like Xerox and General Electric played a major role in expanding the venture capital market. The entry of these companies in this market with separate divisions to deal in the market, encouraged many others. Because of these situations, the venture capital market was expanded beyond the territories of the US and within a short period, it gained ground globally.

Capital Market Theory

Capital Market Theory tries to explain and predict the progression of capital (and sometimes financial) markets over time on the basis of the one or the other mathematical model. Capital market theory is a generic term for the analysis of securities.

In terms of trade off between the returns sought by investors and the inherent risks involved, the capital market theory is a model that seeks to price assets, most commonly, shares.

In general, whenever someone tries to formulate a financial, investment, or retirement plan, he or she (consciously or unconsciously) employs a theory such as arbitrage pricing theory, capital asset pricing model, coherent market hypothesis, efficient market hypothesis, fractal market hypothesis, or modern portfolio theory. The most talked about model in Capital Market Theory is the Capital Asset Pricing Model.

In studying the capital market theory we deal with issues like the role of the capital markets, the major capital markets in the US, the initial public offerings and the role of the venture capital in capital markets, financial innovation and markets in derivative instruments, the role of securities and the exchange commission, the role of the federal reserve system, role of the US Treasury and the regulatory requirements on the capital market.

The Capital Market Theory deals with the following issues:

- Importance of venture capital in the capital market
- Initial public offerings
- Role of capital market
- Major capital markets worldwide
- Markets and financial innovations in derivative instruments
- Role of Federal Reserve System
- Role of securities
- Capital market regulatory requirements
- Role of the government treasury.

Assumptions of Capital Market Theory

The capital market theory builds upon the Markowitz portfolio model. The main assumptions of the capital market theoryare as follows:

- *All Investors are Efficient Investors*: Investors follow Markowitz idea of the efficient frontier and choose to invest in portfolios along the frontier.
- *Investors Borrow/Lend Money at the Risk-Free Rate*: This rate remains static for any amount of money.
- *The Time Horizon is equal for All Investors*: When choosing investments, investors have equal time horizons for the chosen investments.
- *All Assets are Infinitely Divisible*: This indicates that fractional shares can be purchased and the stocks can be infinitely divisible.
- *No Taxes and Transaction Costs*: It is assumed that investors results are not affected by taxes and transaction costs.
- *All Investors Have the Same Probability for Outcomes*: When determining the expected return, assume that all investors have the same probability for outcomes.

- *No Inflation Exists*: Returns are not affected by the inflation rate in a capital market as none exists in capital market theory.
- *There is No Mispricing within the Capital Markets*: It is assumed that the markets are efficient and that no mispricings within the markets exist.

Mortgages, equities, bonds, and other investments are traded in the capital market. The financial instruments in this market have long maturity periods. Capital market theory states that federal funds, federal agency securities, treasury bills, commercial papers, negotiable certificates of deposits, repurchase agreements, Eurocurrency loans and deposits, options and futures are merchandised in the capital market.

When one has to put a price on a security, one has to determine the risk and return of the security both for single assets, as well as a portfolio of assets. The uncertainty and variability of returns on assets and the possibilities of losses can be defined as risks. The theory of capital market defines returns in the following manner:

$$K = Pt + Ct - Pt\text{-}1/\ Pt\text{-}1$$

Where the time of purchase of the asset of price Pt-1 is t-1. If this be the case, then the return (K) from the time period t-1 to t is the above mentioned formula. Ct is the cash gotten from assets between t-1 and t. Pt is the price of the asset at time t.

For practitioners of the capital market theory, it has not lost its significance. It is still as important for retirement, financial, and investment plans.

INVESTMENT OPTIONS

Various options available are described in the following paragraphs and evaluated broadly on criteria such as

- Liquidity
- Safety
- Returns

- Tax savings
- Active involvement required to manage the investment
- Minimum amount that can be invested

Equity Shares

An equity share, commonly referred to as ordinary share represents a fractional ownership of the company in which a shareholder, as a fractional owner, undertakes the entrepreneurial risks and rewards associated with a business venture. The holders of such shares are members of the company and have voting rights. Equity Shares can be purchased in the Primary and Secondary Markets.

Primary Market: Primary market refers to issue of securities by companies/entities to the public. Apart from shares, other instruments commonly issued in the primary market are debentures, convertible debentures, shares with attached options like warrants etc.

Secondary Market: Secondary market refers to the stock exchanges where an investor can buy (or sell) shares which are listed on them. As a result of significant changes in the recent past, particularly computerization, online trading, dematerialization and depository participation, investors are dealing with a much more transparent and efficient secondary market.

Equity Shares yield returns in two ways: one, dividends declared by companies usually at the end of a year (and sometimes during the course of the year) and, two, capital gains on selling. Liquidity of investments in equity shares depends upon the trading volumes of the share. If the share is actively traded, an investor can easily sell the shares and realize the sale proceeds. However, if the share is not traded (or is delisted), then liquidity is a constraint. Technically, it is possible to buy even one share in the dematerialized securities regime.

Equity is a volatile instrument. It is an appropriate investment avenue for an investor who is prepared to take risks in order to generate higher returns. Over the long term, returns from equity shares at aggregated levels have been historically higher than most other avenues. However, individual investors could gain or lose depending on the shares they invest in and when they buy and sell. An investor needs to be aware of the companies in which he invests and continuously monitor their performance. For this, he should have some basic knowledge of finance and of the market processes.

The trends in equity market are reflected in the movement of the equity indices and the volume of the trading activity.

Preference Shares

- Preferred Stock/ Preference Shares: Owners of these kinds of shares are entitled to a fixed dividend or dividend calculated at a fixed rate to be paid regularly before a dividend can be paid in respect of equity share. These also enjoy priority over equity shareholders in payment of surplus. However, in the event of liquidation, their claims rank below the claims of the company's creditors, bondholders/ debenture holders.
- Cumulative Preference Shares: A type of preference share on which dividend accumulates if it remains unpaid. All arrears of preference dividend have to be paid out before paying dividend on equity shares.
- Cumulative Convertible Preference Shares: A type of preference shares where the dividend payable on the same accumulates, if not paid. After a specified date, these shares will be converted into equity capital of the company.
- Participating Preference Share: The right of certain preference shareholders to participate in profits after a specified fixed dividend contracted for, is paid. Participation right is linked with the quantum of dividend paid on the equity shares over and above a particular specified level.

Security Receipts

Security receipt means a receipt or other security, issued by a securitization company or reconstruction company to any qualified institutional buyer pursuant to a scheme, evidencing the purchase or acquisition by the holder thereof, of an undivided right, title or interest in the financial asset involved in securitization.

Debt Instruments

Debt instruments represent contracts where one party is the lender (investor) and the other party is the borrower (issuer). The debt contract specifies the rate of interest, time of interest payment, repayment of principal, etc. In India, the term "bond" is used to represent the debt instrument issued by the central and state governments and PSUs. The term "debenture" is used for debt issues from the private corporate sector.

The principal features of a debt instrument are:

- Maturity
- Coupon
- Principal

Maturity refers to the date on which the principal would be repaid. Coupon is the rate at which interest is calculated with reference to the face value. For example, a 10 per cent 2010 bond refers to face value of ₹ 100, coupon rate of 10 per cent p.a., and repayment of the face value in the year 2010.

The coupon rate may be fixed for the entire period or may be related to a benchmark rate. In the latter case, the coupon rate changes as the benchmark rate changes. This instrument is called a floating rate debt instrument. There are debt instruments that come with options to redeem the principal earlier than the maturity date. If the option rests with the issuer, it is a bond that is callable. If the option to redeem rests with the investor, it is puttable.

There are many different types of debt instruments in India. These are:

- Bonds (from PSUs and Financial Institutions)
- Government (Central or State) Securities
- Treasury Bills
- Company Debentures

- Commercial Paper
- Certificates of Deposit

The secondary market activity for debt instruments takes place in the debt segment of the exchange. The trends in the debt market are reflected in the debt indices and the turnover data. In India, the debt market activity is dominated by banks and institutions.

Bonds

A Bond is a loan given by the buyer to the issuer of the instrument. Bonds may be issued by companies, financial institutions or the government. Over and above the scheduled interest payments, the holder of a bond is entitled to receive the redemption value of the instrument at the specified maturity date. In simple terms, a bond investor lends money to the issuer and in exchange, the issuer promises to repay the loan amount on a specified maturity date and usually pay the periodic interest payments over the life of the loan. Few more popular types of Bonds are as follows:

- Zero Coupon Bonds: Bonds issued at a discount and repaid at a face value. No periodic interest is paid. The difference between the issue price and redemption price represents the return to the holder. The buyer of these bonds receives only one payment at the maturity of the bond. These are also sometimes referred to as deep-discount bonds.
- Convertible Bonds: Bonds giving the investor the option to convert the bond into equity at a fixed conversion price.
- Tax-Saving Bonds: Tax-Saving Bonds offer tax exemption up to a specified amount of investment.
- Regular Income Bonds: Regular-Income Bonds, as the name suggests, are meant to provide a stable source of income at regular, pre-determined intervals.

Similar instruments issued by companies are called debentures. Bonds are usually not suitable to achieve capital appreciation. Sometimes, an investor buys bonds at a lower price just before a decline in interest rates, and the subsequent drop in the interest rates leads to an increase in the price of the bond, thereby facilitating capital appreciation.

Bonds are suitable for regular income purposes. Depending on the type of bond, an investor may receive interest semi-annually or even monthly, as is the case with monthly-income bonds.

Bond prices are dependent on the face value of these instruments. The most common face value is ₹ 100. Minimum amount of investment is generally around ₹ 5,000. An investor need not be actively involved in investment management.

Public Sector Undertakings and Financial Institutions Bonds:

Various bonds are floated from time to time by Public Sector Undertakings as well as Development Financial Institutions. Most such bonds offer attractive schemes like monthly interest, quarterly interest, various redemption options, deep discount bond options etc.

Government Securities (G-Secs)

These are sovereign (credit risk-free) coupon bearing instruments which are issued by the Reserve Bank of India on behalf of the Government of India, in lieu of the Central Government's market borrowing programme. These securities have a fixed coupon that is paid on specific dates on half-yearly basis. These securities are available in a wide range of maturity dates, from short dated (less than one year) to long dated (up to twenty years).

RBI Tax Free Bonds

RBI Tax Free Bonds are special bonds issued by the RBI offering tax-free facility. The rate of interest in such bonds is generally lower than regular bonds and hence these attract only high taxpayers. These bonds tend to be long-term instruments.

RBI Tax free bonds are very safe as they come from the country's central bank. Returns from the bonds are steady and can be ascertained clearly in advance based on the YTM.

Treasury Bills

Short-term (up to 91 day) bearer discount securities issued by the Government as a means of financing its cash requirements.

Company Debentures

Instruments issued by a company bearing a fixed rate of interest usually payable half yearly on specific dates with the principal amount repayable on a particular date on redemption. Debentures are normally secured/ charged against the assets of the company in favour of the debenture holder. Companies borrow from debenture-holders and generally offer a fixed rate of interest to such investors. Most debentures are redeemed after a specified period. The period could be short (less than 18 months) or long depending on the terms of issue. In some cases, companies also pay a premium on maturity.

Investors can subscribe to public issue of debentures by companies or buy debentures from the secondary market. In view of the fixed returns from these securities, prices of debentures are generally much less volatile relative to shares. Investors earn interest and capital gains (difference between the purchase price and the sale price or if held till redemption, the difference between purchase price and the redemption price).

Yields on debentures could be higher or lower than the specified rate of interest depending on the correlation between face value and market value.

For example, assume that a ₹ 100 debenture carrying 15 per cent interest is bought for ₹ 90. The price paid is ₹ 90 whereas the interest earned is ₹ 15. This would translate to a yield of 16.67 per cent.

In the above example, the investor would get back ₹ 100 from the company (face value) if he holds the debentures up to maturity. Hence, apart from the interest yield of 16.67 per cent, he would also gain ₹ 10 by way of capital gain. When this capital gain is also considered for computing the yield, it is termed as Yield to Maturity (YTM).

Most debt issues are required to be rated by credit rating agencies. Rating indicates the quality of the instrument. An indication of credit rating is given below:

Table. Credit Rating Symbols and What They Mean

High Investment Grades	
AAA	Highest Safety
AA	High Safety
Investment Grades	
A	Adequate Safety
BBB	Moderate Safety
Speculative Grades	
BB	Inadequate Safety
B	High Risk
C	Substantial Risk
D	In Default

Different rating agencies might have different symbols than the ones given above.

Returns from high quality debentures are steady and can be ascertained in advance based on the YTM. These returns would vary only if the company were to renege on its payment obligations. An investor need not be actively involved in investment management, except to the extent of keeping basic track of companies, which might be performing badly and could fail to fulfill their interest or repayment obligations.

Commercial Paper

A short term promise to repay a fixed amount that is placed on the market either directly or through a specialized intermediary. It is usually issued by companies with a high credit standing in the form of a promissory note redeemable at par to the holder on maturity and therefore, doesn't require any guarantee. Commercial paper is a money market instrument issued normally for a tenure of 90 days.

Certificate of Deposit

A time deposit with a bank. CDs are generally issued by commercial banks but they can be bought through brokerages. They bear a specific maturity date, a specified interest rate, and can be issued in any denomination, much like bonds. Like all time deposits, the funds may not be withdrawn on demand.

MUTUAL FUND SCHEMES

Mutual Funds are entities which collect funds from small investors, pool these funds together and invest into various equity and debt instruments (or even money market instruments and government securities). Mutual Funds employ competent finance professionals who research the markets effectively, which an individual investor might not successfully manage. Further, these entities are taken seriously by a company's management in view of their large fund base. Mutual fund schemes can be open-ended or close-ended. Open-ended schemes do not have a fixed maturity. Investors can buy/sell units of such schemes from/to the fund itself at prices determined by the Net Asset Value (NAV) plus or minus a load, applied either at the point of purchase or sales by the fund. Liquidity in open-ended mutual funds is very high.

In case of close-ended mutual funds, liquidity depends on the availability of buyers and sellers in the stock exchange where these units are listed. Thus, liquidity is similar to that of listed shares. Close-ended schemes may be listed on stock exchanges and traded at listed prices. If it is not listed, regular repurchase facility will be provided by the mutual Funds. These prices could vary substantially from the NAV due to investor perceptions, demand and supply situations etc. NAV is a common expression in the mutual fund industry and denotes Net Asset Value. NAV per Unit is equal to the Market value of the assets of the scheme less liabilities divided by number of units outstanding.

Mutual Fund Schemes are floated with objectives that determine their investment pattern. A growth-oriented scheme would predominantly invest in equities and would seek capital appreciation as its major objective. A debt-oriented scheme would predominantly invest in debt instruments and would seek regular income as its major objective. A balanced scheme would invest partially in equity and rest in debt and would balance the objectives of growth and income. Tax Saving Schemes are designed to provide tax shelter to the investors.

Equity-oriented Mutual Funds

These funds invest in equities and generate capital appreciation. Redemptions are effected within 2-3 days in most such mutual fund schemes. Safety levels are low though slightly better than direct investment in shares by investors, as most funds invest in a basket of equities thus hedging their individual risks partly through the basket approach.

Returns in equity funds are volatile and would depend on the market movement in general and investment expertise of the mutual fund in particular. An investor need not be actively involved in investment management. However, the investor should watch the NAV and the load.

Debt-oriented Mutual Funds

These funds seek to provide a regular return to investors and would invest in debt instruments where risk levels are lower (relative to equity), and would generate regular returns for the fund and consequently for its investors.

In view of the nature of the fund's investments, safety levels are relatively high in debt-oriented funds. An investor need not be actively involved in investment management. However, the investor should be watchful about the NAV movements. While generally the returns from debt funds are expected to be steady, there could be NAV volatility if the interest ranges change.

Mutual Funds also float innovative schemes like index funds, specific sector funds, money market funds, gilt funds, etc. Index funds seek to invest in index stocks (*e.g.* only those stocks which are used to determine the Sensex, Nifty etc.).

Specific sector funds seek to invest into specified sectors like Pharmaceuticals or Software. Money market and gilt funds seek to invest into those markets alone.

Tax Saving Schemes of Mutual Funds and Financial Institutions

These schemes are floated by mutual funds and financial institutions after obtaining government approval for offering specified tax benefits to investors. An investor thus gets an additional sweetener. Other features of these investment options are on par with the regular features of mutual funds and financial institutional options.

INVESTMENT AND CASH FLOW WITH IMPERFECT CAPITAL MARKETS

Many models of capital market imperfections reach the conclusion that financing an investment project is cheaper with 'internal' than with 'external' funds. (Internal funds are those that the firm owns, for example, in its bank account; external funds are obtained from outsiders like banks or new investors).

Such models tend to be highly specialized, with entrepreneurs who miraculously receive exogenously specified endowments of 'internal' cash and who make a one- (or at most two-) period investment decision.

This is a striking contrast with the generality of the canonical q model of investment in which optimizing firms make investment decisions that take into account infinite future paths of adjustment costs, marginal products of capital, taxes, and all other features of the environment.

But models with imperfect capital markets are always very clear on who receives what cash, when, and why. In contrast, the power of the q model comes at a high cost: The model has no implications whatsoever for the firm's decisions about when and how to make payments to shareholders and lenders.

Modigliani-Miller

To see this, consider the benchmark discrete-time framework qModel without taxes or depreciation, and (as in that handout) assume that the firm issues or repurchases shares to maintain a number of shares s_t outstanding equal to the size of the physical capital stock (so $s_t=k_t$ in every period). Suppose we assume that the firm has a 'dividend policy': In every period, it pays to each shareholder a dividend equal to the flow of revenues per share.

In this case, the value of all the firm's shares s_t (the equity value of the firm) will be,

$$\hat{e}_t(s_t) = \max_{\{i\}_t^{\infty}} \mathbb{E}_t \left[\sum_{n=0}^{\infty} \beta^n (\pi_{t+n} - \xi_{t+n}) \right]$$

(Notice that because the firm always has $s_t = k_t$ the value of the firm's shares defined here $\hat{e}_t(s_t)$ is identical to the value of the firm's capital $e_t(k_t)$ defined in q Model.)

Now suppose the firm decides to deviate, just a little bit, from this dividend policy. It issues an extra share in period, which (assuming capital markets are efficient) raises an amount of money equal to the share price λ_t; it invests the proceeds in the riskless asset, earning return R, then pays out the resulting cash to shareholders in the next period. However, we assume that the firm continues to maximize its value. This modifies the infinite sum to:

but since by assumption $\beta=R^{-1}$ this expression reduces to the original expression.

The point can be extended to show that the firm can raise an arbitrary amount of money in one period, paying it back in another, or vice versa, without having any effect on its value or its optimal investment plans.

This is an example of the famous theorem by Modigliani and Miller, who showed that under perfect capital markets the value of the firm is identical whether its investment is financed by equity, debt, or any combination of the two.

It is precisely to get around this result that models of imperfect capital markets were invented, since from the beginning many economists did not believe that the result is a plausible description of reality (including, I believe, Modigliani and Miller). Indeed, the existence (and high salaries) of corporate financial officers constitute a proof that the proposition is not true – if it were true, CFOs would have no effect on the value of the firm, and could all be fired (thus saving the firm their salaries!). What remains true, however, is that models of investment that relax the assumption of perfect capital markets are much more difficult to work with and harder to extract implications from than the perfect capital markets versions.

A testable result that generally emerges from these models, however, is that the amount of a firm's investment depends on the amount of cash the firm has on hand with which to finance that investment.

Testing for the Failure of Modigliani-Miller

qModel shows that the q model can be manipulated (abstracting from depreciation, taxes, and other complications) to yield an implication for investment dynamics of approximately the following kind:

$$i \approx (q - 1)/\omega$$

The simplest class of imperfect capital markets models is one in which the firm is constrained to pay dividends to shareholders equal to whatever is its flow of cash after subtracting off expenses. But the rate of return that the firm must pay for external funds exceeds the return it can earn on internal funds. Without going into details, the rough implication of this is that an empirical model of the firm's investment choices should augment with a measure of the funds the firm has in its hands at the time the investment decision is made:

$$i \approx \psi_0 + \psi_1 q + \psi_2 \pi$$

A large literature spurred by the seminal paper of Fazzari, Hubbard, and Petersen estimates equations like this, and virtually always finds a statistically significant estimate of ψ_2, interpreted as indicating the importance of 'cash flow' for investment decisions. But there are many criticisms of this literature, and the importance of imperfections in capital markets remains a lively area of debate. My own view is that the most persuasive evidence of large deviations from the benchmark of the MM theorem is the fact that the financial services industry (including corporate CFOs) absorbs a very substantial amount of resources every year. Why would such a large industry exist if the informational problems were easy to solve? It wouldn't - especially in the internet era, where it would be a trivial matter to match up borrowers and lenders in the absence of informational and enforcement difficulties.

MARKET EFFICIENCY IN INTERPRETING INFORMATION

Investors with different information sets may value an asset differently, and even investors with the same set of fundamental information may disagree on asset values because of different subjective interpretations of that information and different expectations about an uncertain future. Poor information interpretation and expectations can lead to some investors being willing to trade assets at prices much different from the intrinsic value that can be computed from the best or most efficient interpretation and set of expectations.

When transaction prices deviate from the intrinsic value, the opportunity for abnormal profits exists for investors who are operating with the best interpretation and set of expectations. Abnormal profits exist by buying assets below their intrinsic value and selling them above their intrinsic value, thereby earning returns above the required return. Required returns are typically measured using the CAPM equation which indicates that, for any asset j:

$$i_j = R_f + (B_j [E(R_m) - R_f]), \quad (18\text{-}1)$$

where R_f is the risk-free rate, $E(R_m)$ is the expected return on the market portfolio, and B_j is the beta of asset j.

Investors with the best information, analysis, and set of expectations may not only be able to obtain abnormal profits for themselves but may also be able to sell investment advice for a fee that would enable other investors to also earn abnormal profits. Theoretically, they can continue to do so until the market prices approach intrinsic value (although it is often difficult to convince other investors that one has the best investment recommendations, since anyone, including poor analysts and even swindlers, can sell investment advice). This process can result in the price of assets selling below intrinsic value being bid up towards intrinsic value, while sales of assets selling above intrinsic value result in the price falling towards intrinsic value (although trading based on poor investment analysis can cause the opposite price reaction). When market prices approximately equal intrinsic value, there are no longer any opportunities for abnormal profits, and the market is defined to be efficient. In other words, market efficiency means that V=P, and $E(R_{j)}$=i.

There are two major degrees of market efficiency: semi-strong and strong. With semi-strong market efficiency, abnormal profits are not obtainable using all public information. With strong market efficiency, abnormal profits are not obtainable using any information, including inside information not made public. Differences between semi-strong and strong market efficiency are smaller when more information is made public (either voluntarily or due to government requirements of full disclosure) because less inside information then exists.

Tests Of Market Efficiency And Investment Performance

Tests of market efficiency in interpreting information generally focus on the performance of some set of assets, portfolios, strategies, or managers to see if they generate abnormal profits. If these tests reveal that a set of assets is more likely to outperform the risk-return relationship in equation, the implication is that those assets are mispriced, and that the market for those assets is inefficient.

Similarly, if a test reveals that a portfolio or portfolios run by an investment managerare likely to outperform the risk-return relationship in, the implication is that the manager can find mispriced assets in what appears to be an inefficient market. That indeed is one of the goals of investment management..

Measurement of Performance

The investment performance of an asset, strategy, or manager can be measured by several different criteria. These performance measures include the investment alpha, the Treynor ratio, the Sharpe ratio, and the geometric mean.

The Investment Alpha (Jensen Alpha)

Computation of abnormal profits frequently employs an investment alpha, which is calculated using some form of the following regression equation:

$$R_j - R_f = a_0 + a_1 B_j [R_m - R_f] + z_j$$

where a_0, is the regression intercept often called the investment alpha, a 1, is the regression coefficient, z_j is the regression residual, and actual periodic returns R for each investment are measured over some time interval (such as monthly returns over 60 months). Given the CAPM equation (18-1), a0 should equal 0, and a1 should equal I (and is often restricted to equal I in many tests). Tests of market efficiency focus on the a, term, which measures the abnormal return that exists that expected by CAPM equation (18-1). Using average returns, the investment alpha can also be written as

$$a_0 = R_j - R_f - B_j [R - R_f]. \quad (18\text{-}2b)$$

Although the a_0, term is often referred to as the investment alpha, it is also sometimes named the Jensen alpha after one of the earliest researchers in this field. If a, is found to be statistically significant from 0 for some set of assets or portfolios, there is evidence of abnormal profits. The abnormal profits can be earned by buying the assets if $a_{00} > 0$).

Because the regression factors out the return required on the asset for beta risk, the investment alpha evaluates the contribution of the asset to the performance of a diversified portfolio. As a result, the investment alpha may be used to evaluate the performance of both diversified and undiversified portfolios.

The Treynor Ratio

A similar measure of performance is the Treynor ratio, which computes the average return the risk-free rate per unit of beta risk. In particular,

$$\text{Treynor Ratio} = (R_j - R_f)/B_j.$$

Like the investment alpha, the Treynor ratio may be used to evaluate the performance of both diversified and undiversified portfolios, although it suffers the problem of potentially being a meaningless performance measure when the beta is zero, very small, or negative.

The Sharpe Ratio

Another measure of performance is the Sharpe ratio, which is named after another one of the earliest researchers in this area. This ratio measures return the risk-free rate per unit of total risk, i.e.,

$$\text{Sharpe Ratio} = (R_p - R_f)/S_p,$$

where s_p is the standard deviation of return on portfolio p. Because much of the standard deviation of return on individual assets is diversified away in most portfolios, this measure of performance is not relevant for isolated parts of a portfolio (such as a single asset). Instead, this measure of performance is only relevant when applied to an investor's total risky portfolio p.

The Geometric Mean Return (Compounded Return)

Other tests of market efficiency and performance also exist. For instance, some researchers (such as 1970 and 1971 research by Hakansson) have suggested simply measuring performance by the geometric mean or compounded return over time, which is computed as,

$$\text{Geometric mean} = [(1+R_1)(1+R_2)\ldots(1+R_{T-1})(1+R_T)]^{1/T}-1. \quad (18\text{-}5)$$

If the geometric mean or compounded return on a portfolio exceeds that of the return on the market portfolio, the performance of the portfolio is deemed to be superior. Although risk and return variation dc affect compounded returns are therefore implicitly incorporated into the performance criteria, the different risk aversion levels and diversification needs of many investors make the framework in more generally applicable (because it explicitly incorporates systematic risk).

Use of the Performance Measures

Measures of investment performance may be used to evaluate whether a particular market for a particular set of assets is efficient or not. If a market is found to be inefficient, the implication is that opportunities for abnormal rates of returns exist, although it may take years, or even decades, to realise such abnormal returns if prices move towards value very slowly.

Measures of investment performance may also be used to evaluate investment managers. If the portfolio managed by an investment analyst earns abnormal returns, the implication is that the market in which the analyst invests is inefficient and that the analyst is skillful in picking out the mispriced assets. Individuals and institutions who decide not to make their own investment decisions should choose managers who can generate abnormally high rates of return.

When using the foregoing performance measures, it is usually wise to make comparisons with a peer group. Such a comparison is especially important when using the geometric mean compounded rate of return (which does not explicitly adjust for risk). For example, the compounded return of a bond mutual fund could be compared with the average compounded return of all bond funds, the returns of an international fund could be compared to that of the average international mutual fund return, the returns of a specialty mutual fund that invests into telecommunications stocks could be compared with other funds that specialize in that sector, etc.

Empirical Evidence Of Market Efficiency

The overall evidence from empirical tests indicates that some markets may be inefficient and that opportunities for abnormal profits may exist. However, the pricing efficiency is fairly high in liquid markets, implying limited opportunities for abnormal profits there.

Primary Markets

Pricing efficiency in the primary market is often a function of the amount and quality of analysis done by investors and issuers. A failure to properly conduct fundamental analysis can lead to substantial differences between value and price. Such mispricing can be especially large in negotiated and private placement markets where a limited number of investors may be involved on any one particular issue (such as in the case of a bank providing a loan).

Even in auction and underwritten markets where there are a large number of investors participating, the efficiency of the initial issue price in incorporating all public information can be low. For instance, prices of new stocks being issued to the public for the first time, called Initial Public Offerings (IPOs), tend to vary widely on the first day of trading in the secondary market. It is not totally unusual for prices of IPOs to rise more than 100% by the end of the first day, or to fall substantially.

Often, fundamental analysis of information on a new security can indicate the direction and magnitude of returns. One study has indicated that positive recommendations on an IPO by analysts at an investment bank not associated with underwriting the IPO are associated with returns that far exceed market returns. In addition, there are sometimes more subtle information clues in an IPO prospectus. For instance, when employees sell some of their own stock in conjunction with a new stock offering by the corporation, there is empirical evidence of investors suffering negative abnormal returns following issue. Although many employees (especially those in a closely held corporation) may sell stock of their corporation in order to reduce their portfolio concentration in one asset, employee stock sales may also indicate that they feel the price is greater than the value. Since employees may possess inside information not available to investors, their decisions to sell stock may have significant information content. There is some evidence of underpricing in the primary issue market on average.

For instance, for IPO stocks going public for the first time, abnormal returns average approximately 10% on the first day. This underpricing may represent compensation for the uncertainty of the pricing, as well as serve to facilitate floatation of the issue. Because of this average underpricing, there is usually an excess demand from investors for an IPO (investors are also typically not charged a transaction cost for buying in the primary market, as this cost is borne by the issuer, as are the administrative costs of registering with the SEC and the implicit costs associated with underpricing). To ration the stock in the face of excessive demand at the IPO price, investment bankers generally give the first choice of an IPO purchase to their "best" customers (i.e., those who have paid them the most commissions in the past), who may also qualify for special non-public information. However, it should also be the "best" customers pass some IPOs by because they perceive them to be overpriced, and such IPOs that might therefore be available to other customers may be less likely to perform well. Moreover, there is some empirical evidence that, longer-term, the average IPO tends to underperform the average stock (especially after the first day).

Secondary Markets

As has been summarized by 1970 and 1991 studies by Fama, tests of various secondary investment markets indicate a fair amount of efficiency in incorporating fundamental information into price, especially for liquid markets where there is a substantial amount of trading and investment advisory information. For instance, cosmetic changes in accounting procedures that do not affect cash flows, or stock splits that merely divide value into more pieces (without an increase in earnings or dividends), have not been found to result in abnormal returns. In addition, empirical evidence exists to indicate that stock prices already incorporate much fundamental information about stocks, and when there is an announcement that is different from expectations, a market price reaction occurs in the direction of the deviation from expectation within a few minutes of the announcement. For instance, a 1997 study by Kim, Lin, and Slovin indicated that professional purchase recommendations on a stock, on average, drive up the price by 4% on the NYSE and ASE and by 7% on the NASDAQ, with the movement taking place within 5 and 15 minutes, respectively.

However, there is also substantial evidence of stock returns being positively related to past returns and fundamental information announcements for months. There is also some evidence of a reversal from a trend after time periods of over one year. In a 1998 study, Daniel, Hirshleifer, and Subrahmanyam developed a psychological theory of investor behaviour to explain this phenomenon, whereby investors tend to become overconfident when stock prices and information reinforce their prior beliefs and trading decisions, so that they drive stocks in waves in one direction until they become so mispriced that they begin to move in an opposite trend, which itself feeds on a loss of confidence and pessimism that fuels further price moves in that opposite direction. In a 1998 study, Olson et al. have shown empirically that some of the technical trading signals advocated by are successful enough in picking up such trends to permit profitable trading strategies.

There are also other exceptions to market efficiency. For instance, research indicates that stocks with lower P/e ratios (and higher earnings yields) tend to outperform stocks with higher P/e ratios (and lower earnings yields) on a risk-adjusted basis. In addition, higher yielding bonds (junk) tend to outperform lower yielding bonds (investment grade and Treasury bonds) even over periods when general credit conditions are detrimental to bonds subject to high default, and even over periods when falling interest rates would cause greater appreciation on T-bonds with no call risk and on lower coupon bonds in general with longer durations. Such findings provide evidence that some yield information is not fully reflected in market prices. It is, however, possible that a portion of such abnormal returns reflect transaction cost premiums related to the illiquidity of trading many junk bonds and small company stocks.

Studies of the performance, of professional investment managers provide evidence that market prices do not fully incorporate all fundamental information. In particular, some tests have indicated that professional investors (like mutual fund managers, pension fund managers, and stockbrokers) in the U.S. are able to outperform the market average on a risk-adjusted basis by earning about a 1% higher return per year net of management fees and transaction costs over the long term. With annual management fees averaging about 1% of assets managed, with annual trading turnover averaging about 100% of the size of the portfolio being managed, and with transaction costs for institutions trading NYSE stocks ranging between 1% and 4%, the total expenses incurred by professional investment managers may be 2-5% (with higher transaction costs for more illiquid stock investments like in the OTC market).

The managers must be able to beat the market by 3-6% gross of expenses in order to beat the market by 1% net of expenses. In a 1996 study, Womack has reported results which indicate that investment banker recommendations are able to beat the market by such amounts (this finding is consistent with that reported by the *Wall Street Journal* in its quarterly review of the leading brokerage house, recommendations that generally indicates virtually all of the investment banks make stock selections which greatly outperform the stock indexes over 5-year periods).

There also exists some evidence that investment managers who have outperformed the average over a fairly long past time interval (such as at least 4 years) tend to perform above average in the future.In particular, studies of mutual fund performance indicate that returns over one 5-year interval are positively related to the returns over a subsequent time interval. These results provide some support for the hypothesis that above-average performance over a past interval may not be due solely to luck. However, it should be emphasized that there are many cases of inconsistent performance among investment managers, and that past performance is no guarantee of future performance.There is also evidence that better-trained managers are able to outperform those that are not so well educated. For instance, a 1994 study by Shukla and Singh found that mutual funds managed by Chartered Financial Analysts (CFAs) outperformed those that were not run by CFAs.

Although some studies have found evidence that some sets of professional managers are not able to beat the market over some time intervals net of expenses, the general results indicate that some investment managers are able to beat the market before expenses. These results imply that good professional investment managers can identify securities whose values differ significantly from market prices, and that it is possible to profit from such opportunities. These findings compare favourably to those for investment clubs and discount broker customers who generally do not have access to professional investment management and whose average risk-adjusted returns are lower than for market indexes, both before and after transaction costs

In addition, some studies have found that managers with low operating costs are, net of expenses, able to outperform managers with high operating costs. Here, total costs include management expenses, turnover or transaction costs, and load fees. Thus, although net abnormal profit opportunities may exist in investments, the gains can be partially (if not fully) eaten up by high expenses. For example, for futures funds, whose annual expenses often exceed 20% of the value of the funds, returns net of expenses average no better than those obtainable from a buy-and-hold strategy, although gross returns are much higher. Even investors without professional investment management (such as customers of discount brokers) tend to perform better (but still worse than market indexes) when they trade less actively and have less transaction costs (e.g., in a 1998 report, Simon explains that female customers of discount brokerage firms tend to perform worse than male customers after transaction costs largely because they tend to trade less actively). There is some evidence that the market for stocks of smaller companies are more inefficient than the market for stocks of larger companies that are more widely traded and analysed. Just for example, a 1998 report by Tam indicated that each of the largest 10 mutual funds which invest predominately into U.S. small company stocks earned higher risk-adjusted returns than an index of small stocks (the Russell 2000) over the last 10 years. This finding implies that it is possible to exploit the inefficiencies in market pricing of stocks of smaller companies even after the typically larger transaction costs and management fees (which compares very favourably to the studies that indicate even the average mutual that invests into U.S. large company stocks is not able to outperform an index of large company stocks net of management fees and transaction costs over some time intervals). The fairly illiquid OTC Bulletin Board and pink sheet markets are widely perceived as having the greatest market inefficiencies (and therefore the greatest potential for profitable trading and investment).

Even in the most liquid U.S. markets, lawyers frequently challenge the concept of value equaling market price, citing widespread evidence of market inefficiency there. In addition, the Internal Revenue Service (IRS) does not accept a market price as a conclusive appraisal. In particular, tax courts have accepted appraisals of securities at a value substantially different from market price when the market price was based on the sale of only a small portion of the total amount of a security outstanding, or when a sale occurs during special circumstances (including when the general market is considered to be greatly under- or overpricing securities, as often occurs just prior to or after stock market crashes).

In addition, even in the liquid markets where prices are fairly efficient in reflecting all public information, market prices are often fairly inefficient in reflecting inside information. As a result, although illegal in the U.S. (and in many other countries), it has been found that high abnormal returns (net of costs) are available from trading on nonpublic inside information (even in liquid markets). Decisions by insiders to buy or sell stock often provide clues to public investors concerning the fundamental value of the company given inside information. Similar information effects have also been found to occur when the corporation itself buys or sells its own stock, with a rise in price occurring following an announcement to repurchase stock and a fall in price occurring following an announcement to sell new stock.

Evidence of market inefficiency has also been found in some foreign markets. For instance, some evidence has been found of abnormal profits being available from trading stocks based on the existence of a positive or negative information announcement that has been public for several months. Following brokerage recommendations has also been found to result in abnormal profits in some foreign markets. As in the U.S., the more illiquid the market and the less sophisticated the investor, the more inefficient the market is in reflecting value

Interpretation Of Market Price

Although the market price of an investment may not represent a totally accurate or objective indicator of value, it does represent a sort of consensus view on the value of an asset. Many may feel the asset is worth more, while others may feel it is worth less, and the market price is the average of those valuation estimates weighted by the dollar amount of orders placed. For liquid securities that are widely and heavily traded, the market price represents the consensus value of a large number of investors. For illiquid securities that are infrequently traded, the market price represents the consensus value of a limited number of investors.

As a consensus estimate of value, the market price is often a reasonable indicator of value if one has no other information. It is thus similar to the expectations theory forecast of interest rates, which is based on a consensus forecast of interest rates and bond prices. The consensus estimate is invariably wrong and frequently by a large amount, but it is often difficult to produce a more accurate estimate.

Implications For Investors

The major implication for investors is that fundamental analysis may be useful (and necessary) in markets that are not totally efficient (whereas indexing may be appropriate in efficient markets). In addition, regardless of whether markets are efficient or inefficient, it is always necessary to analyse risk, taxes, and transaction costs.

Selecting Investments or Managers in Secondary Markets

The analysis of market pricing efficiency indicates that market prices can deviate from value, even in the secondary market. As a result, it may be possible to locate underpriced investments, and, with sufficient skill, the time and expense associated with fundamental analysis may be justified. However, efficiency in analysis and trading is required to generate profits net of costs.

Choosing a Money Manager

Many investors may feel that they do not possess the expertise to find prices that deviate from value (and thereby "beat" the market). In addition, many investors with smaller portfolios and/or with insufficient time (because of other job constraints) may not have the economies of scale and scope to earn abnormal returns in excess of the management and trading costs incurred in an active investment strategy. Such investors may optimally select investment managers and advisors, who do have the expertise and economies of scale and scope. For instance, such investors might consider investing through actively managed mutual funds, subscribing to an investment advisory newsletter, and/or investing through full service brokers and financial planners who can provide the necessary advice.

The choice of manager or advisor can be made using the performance criteria described If investors choose different managers or advisors for different portions of their portfolios, they may still need to determine how much to allocate to each investment category.

For instance, if an investor believes that she or he has superior skill in selecting between different investment categories, that investor can justify performing an analysis.if she or he wanted to let investment managers choose specific securities within each asset category. On the other hand, if an investor does not wish to make any investment decisions at all, it is also possible to let a single mutual fund allocate money across all asset categories by investing into a superior-performing asset allocation fund.

Indexing

Some investors may not feel that they can pick out an honest investment manager or advisor who will sell services for a fee that is less than the value of those services. Such investors should consider investing into index mutual funds that track the market portfolio. In particular, if P approximates V, and if $E(R_j)=i$ after management and trading costs are subtracted from the gross returns that can be generated through fundamental analysis, the optimal portfolio p equals the market portfolio.

Because many index funds are indexed only within a specific asset category (such as a stock index fund or a bond index fund), investors following an indexing strategy would still have to allocate funds between stocks, bonds, foreign assets, and real assets. In order to attempt to match the return on the entire market portfolio, investors may allocate the risky portion of their portfolios to each investment category according to the weights in the market portfolio of all assets.Besides reducing the time and expense of evaluating investments, indexing also reduces the tax and transaction costs of trading. Nevertheless, indexing does incur some transaction costs and capital gains taxes, as securities that are replaced in the index must be sold and new securities in the index must be purchased. One study has indicated that the tax costs associated with tracking the S&P 500 index reduced after-tax returns by about 0.25% per year over the 1988-97 interval. While such costs could be reduced slightly by buying and holding the original stocks in the index, cash acquisitions would still result in some tax and transaction costs.

It should also be no matter how broad the index or set of indexes in which an investor takes a position, it is unlikely that all assets in the world will be purchased. As a result, the very many investors who do index their investments could drive up the prices of assets in the indices beyond their fundamental value, implying more lucrative investment opportunities on assets not included in major indices.

The Necessity of Security Analysis in Primary Markets

Even if investors do not believe they can earn abnormal profits in the secondary market, it is still necessary for financial analysts to be able to analyse the value of new securities issued in the primary market. Poor security selection and poor pricing in the primary market can occur if either the seller or the buyer of the new security fails to analyse the value of the investment.

An Example of Mortgage Valuation

Because the average homeowner is not equipped with computer models of mortgage pricing, and because the average homeowner is usually not able to monitor refunding opportunities on a daily basis, most homeowners are unable to determine the most appropriate time to prepay their mortgages. Some may prepay earlier than is optimal, but most tend to prepay later than is optimal. As a result, the prepayment right in a mortgage has less value to the average homeowner than it would to a more sophisticated mortgagor. This lower value is typically incorporated into standardized residential mortgage pricing, as lenders usually price mortgages based on some expected prepayment pattern that is normally based on the past behaviour and evidence on average mortgagor prepayments. Thus, the lower value of the prepayment rights given an expectation of mortgagors suboptimally prepaying is passed on to all mortgagors in the form of a lower coupon rate.

For sophisticated mortgagors, this lender practice represents an opportunity to sell an asset for a price that is in excess of its value. In particular, sophisticated mortgagors, who will prepay their mortgages when it is optimal to do so, generally are offered the lower interest rate on their mortgages just like any other mortgage or (because the lenders cannot differentiate between sophisticated and other borrowers). By prepaying the mortgage only at optimal times, mortgagors obtain the full value of the prepayment rights in the mortgage but do not have to pay for them with a higher coupon rate.

Sophisticated mortgagors can also differentiate between different mortgage offers from different lenders. For instance, sophisticated mortgagors can determine whether a lender's offer to borrow at a specified fixed rate is better than another offer to borrow at a specified adjustable rate (that typically varies with some market interest rate like the T-bill rate).

In addition to being able to analytically compare fixed-rate mortgages (FRMs) and adjustable rate mortgages (ARMs), sophisticated borrowers can evaluate differences in other mortgage terms such as maturity, points, ARM teaser rates, and ARM caps. Points represent the percentage by which the mortgage is sold to the lender at a discount.

In addition to subtracting out points, the closing costs of entering into a mortgage (including title insurance, application fees, appraisal fees, and tax escrow waiver fees, together which average about 1% of the value of the mortgage) must also be subtracted from the face value of the mortgage in order to compute the net amount of cash received by the borrower. For ARMS, teaser rates represent an initially low coupon payment on an ARM, which is subsequently set to increase substantially even if interest rates do not change. Annual ARM caps represent the maximum percentage increase in ARM rates allowed per year. A lifetime ARM cap represents the maximum ARM rate that can be charged.

Let's take an example for October 19, 1998. Assume a homeowner has about 28 years in payments left on a 7.875% fixed-rate mortgage. The homeowner estimates his probability of default to be 0.2%, with a 50% expected value of the mortgage in default (because of the typical high value of the home used as collateral). The expected loss rate is therefore 0.2(1-.5)=0.10%. The homeowner also estimates a 5% chance of moving to a new home each year.

Plugging these numbers into the SIA software indicates the value of the homeowner's mortgage to be $1000 per $1000 in principal but to be $1016.55 if it were not currently callable (implying that the mortgage should optimally now be prepaid). Because the mortgage value exceeds the normal mortgage prepayment price of par value plus normal refunding costs of 1.2% of par value, the homeowner should consider refinancing the mortgage. By doing so, the borrower saves the difference between what the mortgage would be worth if it were not currently prepayable, 101.66%, and the prepayment price of 100% of par.

The difference here is 1.66% of par, which exceeds normal 1.2% refunding costs, and so prepayment of the bond should be considered. therefore enables the homeowner to evaluate the optimal time to prepay. Using intuition or rules of thumb such as "prepay whenever mortgage rates fall 2% below the mortgage coupon rate" generally result in prepayments that are later than optimal.

At this time, the homeowner shops around and finds a lender who is offering a 30-year fixed-rate mortgage with a 6.75% coupon and 1.5 points plus closing costs equal to 0.5% of the mortgage par value. The fixed-rate mortgage offer is valued using the SIA software as 97.46% of par. After deducting the 1.5+0.5=2% in points and closing costs for the fixed-rate mortgage, the borrower receives 98% of par in cash, which, compared to the present value for the obligation of 97.46% of par, represents a net present value gain of 0.54% of par.

In this example, the net proceeds to the borrower from the new loan (after deducting points and fees) exceeded the present value of the future loan payments, while the present value of the future payments on the old loan was greater than the prepayment price. As a result, it was clear that the mortgage should be refinanced. However, such a clear situation may not always exist, in which case a decision rule may be used. In particular, if the present value of the future payments on the new loan exceed the net proceeds to the borrower, it may still be optimal to refinance if the net gain from refinancing exceeds zero, i.e., if

Net Cashnew loan - Vnew loan + Vold loan - Prepayment Priceold loan > 0. (18-6)

Although this framework may not be necessary in obvious cases like the foregoing 30-year fixed-rate mortgage offer, the methodology can be useful for measuring the gain from the refinancing: Gain from refinancing with the fixed-rate = 98 - 97.46 + 101.66 - 100 = 2.20% of par > 0. (18-7)

In addition to helping to determine whether it is optimal to refinance, this type of analysis can also be used to choose from different refinancing alternatives. For instance, in the foregoing example, assume that lenders are also offering at this time a 30-year ARM with a coupon that equals the 1-year T-bill rate plus 1%, an initial rate of 4.75%, a 2% annual cap, an 10.75% lifetime cap and two points plus closing costs equal to 0.5% of the mortgage principal. For the ARM here, the cap restricts the coupon rate from going up more than 2% per year (i.e., the maximum rate is 6.75% in the second year) and restricts the coupon rate from going above 10.75% at any time. The SIA software, the value of this ARM is 97.74% of par.

The computer analysis indicates that the fixed rate mortgage is the better deal for the sophisticated mortgagor. In particular, after deducting 2.0+0.5=2.5% in points and closing costs for the ARM, the borrower receives 97.5% of par in cash, while the payments on the variable-rate debt have a present value of 97.74% of par, for a net present value loss of 0.24%. The borrower should therefore take the 30-year fixed-rate mortgage which provides the 0.54% gain.

Nevertheless, if the borrower had not found such advantageous terms on the 30-year fixed-rate mortgage, the ARM might have been acceptable, even though it has an estimated net present value loss before considering the benefits of refinancing.

In particular, even though the ARM results in the borrower receiving a cash amount that is lower than the present value of his debt, refinancing would still be optimal to doing nothing, as the loss on the ARM would be more than offset by the gain from prepaying the old 7.875% mortgage:

Refinancing gain with the ARM = 97.5 - 97.74 + 101.66 - 100 = 1.42%, (18-8) although it is clearly not as profitable as refinancing with the existing fixed-rate mortgage offer.

It should also be noted that, for different homeowners, the value and choice of mortgages may be different. For instance, for homeowners with a much greater probability of moving to a new home (which is a probability estimate that the SIA software incorporates into the valuation analysis), ARMs frequently have more favourable value-to-price ratios (as the ARM teaser rate is worth relatively more in such circumstances whereas the call option on the fixed-rate mortgage is worth relatively less).

Although the mortgage lender will often be losing on the sophisticated mortgagors who prepay optimally and choose the best mortgages, the lenders more than make up for the losses by lending to mortgagors who are not sophisticated, who do not prepay optimally, and who cannot choose the best mortgage offer. If more mortgagors become sophisticated, lenders will either begin to start earning lower profits, or mortgage rates will have to rise relative to treasury rates.

Analysis of Taxes, Transaction Costs, and Multiperiod Risk

Regardless of whether investors believes they are capable of picking superior-performing investments or managers, it is still necessary for them to analyse transaction costs, taxes, and risk. Such analysis must be customised to meet the needs of each different investor.

Tax and Transaction Cost Management

To maximize net returns, the taxes on investment income and the transaction costs of conducting trades must be considered. Strategies that may maximize returns after transaction costs are discussed, which describes the markets with the lowest transaction costs. Guidelines for maximizing after-tax returns are provided, which shows how to select the optimal investment or type of account in which to make investments. Because each investor may have different cash inflows and outflows, different tax and trading strategies may be appropriate for different investors.

In all cases, a trade should be undertaken only if the gains from trading more than cover the transaction costs and taxes that arise from trading. For instance, assume an investor owns a stock with a price of $80 and assume that the investor would have to pay $2 per share in transaction costs and $15 per share in capital gains taxes if she sold it (because the investor had bought the stock at a much lower price of $4 fifteen months ago). The investor should generally hold onto this stock unless she believes that the stock's value is worth at least $15+$2=$17 less than the market price (i.e., only if the investor believed the stock was only worth less than $80-$17=$63 would it be optimal to sell the stock). Alternatively, if the investor could find another stock that was underpriced by enough to make up the difference, it might be optimal to sell the stock (e.g., if the investor found a stock selling for $70 that she thought was worth $95, she could justify selling the original stock just to be able to take advantage of the lucrative investment opportunity even if the original stock had a value equal to its $80 price).

Multiperiod Risk Management

The different cash needs and resources of different investors make evaluation of portfolio risk even more complex. many investors have complex needs and wishes, for which a Multiperiod analysis is necessary. Such an analysis is similar to the single period analysis describe that merely attempted to maximize expected return for a given constraint on the maximum annual loss an investor could afford. The analysis involves choosing that level of leverage that maximizes the statistical probability of the investors having enough cash to achieve their personal consumption and financial needs and wishes. However, the existence of Multiperiod needs and wishes necessitates the use of a computer.

Regardless of whether individual assets are selected directly by the investor, whether active mutual funds are used to choose individual assets, or even whether index funds are employed, it is possible to utilize the PORTFOLIO portion of the SIA software to determine the optimal amount to be put into the risk-free asset. The PORTFOLIO programme makes the conservative assumption that the expected return on each asset in a portfolio will equal the naive expected return given by (3-2). If the market is efficient, this estimate is the actual expected return. On the other hand, if the market is inefficient, and if superior analysis is used, the expected return should actually be greater than this expected return (thus making it a conservative estimate).

EFFICIENT MARKET THEORY

The fundamental approach, the security analyst or prospective investor is primarily interested in analyzing factors such as economic influences, industry factors, and pertinent company information such as product demand, earnings, dividends, and management, in order to calculate an intrinsic value for the firm's securities. He reaches an investment decision by comparing this value with the current market price of the security.

Technical analysts believe that they can discern patterns in price or volume movements, and that by observing and studying the past behaviour patterns of given stocks, they can use this accumulated historical information to predict the future price movements in the security. Technical analysis,, comprises many different subjective approaches, but all have one thing in common- a belief that these past movements are very useful in predicting future movements.

Financial Markets are influenced by money flows and information flows. In free and highly competitive markets, demand and supply pressures determine the prices or interest rates. In a theoretical sense, markets are said to be efficient, if there is a free flow of information and market absorbs this information fully and quickly. James Lorie has defined the efficient security market as follows:

"Efficiency...means the ability of the capital market to function, so that prices of securities react rapidly to new information. Such efficiency will produce prices that are appropriate in terms of current knowledge, and investors will be less likely to make unwise investments."

What will happen is that market making mechanism is free and unfettered. There are no pockets with holding information or interested parties making undue gains by insider information by manipulation of supply and demand forces. There will be no monopoly elements and malpractices or corruption etc. are not prevalent.

Information flow is free and costless. In the normal course, capital or money flows into areas which are most profitable which in turn depends on their efficiency and competitiveness.

Money flows also from less profitable to more profitable avenues if information flow is free, fast and costless. In such market scenario, all investors will have the same information, which is immediately reflected in the stock prices and nobody can gain extra profits.

Al instru- ments in the market will be correctly priced, as all the available infomration is perectly absorbed and any investor entering the market any time will have the same advantage or returns. No excess profits are possible in this scenario. As the demand and supply forces are playing their role freely, the emerging prices are fair and move in a randon manner.

Prices of today are no more a function of the prices in the past as the day-to-day forces move in an independent and random manner. This concept of randomness has led to the theory of random Walk in the determination of prices. This Random Walk hypothesis is thus a special case of the Efficient Market Theory.

Assumptions

For the capital market efficiency theory to operate, the following assumptions are made

- Infomration is free and quick to flow.
- All investors have the same access to information.
- Transaction costs, taxes and any bottlenecks are not there and not hampering the free forces of market.
- Investors are rational and beahve in a cost effective competitive manner for optimization of returns.
- Every investor has access to lending and borrowing at the same rate.
- Market prices are not stickly and absorb the market information quickly and the market responds to new technology, new trends, changes in tastes, habits of consumers etc., efficiently adn quickly.

In essence, the technician says that it is somewhat an exercise in futility to evaluate accurately a myriad of detailed information as the fundamentalist attempts to do. He chooses not to engage in this type of activity, but rather to allow others to do it for him.

Thus, after numerous analysts and investors evaluate this mountain of knowledge, their undoubtedly diverse opinions will be manifested in the price and volume activity of the shares in question. As this occurs, the technician acts solely on the basis of that price and volume activity, without cluttering his mind with all the detail that he feels is superfluous to his analysis. He also believes that his price and volume analysis incorporates one factor that is not explicitly incorporated in the fundamentalist approach-namely, the psychology of the market.

Random Walk Theory

Random walk theory poses a question- Can a series of historical stock prices or rates of return be an aid in predicting future stock prices or rates of return?

As per this theory, changes in stock prices are independent of each other. The prices of today are independent of the past trends. The present price is randomly determined and only information flow can influence prices. As information is free and independent, the resulting prices are free and independent.

A word of caution is necessary here. This Random walk hypothesis was postulated by researchers on the basis of empirical work on the market price behaviour. It does not therefore tantamount to the same theory as the capital market efficiency theory. Only market efficiency promotes randomness and is therefore not a necessary condition. The fact that prices move independently has been found empirically and the analysts found an explanation for this in the efficient function- ing of the markets and the market absorption of the information quickly and efficiently. The equilibrium price of a stock is determined by demand and supply forces, based on the available information. Quickly as the fresh information becomes available, a new equilibrium point is reached and the resultant price is thus independent of the part. This Random walk hypothesis contradicts the Chartist and Technical School which believes that the present prices are the result of the past trends and that averages discount all fluctua- tions and that the average trends move in a predictable manner as the history of trends repeats itself. On the other hand, fundamental school postulates that the prices are a function of the intrinsic value pf the stock and prices result from changes i the intrinsic value and information relating to fundamental factors influence the equilibrium prices. Random walk hypoth- esis is an offshoot or a phase of the capital market efficiency theorem. The market efficiency theory postulates that prices are the result of free flow of information which the market absorbs quickly and efficiently.

Assumption of Random Walk Theory

- Market is supreme and no individual investor or group can influence it.
- Stock prices discount all information quickly.
- Markets are efficient and that the flow of information is free and unbiased.

- All investors have free access to the same information and nobody has superior knowledge or expertise.
- Market quickly adjusts itself to any deviation from equilibrium level due to the operation of free forces of demand and supply.
- Market prices change only on information relating to the fundamentals, when the equilibrium level itself may shift.
- These prices move in an independent fashion, witin undue pressures or manipulation.
- Nobody has better knowledge or insider information.
- Investors behave in a rational manner and emand and supply forces are the result of rational investmnt decisions.
- Institutional investors or any major fund managers have to follow the market and market cannot be influenced by them.
- A large number of buyers & sellers and perfect market conditions of competition will prevail;

Random Walk and Efficient Market Theory

Random Walk hypothesis is considered as restatement or a form of Efficint Market Theory by some Analysts. The EM - (Efficient Market Hypothesis) is based on the flow of free and correct information and the market absorption of it. This information flow and its absorption by the market are the critical elements of this theory. There are three types of information affecting the market, namely, pst Prices and trends, other public information and inside information. If all these types are not absorbed perfectly by the market, there is a possibility of some gaining above average returns, from the investments. Based on the three types of information, the analysis have placed the market absorption and the related theory under three heads; namely:

- Weak Form of EMH, which absorbs only market price information,

- Semistrong Form which absorbs price information and also all other public information and
- Strong Form which absorbs all types of information including insider information.

Weak form of EMH is closely related to the Random Walk Hypothesis, as the past prices are already absorbed by the market and the present prices move therefore independently of the pat, which is the same as the Random walk hypothesis. The present trends are thus random variables, and past data cannot be used to predict the future. All the information on the past data on price trends and volumes was already absorbed earlier. As prices have no memory of the past, yesterday prices have nothing to do with today's prices. To give an example from BSE quotation Dr. Reddy Labs has yearly low of Rs. 190 and a high of Rs. 333; its price at close on Oct. 15, 1996 was Rs. 215, but it opened on Oct. 16, at Rs. 212 and closed at Rs. 210. A day later it opened again at a higher price, independent of the last closing. It is futile exercise that the present day price can be derived by any past data, at least in short run. If that is proved empirically, then prices move in a random fashion like the walk of a Drunkard, each move independent of the other. It is anybody's guess or the result of a toss of coin of what will be the price of TISCO today or Dr. Reddy Labs tomorrow. Thus the Random Walk hypothesis states that prices move in random manner, independent of the past prices.

In the real world, the weak form of market efficiency may exist, as prices do move in an independent manner which the empirical evidence has shown as the past prices are already absorbed by the market. However, it is to be canceded that market imperfections, costs of information and blocks to the free flow of information may stand in the way of free play of market forces. Speculators and groups of interested parties or even brokers may manipulate the prices through corneing of shares and reducing the flating stock of the market The empirical evidence in the random-walk literature existed before the theory was established. Empirical results were discovered first, and then an attempt was made to develop a theory that could possibly explain the results. Both the Random walk hypothesis and weak form of EMH, state almost the same thing, namely, that knowledge of the past stock price does not aid the investors to gain any improved performance.

The prices move independent of the other; although they may move in a random manner they move around a trend line decided by the anticipated real earnings of the company and its fundamentals. Both EMH in weak form and the Random Wal;k Theory thus postulate that analysing the past does not improve the forecasting ability of stock prices and new information and prices that result from them cannot be predicated. After these initial occurrences, more results and more theory were uncovered. This has led then to a diversity of theories, which are generically called the random-walk theory. A good deal of confusion resulted from the diversity of the literature; and only recently has there been some clarification of the proliferation of empirical results and theories.

Empirical Tests

There were several empirical tests on the Random Walk Theory. The question tested was whether the security prices follow a "Random Walk, whether today's prices are in any way a function of the past prices. Similarly weak form of Market efficiency also states that no investor can use the price information of the past to earn superior return on investment. Investors who analysed the past fundamentals involving price behaviour of the past did pick up good blue chips in their portfolio, but that did not give them superior portfolio Empirical tests were conducted both in the past and the present and in India and abroad on the validity of Random Walk hypothesis.

These tests to some extent support the hypothesis that price changes of today are independent of the past price changes. But the evidence is not conclusive and results varied with the time period's chosen and the data used. Cowles (1934) and JOnes (1937) and Kendall (1953) etc. have shown in their research that security prices moved in a random fashion.

Filter Tests

Filter tests are based on the principle of fixing a filter level varying from 0.5% to 5%, and then examine how well pick up both trends and reversals.Thus, if a stock moves up a filter point say 5%; then buy it and hold it long; when it reverses by the same filter point, 5%, sell it and take a short position in it. A short position is one where on sells even without holding shares to deliver. When the stock price reverses again at the filter point, cover the short position by buying the shares in the market. By this process, the contention of chartists that prices and volume data of the past are supposed to tell the entire story and our approach is to forecast the trends and reversala only. Filterig is the screening of the important information affecting the prices from unimportant and see how well the price changes pick up the trends and reversals. The results of tests conducted by Fama, Blume and Alexander on the basis of filter points also did not gie conclusive proofs. If the filter level is low, the market swings capture these levels, but if the filter level is taken to be large, then results did not prove the hypothesis. Even in case of smaller filters, if transac- tion costs and other charges are taken into account the investors did not profit by using the filter tests. In sum, the results of filter tests did not prove the chartist school's validity. Stock prices do not move in a predictable fashion of movement and reversals and one cannot make return in excess of the results warranted by the risks assumed by the investors. These reults prove that the weak form of market efficiency holds good as it is not possible to gain more from the price infomration of the market.

Serial Correlation Tests

Mr. Moore tested the movement of stock prices through serial correlation tests. Serial correlation is used to measure the extent of association of one series of security prices with a series in the past. Moore measures the correlation coefficient of price changes of one week with the price changes a week later and so on down the line. Its results showed that the correlation coefficient is very low indicating that a price rise did not show the tendency to the price fall and vice versa in any predictable manner. The price changes of this week do not therefore depend on the past price changes to any significant extent.

Fama did the same correlation tests on daily price changes in 1965. He studied the companies included in the Dow Jones Industrial average for five years.

His research showed low correlation and this proved that there is no significant relation between price changes in successive periods. Serial correlation or auto correlation of price data of different time periods did not show significant positive results. This proves that prices move in an independent fashion to a large extent.

Run Tests

A run is a set of consecutive price changes in the same direction. The time series data on price changes of stocks are used to test whether there are dependencies among these series in terms of signs and reversal of signs. Fama made Run Tests to examine whether the price changes were likely to be followed by further price changes in the same direction. Run tests are conducted by the following method:

Example Elecon Engi

Suppose the price changes are as follows: Rs. 40, 40.5, 41.50, 41.5, 45.0, 44.0, 44.0, 44.5, 46.0, 45.0 - 10 observations for ten days, then count the number of consecu-tive signs in the same direction which will have (+) sign.

Then count the number of signs with no change with a zero sign and those with consecutuve price declines (with Minus sign). In the example we have two positive, two zero sign and then one positive, one negative sign, two with zero sign and two again the positive sign and the last with a negative sign. These data show that there are no price dependencies. Yesterday's prices neither tell us of today's price nor today's price of to- marrow's price.

There is no consistency in the price changes. This cease also gives support to Random Walk hypoth- esis. Hagerman and Richmand made a similar study for prie changes observed on securities traded on O.T.C. (Over the Counter). The efficiency of options Market was tested by Black and Scholles. Their research showed that the market was not perfect and that the transactions costs are so high that those tradign in the market could not make abnormal returns. Granger and Morgenstern used a method known as Spectral Analysis in 1963 to test the Random nature of the stock prices. They did not notice any worthwhile relationship between the returns of security in one period and the returns in the previous periods.

Most of these research results proved that security prices moved in a random manner and are not amenable to any precise forecast.

Other Testsher

Brownian motion in physics is a kind of Random Walk. The research conducted by Osborne showed that stock prices moved in a Brownian fashion. This means that simulation tests conducted by some authors showed that the mechanism of Random Walk generated variables which are similar to movement of stock prices. Robert's research in simulation tests in particular confirmed that price changes in the present period are independent of the past trends. Research conducted by Levy in 1967 and be Jensen and Bennington in 1970 and many others did not find any signifi- cant abnormal returns due to a study of past price and volume data used in portfolio selection.

Mutual Fund Performance

Similarly mutual fund performance based on insider information is also not found to bear any superior returns. Friend in 1972, Sharpe in 1966 and Jensen in 1969 studied relative performance of mutual funds. It was for that their results are no better. The hypothesis tested and found void is that mutual funds could earn extra ordinary returns and constantly achieve a higher average performance, because they have better access to insider information. Research studies made by Blume, Williamson and others in this line proved that the mutual-fund performance was not extra ordinary or superior to average market performance. They have probably no insider information or their expertise is not superior or their administrative costs are higher than for individuals.

Misconceptions of the Random Walk Model

Our generalisation of the random-walk model, then, says that previous price changes or changes in return are useless in predicting future price or return changes. That is, if we attempt to predict future prices in absolute terms using only historical price-change information, as suggested, not be successful.

Note that random walk says nothing more than that successive price changes are independent. This independence implies that prices at any time will on the average reflect the intrinsic value of the security. (Often one will find this intrinsic worth referred to as the present value of the stock's price or its equilibrium value). Furthermore, if a stock's price deviates from its intrinsic value because, among other things, different investors evaluate the available information differently or have different insights into future prospects of the firm, professional investors and astute non-professionals will seize upon the short-term of random deviations from the intrinsic value, and through their active buying and selling of the stock in question will force the price back to its equilibrium position.

Bibliography

Aliber, R. Z.: *The International Market for Foreign Exchange,* New York, Praeger, 1969.

Alpha C.: *Fundamental Methods of Mathematical Economics,* McGraw-Hill, 1984.

Amar Jesani: *Narco Analysis, Torture and Democratic Rights*, Delhi: Peoples Union for Democratic Rights, 2008.

Ashok, Vasant: *Indian Economy in the World Setting*, Bombay, Himalaya, 1988.

Behari, Madhuri: *Indian Economy since Independence: Chronology of Events*, Delhi, D.K. Publications, 1983.

Belenky Gregory: *Contemporary studies in combat psychiatry*, New York: Greenwood Press, 1987.

Bhuleshkar, Vasant: *Indian Economy in the World Setting*, Bombay, Himalaya, 1988.

Bunn, Geoffrey C: *The Truth Machine: A Social History of the Lie Detector,* Johns Hopkins University Press; 2012.

Cencini, A.: *Time and the Macroeconomic Analysis of Income*, London and New York, Pinter Publishers, 1984.

Dershowitz Alan M.: *Why Terrorism Works: Understanding the Threat, Responding to the Challenge*, New Haven: Yale University Press, 2003.

Fienberg Stephen E., Blascovich James J: *The Polygraph and Lie Detection,*Washington DC: The National Academic Press, 2003.

Gerald Posner: *Why America slept: the failure to prevent 9/11*, New York: Random House, 2003.

Inbau F. G.: *Self-incrimination*, Springfield: C. C. Thomas, 1950.

Jacob Joseph M.: *Doctors & Rules: a Sociology of Professional Values*, New Bruswick: Transaction Publisher, 1999.

Kant Immanuel, *Kant's Critique of Practical Reason and Other Works on the Theory of Ethics*, trans. Thomas Kingsmill Abbott, B.D., 4th revised ed., London: Kongmans Green and Co., 1889.

Louis B. Schlesinger: *Sexual Murder: Catathymic and Compulsive Homicides*, Massachusetts: Taylor & Francis LLC, 2003.

Madhava Menon N. R.: *Draft National Policy on Criminal Justice*, Delhi: Ministry of Home Affairs Government of India, 2007.

Matté James Allan: *Forensic psychophysiology using the polygraph: scientific truth verification – Lie Detection*, New York: JAM Publications, 2000.

Morgan Michael L.: *Classics of Moral and Political Theory*, Indiana: Hackett Publishing Compaby, 2005.

Parker Philiph M.: *Blink: Webster's Quotations, Facts and Phrases*, California: ICON Group International, 2008.

Rudin Norah, Inman Keith: *An Introduction to Forensic DNA Analysis*, Florida: CRC Press, 2002.

Spiegel John: *War Neuroses in North Africa: The Tunisian Campaign*, New York. the Josiah Macy Jr. Foundation, 1943.

Stuart H. James, Nordby Jon J.: *Forensic science: an introduction to scientific and investigative techniques*, Massachusetts: Taylor & Francis LLC, 2005.

Subhash, C.: *National Policy Studies*, New Delhi, Tata McGraw-Hill for the Lok Sabha Secretariat, 1990.

Swoboda, A. : *Monetary Problems of the International Economy*, Chicago, University of Chicago Press, 1969.

Terence, J.: *The State and Development Planning in India*, Delhi, Oxford University Press, 1994.

Ullman, D. G.: *Making Robust Decisions,* Trafford, 2006.

Vines, David and Christopher Gilbert: *The IMF and its Critics: Reform of the Global Financial Architecture*, Cambridge, Cambridge University Press, 2004.

Index

❑❑❑